How Statin Drugs *Really* Lower Cholesterol

And Kill You One Cell at a Time

A matter of public record

Plus Update:

2018 Neuropathy Treatment Protocol

James B. and Hannah Yoseph

ISBN-13: 978-0-615-61817-3

Published 2012 by James and Hannah Yoseph
jandhyoseph@yahoo.com

Printed in the USA

VCell images of ATP production by Virtual Cell Collection

To order wholesale copies, please contact Hannah at:
Doc@DocWise.net

Second Edition, 2018

Table of Contents

To caring physicians, concerned attorneys and all statin-injured victims

In memory of Marvin Siperstein, MD, PhD and true scientist

Marvin D. Siperstein

Special thanks:

To Marvin Siperstein, David Graham, Robin Fears, John Yudkin, Sir John McMichael, Van Rensselaer Potter and all those unnamed scientists who have worked diligently in the pursuit of knowledge over fame, money and power.

It is they who made this book possible.

Preface

Seventy million Americans and over two hundred million people worldwide are taking a deadly drug called statins. How did this happen? Whose fault is it?

The record reads like an Edgar Allen Poe novel. It did not start with some grand conspiracy. It became one.

It was an insidious creeping cancer, a combination of events and history. It was capitalism running amuck. It was the rise to power of one true believer. It was competition and greed. It was corruption of good science and good scientists. It was deregulation of the FDA. It was pride and prejudice and the residual of WWII.

It was a poison so tiny it went unnoticed. It crept into the culture in the name of good and infected everyone it touched with evil.

By 1930, cardiovascular disease (CVD) had become the leading cause of death of Americans. It was an enemy to be stopped.

In 1913, a Russian scientist named Nicolay Anitschkow released a study that grass-eating rabbits developed CVD when force-fed an all-cholesterol diet.

The evil seed was planted.

When WWII broke out the "Japs" became America's archenemy. Movies, news articles and newsreels portrayed them as diabolical "slant-eyed" demons. It was a national agenda: "Beat the Japs". The residual prejudice of that war would play into the development and widespread acceptance of statins.

In 1948, the largest tax-paid study ever mounted on heart disease began in a small town called Framingham. The cost of it would eventually amount to hundreds of millions of dollars. It was established on a flawed agenda. It set out to prove the relationship of high LDL cholesterol to heart disease (the lipid theory). It failed. But millions of taxpayer dollars had been spent and reputations and jobs were on the line; it had to succeed.

The evil began to grow.

The Framingham study proved that if you were male, between the ages of 28 and 45, lived in Framingham and had high LDL cholesterol levels, you had a 2% greater chance of dying from a heart attack or stroke than the national average. On that one statistic, a national health agenda began: stamp out high LDL cholesterol in everyone. The lower the better.

The evil began to spread.

In 1957, a young Japanese scientist named Akira Endo graduated from Tokyo Noko University and joined Sankyo – a Japanese drug company. His part in the coming travesty would not be known until much later.

In 1959, the William S. Merrell Company pushed through the FDA, in record time, a drug called triparanol (MER/29). It lowered cholesterol by blocking the same biochemical path as statins.

Cataracts, skin lesions, hair loss, impotence and neuropathy began to develop in the patients. Whistle-blowers came forward. Merrell Co. had lied and withheld information pertinent to approval. Heads rolled, people were convicted, lawsuits abounded and the drug was withdrawn in 1962.

MER/29 was a hugely profitable and popular drug.

Enter Daniel Steinberg MD, PHD, NIH investigator, egomaniac and true believer. He led the science team that dismantled MER/29 and had advised the FDA against approval. His stature rose far beyond that of a public servant just doing his job. In time, he became an NIH chief with far-reaching influence. In third-person language of a narcissist, he would later publicize himself as a hero in structuring FDA's approval of statins: "Daniel Steinberg did this. Daniel Steinberg did that."

Steinberg hails Nikolai Anitschkow as the first lipid theorist worthy of the Nobel Prize – having supposedly first proved that LDL cholesterol is the cause of heart disease. He would spend hundreds of millions of taxpayer dollars on the CPPT (Coronary Primary Prevention Trial). It failed.

Undaunted, he would manipulate the statistics to be right regardless the true results. That had already been done with the Framingham study. He perverted an absolute statistic of less than two percent in the CPPT study into a 19% relative statistic. He then declared the cholesterol wars over and the lipid theory factual science. He gathered like-minded true believers and formed the NIH "consensus panel" on cholesterol.

In 1980, statin development came to a screeching halt due to cancer in Sankyo's lab animals. Daniel Steinberg and Akira Endo would resurrect its development.

In 1981, Endo published the results of clandestine human studies in Japan. Steinberg consulted Merck and the FDA, discredited Sankyo's findings of cancer in more than half their statin-fed dogs and helped pave the way for starting human trials in the U.S. so as to beat Japan in a "knock-down drag-out race" – an ugly leftover from WWII.

In 1982, human studies began on Merck's lovastatin at a university in Dallas using NIH grant funds. The taxpayers would pay for Merck's trials.

In February 1987, Daniel Steinberg, the former NIH chief turned Merck's advisor, would be the first speaker at the FDA advisory committee meeting on statins, held at the NIH.

In August 1987, the FDA approved lovastatin.

In October of 1987, the National Heart, Lung and Blood Institute (of the NIH) launched the largest free advertising program ever devised: The National Cholesterol Education Program (NCEP). Steinberg again led the way. At taxpayer expense, Americans were screened and 25% prescribed statins to take the rest of their lives. The taxpayers would pay another 150 million dollars to advertise for Merck. Steinberg would brag of his involvement in his later writings.

The evil had overcome the land like the creeping vines of Japanese kudzu had swept over southern farmlands and immersed them in a tangled impenetrable web.

Even leeches and bloodletting have proved more useful and safe than statins.

Never in the history of medical science has one man and his followers done so much harm to so many. Steinberg *et al.* have been beating a dead horse. The myopia of their dead science and findings have harmed and killed too many to count.

Akira Endo is another dangerous and driven man.

There was only one thing certain about Anitschkow's rabbits: they are natural vegetarians that do not normally suffer cardiovascular disease. The cholesterol they were fed was never the enemy. The quantum leap that even Anitschkow did not make linking cholesterol to heart disease was not just bad science.

It was, and remains, insane.

James and Hannah Yoseph
March 12, 2012

"Quoth the raven, nevermore."

Introduction

While investigating statins, we were faced with big words like "3-Hydroxy-3-Methyl-Glutaryl Coenzyme-A reductase", sometimes shortened to "HMG-CoA reductase" or better yet "reductase". What to do?

To be understood, this report had to be simple.

Here is simple: we got shafted. The NIH and associated agencies blew over a half a billion dollars of our money. The FDA may as well have not existed. We have been lied to, stolen from and poisoned by the pharmaceutical industry.

No surprises here; business as usual.

Another part of biochemical language became apparent. Biochemistry is riddled with words and phrases like, "may, might, could, this might mean, putative (supposed), pleiotropic (many) and unknown mechanism". The chemist might describe it something like this: "a proliferation of putative, pleiotropic inexactitudes".

Is biochemistry an inexact science?

No. It is a science of proven results that are reproducible, consistent and understandable.

When it comes to approving drugs for profit it is easy to obscure proven results with caveats like "may or might or unknown mechanism". After all, that is the language of biochemistry. When seeking FDA approval, those words become the lies of the pharmaceutical industry. Those words are honest words for unproven science; those are words that cannot be trusted when money is involved.

When it comes to drugs versus sound science, absolute science can be quickly obscured by the smoke screen of relative statistics.

Statistics don't lie, but liars use statistics.

Conflicts-of-interest become the enemy of a universally accepted proven scientific body of evidence. Absolute truths are buried by relative lies.

All of lipid theory "evidence" linking cholesterol to cardiovascular disease is based on relative statistics. True believers like Steinberg have agendas.

True believers are a dangerous lot. They fought on both sides in the crusades and presided over the Spanish Inquisition. They brought the Nazis to power in Germany and brought down the twin towers on 9/11.

Steinberg and his comrades are the true believers of this report. They skewed the statistics to save us from ourselves – even if it kills us. They are like the religious right that brought us prohibition, Al Capone, segregation and lynch mobs.

Scientists free of hidden agendas like Siperstein had proven statins were deadly long before a corrupted FDA approved them. Steinberg infected his colleagues and convinced the FDA that a deadly fungal toxin was good for all of us.

The drug companies that sell statins benefit from relative statistics used to obfuscate hard science. They dress it up with phrases like "evidence-based medicine", "peer-reviewed report" and "double-blind study." Dress up a pig, it is still a pig.

Misuse of statistics is a malignant cancer on medicine.
Two hundred million users at $2 per toxic dose and $400,000,000 per day yields enough gross resources to hire a whole army of ghostwriters to publish bogus claims and bury absolute science with relative statistics. This "malignancy" props

up a $146,000,000,000 per year windfall to the drug industry—all built on lies.

This report tracks the liars and the lies about one of the statin drugs (lovastatin) from one of the drug companies (Merck). This is because lovastatin was the first of all the currently prescribed statins and Merck is responsible for its approval.

In short:

- Statin research was founded on scientific assumption and an agenda.
- Statins are dangerous drugs developed in error for profit.
- Scientific evidence had proven that statins were lethal years before lovastatin's approval.
- Merck corrupted the science and the scientists.
- The approval process was so corrupted by Merck that lovastatin was bound to be approved.
- Merck lied.
- The FDA shirked its duty; neither safety nor efficacy was proven for statins.
- Statins are derived from fungal toxins that block cell growth and replication.
- Untold harm is being done to millions of human beings.

All of this is recorded in and gleaned from the public record.

In 1989, Thomas J. Moore wrote an investigative report called "*The Cholesterol Myth*". He reviewed all the statistics published on three major NIH studies mounted with public funds (costing us over $500,000,000). He converted those relative statistics into their most understandable and absolute form. From his work, the following is clear:

- There is no credible proof that high blood cholesterol and cardiovascular disease (CVD) have a causal connection.
- Diet and exercise do not help.
- There is no good reason to prescribe statins to anyone.

If there was any justification for lowering cholesterol from NIH's $500,000,000 studies, and a safe way could be found, it should be administered to only one small group of men aged 28 to 45. The entire myth was built around that group.

Irrefutable, reproducible science proves statins are deadly and LDL cholesterol is vital for life. Universal biochemistry convention proves statins kill organs and organisms, one cell at a time.

This report expands on the following publicly recorded events:

1. 1957: Japanese biochemist Akira Endo graduates from Tohoku University and joins Sankyo Pharmaceuticals in Tokyo. He receives a PhD in 1966 from Tohoku for his work at Sankyo.

2. 1959: FDA approves MER/29 as the first cholesterol-lowering drug that blocked the mevalonate pathway and is an instant success.

3. 1959-1961: Multiple reports are published hailing the benefits of MER/29 for lowering cholesterol.

4. 1961: A MER/29 lab worker complains to her husband that lab animal data is falsified. Her husband, who car-pools with an FDA investigator, reports his wife's complaint. FDA performs an unannounced record search.

5. 1962: MER/29 is removed from the market after FDA discovers the William S. Merrell Company had omitted preclinical findings of cataracts in rats and dogs, muscle wasting in monkeys and other falsified or unreported data.

6. 1963: A federal grand jury indictment is issued against Merrell Co. and some of its employees. Scientists and executives plead "no contest", which protects them against the grand jury findings in subsequent class-action civil suits. Multi-millions are awarded to the victims.

7. 1960-1975: Drug companies enter the "mycotoxin gold rush" after a fungal toxin (aflatoxin) was found to cause cancer epidemics in grain-fed domestic trout and turkeys.

8. 1970: Marvin Siperstein publishes his discovery that aflatoxin disrupts cholesterol synthesis in cells.

9. 1971: Endo searches for cholesterol-lowering agents from fungal mycotoxins.

10. 1976: Endo extracts citrinin, a disease-causing mycotoxin from *Penicillium citrinum*. He discovers that citrinin lowers blood cholesterol and publishes his report.

11. 1976: Endo abandons his work with citrinin because it is too toxic. He extracts another mycotoxin from *Penicillium citrinum* called "ML-236B" which proves less toxic than citrinin and also lowers blood cholesterol. ML-236B becomes the first experimental statin.

12. Endo contacts Dr. Goldstein at a Dallas-based Merck supported lab. Goldstein expresses interest in ML-236B.

13. 1976: Merck contracts with Sankyo for the disclosure of information on ML-236B. Sankyo believes that both companies will jointly develop ML-236B.

14. 1977: Endo, Brown and Goldstein publish a paper documenting how statins cause an increase in reductase. Statins are yet called "reductase inhibitors" instead of "reductase stimulators".

15. 1978: Merck develops their own statin. Sankyo cancels work with Merck. Endo leaves Sankyo.

16. 1979: Endo patents another statin and sells it to Sankyo.

17. 1979: Brown and Goldstein's mentor, Marvin Siperstein, co-authors a paper with astronaut Millie Hughes-Fulford. They explain how Endo's statin blocks DNA replication in cells and kills them.

18. 1980: Brown and Goldstein co-author a paper explaining how statin-fed cells mutate and make more reductase or die.

19. 1980: Sankyo cancels clinical trials on humans after half their lab dogs develop cancer.

20. 1980: After receiving news of Sankyo's decision to stop statin development, Merck calls Sankyo. Sankyo refuses to talk with Merck. Merck stops statin development.

21. 1981: Brown and Goldstein report on cell mutations induced by statins.

22. 1982: Under arrangements approved by the FDA, Merck makes lovastatin available to Grundy, Bilheimer and Brown at Dallas for FH patients who had failed known treatment modalities. An IND (Investigational New Drug) permit is granted for human experimentation in Dallas.

23. 1984: Merck applies for an IND for lovastatin and a new drug application (NDA) is approved in nine months – one of the shortest approval times for the FDA since MER/29.

24. 1985: The NIH launches the National Cholesterol Education Program (NCEP). Steinberg positions his colleague Grundy to chair the NCEP.

25. 1985: Merck consultants Brown and Goldstein receive the Nobel Prize in Medicine for statin-related research. Their papers no longer report on statins' deadly effects.

26. 1987 (February 19): Brown and Steinberg represent Merck at the FDA advisory committee meeting on lovastatin. There is no disclosure on the increase in reductase and resultant cell injuries from mevalonate deprivation that are said, by Merck's MacDonald and Tobert, to be due to an unknown mechanism.

27. 1987 (August): Lovastatin is FDA approved.

28. 1987 (October): NCEP publishes cholesterol (statin) treatment guidelines in the American Heart Association's (AHA's) widely read "Circulation" magazine. The president of the AHA, Tony Gotto, is Merck's consultant.

29. 1990: The NIH convenes a panel to discuss the possibility that decreasing cholesterol levels might be intrinsically dangerous. The panel concludes that the evidence cannot be ruled out but dismisses it anyway.

30. 2001: Bayer's "super-statin" Baycol is recalled after multiple deaths are attributed to the drug.

Greed smothers the conscience. Drug cartels, legal or illegal, pursue another agenda that rivals the evil of true believers. The vampire turns his hypnotic gaze on his victim: "You will live forever," he whispers. He does not rightfully hiss, "You will sleep alone in a casket and never see the sun again."

Today, statins remain the most insidiously dangerous and best-selling drug in the world.

In this book, "cardiovascular disease" is abbreviated as CVD. CVD includes coronary heart disease, atherosclerosis (hardening of the arteries), heart failure, high blood pressure and stroke.

One author is a medical doctor; the other is a carpenter.

PART ONE: HOW STATINS KILL CELLS

Chapter 1: Living Cycles

"To be or not to be" is not the question. Life is wired to be.

Our brain keeps us from starving to death. The hunger craving begins there and signals us to get life-sustaining food.

Every cell has a similar mechanism. The cell says, "I'm hungry," and makes a protein called "reductase". Reductase activates the mevalonate pathway that makes mevalonate to sustain the cell.

A key turns the ignition and an engine starts. Reductase starts the mevalonate pathway and cells have life.

Mevalonate is cell food as glucose is brain food. The body makes glucose from any food type. The brain survives. The cells make mevalonate from any food type. Cells survive.

Mevalonate is the essence of cell renewal. In all cells, mevalonate travels down the mevalonate pathway to make cholesterol and isoprenoids (five-carbon molecules). Both stimulate the cell to grow, replicate its DNA and divide into two cells. This is the "cell cycle". This is life.

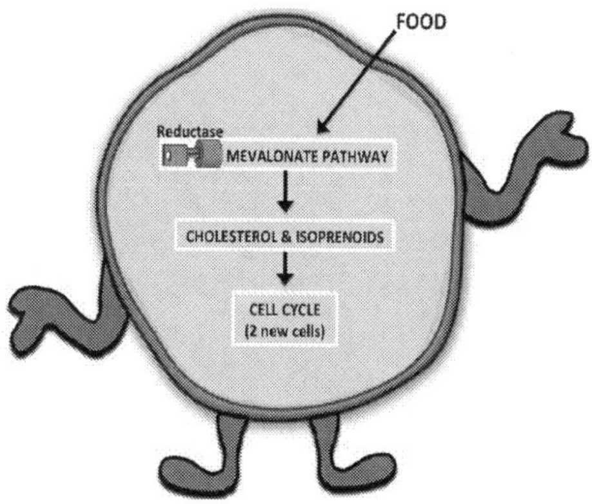

Cell renewal, or turnover, varies for different types of cells. Turnover for cells lining the gut is every 10 hours to five days; skin cells are recycled every two weeks; red blood cells last only four months; bone cells last a decade; cells from the brain's vision center are as old as the individual. Liver cells – the body's detoxifiers – have short lives of 300 to 500 days.

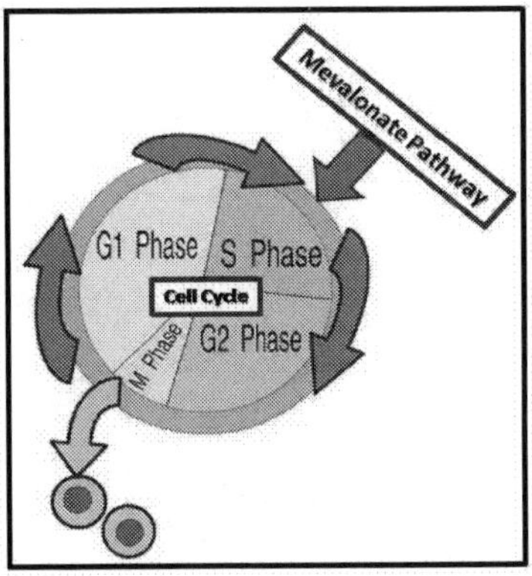

For a cell to cycle, it must grow (G1 phase), replicate its DNA (S phase for DNA "synthesis"), grow some more (G2 phase) and divide into two new cells (M phase for "mitosis").

Without mevalonate's cholesterol and isoprenoids, none of this happens. No cell cycle, no cell life.

DNA is the blueprint of a cell. Before a cell divides, it replicates its DNA – a spiral-staircase shaped protein. DNA "unzips" down the middle. Each half becomes two new DNA molecules. Each new cell receives a blueprint.

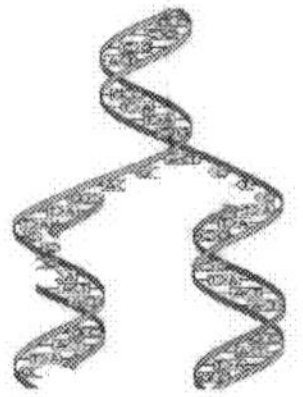

Cell cycles work in concert with cholesterol and isoprenoids made from the mevalonate pathway.

Ah…life's marvelous isoprenoids! Isoprenoids are the largest and most diverse class of over 25,000 molecules made by plants and animals. Because of isoprenoids, we can wake up and smell the roses, enjoy the spice of life (cinnamon, cloves and ginger), relish color (orange carrots and red tomatoes) and see it all clearly (vitamin A). Isoprenoids also include powerful antioxidants (vitamin E) with anti-cancer and heart-protective properties.

Isoprenoids make our cells replicate and renew.

Isoprenoids include isopentenyl adenine for DNA replication. Without isopentenyl adenine for DNA replication there is no cell cycle. Without cell cycles, cells age and die.

Proc. Natl. Acad. Sci. USA
Vol. 76, No. 10, pp. 5056–5060, October 1979
Biochemistry

Essential role for mevalonate synthesis in DNA replication

VALERIA QUESNEY-HUNEEUS, MILLIE HUGHES WILEY, AND MARVIN D. SIPERSTEIN*

Other isoprenoids from the mevalonate pathway include CoQ10, heme-A, dolichol and signaling proteins. ***Like cholesterol, these molecules from mevalonate are vital for normal cell cycles and normal cell function.*** Some of these vital isoprenoids are:

- **Isopentenyl adenine (tRNA)**: For normal cell cycles
- **CoQ10:** For cell energy
- **Heme-A:** For cell energy and drug metabolism
- **Dolichol:** For membrane, nerve and fetal development
- **Signaling proteins:** For normal cell cycles

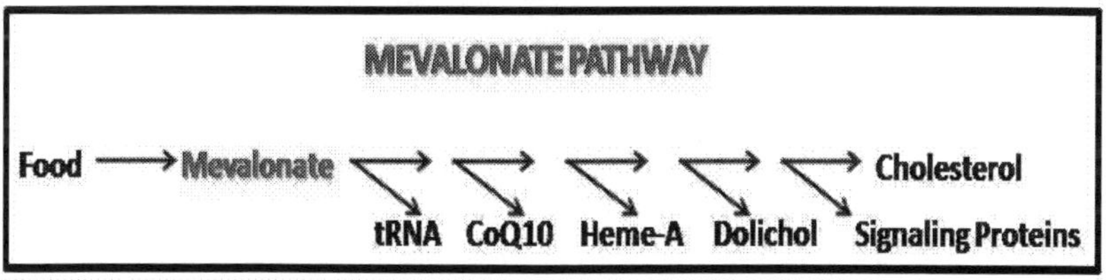

Cholesterol is a major part of the cell cycle. It is part of the mortar and clay that builds cell membranes. Before a cell replicates, the cell and cell membranes grow.

Cholesterol is as key to cell life as isoprenoids. Both are needed just as fuel and electricity are both needed to start a car. Without mevalonate to make cholesterol and isoprenoids, cells die.

Because statins block mevalonate metabolism, Parke-Davis warned the FDA that, ***"Cellular depletion of any or all of these metabolic products could theoretically be deleterious."***

Lipitor New Drug Application (NDA)

Orloff

Medical Reviewer: Dr. David G. Orloff
NDA #20-702 submission date: 6-17-1996
Review completed: 10-28-96

Parke Davis to the FDA: "Mevalonate is an intermediate not only in the pathway to cholesterol, but also in the synthesis of the prenyl, geranyl and farnesyl pyrophosphates (used in post-translational modifications of proteins), ubiquinones (compounds of the electric transport chain and critical in energy metabolism, dolichols (used in the maturation of glycoproteins), and isopentenyladenine (a compound of tRNA). ***Cellular depletion of any or all of these metabolic products could theoretically be deleterious"*** (emphasis added).

For any factory to operate smoothly, all the components must be in the right place at the right time. Similarly, all the components of the mevalonate pathway must be in the right place at the right time for cells to cycle normally. Any error in this process can be dangerous. Without the mevalonate pathway fully functioning, a cell cannot replicate and prematurely dies.

MEVALONATE PATHWAY

One biochemical pathway that a pharmaceutical drug should never touch is the mevalonate pathway. Leave our cells' reproductive, rejuvenating and life-restoring cycles alone, thank you very much!

There is a simple word for healthy cell cycles: life.

Cell turnover decreases with age. We age and die.

There is a simple word for blocked cell cycles: death.

Do **NOT** touch the mevalonate pathway.

Chapter 2: Marvelous Mevalonate

Like keys that turn on ignitions, human cells make enzymes that turn on and speed up chemical reactions. One of the enzymes made by cells is called "reductase" (short for "HMG-CoA reductase"). Reductase converts food into mevalonate.

Statins disable reductase.

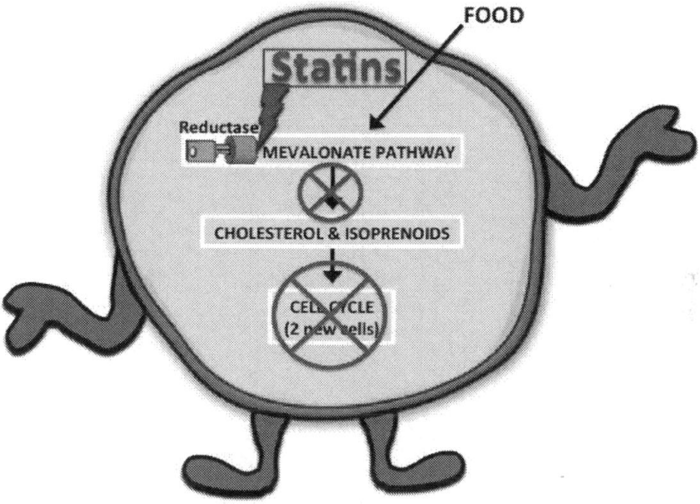

Any drug that blocks reductase likewise prevents it from making mevalonate. Because statins disable reductase, they are called "reductase inhibitors". ***Statins block mevalonate production.*** In so doing, statins block the mevalonate pathway required for cell cycles.

Disabling reductase blocks the mevalonate pathway and its products. No isoprenoids means no growth and no cell cycle. No isopentenyl adenine means no DNA replication. No signaling proteins means no cell-to-cell communication. ***Human cells cultured in nutrients infused with a statin inevitably stop growing, stop replicating, lose their normal appearance and die without making progeny.***

The cells first and most affected by a drug-induced blockage of cell cycles are those with the fastest turnover rates. Again, from chapter one, these are:

- Intestinal cells: 10 hours to 5 days
- Skin cells: 2 weeks
- Red blood cells: 4 months
- Liver cells: 300-500 days

In 1953, Watson and Crick discovered the structure of DNA. In 1979, while investigating the effects of statins on the mevalonate pathway, Marvin Siperstein discovered that DNA replication required isoprenoids from mevalonate.

Siperstein was a pioneer in studying mevalonate synthesis. While working at the University of Texas Southwestern Medical Center at Dallas, he developed techniques for investigating the mevalonate pathway. Statins were useful. Initially his main interest was in cholesterol synthesis – until he discovered that the mevalonate pathway was connected to cell cycles and was broken in cancer cells. In 1972, Drs. Brown and Goldstein joined him in this work.

In 1973, Siperstein moved his lab to San Francisco. Astronaut Millie Hughes-Fulford (formerly Hughes Wiley) joined him. From 1979 to 1980, they performed two experiments with the first statin called "compactin". They found that compactin blocked the S-phase (DNA replication) of the cell cycle.

Essential role for mevalonate synthesis in DNA replication

Proc. Natl. Acad. Sci. USA
Vol. 76, No. 10, pp. 5056–5060, October 1979

VALERIA QUESNEY-HUNEEUS, MILLIE HUGHES WILEY, AND MARVIN D. SIPERSTEIN

They also found that mevalonate, and later more specifically one of the isoprenoids from mevalonate (isopentenyl adenine), restored statin-blocked DNA replication in cells and thus restored cell cycles.

Isopentenyladenine as a mediator of mevalonate-regulated DNA replication*

Proc. Natl. Acad. Sci. USA
Vol. 77, No. 10, pp. 5842–5846, October 1980
Biochemistry

VALERIA QUESNEY HUNEEUS, MILLIE HUGHES WILEY, AND MARVIN D. SIPERSTEIN†

Siperstein's team had made one of the most amazing discoveries about DNA since Watson and Crick. ***He revealed that mevalonate was required for DNA synthesis, cell growth and replication.*** Despite the magnitude of the find that neither DNA nor cells can replicate without an intact mevalonate pathway, his work remains largely ignored.

Role of cholesterogenesis and isoprenoid synthesis in DNA replication and cell growth

Journal of Lipid Research Volume 25, 1984

Marvin D. Siperstein[1]

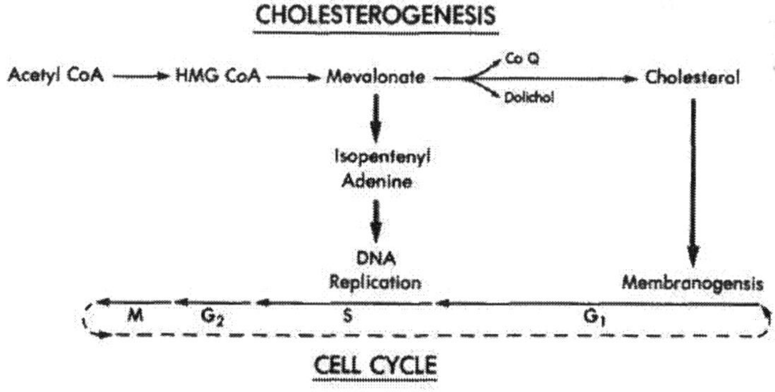

Fig. 2. Role of cholesterogenesis in the cell cycle and DNA synthesis.

By 1979, Siperstein was able to discover that blocking mevalonate blocks cell replication because:

1. In 1964, he had developed a gas-liquid chemical separation tool to measure mevalonate in cells.

2. By 1976, Beecham Labs in the U.K had discovered the statin "compactin" (Sankyo Pharmaceuticals in Japan discovered the same statin as Beecham and called it "ML-236B" or "mevastatin"). With samples of compactin, Siperstein could block reductase and therefore stop mevalonate synthesis. This allowed him to observe the deadly effects of blocking mevalonate with a statin ("stat" in "statin" means "to stop"; "mevastatin" means "to stop mevalonate").

Within one hour of adding compactin to cholesterol-fed cells, the S-phase of cell cycles was *completely stopped*; within minutes of adding back a miniscule amount of mevalonate, DNA replication and cell cycles were *completely restored.*

Because statin-fed cells were given ample cholesterol, it was clear that it was not cholesterol deprivation but, rather, isoprenoid deprivation that prevented DNA replication and cell cycles (DNA must replicate before cells can divide).

Essential role for mevalonate synthesis in DNA replication

Proc. Natl. Acad. Sci. USA
Vol. 76, No. 10, pp. 5056–5060, October 1979

VALERIA QUESNEY-HUNEEUS, MILLIE HUGHES WILEY, AND MARVIN D. SIPERSTEIN

Despite the presence of such ample amounts of cholesterol, blockage of mevalonate synthesis for only 1 hr completely prevented DNA replication. No detectable depletion of cellular cholesterol occurred during this brief exposure to compactin. On the other hand, the restoration of S-phase DNA synthesis was observed within minutes after addition of mevalonate, during which time only picomole amounts of mevalonate were incorporated into a cellular cholesterol pool of more than 30 nmol.

Cells are poisoned by statins because statins block the making of isoprenoids from mevalonate. If cells cannot replicate, they inevitably die.

How long does it take a cell to die if cell cycles are blocked?

Again, that would depend on the turnover rate of any particular cell: 10 hours to five days for intestinal cells, two weeks for skin cells, etc.

After Siperstein moved to San Francisco in 1973, work on the mevalonate pathway continued out of Dallas by two of his junior colleagues: Michael Brown and Joseph Goldstein. They would later betray him and the science he discovered by consulting for Merck and obfuscating the deadly effects of statins.

From 1976 to 1984, Roy Vagelos directed statin research at Merck; by 1985, he was CEO. Vagelos had strong ties with Dallas; he and Brown had graduated from Pennsylvania University. Both had studied under Earl Stadtman at the NIH.

Discoveries came out of Dallas and NIH funds flowed in; Merck benefitted from the NIH taxpayer monies that supported the Dallas-based lab. Brown and Goldstein's work on the regulation of mevalonate would help develop Merck's lovastatin.

In 1980, Sankyo's statin development stopped in Japan after cancer developed in lab animals. Merck followed suit, called an "all stop" and informed the FDA and Dallas of their decision.

After Endo resumed human studies in Japan with a new statin, former NIH-director Daniel Steinberg advised Merck to resume lovastatin's development. With his support, the FDA endorsed human trials at Dallas in 1982. Five years later, Nobel laureates Brown and Goldstein (now Merck consultants) would be recommending FDA's approval of lovastatin (got to "love-a-statin") at the FDA advisory committee. Two years later, lovastatin was on the shelves.

Siperstein's work was buried; it conflicted with statin approval.

Brown and Goldstein were funded and headed for fame. Earl Stadtman at the NIH and Roy Vagelos at Merck both hovered over them like a pair of brood hens. Vagelos and Stadtman made sure their papers were promptly published:

Evidence for regulation of 3-hydroxy-3-methylglutaryl coenzyme A reductase activity and cholesterol synthesis in nonhepatic tissues of rat

Proc. Natl. Acad. Sci. USA
Vol. 73, No. 8, pp. 2564–2568, August 1976

S. Balasubramaniam, Joseph L. Goldstein, Jerry R. Faust, and Michael S. Brown

Division of Medical Genetics, Department of Internal Medicine, University of Texas Health Science Center at Dallas, Dallas, Texas 75235

Communicated by P. Roy Vagelos, April 23, 1976

Squalene synthetase activity in human fibroblasts: Regulation via the low density lipoprotein receptor

Proc. Natl. Acad. Sci. USA
Vol. 76, No. 10, pp. 5018–5022, October 1979

Jerry R. Faust, Joseph L. Goldstein, and Michael S. Brown

Departments of Molecular Genetics and Internal Medicine, University of Texas Health Science Center at Dallas, Dallas, Texas 75235

Communicated by E. R. Stadtman, July 18, 1979

Additional financial support came from the American Heart Association (AHA) via Merck consultant and AHA president Tony Gotto. Just a stone's throw away (six-mile toss), AHA lent a revolving door for Brown and Goldstein to publish in AHA's popular "Circulation" magazine. With the NIH, Merck and AHA's blessings, varied interests encircled Brown and Goldstein. Each had an agenda. In time those interests would surface, with Brown and Goldstein in first-class seats leading the way.

Merck's interest in statins was tied to blocking cholesterol synthesis in cells. But blocking mevalonate to block cholesterol had a serious design flaw: isoprenoid blockade and cell death.

Defective macromolecule biosynthesis and cell-cycle progression in a mammalian cell starved for mevalonate

(restriction point)

Proc. Natl. Acad. Sci. USA
Vol. 82, pp. 3257–3261, May 1985
Cell Biology

Michael Sinensky and Judith Logel

Eleanor Roosevelt Institute for Cancer Research, 4200 East Ninth Avenue, Box B129, Denver, CO 80262

Merck knew the risks. Merck's toxicologist, James MacDonald, reported that Merck actually anticipated the toxic effects of blocking the "non-sterol precursors" (isoprenoids). Merck would later disguise this as "an exaggeration of the desired biochemical effect".

The Toxicology of HMG—CoA Reductase Inhibitors: Prediction of Human Risk
James S. MacDonald and Margaretann M. Halleck
Toxicol Pathol 2004 32: 26

As statins inhibit an enzyme that is essential not only for cholesterol biosynthesis but also for the synthesis of several other nonsterol precursors essential for normal cellular function (Figure 1), it was hypothesized early on that some or all of the toxicity seen at high exposure levels in animals could be related to an exaggeration of the desired biochemical effect (MacDonald et al., 1988).

MacDonald also reported that Merck was "not surprised" to find birth defects in fetuses of lovastatin-fed animals. After all, isoprenoids – cell cycles – are crucial for normal egg cell, sperm cell and embryo development:

The Toxicology of HMG—CoA Reductase Inhibitors: Prediction of Human Risk
James S. MacDonald and Margaretann M. Halleck
Toxicol Pathol 2004 32: 26

In addition to cholesterol, HMG-CoA reductase is responsible for the synthesis of nonsterol intermediates essential for cellular function (Figure 1). Thus, it was not surprising when decreased body weights and skeletal malformations were first observed in fetuses of rats and mice given lovastatin during pregnancy (MacDonald et al., 1988).

Over the next decade, Brown, Goldstein and others duplicated Siperstein's 1979 discovery that statins block DNA replication. The scientific literature is packed with reports of cells, tissues and animals dying when exposed to a statin – and then rescued from ultimate demise with mevalonate:

The Journal of Biological Chemistry
Vol. 258, No. 1, Issue of January 10, pp. 378-385, 1983
Printed in U.S.A.

The Dual Role of Mevalonate in the Cell Cycle

It is well established that either exogenous or endogenous cholesterol is required for both cell growth and proliferation. This laboratory has recently discovered that, in baby hamster kidney-21 cells, independent of its role as a cholesterol precursor, mevalonic acid plays an essential role in S phase DNA replication.

The Journal of Biological Chemistry
Vol. 255, No. 14, Issue of July 25, pp. 6546-6548, 1980

Synthesis of Δ^2-Isopentenyl tRNA from Mevalonate in Cultured Human Fibroblasts*

(Received for publication, April 14, 1980, and in revised form, May 21, 1980)

Jerry R. Faust, Michael S. Brown, and Joseph L. Goldstein

When HMG CoA reductase[1] is inhibited by compactin, mevalonate formation is blocked and cultured cells die.

Merck knew. And Merck blocked the marvelous mevalonate pathway anyway without any informed consent.

It is deadly awful.

Chapter 3: Ground-Zero

All cells die; that is why they replicate.

Siperstein used compactin to discover that a statin quickly stopped all cell cycles. Beecham never brought compactin to market.

In 1980, Sankyo discontinued development of ML-236B after half of their lab dogs developed a rare cancer of the gut. Nevertheless, ML-236B and compactin were used as experimental statins to further investigate the lethal effects of blocking mevalonate.

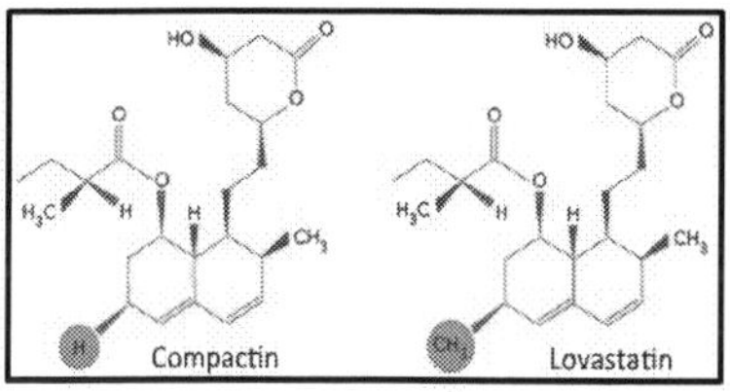

Lovastatin, the first statin to be approved by the FDA, is more potent than compactin/ML-236B. Lovastatin looks exactly like compactin with the exception of one (CH_3) group.

Isoprenoids from mevalonate are indisputably vital for cells to reproduce. This is uncontested scientific *fact* that has been repeatedly demonstrated both in-vitro (in living tissues) and in-vivo (in living animals). Statins block the mevalonate pathway. Statin-fed cells stop growing and stop reproducing. Cells die.

Cell death occurs in two ways: necrosis (normal cell death) and apoptosis (death triggered by DNA damage).

Siperstein and others established that compactin interrupts cells cycles by blocking DNA replication. It is no surprise that statins kill cells by apoptosis.

Glial cells make up to 90 percent of the brain and support the entire nervous system. They rapidly cycle when there is injury.

Lovastatin blocks glial cell cycles. Lovastatin also induces apoptosis in glial cells. Bad juju.

0022-3565/99/2891-0572$03.00/0
The Journal of Pharmacology and Experimental Therapeutics
Vol. 289, No. 1
Printed in U.S.A.

JPET 289:572–579, 1999

Lovastatin-Induced Proliferation Inhibition and Apoptosis in C6 Glial Cells[1]

JAE W. CHOI and SUNG E. JUNG
Department of Pharmacology, Yonsei University College of Medicine, Seoul, Korea

In this study we demonstrated that the cytotoxic effects of lovastatin fall into two categories: suppression of cell growth and induction of apoptosis of C6 glial cells...In conclusion, our data demonstrate that lovastatin can inhibit cell proliferation and induce apoptosis in C6 glial cells, which highlights the importance of the mevalonate pathway on the regulation of cell proliferation and prevention of apoptosis.

In apoptosis, the normally compact DNA begins to fragment and protrude from the nuclear membrane that houses the DNA. Within 24 hours after lovastatin treatment, glial cells use up mevalonate. Like disintegrating twin towers, DNA falls apart.

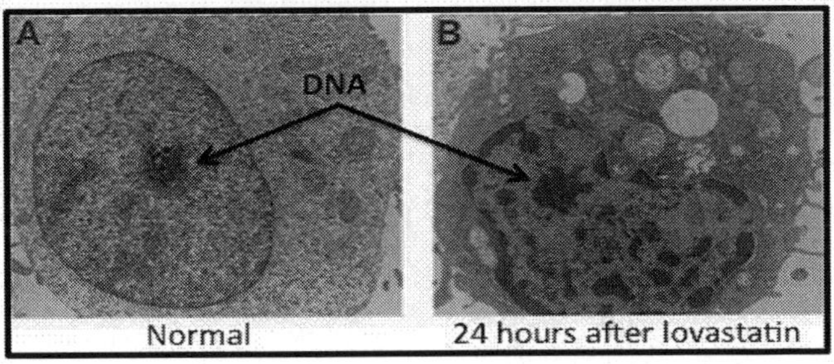

Left above: Normal twin-strands of condensed DNA before lovastatin. Right above: "Ground-zero" after lovastatin.

DNA contains genes. Lovastatin is clearly genotoxic.

The amount of lovastatin that is genotoxic to glial cells depends on the type of glial cells. A tiny dose of 0.1-μM lovastatin induces apoptosis in glioma cells; one hundred times that dose causes apoptosis in "C6-type" glial cells.

Lovastatin fragments DNA and leaves the nucleus looking as if hit by an atomic bomb. Merck's Research Director, Jonathan Tobert makes the absurd claim that lovastatin "is clearly not genotoxic" yet admits it causes liver tumors, shrunken testicles, bleeding on the brain, blindness, muscular flaccidity and liver cell damage:

LOVASTATIN AND BEYOND: THE HISTORY OF THE HMG-COA REDUCTASE INHIBITORS

Jonathan A. Tobert

Adverse effects of statins

Statins produce significant toxicity at high doses in a variety of animal species. These effects include increases in hepatic transaminases, atypical focal hyperplasia of the liver, squamous epithelial hyperplasia of the rat fore stomach (an organ not present in man), cataracts, vascular lesions in the central nervous system (CNS), skeletal muscle toxicity, testicular degeneration and, although the statins are clearly not genotoxic, tumours of the liver and other sites (details can be found in the product circulars of the individual statins). It has been shown, where it has been practical to conduct the experiment, that these effects can be prevented by administering mevalonate[29,30], the product of the reaction catalysed by HMG-CoA reductase.

?

Tobert lies when the truth sounds better.

Statins kill muscle cells (myoblasts). In keeping with the known functions of the mevalonate pathway, statins also stop muscle cell cycles.

Action of lovastatin, simvastatin, and pravastatin on sterol synthesis and their antiproliferative effect in cultured myoblasts from human striated muscle

van Vliet AK, Nègre-Aminou P, van Thiel GC, et al.

The more portent inhibitors of sterol synthesis, lovastatin and simvastatin, were able to inhibit the proliferation of these (skeletal muscle) cells during 3 days of incubation with drug concentrations of 1 uM for lovastatin and 0.1 uM or 1 uM for simvastatin. DNA synthesis was decreased by more than 80% in the presence of 1 uM of lovastatin or simvastatin.

Biochem Pharmacol 1996 Nov 8; 52(9) :1387-92.

The anti-life effects of six statins have also been studied on four common types of human cells: smooth muscle cells, fibroblasts, endothelial cells and myoblasts. All cell types stopped replicating in the presence of all six FDA-approved statins in the following order of increasing potency (and increasing risk of injury):

- Pravastatin
- Lovastatin
- Simvastatin
- Atorvastatin
- Fluvastatin
- Cerivastatin (removed from the market in 2001)

> **Inhibition of proliferation of human smooth muscle cells by various HMG-CoA reductase inhibitors; comparison with other human cell types**
>
> Pascale Nègre-Aminou, Ariane K van Vliet, Monique van Erck, G.Christa F van Thiel, Rick E.W van Leeuwen. Louis H Cohen
>
> **Abstract**
>
> The anti-proliferative effects of these 6 drugs were analyzed by measuring cell number...(statins) block various steps of the cell cycle and this effect depends on the cell type and the growth signaling pathway activated.
>
> Biochimica et Biophysica Acta (BBA) - Lipids and Lipid Metabolism
> Volume 1345, Issue 3, 21 April 1997, Pages 259-268

Statin this, statin that; they *all* stop (stat) cell cycles. That is why statins were called “statins”.

The speed that statins interrupt growth and replication of cells – which advances aging and death – depends on the strength of the statin. For example, “super-statin" Baycol (cerivastatin) by Bayer was recalled in 2001 after a series of rapid fatalities. Bayer boasted that Baycol was the *most potent* statin on the market and never warned that it was therefore the most potent blocker of the cell life cycle.

The more potent the statin, the faster cells die.

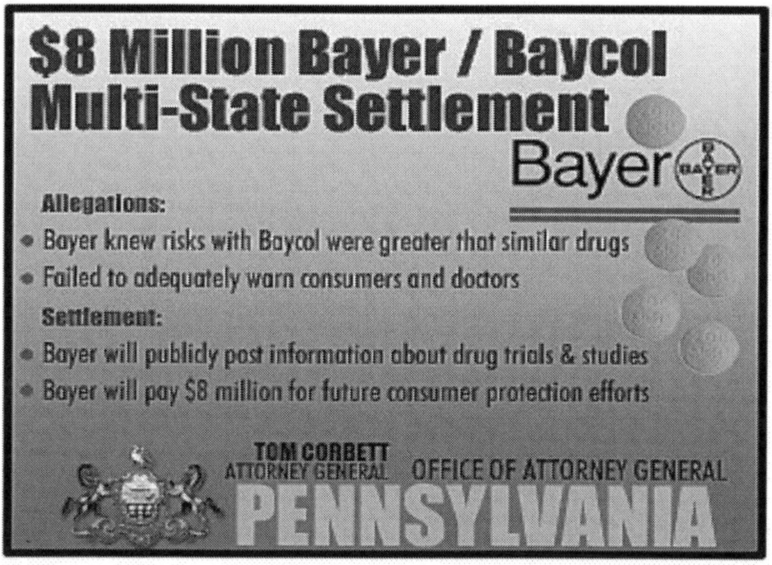

Most doctors never heard about the Baycol deaths and recall.

Chapter 4: Mevalonate's Captain Marvel

Space stations provide a platform for spaceships to link together. Similarly, enzymes provide a dock to bring molecules close together so they can react and chemically link. Without enzymes, some chemical reactions never take place or happen very slowly.

Reductase, an enzyme, provides the site for HMG-CoA (from food) to react with two hydrogen atoms to make mevalonate.

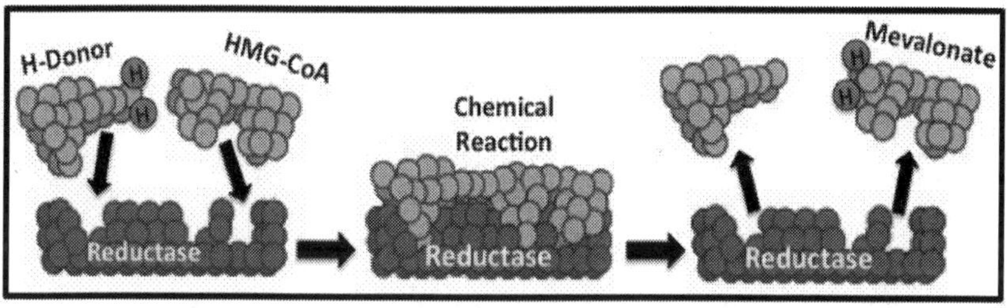

Reductase is 655 times heavier than mevalonate (above is depicted just a small part of it). When a cell needs more mevalonate, it makes more reductase. This takes time. Reductase is the rate-limiting (slowest) step of the mevalonate pathway.

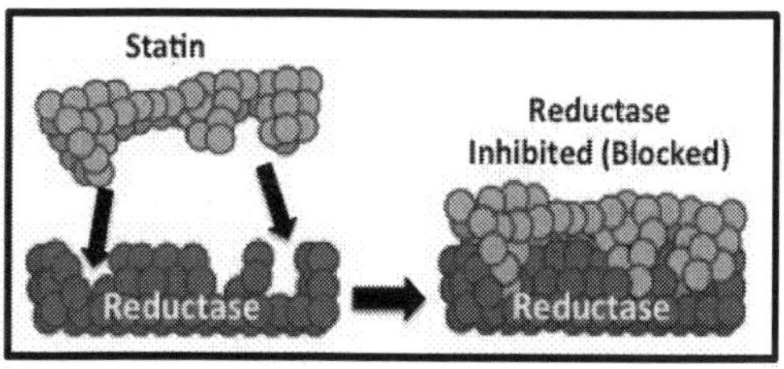

Statins are called "reductase inhibitors." The active site of reductase, where mevalonate is formed, is replaced by the statin.

In 1970, Siperstein discovered that reductase was located in specialized membrane-bound flat structures inside cells called "endoplasmic reticulum" – or "ER" for short.

CHOLESTEROL AND CANCER

By MARVIN D. SIPERSTEIN, M.D., Ph.D.

The enzyme responsible for this control mechanism has been shown in our laboratory to be a lipoprotein, which is located in the endoplasmic reticulum...

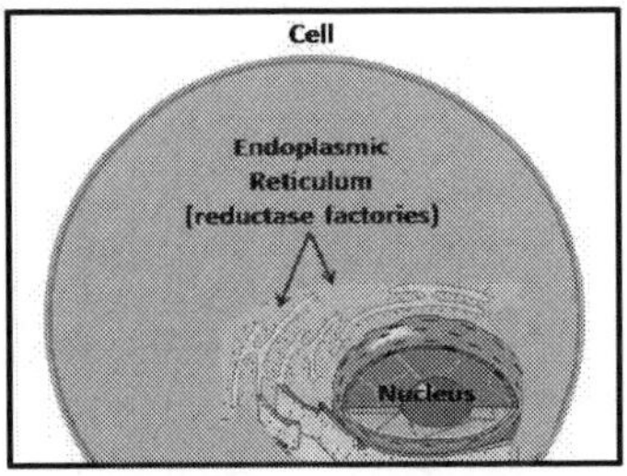

The ER is the cell factory where reductase is made. The pancake-shaped ER membranes connect with the nuclear membrane.
The "order" to make reductase comes from the nucleus with the genetic code for making reductase.

Like a long thread, reductase weaves in-and-out of ER membranes. Part of it is made of lipid (fat), part of it is protein – hence reductase is a "lipoprotein." The part that is made of lipid weaves through and anchors seven times within ER membranes. The part that is protein and water-soluble sticks out into the watery cell; this is where mevalonate is made.

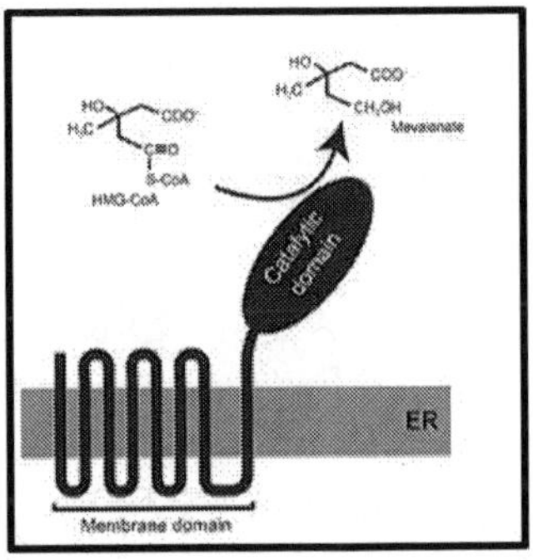

Only a small portion of reductase controls mevalonate synthesis. The seven loops of reductase are involved with the "feedback control" mechanisms (that increase and decrease reductase). These loops are "wired" into the ER membrane that is contiguous with the nuclear membrane.

Less is known about reductase than known. Is reductase under higher-order control from the nucleus through the network of membranes that connect the ER to the nucleus? Many questions are still asked about reductase by Brown and Goldstein, who know more about reductase than anyone else (reference 1).

Controlling cell growth, communication, DNA replication and cellular division, reductase is tightly regulated. Much more remains to be discovered about how it all works.

MEVALONATE PATHWAY

But we *do* know is its full name: "Hydroxy-3-Methyl-Glutaryl Coenzyme-A reductase", also known as "HMG-CoA reductase" or, reduced to its simplest name, "reductase". Its name is as complex as its function in regulating the mevalonate pathway. ***Reductase is "Captain Marvel" of the marvelous mevalonate pathway of life.***

In 1972, Siperstein and Brown developed a new method for isolating reductase. Until then, reductase had never been isolated because it could not be separated from the ER membranes in which it weaves. Their experiment failed; but they *were* able to identify that unlike other known enzymes, reductase was sensitive to cold and *very* large.

3-Hydroxy-3-methylglutaryl Coenzyme A Reductase

SOLUBILIZATION AND PURIFICATION OF A COLD-SENSITIVE MICROSOMAL ENZYME*

(Received for publication, December 18, 1972)

MICHAEL S. BROWN, SUZANNA E. DANA, JOHN M. DIETSCHY‡, AND MARVIN D. SIPERSTEIN§

HMG-CoA reductase has not yet been purified sufficiently to allow determination of the exact molecular basis of cold inactivation. The apparent molecular weight of 200,000 suggests, however, that the enzyme is composed of subunits, and it is probable that cold inactivation involves dissociation of these subunits.

THE JOURNAL OF BIOLOGICAL CHEMISTRY
Vol. 248, No. 13, Issue of July 10, pp. 4731-4738, 1973

In 1976, Brown and Goldstein learned of "compactin" made by Beecham Labs in the United Kingdom. In the same year, Akira Endo of Sankyo Pharmaceuticals in Japan extracted the same statin but from a different fungus; this was called "ML-236B". Because compactin and ML-236B reportedly disabled reductase, Brown and Goldstein wanted to test it. In 1977, Endo brought samples to Dallas and joined them for an experiment.

After adding Endo's statin to live human cells growing in petri dishes, they watched the cells "round up" and then stop growing. Then unexpectedly, the abnormal cells started to make *more* reductase!

Induction of 3-Hydroxy-3-methylglutaryl Coenzyme A Reductase Activity in Human Fibroblasts Incubated with Compactin (ML-236B), A Competitive Inhibitor of the Reductase*

MICHAEL S. BROWN‡ JERRY R. FAUST, AND JOSEPH L. GOLDSTEIN
From the Department of Internal Medicine, University of Texas Health Science Center at Dallas, Dallas, Texas 75235
ISAO KANEKO AND AKIRA ENDO
From Sankyo Company, Ltd., Tokyo, 140, Japan

An unexpected finding in the current studies was the striking increase in the cellular content of HMG-CoA reductase that occurred in fibroblasts when the activity of the enzyme inside the cell was inhibited by compactin.

THE JOURNAL OF BIOLOGICAL CHEMISTRY
Vol. 253, No. 4, Issue of February 24, pp. 1121-1128, 1978
(Received for publication, August 11, 1977)

As the mevalonate was used up, cholesterol synthesis slowed down and then stopped. ***As cholesterol synthesis went down, more and more reductase was made!***

Induction of HMG-CoA Reductase by Compactin

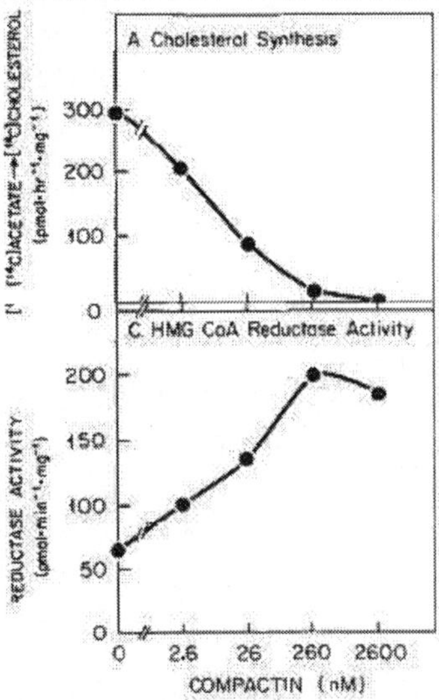

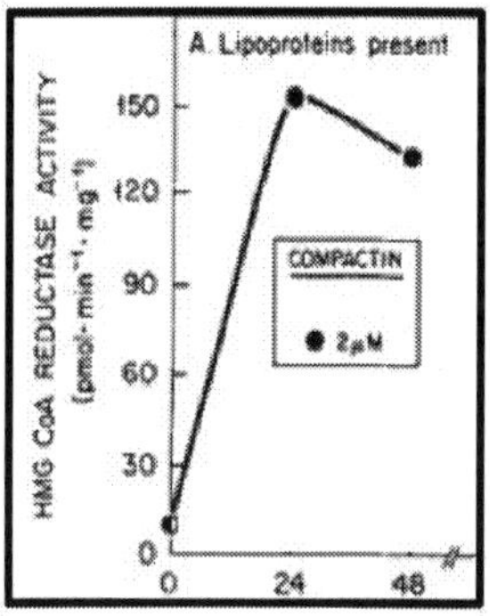

They added LDL cholesterol back to the cells to see what would happen with reductase. ***Reductase remained significantly elevated.*** The only logical explanation was that the cells needed isoprenoids. ***The increased reductase was a life-saving response to make isoprenoids – and not just cholesterol.***

Twenty-three months later, Siperstein (in San Francisco) obtained his own statin samples and reproduced Dallas' results – only he did not report on the reflexive increase in reductase. His experiment, nevertheless, provided an answer for the increase in reductase found in Dallas. ***By blocking mevalonate, statins killed cells unless reductase increased enough to re-open the blocked mevalonate pathway.***

> If reductase activity cannot increase sufficiently to overcome the compactin inhibition, the cells die (Kaneko, Hazama-Shimada & Endo, 1978; Goldstein, Helgeson & Brown, 1979). *J. Cell Sci. 63, 1-20 (1983)*

Life-preserving reflexes are hard-wired at the cellular level. Because reductase is the "master regulator" of reproductive cell cycles, blocking reductase with a statin stimulates a reflexive increase in reductase to re-open the mevalonate pathway. Otherwise, cells die.

Reductase has a 10,000 times greater affinity for a statin than it does for HMG-CoA, making statins potent reductase poisons.

> **The discovery and development of HMG-CoA reductase inhibitors**
>
> Akira Endo
> Department of Applied Biological Science, Tokyo Noko University, Fuchu, Tokyo, 183 Japan

> Thus, the affinity of HMG-CoA reductase for compactin is 10,000-fold higher than its affinity for the natural substrate HMG-CoA, showing mevastatin to be a highly potent inhibitor.
>
> Journal of Lipid Research Volume 33, 1992

Statins block mevalonate's products from being made; but cholesterol and isoprenoids are vital to cell life! This life-saving reflex by cells to make more reductase is a failsafe response to restore a crashed central computer on a captain's bridge. How the cells make more reductase remains a mystery.

In 1982, Brown and Goldstein used the reductase-stimulating property of statins to make a line of mutant cells that produced *500 times* the normal amount of reductase. These cells overcame statin-induced death. Because the cells made massive amounts of reductase, Brown and Goldstein were able to isolate a large enough sample to further their research on the elusive enzyme.

Here's their reductase-cloning recipe: "Add enough statin to living, growing cells until 90% die. Add another dose of statin to the 10% surviving cells until 90% die again. Repeat until a statin-resistant reductase-producing mutant strain of cells is produced. Scan cells with an electron microscope; be amazed."

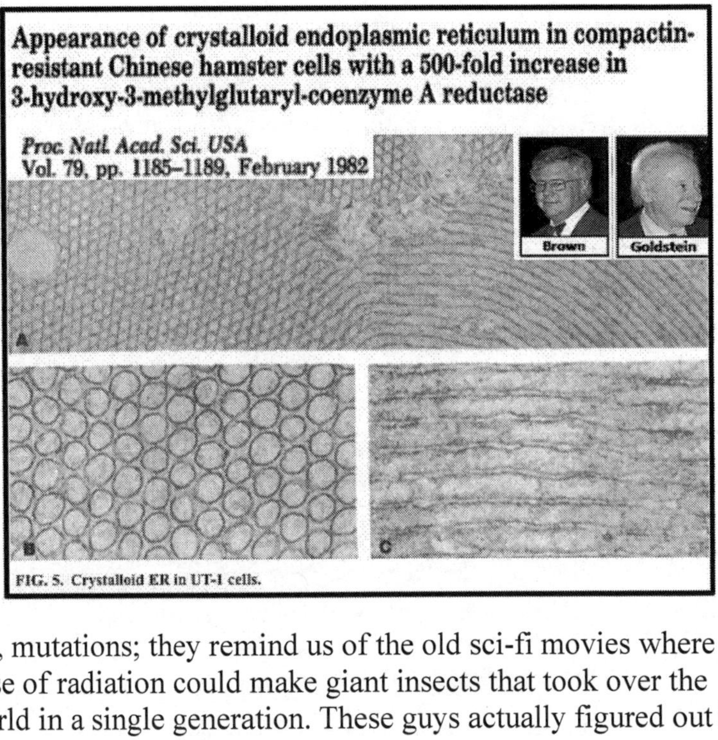

Ah, mutations; they remind us of the old sci-fi movies where a dose of radiation could make giant insects that took over the world in a single generation. These guys actually figured out how to mutate cells into reductase-producing factories. They didn't prove much at that time other than statins are mutagenic but that was not the goal so no grand announcements.

But what they *did* get from these mutant cells was massive amounts of crystal-shaped ER filled with massive amounts of reductase. The ER are the cell "factories" where reductase is made. Reductase is so well regulated that if a cell needs more reductase – or die – ***then the cell can even make more reductase-factories (ER) so as to overcome death.*** Life is wired "to be".

Using fluorescent dye, Brown and Goldstein found 500 times the normal amount of reductase in the copious and abnormally-shaped ER crystals – all made in effort by cells that had mutated to escape the lethal effect of a statin.

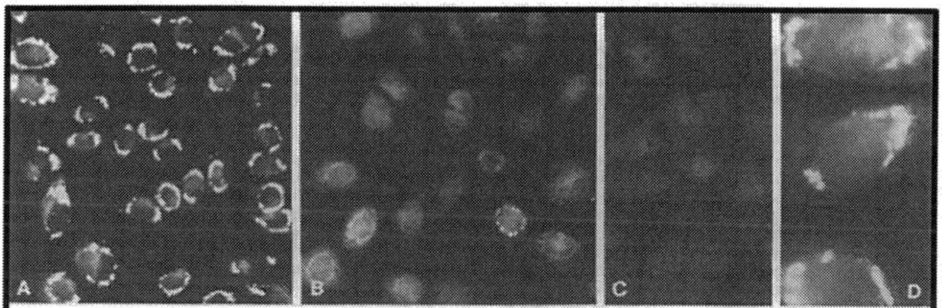

FIG. 4. Localization of reductase in UT-1 cells by indirect immunofluorsence.

They gathered up all the reductase, and in a collaborative work with San Francisco they isolated and identified reductase.

THE JOURNAL OF BIOLOGICAL CHEMISTRY
© 1985 by The American Society of Biological Chemists, Inc.
Vol. 260, No. 1, Issue of January 10, pp. 522-530, 1985
Printed in U.S.A.

Domain Structure of 3-Hydroxy-3-methylglutaryl Coenzyme A Reductase, a Glycoprotein of the Endoplasmic Reticulum*

(Received for publication, June 26, 1984)

Laura Liscum‡§, Janet Finer-Moore¶, Robert M. Stroud¶, Kenneth L. Luskey‡‖, Michael S. Brown‡, and Joseph L. Goldstein‡

From the ‡Departments of Molecular Genetics and Internal Medicine, University of Texas Health Science Center at Dallas, Southwestern Medical School, Dallas, Texas 75235 and the ¶Department of Biochemistry and Biophysics, School of Medicine, University of California, San Francisco, San Francisco, California 94143

Finally, the reductase molecule was unveiled to mankind:

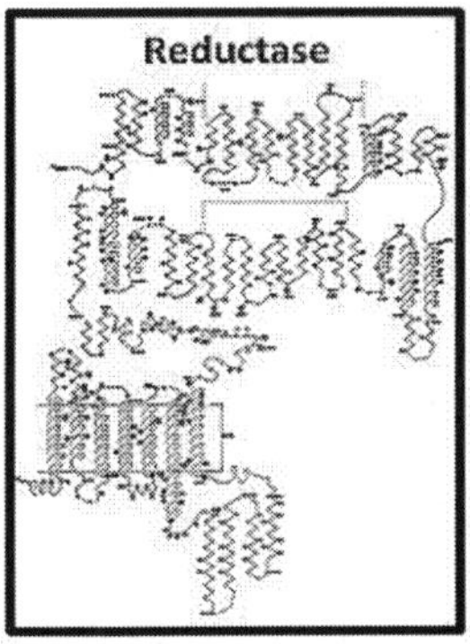

What a molecule! That looks more like a complex wiring diagram than an enzyme. And statins inhibit *that?*

The cell-killing property of statins has helped molecular biologists to crack the reductase "code" and unravel how it regulates the mevalonate pathway. By blocking mevalonate and causing "cardiac arrest" in cells, scientists can add back to dying cells the various isoprenoids normally made from mevalonate, to figure out how to resuscitate them.

So far, they have not figured out how to save statin-fed dying cells except by adding back mevalonate.

But what makes a useful tool for scientific discovery in a controlled laboratory setting can make for an uncontrolled mess when given to a living organism. Mutate – or die. That is what Brown and Goldstein discovered when cells were fed a statin to the brink of extermination.

Just as a person who is continuously hungry eats more and more food until he no longer resembles his former self, cells intentionally starved of reductase with a statin produce more and more reductase until they no longer resemble normal cells. And because statins block isoprenoids such as dolichol that are needed to make normal ER membranes, the ER are abnormal. Even so, cells manage to make more ER *anyway*. Cells don't die easy – not without a good fight; better to mutate than die.

Statins are reductase inhibitors-stimulators. By disabling reductase, statins induce normal cells to mutate into isoprenoid-starved reductase-making factories. If cells don't increase reductase, they die from broken cell cycles. We have been told that statins are just "reductase inhibitors" – a half-truth (lie of omission).

The cell is a nucleus-powered complex mini-universe. Like a nuclear-power plant, reductase is wired with multiple failsafe measures to ensure it remains operational. Its complete function remains unknown, but what we do know about reductase is:

- It is vital to life.
- It is required to make isoprenoids and not just cholesterol.
- Once increased with a statin, reductase cannot be turned back to baseline levels except with mevalonate.
- It weighs 655 times more than mevalonate (a 20-ton whale weighs 230 times more than a man).
- It has seven arms that interweave through membranes that are involved in its yet-unknown control.
- It is made in the ER and linked to the nucleus.
- It is so vital to life that if it begins to fail the nucleus signals the cell to make more reductase – *and more ER.*
- The entire cell will mutate to keep reductase on board.

It is common sense to not inhibit reductase. If anything, pharmaceutical drugs should be targeted to correct its normal function when gone awry as in cancer cells (chapter 9).

What we know about reductase is yet in its infancy. Granting license to tamper with reductase, in ignorance, is like turning a bunch of six-year-olds loose in a nuclear-power plant – and then trusting that the computers' redundant systems will somehow compensate for whatever controls they push or turn.

In 1981, the "recipe" for developing statin-resistant reductase-producing mutant cells was first published in Japan by Sankyo's statin-inventor Akira Endo – one year before Brown and Goldstein. This mirroring of work between Merck consultants Brown and Goldstein in Dallas and Sankyo's Endo in Tokyo marks the start of a trend between East and West to copy one another's work.

THE JOURNAL OF BIOLOGICAL CHEMISTRY
Vol. 256, No. 13, Issue of July 10, pp. 6762-6768, 1981
Printed in U.S.A.

Isolation and Characterization of Cells Resistant to ML236B (Compactin) with Increased Levels of 3-Hydroxy-3-methylglutaryl Coenzyme A Reductase*

(Received for publication, December 22, 1980, and in revised form, March 16, 1981)

Judith Ryan‡, Edna C. Hardeman§, Akira Endo¶, and Robert D. Simoni‖
From the Department of Biological Science, Stanford University, Stanford, California 94305 and the ¶Department of Agricultural and Biological Chemistry, Tokyo Noko University, Tokyo 183, Japan

We conclude that the variant cell lines are able to overcome the cytotoxic effects of ML236B by a mechanism which leads to overaccumulation of HMG-CoA reductase which in turn permits normal mevalonate metabolism and cholesterol synthesis to take place.

Endo's clear report on the cytotoxic effect of ML-236B was made during the last of the years when Brown, Goldstein, Siperstein and others were using statins to investigate statins' deadly effects on cells. It was a time of great discovery and white powder was flying off the chalkboards! Statin-associated toxicity such as DNA-alteration and cell death was no secret – at least not until 1982 when Dallas got a green light from the FDA to start experimenting with statins on humans.

With a bit of back-engineering and human experimentation, Brown and Goldstein found that elevated reductase – the cells' response to extermination – ***also lowered blood cholesterol.***

Merck got wind of it. Dallas' discoveries would need to be tweaked. Drug-induced cell death by inhibiting reductase with a statin became something "good" – not for us, but for Merck.

After 1982, reporting on statin toxicity by Brown and Goldstein stopped. Human experimentation began. No more transparency on how statins block DNA replication, cause cells to "round up" and stop growing. Not a word on how blocking reductase, and therefore mevalonate synthesis, killed cells.

Reductase's importance was reduced to "the rate-limiting step of cholesterol synthesis" rather than the rate-limiting step to a captain's bridge where nothing happens *at all* in the mini-universe of a cell until reductase, mevalonate's Captain Marvel, shouts," ENGAGE!"

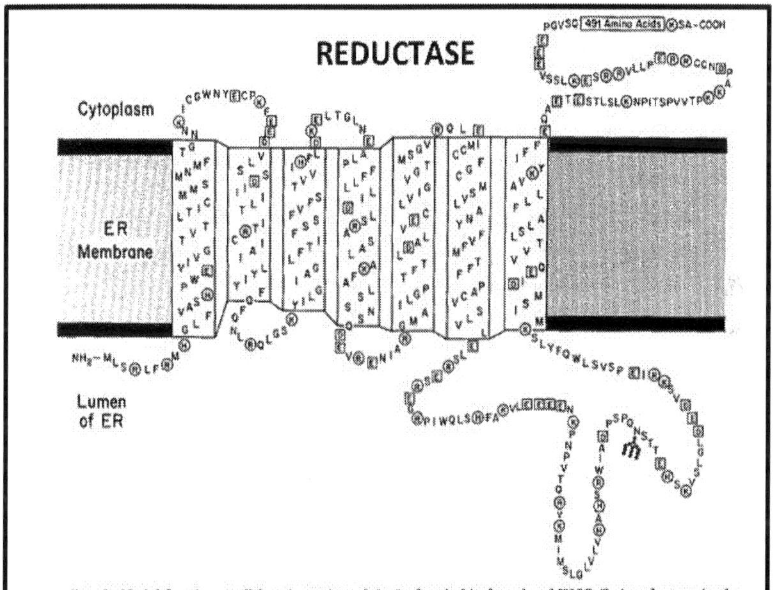

FIG. 6. Model for the possible orientation of the hydrophobic domain of HMG-CoA reductase in the membrane of the endoplasmic reticulum.

Pulling the political strings and removing all the stops was former NIH chief Daniel Steinberg. He devised the first obfuscations.

According to Steinberg, FDA statin advisor/Merck consultant, it's okay for statins to mutate cells because it's not cancer.

An interpretive history of the cholesterol controversy, part V: The discovery of the statins and the end of the controversy[1]

Journal of Lipid Research Volume 47, 2006

Daniel Steinberg[2]

Department of Medicine, University of California-San Diego, La Jolla, CA

Steinberg

A few years later, the Goldstein/Brown laboratory showed that this huge overproduction of reductase protein, representing an attempt by the cell to overcome the statin inhibition, is accompanied by a huge buildup of endoplasmic reticulum, the organelle in which the reductase resides (32). As a result, the cells look "abnormal," but of course they are not cancer cells. As discussed below, in retrospect, this may be what led the pathologists at Sankyo at a later date to conclude, incorrectly, that high doses of compactin were possibly carcinogenic.

Steinberg says that the huge build-up of ER crystals likely represents why Sankyo stopped statin development in 1980 due to an "incorrect" diagnosis of "possible cancer." Steinberg seems to know it all; those dumbass Japanese pathologists don't know cancer when they see it.

Sankyo *almost* stopped statin development in 1977 due to "toxic crystals" seen in statin-fed cells. In 1980, Sankyo *definitively* stopped developing ML-236B (which Endo sometimes calls "compactin") after discovering cancer in half their dogs. It was the huge buildup of ER crystals and reductase found by Brown and Goldstein that explains, therefore, why Sankyo almost stopped statin research in 1977 and not 1980. In 1980, Sankyo found lymphomas in their dogs; they certainly did not confuse lymphomas for previously identified "toxic crystals".

> **A gift from nature: the birth of the statins**
>
> Akira Endo
>
> We encountered a second challenge in April 1977. The issue was the detection of microcrystalline structures in the liver cells of rats that had been fed extremely large amounts of compactin (more than 500 milligrams per kilogram body weight per day (mg/kg/d)) for 5 weeks. The toxicologists insisted that these structures were toxic substances. It took us 9 months to identify these microcrystalline structures as nontoxic cholesterol.

Endo and Steinberg turn blind eyes to multiple "DANGER!!" signs. Endo concludes about the toxic crystals, "Nothing wrong here, shipmates! Just some non-toxic cholesterol! Full speed ahead; we have a race to win!" (Say what?) As if with numbed conscience, they both repeatedly turned away from the microscope to instead focus on numbers: statins lower cholesterol by more than 20%! WOW! They ignored the awkward truth: cells increase reductase and ER *and* become saturated with "cholesterol crystals". What an absolutely monstrous out-of-control mutational mess. These men are foxes in the hen house.

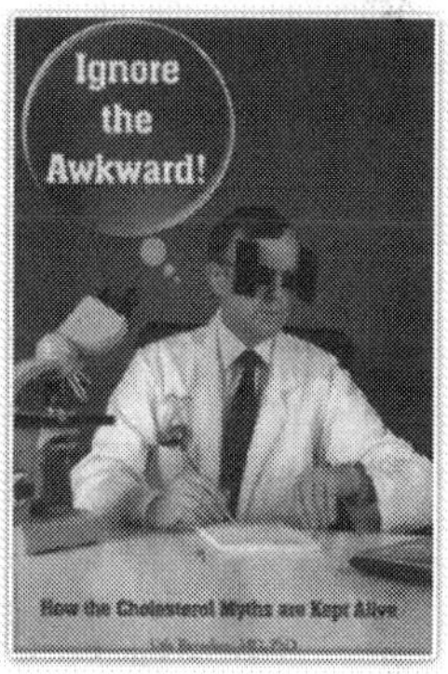

When news of Sankyo's canceled trials reached Merck in 1980, a nervous Merck promptly dropped out of the "race". If all was well in Merck's labs, there was no reason for them to stop developing lovastatin simply because of rumors that Japan had quit the "statin race" – as Steinberg likes to call it. The truth is that there were already clear DANGER signs in Merck's dogs, rabbits and rats; Merck did not want to face the mounting evidence – nor would they want to disappoint their investors. Thanks to Endo, the unrestrained statin inventor in the East, all of that would quickly change. In the dark and late-night hours, Endo continued clandestine human trials in Japan. It was easy; there was no FDA to stop him. After 1980, he published his results in U.S. journals and Merck got wind of it.

With Japan back on-line with human experimentation, the FDA was apprised and took an active interest in resuming statin development (reference 2). This interest was influenced by urgent pleas from Steinberg whom the FDA trusted and consulted (reference 3). Japan had already beaten the U.S. to the international patent and now they had beaten the U.S. on human testing. Numbers – human statistics – were rolling in for Japan, and looking pretty impressive.

A "knock-down drag-out" war began (reference 4). Steinberg sounded the battle cry.

The FDA responded to the urgency of the moment. In 1982, the FDA neither passed go nor collected $200 from Merck; instead, the FDA joined the race and *directly* granted an Investigational New Drug (IND) license to Dallas physicians (Brown, Bilheimer and Grundy). The U.S. had to beat Japan. This gave way for the U.S. to quickly reproduce Japan's results with NIH grant (taxpayer) monies – two years before Merck received an IND from the FDA to perform their own trials at their own expense.

Statins lowered blood cholesterol and that was a good thing: *that* was the new mantra after 1982. It echoed out of Dallas (Brown/Goldstein lab and the AHA), California (Steinberg), New Jersey (Merck) and the NIH lipid labs that had participated in Steinberg's NIH cholesterol trials. Like a well-oiled protection racket, the NIH created the problem ("bad" cholesterol) and insiders would profit from the solution. They would set into motion a series of events that made statin-approval by the FDA a sure-deal.

Positions were taken and pockets pre-lined for the coming windfall. The absolute hard science – that blocking reductase killed cells and/or evoked a life-restoring response that mutated cells – would be traded for Steinberg's and Tobert's relative statistics to prove that statins were such a great idea for the world that they should even be added to public water supplies.

A word from our sponsor:

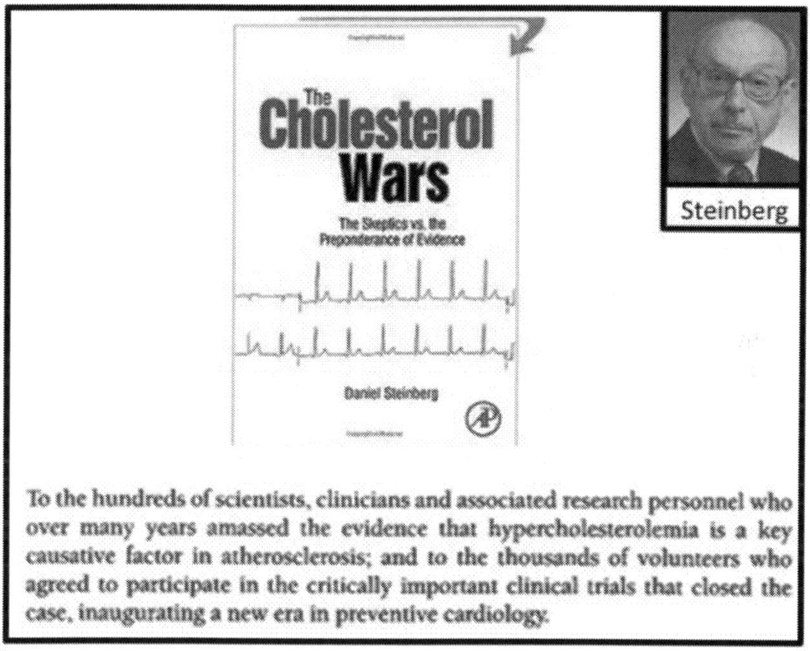

Comments posted at Amazon.com by readers of "The Cholesterol Wars" shows that the literate public doesn't buy Steinberg's propaganda, although the FDA did.

Relative statistics put aside, here's how statins *really* work...

Chapter 5: How Statins *Really* Work

Statins lower cholesterol unnecessarily (see chapter 12) and slowly rob you of life, energy, immune function, sex drive and mental faculties.

The human body is an incredibly-complex biological machine, designed with innumerable redundancies so as to suffer insult and function normally: we have two eyes, two ears, two arms, two legs, two kidneys, ten fingers, ten toes; you can lose any one of them and still see, hear and function.

Redundant life-preserving mechanisms are also intricately "wired" throughout organ-to-cell communication pathways. The hunger reflex serves as an example: the mid-brain detects low blood sugar and sends multiple signals to the stomach (acid release causes hunger pangs), olfactory nerve (food smells are heightened) and salivary glands (the mouth "waters" at the sight of food). When blood sugar levels return to normal, feedback signals sent to the mid-brain turn off the hunger reflex.

When Brown and Goldstein collaborated with Endo in 1977, they had uncovered such a redundant system within cells – but didn't know it at the time. When cells need cholesterol to meet growth requirements, the central command station of the cell (nucleus) stimulates production of both reductase and LDL cholesterol receptors. ***In 1977, they detected the elevated reductase, but not the increase of cholesterol receptors.***

Cholesterol provides support for cell membranes and is converted by cells into life-essential hormones such as testosterone, progesterone, aldosterone, cortisol and vitamin D. When it's needed, there can be no time to waste.

Cholesterol is *so vital to life* that, when needed, cells almost-instantly obtain it in two ways:

1.) Cells "make it" from scratch via the mevalonate pathway.

2.) Cells "take it" from the blood in ready-made form.

When cells are hungry for cholesterol, reductase turns on the mevalonate pathway. At the same time, the nucleus that houses the genetic code sends the order to make more LDL cholesterol receptors. ***Cholesterol synthesis and LDL cholesterol receptor synthesis are co-regulated.***

Cholesterol is not soluble in blood. When combined with LDL protein, LDL cholesterol dissolves and travels in the blood.

LDL cholesterol receptors are like catcher's mitts sitting on top of cell membranes that "catch" LDL cholesterol in the blood. (Most of the cholesterol in the blood is made by the liver and provides other tissue cells with a ready-made supply of LDL cholesterol.) The "caught" ready-made LDL cholesterol is then pulled into a cell.

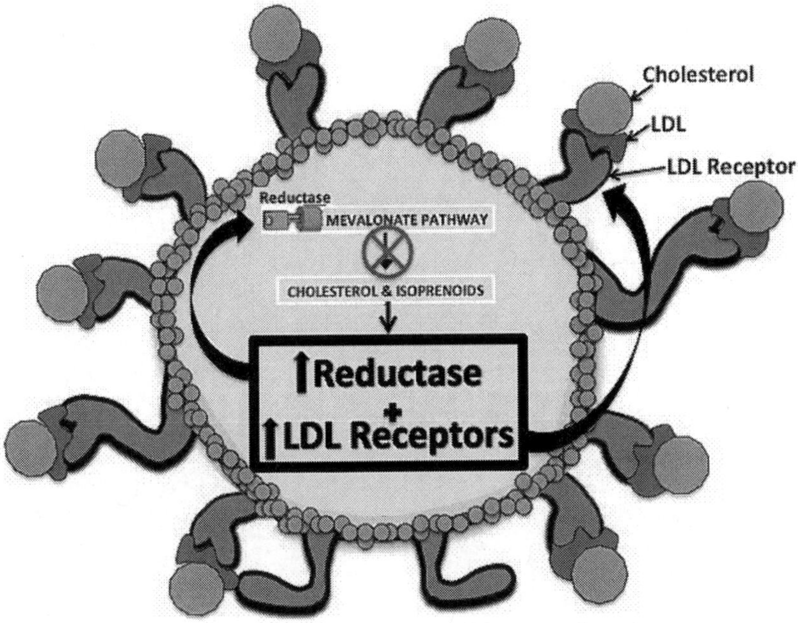

The net result is that cholesterol in the blood is lowered.

The liver will later replace the removed blood cholesterol, but for immediate use cells grab up what is needed from the blood. Peter (blood LDL cholesterol) is robbed to immediately pay Paul (cellular needs for LDL cholesterol inside tissues and organs).

As cells snatch up the ready-made LDL cholesterol circulating in the blood, reductase is reduced because the burden to make cholesterol from scratch via the mevalonate pathway is reduced.

Feedback information that is sent to the nucleus and ER where reductase is made results in decreased cholesterol synthesis *and* decreased LDL cholesterol receptor (LDL receptor) synthesis.

Again, all of this happens together because cholesterol synthesis and LDL receptor synthesis are co-regulated. Reductase, cholesterol synthesis and LDL receptor synthesis are turned up and down *together*. They are hard-wired.

When statins are ingested, the liver absorbs most of it. Mevalonate synthesis in liver cells is blocked and liver cells are robbed of cholesterol and isoprenoids. The cells respond to the death threat and start making more reductase to try to turn the mevalonate pathway back on. ***Because reductase is elevated, the nucleus wrongly thinks more LDL receptors are needed.*** (What cells really need is more mevalonate.)

More LDL receptors are made anyway that snatch up cholesterol from the blood and pull it into the liver cells. Reductase is then decreased and so LDL receptor synthesis is decreased.

But...and here's the big BUT! "Wait a minute!" exclaims a liver cell as it detects that cholesterol has been increased through the LDL receptors. "*Where are my isoprenoids?* I turned on the mevalonate pathway and didn't get any isoprenoids. All I got was cholesterol. What the...?"

Cells respond appropriately as wired. Reductase is turned back up again to try to make isoprenoids. LDL receptor synthesis is also turned up again (hard-wired). More blood cholesterol is lowered as it is shoved into liver cells via LDL receptors.

Seen: Blood cholesterol lowers. Unseen: Blood cholesterol is being shoved into cells via the LDL cholesterol receptors.

In 1977, Endo and Sankyo toxicologists looked inside cells and found "cholesterol crystals". But blood cholesterol came down 40 percent in lab animals. Ignore the awkward! Accentuate the positive and avoid the negative!

In vivo – in humans – are undetected cells throughout the rest of the body choking to death from isoprenoid deprivation. Worse are cells that do not make LDL cholesterol receptors; these are starved of *both* isoprenoids and cholesterol. Even harder hit are cells that do not make LDL cholesterol receptors *and* have fast turnover rates.

Proc. Natl. Acad. Sci. USA
Vol. 83, pp. 8370–8374, November 1986
Medical Sciences

Mevinolin, an inhibitor of cholesterol synthesis, induces mRNA for low density lipoprotein receptor in livers of hamsters and rabbits

(3-hydroxy-3-methylglutaryl CoA reductase/S1-nuclease assay/regulation of cell surface receptors/Watanabe-heritable hyperlipidemic rabbits)

Patrick T. S. Ma, Gregorio Gil, Thomas C. Südhof, David W. Bilheimer, Joseph L. Goldstein, and Michael S. Brown

Low Density Lipoprotein Receptor and 3-Hydroxy-3-Methylglutaryl Coenzyme A Reductase Gene Expression in Human Mononuclear Leukocytes Is Regulated Coordinately and Parallels Gene Expression in Human Liver

Elizabeth E. Powell and Peter A. Kroon
Department of Biochemistry, The University of Queensland, Brisbane, Queensland 4072, Australia
Received for publication 17 July 1993.

Irrespective of the mechanisms involved, the current data suggest that liver cells and mononuclear leukocytes respond to an increased demand for cholesterol by increasing the number of copies of LDL receptor and HMG CoA reductase mRNA molecules simultaneously.

Biochem. J. (1989) 260, 731–736 (Printed in Great Britain)

Co-ordinate regulation of low-density-lipoprotein receptor and 3-hydroxy-3-methylglutaryl-CoA reductase and synthase gene expression in HepG2 cells

David T. MOLOWA and George M. CIMIS
Department of Molecular Pharmacology and Biochemistry, Merck Sharp & Dohme Research Laboratories,

We conclude that the expression of the LDL receptor, HMG-CoA reductase and HMG-CoA synthase is co-ordinately regulated in HepG2 cells.

Three years later and with a bit of back engineering in Dallas after experimenting with statins on humans from 1982 to 1984, the data began to make sense. Dallas figured out how "reductase inhibitors" both raise reductase and lower blood cholesterol. ***It was the increased LDL receptors!***

In 1985, Brown and Goldstein wrote a treatise on cholesterol synthesis and explained how statins lower blood LDL cholesterol. They said nothing about the isoprenoid synthesis blockade by statins that resultantly kills cells.

They were awarded the Nobel Prize in medicine for this work.

By blocking mevalonate, cells are "tricked" into thinking the cholesterol (and isoprenoid) levels are low. More reductase and more LDL cholesterol receptors are made – and the latter remove blood cholesterol and lower it.

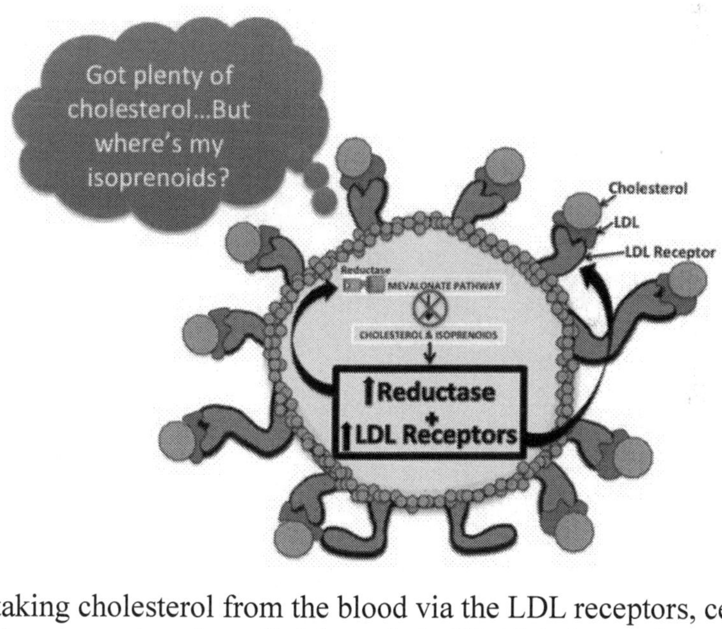

By taking cholesterol from the blood via the LDL receptors, cells that have receptors (not all do) get their fill of cholesterol; cholesterol needs are met. Blood cholesterol is lowered; your lab report looks great. Your doctor, ignorant of the facts, is happy.

But that is only half the story. Cells get more than their fill of blood (dietary) cholesterol by the LDL cholesterol receptors – but cells remain deprived of isoprenoids. Isoprenoid synthesis remains blocked. ***Reductase stays elevated – because the mevalonate pathway remains blocked and cells are starving for isoprenoids.*** That cannot be good, right?

That is a relative truth. Whether or not all of that is good depends on who you are.

For Merck and the statinic scientists who lined their pockets with the hat trick, it's good. As long as cells remain forever blocked from making isoprenoids, reductase remains elevated. And as long as reductase remains elevated – LDL receptors are made. And as long as LDL receptors are made, blood cholesterol is lowered. And as long as blood cholesterol is lowered, Merck and Merck's cronies' make money – lots of it. ***They make lots of it by telling consumers and prescribers only half a story.*** Brown and Goldstein's 1985 Nobel speech (available on line for the public record) tells half the story on how statins work. Statin prescriber information sheets tell half the story.

Merck and Dallas spared consumers and prescribers from confusing "details" – ***that statins block both isoprenoids and cholesterol synthesis.*** Most people – heck, most physicians – can't even pronounce "isoprenoids" never mind know what they do!

So a plan was devised, using half-truths, to keep us all from confusing details that would bias us against statins. Statins would be called "reductase inhibitors". Statins would be marketed as drugs that block "the rate-limiting enzyme of cholesterol synthesis" (not mevalonate synthesis). Brown and Goldstein's 1985 Nobel speech would become the "standard" taught in medical school on how statins work.

Telling half-truths would yield two hundred million consumers (and growing). That's enough to support a whole army of ghostwriters to publish bogus claims, bury absolute science with relative statistics, keep all the players silent about the science that proves the harmful effects and pay off any injury claims that manage to sift through the obfuscations.

Marvin Siperstein, you and your life-propelling discoveries were destined for obscurity. There was no money in them.

So, voila! Take statins, choke off the life cycle of liver cells so that reductase kicks into overdrive to "trick" liver cells into mass-producing cholesterol receptors that soak up supposedly-bad blood cholesterol – most of which is normally made by the liver via the mevalonate pathway in the first place. Get blood tested and "WOW!" – just like magic – LDL "bad" cholesterol is lower.

CBC news

Home World Canada Politics Health Arts & Entertainment Technology & Sci

Story Tools: EMAIL | PRINT | Text Size: S M L XL | REPORT TYPO | SEND YOUR FEEDBACK | SH

Statins: the Aspirin of the 21st century?

Last Updated: Tuesday, July 7, 2009 | 12:51 PM ET Comments 19 Recommend ✓ 38
CBC News

Those refined foods help your body produce the bad kind of cholesterol. That's where statins come in. They work by blocking an enzyme in the liver that is involved in producing cholesterol within liver cells.

"This tricks the liver cells into thinking the cholesterol levels are too low within the cell and the cell puts more receptors onto its surface, which drag the bad LDL cholesterol out of the blood," explains Dr. Rory Collins, professor of epidemiology at Oxford University.

WAIT A MINUTE!! STOP!!!

Like the magic trick with the disappearing-dove, lowering blood LDL cholesterol with a statin comes with a death sentence. The bird didn't disappear. As the cage was crushed, it was shoved into a secret box in the bottom of the cage. It happened so fast, and you were so distracted, you didn't hear the dove cry, the bones crunch or see the blood splatter.

Watch again. Closer.

Did you see it this time?

Chapter 6: The Mycotoxin Gold Rush

Americans do not understand Japanese culture and tradition; they are European descendants with an entirely different mindset.

American soldiers witnessed mass suicide by Japanese soldiers and their families. They fought Kamikazes and never understood the sacrifice. Only 250 years old at the time of WWII, it was not possible for such a young culture to understand a 2,500-year-old culture that values some things more than life.

The Japanese held honor above life.

As a nation, the Japanese would not have surrendered in 1945. They were prepared to withstand a twenty-year siege by the allies.

It took an atom bomb to change their minds.

Once surrendered, they were the most compliant nation ever occupied by a foreign army. It was a matter of honor. The entire society shifted gears and started the prodigious task of rebuilding and becoming westernized.

Akira Endo was 12 years old when the war ended. He was indelibly steeped in honor and tradition. He was also in agreement with his nation. They must westernize.

Japan did not have a counterpart to the FDA. An honorable people do not need such regulatory agencies. They would need one before Endo was done.

In 1957, after receiving his Bachelor of Arts degree, Akira Endo joined Sankyo, a Tokyo-based drug company. In time, after studying cholesterol at the Albert Einstein College of medicine, the young scientist was set to the task of discovering a drug to lower cholesterol. He knew from the scientific literature that some toxic chemicals and fungal metabolites (mycotoxins from disease-causing molds) did the trick.

In 1960, the term "mycotoxin" ("myco" means "fungus") was coined after a fungal toxin in commercial nut feed was found as the source of rapid and deadly cancer epidemics in farm-raised turkey and trout. The discovery spawned the "mycotoxin gold rush" for the next 15 years as drug companies searched for more toxigenic agents from food molds.

In 1971, Endo joined the mycotoxin prospectors.

Having developed fungal enzymes for the food industry, Endo knew how to extract chemicals from fungi. On his walk to work, he treasure-hunted for samples of mold-contaminated grains from Tokyo's street vendors. He could do no less for his honorable employers.

Set on finding Sankyo's golden egg, Endo dedicated long-night hours to extracting mycotoxins from thousands of fungal brews. At times the smell was awful; ever-present was the possibility of inhaling volatilized airborne toxins. He donned safety gear to protect himself from the mushroom clouds.

In 1959, the first FDA-approved cholesterol-lowering drug called MER/29 hit the streets. Scientists reported their finds; Akira kept abreast of the literature.

MER/29 was an estrogen; insiders joked that men with breasts would enjoy less CVD. It blocked the tail of the mevalonate pathway – not isoprenoids – and so the cell cycle was preserved.

Bad effects were limited to cholesterol-deprivation: cataracts and blindness, hair loss, skin disease, impotence and nerve damage.

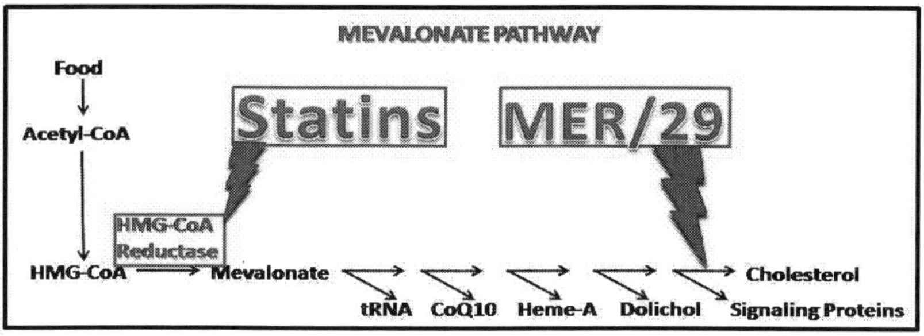

From 1959 to 1961, multiple peer-reviewed double-blind studies hailed MER/29's benefits. MER/29 was an instant success.

Until then, the lipid theory – the belief that lowering cholesterol lowers the incidence of heart disease – was hotly debated. But with FDA approval of MER/29, and "evidence-based medicine" (drug company and NIH engineered "statistics") to back them up, doctors started handing out MER/29 like candy.

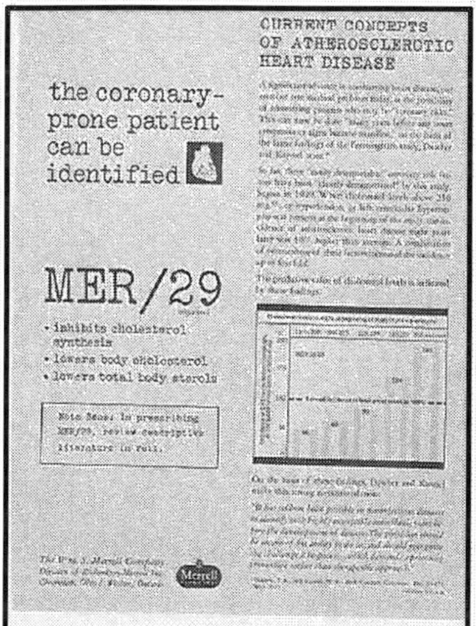

Advertisement which appeared in seven major medical journals in March and April 1962, including the April 16th issue *of Modern Medicine.*

MER/29 was fast on its way to becoming a top-seller. Then one woman ruined it for everybody.

In February 1962, a MER/29 lab worker named Beulah Jordan complained to her husband that her boss, Dr. William King, had ordered her to falsify lab animal data on MER/29's toxic effects. One cold, Cincinnati evening in late February, Thomas Rice, a local FDA inspector, was riding home with Beulah's husband who conveyed to Rice his wife's complaint.

On April 9, 1962, the FDA paid the MER/29 manufacturer a surprise visit and searched the records. They found that Dr. King, who ran the toxicology lab, was not a doctor (Beulah had wasted all that breath calling her boss "doctor"), that preclinical findings of cataracts in rats and dogs had been omitted and that muscle wasting in monkeys had not been reported to the FDA.

Cincinnati, home-city to MER/29's development, got an enema.

A federal grand jury criminal indictment promptly fell on three MER/29 scientists' heads. Civil suits followed and juries awarded multi-millions to the victims. After that, most suits quickly settled out-of-court.

After the MER/29 exposé, a leading trial lawyer documented the story on the criminal indictment of the MER/29 scientists in a light that cast the lipid theory at the heart of the disaster – a fad of the 1950's and stamped out by the MER/29 civil litigation of the 1960's – for good.

The medical community had been duped by a bunch of shysters.

Physicians were ashamed.

Attorneys sounded the alarm and responded to the mass disaster.

The lipid theory was dead.

> ## The MER/ 29 Story—An Instance of Successful Mass Disaster Litigation
>
> *Paul D. Rheingold**
>
> *A. The Medical Background*
>
> In the mid-1950's many physicians believed that high levels of cholesterol, a fatlike substance in the blood and tissue, significantly contributed to atherosclerosis, or hardening of the arteries. Since atherosclerosis in turn led to heart attacks, these physicians believed that lower cholesterol levels would mean fewer deaths from heart attacks.[2] Because low-cholesterol diets were generally recognized as inefficient in reducing cholesterol, many pharmaceutical houses and scientists were searching during the 1950's for a drug either to prevent the formation of cholesterol in the body or to destroy it after formation.

Like a dog returning to its vomit, the AHA-NIH-Pharmaceutical Complex resuscitated the lipid theory. Like a three-pronged racketeering operation, it was foisted again on an unsuspecting public by a voracious pack of wolves returning to its kill.

By the 1970's, MER/29 was humiliating forgotten old news – a topic as popular as flies on feces.

But the NIH maintained the lipid theory was correct. The Framingham study was still on going and more taxpayer-paid studies would begin. The NIH (Steinberg *et al.*) led the march. The public needed rescue from their "bad" LDL cholesterol.

Drug companies responded to the call to replace MER/29. Reports surfaced on various fungal toxins and chemicals that lowered cholesterol.

Familiarized with a report by Raistrick and Smith on the fungal toxin citrinin, Akira Endo extracted some. He wanted to see if, like other known mycotoxins, it too lowered blood cholesterol in lab rats. Citing other scientists in his papers, Endo also knew that

Boots, Noble and Guyer found that some chemicals lower cholesterol by blocking reductase. He wondered if citrinin did the same.

Hypocholesterolemic agents II: Inhibition of β-hydroxy-β-methylglutaryl coenzyme a reductase by arylalkyl hydrogen succinates and glutarates

Marvin R. Boots, Sharon G. Boots, Carole M. Noble*, Kenneth E. Guyer*

Article first published online: 16 SEP 2006

DOI: 10.1002/jps.2600620620

Copyright © 1973 Wiley-Liss, Inc., A Wiley Company

Issue

Journal of Pharmaceutical Sciences

Volume 62, Issue 6, pages 952–957, June 1973

Citrinin, a mycotoxin first isolated in 1961 from the fungus *Penicillium citrinum,* was a proven kidney toxin in all-animal species tested.

Endo extracted it anyway. He had extracted thousands of fungal toxins that were too toxic or did not work. He was tired of coming up empty-handed. It worked. Citrinin lowered blood cholesterol.

CITRININ, AN INHIBITOR OF CHOLESTEROL SYNTHESIS

AKIRA ENDO and MASAO KURODA

Fermentation Research Laboratories,
Sankyo Co., Ltd.,
Shinagawa-ku, Tokyo 140, Japan

(Received for publication April 28, 1976)

It is evident from Table 2 that citrinin administration to normal rats for 7 days considerably lowered the plasma and liver cholesterol levels.

VOL. XXIX NO. 8 THE JOURNAL OF ANTIBIOTICS

Primary fungal metabolites are pro-life. Secondary fungal metabolites are anti-life. In the cutthroat world of fungi, secondary metabolites like citrinin are mycotoxins. Mycotoxins block the growth and reproduction of competing organisms. The mycotoxin gold rush diggers knew these anti-life secondary fungal metabolites had potential use in a drug industry designed to primarily treat symptoms rather than cure disease.

Evaluation of toxicity of the mycotoxin citrinin using yeast ORF DNA microarray and Oligo DNA microarray

Hitoshi Iwahashi[1 *], Emiko Kitagawa[1], Yoshiteru Suzuki[1], Youji Ueda[2], Yo-hei Ishizawa[2], Hitoshi Nobumasa[3], Yoshihide Kuboki[4], Hiroshi Hosoda[5] and Yumiko Iwahashi[5]

Background

Mycotoxins are fungal secondary metabolites commonly present in feed and food, and are widely regarded as hazardous contaminants. Citrinin, one of the very well known mycotoxins that was first isolated from *Penicillium citrinum*, is produced by more than 10 kinds of fungi, and is possibly spread all over the world. However, the information on the action mechanism of the toxin is limited. Thus, we investigated the citrinin-induced genomic response for evaluating its toxicity.

Results

Citrinin inhibited growth of yeast cells at a concentration higher than 100 ppm.

BMC Genomics 2007, 8:95

Statins are secondary fungal metabolites like citrinin; these mycotoxins are poisonous to microbes and human cells.

Chem. Rev. 2009, *109*, 3903–3990 3903

Chemistry and Biology of Mycotoxins and Related Fungal Metabolites

Stefan Bräse,* Arantxa Encinas,† Julia Keck,‡ and Carl F. Nising§

Institut für Organische Chemie, Karlsruhe Institute of Technology, Fritz-Haber-Weg 6, D-76131 Karlsruhe, Germany

Received October 1, 2007

Table 2. Mycotoxins Produced by *Aspergillus* sp.

fungus	mycotoxin produced
Aspergillus terreus	Territrem A,[25] Citreoviridin, Citrinin (**2**), Gliotoxin (**527**), Patulin (**3**), Terrein, Terreic acid, Terretonin, Itaconic acid, Aspulvinone, Asterric acid, Asterriquinone, butyrolactone I, Emodin (**573**), Geodin, Itaconate, Lovastatin,[26] Questin, Sulochrin, Terrecyclic acid.

Most mycotoxins come from four species of fungi: *Aspergillus*, *Penicillium, Proteus* and *Monascus*. These are the same four fungal species used to make statins.

Chem. Rev. 2008, *108*, 3903–3990

Chemistry and Biology of Mycotoxins and Related Fungal Metabolites

Stefan Bräse,* Arantxa Encinas,† Julia Keck,‡ and Carl F. Nising§

Institut für Organische Chemie, Karlsruhe Institute of Technology, Fritz-Haber-Weg 6, D-76131 Karlsruhe, Germany

Table 3. Continued

mycotoxin class	name (stereochemistry) (alternative name)	producing fungus (example)
Statin	Compactin[25] (Mevastatin)	*Penicillium cyclopium*, *P. citrinum*, *P. solitum*[7]

Agendas are the enemy of true science. Endo accentuated the positive and excluded the negative. Citrinin was kidney-toxic, so he didn't report on his rats' kidneys. He instead reported on the positive effects of citrinin on rat liver:

Biochimica et Biophysica Acta (BBA) - Lipids and Lipid Metabolism
Volume 486, Issue 2, 23 February 1977, Pages 254-259

Inhibition of sterol synthesis by citrinin in a cell-free system from rat liver and yeast

Kuroda Masao, Hazama-Shimada Yoko, Endo Akira

Fermentation Research Laboratories, Sankyo Co. Ltd., 1-2-58 Hiromachi, Shinagawa-ku, Tokyo, 140 Japan

At the time, a 150-million-dollar taxpayer-paid NIH-study led by lipid-theorist agenda-driven Steinberg called the Coronary Primary Prevention Trial (CPPT) was in the works. A gritty bile-resin called cholestyramine was being tested on thousands of humans to see if lowering blood cholesterol would reduce CVD. This drug robs the liver of its normally recycled cholesterol-rich bile from the gut, forcing the liver to work over-time to make up the difference. This can cause an increase in liver weight (called hepatomegaly or "big liver").

Endo boasted that unlike Steinberg's bile-resin, citrinin did not enlarge the liver like that other nasty-tasting cholesterol-lowering drug.

Endo confirmed that citrinin, like the toxins reported by Boots *et al.*, also lowered blood cholesterol by inhibiting reductase. But he admittedly had to give up on citrinin. Like cyanide's effect on cellular respiration, citrinin's action on reductase was irreversible. It also blocked respiration. Cells could not breathe.

Citrinin was simply too toxic.

How One Scientist Intrigued by Molds Found First Statin

Endo

By PETER LANDERS
Staff Reporter of THE WALL STREET JOURNAL
January 9, 2006; Page A1

For more than two years, he and his team worked into the night at their lab next to a train depot in southern Tokyo. "We were doing grunt work every day until we got sick of it," he recalls. Some chemicals blocked the enzyme well but were rejected because they were toxic.

Citrinin, like statins, is an antibiotic – albeit a kidney-toxic one. He abandoned citrinin then extracted ML-236B from *Penicillium citrinum*. Like citrinin, ML-236B also lowered blood cholesterol by blocking reductase.

The discovery and development of HMG-CoA reductase inhibitors

Endo

Akira Endo
Department of Applied Biological Science, Tokyo Noko University, Fuchu, Tokyo, 183 Japan

Over a 2-year period, approximately 6,000 microbial strains were tested for their ability to block lipid synthesis. As a result, the antibiotic citrinin was first isolated as an active compound from the mold *Pythium ultimum* (29). Citrinin was shown to irreversibly inhibit HMG-CoA reductase (30). Subsequently, a strain of *Penicillium citrinum* was found to produce active compound(s). To isolate the active component(s), 600 l of culture filtrate was extracted with organic solvents and applied to silica gel chromatography, followed by crystallization, giving crystals (23 mg) of mevastatin (formerly called ML-236B).

Journal of Lipid Research Volume 33, 1992

Endo's tone changed.

After discovering ML-236B, Endo began to use euphemisms like "fungal metabolite" instead of "mycotoxin". Reductase was reduced to the "rate-limiting enzyme" in cholesterol synthesis rather than "master-regulator of cell growth and replication".

Inhibitory Effects on Lipid Metabolism in Cultured Cells of ML-236B, a Potent Inhibitor of 3-Hydroxy-3-methylglutaryl-Coenzyme-A Reductase

Endo

Isao KANEKO, Yoko HAZAMA-SHIMADA, and Akira ENDO
Fermentation Research Laboratories, Sankyo Co. Ltd, Tokyo
(Received January 4, 1978)

The fungal metabolite ML-236B is a potent inhibitor of cholesterol synthesis both *in vitro* and *in vivo* that competitively inhibits 3-hydroxy-3-methylglutaryl-CoA reductase, the rate-limiting enzyme in cholesterol synthetic pathway [1 – 3] ;

Eur. J. Biochem. 87, 313 – 321 (1978)

During the next three years of testing ML-236B, it became clear to Endo that reductase was more than just the "rate limiting step" in cholesterol metabolism. ***In 1981, he acknowledged that reductase was central to cell life.***

The Journal of Biological Chemistry
Vol. 256, No. 13, Issue of July 10, pp. 6762-6766, 1981
Printed in U.S.A.

Isolation and Characterization of Cells Resistant to ML236B (Compactin) with Increased Levels of 3-Hydroxy-3-methylglutaryl Coenzyme A Reductase*

Endo

Judith Ryan‡, Edna C. Hardeman§, Akira Endo¶, and Robert D. Simoni||

HMG-CoA reductase,[1] which catalyzes the conversion of HMG-CoA to mevalonate, has long been established as a key regulatory enzyme in the cholesterogenic pathway (1). More recent studies have emphasized the role of this enzyme in the pathway of other mevalonate-derived products, such as ubiquinone, dolichol, and isopentenyladenine (2–8). It has become increasingly clear that this enzyme is central to both cell growth and division (9–14).

The same toxin as ML-236B (mevastatin) was discovered by Beecham from a different fungus and named "compactin". Except for use in research, compactin was abandoned as a pharmaceutical for its known blockade of cell replication.

In his series, "An Interpretive History of the Cholesterol Controversy", Daniel Steinberg boasts that Beecham abandoned compactin's development in 1980 because it was a weak antibiotic and they didn't know "what a treasure they had in their hands." The truth of the matter, despite the Merck-consultant's claim to the contrary, is that Beecham dropped compactin's development because they knew it was lethal to cells.

In 1981, Beecham had been alerted to the prime importance of reductase and the isoprenoids ("non-sterol intermediates") for normal cell function and embryo development. With exacting detail, Robin Fears explains why Beecham had so many fears about touching "the pathway":

The contribution of the cholesterol biosynthetic pathway to intermediary metabolism and cell function

Robin FEARS

Beecham Pharmaceuticals Research Division, Great Burgh, Epsom, Surrey KT18 5XQ, U.K.

It is the purpose of the present review to consider those aspects of the pathway which have received relatively less attention previously. First, to discuss the role of HMG-CoA reductase in providing non-sterol intermediates required for cell function.

Biochem. J. (1981) 199, 1-7
Printed in Great Britain

Unlike Beecham's Robin Fears, Akira Endo fearlessly continued to develop ML-236B, even after watching cells fizz-out and "round up" after day one (cells deprived of dolichol take on an abnormal round shape) and stop growing after day two.

Inhibitory Effects on Lipid Metabolism in Cultured Cells of ML-236B, a Potent Inhibitor of 3-Hydroxy-3-methylglutaryl-Coenzyme-A Reductase

Isao KANEKO, Yoko HAZAMA-SHIMADA, and Akira ENDO
Fermentation Research Laboratories, Sankyo Co. Ltd, Tokyo
(Received January 4, 1978)

Cell growth in the presence of 5 μg/ml of ML-236B was not detectably affected until after 48 h but most cells became round within 24 h.

Endo pressed on. There were people with high cholesterol due to genetically defective LDL receptors; this birth defect is called Familial Hypercholesterolemia (FH). FH patients with flawed genes from both parents were only one in a million. But the more common type, those with a bad gene from one parent, were one in 500 or 12,000,000 worldwide – potential customers for Sankyo. Those people might be willing to risk killing some cells for less blood cholesterol.

In 1975, Endo contacted Joe Goldstein at Dallas where he and Brown were studying the genetics of FH.

That encounter would prove potentially lethal to us all.

Brown and Goldstein were studying the defective LDL receptor genes in FH. Endo asked Goldstein if he might be interested in testing his ML-236B to lower cholesterol in these patients. Goldstein agreed and sent Endo some diseased cells from their FH patients. Plans were made for future joint research. A new alliance was in the mill with America. Saki time!

Endo wrote to Goldstein in October 1975 and his study interested the American researcher. Goldstein agreed with Endo's idea that mevastatin might work in disease cells, and he also proposed that they conduct joint research. Endo acquired cells from FH patients from the United States and tested mevastatin in those and other mammalian cells by using the techniques Goldstein and Brown developed.

At the time, Brown and Goldstein's lab was connected to Merck via Alexander Bearn and P. Roy Vagelos. Merck learned of Endo's discovery and contacted Japan. Merck and Sankyo signed a one-page contract written by Merck.

With a non-disclosure agreement from Merck and pending plans for Endo to join Dallas to study ML-236B, Sankyo was led to believe they had entered into a joint venture with Merck to develop and market their statin. After Sankyo received samples of FH cells from Goldstein, Sankyo freely gave Merck ML-236B samples and toxicology data.

Merck suddenly stopped calling. Sankyo became worried that Merck had a hidden agenda.

Scientist Finds Drug that Changes the Lives of Heart Patients

"We received no response from Merck and had a feeling of dread that maybe they were contriving a plot of some sort."

-Akira Endo, sometime after Merck asked for and received a sample of compactin for study

Sankyo's worst fears were realized. Merck had taken Sankyo's crystals and quickly isolated an almost-identical mycotoxin from a different fungus. They published their finds in a report with a "thank you" to Sankyo for the generous gift of ML-236B.

Proc. Natl. Acad. Sci. USA
Vol. 77, No. 7, pp. 3957–3961, July 1980
Biochemistry

Mevinolin: A highly potent competitive inhibitor of hydroxymethylglutaryl-coenzyme A reductase and a cholesterol-lowering agent

[fungal metabolites/crystal structure/absolute configuration/cholesterol synthesis/ML-236B (compactin)]

A. W. Alberts*, J. Chen*, G. Kuron*, V. Hunt*, J. Huff*, C. Hoffman†, J. Rothrock†, M. Lopez†, H. Joshua†, E. Harris†, A. Patchett†, R. Monaghan‡, S. Currie‡, E. Stapley‡, G. Albers-Schonberg¶, O. Hensens¶, J. Hirshfield¶, K. Hoogsteen¶, J. Liesch¶, and J. Springer¶

*Department of Biochemical Regulation, †New Leads Discovery Department, ‡Department of Basic & Applied Microbiology, and ¶Department of Biophysics, Merck Sharp & Dohme Research Laboratories, Rahway, New Jersey 07065

Communicated by P. Roy Vagelos, April 18, 1980

We are grateful to Dr. Issei Iwai, Sankyo Co. for the generous gift of ML-236B.

The Americans clearly did not understand. The Japanese would consider it an insult to require hundreds of pages of agreement to protect them. A man was honorable until proven otherwise. Merck operated on the Calvinist European attitude. Honor and honesty were good things but "business was business." It is the American way.

The Japanese way is to shun and ostracize the dishonorable. Since Endo was considered in league with the Americans, he was shunned. Only thirty years earlier he would have been expected to commit suicide (hari-kari).

> A gift from nature: the birth of the statins
>
> Akira Endo
>
> We were, in fact, under the impression that both companies were jointly developing compactin. However, in the fall of 1978, Merck independently discovered lovastatin from another fungus, *Aspergillus terreus*.

After 21 years of dedicated service, at the peak of his career and when his research had been the most valuable to Sankyo, he was expected to leave.

Endo departed Sankyo without anyone so much as lifting a finger to help him move. He experienced a fate worse than death to a Japanese man: he was dishonored. Sankyo immediately canceled "joint ventures" with Merck.

> *Stalking Cholesterol*
> **How One Scientist Intrigued by Molds Found First Statin**
>
> Akira Endo is at Biopharm Research Laboratories, Inc., 3-41-3 501 Shimorenjaku, Mitaka, Tokyo 181-0013, Japan. e-mail: aendo@biopherm.co.jp
>
> By PETER LANDERS
> Staff Reporter of THE WALL STREET JOURNAL
> *January 9, 2006; Page A1*
>
> Dr. Endo figured he had brought it as far as he could, and decided to quit Sankyo for a professor's post at Tokyo Noko University. It wasn't a friendly parting: Dr. Endo still complains that the company ordered the scientists in his lab not to help him carry his boxes of papers to the moving truck.

Endo became a driven man. He had to be vindicated.

Chapter 7: The Fungal War

Endo was onto Merck's game. He had completely grasped the Western doctrine of every man for himself. No longer a company man, he formed a desperate plan to restore his honor. He would become a Ronin, a rogue disgraced Samurai, an outlaw who would sell his sword to anyone – even Sankyo.

He took a job at Tokyo Noko University and continued to sharpen his sword and further his research. Endo the man without honor and Steinberg the master manipulator would bring statins to the world.

Endo prepared a batch of Sankyo's ML-236B to begin the first human tests. He secretly telephoned a physician named Yamamoto from his alma mater and asked if he, like Goldstein and Brown, would also like to test ML-236B on FH patients. With no FDA-like agency to regulate them, this was a chance to out-smart the Americans. Yamamoto agreed.

Stalking Cholesterol

How One Scientist Intrigued by Molds Found First Statin

Akira Endo is at Biopharm Research Laboratories, Inc., 3-41-3 501 Shimorenjaku, Mitaka, Tokyo 181-0013, Japan. e-mail: aendo@biopharm.co.jp

By PETER LANDERS
Staff Reporter of THE WALL STREET JOURNAL
January 9, 2006; Page A1

Akira Yamamoto

With the support of only his boss at the research labs, Dr. Endo embarked on a secret experiment at Osaka University. A doctor at the university hospital named Akira Yamamoto was treating patients who had extremely high cholesterol because of a genetic defect. Dr. Endo recalls phoning Dr. Yamamoto from home at night so colleagues didn't learn about the experiment. He personally prepared the samples of the drug and carried them to Osaka. Nowadays such a trial would typically require permission from a review board and the Japanese equivalent of the FDA, but those steps weren't necessary at the time.

Dr. Yamamoto made an astounding discovery. His first test patient, a woman of childbearing age, had so much muscular dysfunction that she couldn't walk. She never took another statin.

> The first patient in the world to receive a statin, an 18-year-old woman, was also the first to suffer a side effect that occasionally occurs with statins: muscle pain. Because Dr. Yamamoto had given her an extremely high dose, she became so weak she was unable to walk. Dr. Yamamoto says his boss at the university advised him to halt the tests.

Despite being advised by his boss to stop human trials, Yamamoto forged ahead without giving his patients informed consent on the risks of ingesting a mycotoxin:

> Dr. Yamamoto insisted on carrying on. He discontinued the drug on the first patient, and she recovered. He tried compactin on other patients in lower doses. It succeeded in lowering cholesterol in nine patients by an average of 27%, according to a paper he later published. Dr. Yamamoto concedes he didn't give the patients much information about the treatment he was testing on them. "They trusted me, and I think I responded to that trust," he says.

In July 1978, Yamamoto and Endo submitted their report to *Atherosclerosis* magazine, published by Elsevier. For unknown reasons, it was revised in April the following year, officially "accepted" in September 1979 and then finally published in March 1980 – a total of 20 months. While Elsevier was then well respected in the medical world, they were later caught publishing phony medical journals and bogus studies for Merck. Did Elsevier advise Merck of Endo's research and stall the print?

> **Therapeutic effects of ML-236B in primary hypercholesterolemia**
>
> Akira Yamamoto, Hiroshi Sudo, Akira Endo
>
> Received 16 July 1978; received in revised form 24 April 1979; accepted 5 September 1979.
>
> **Abstract**
>
> ML-236B, a competitive inhibitor of 3-hydroxy-3-methylglutaryl CoA reductase, was administered to 11 patients with primary hypercholesterolemia. After 4–8 weeks of drug treatment at doses of 50–150 mg/day, serum cholesterol levels were reduced by 11–37% (27% on average) in cases of heterozygous familial hypercholesterolemia and combined hyperlipidemia.

Nevertheless, Endo had to stop advancing with Sankyo's statin. He donned his mask and went back to extracting mycotoxins.

In February 1979, Endo discovered that the fungus *Monascus* also made Merck's toxin, from *Aspergillus.*

"Tsumi!" ("Check-mate!")

Despite he had extracted Merck's mycotoxin monocolin-K (lovastatin), it was patentable because it was from a *different* fungus.

"Sayonara, Merck."

With results from human tests, Endo sold his Japanese patent to Sankyo. Sankyo promptly applied for an international patent.

The fungal war was on.

In June 1979, Merck applied for the U.S. patent for lovastatin. After applying for an international patent, Merck discovered that Sankyo had beaten them to the spoils.

Sankyo's international patent application predated Merck's!

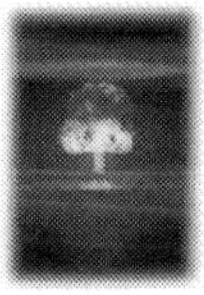

Merck's bridge took a direct hit. Boardrooms were quickly filled with muffled voices, scuffling feet and pounding fists. Merck's office in Japan was put on red-alert.

And then, like the eye of a typhoon passing directly overhead, all went still at Merck in August of 1980. Merck's watchman in Japan had informed Merck's Vagelos in New Jersey that Sankyo canceled all of its statin clinical tests on FH patients. Intestinal lymphomas, a rare cancer of the small intestines, had developed in half their ML-236B experimental dogs.

Still completely ignorant of Japanese values, Vagelos tried to get details from Sankyo executives. No one at Sankyo would talk to him. "Hell," Vagelos must have thought, "Alberts was having trouble anyway with all those dying rabbits."

"ALL STOP!" came the order from Merck's helm. The fungal war came to a screeching halt.

But that was not the End-o the story.

While Sankyo may have given up on Endo's statin, there were other true believers. Like Steinberg, Endo was on a mission and had to be restored. Inadvertently, Endo and Steinberg served one another. Both were bonded brothers in the war to stamp out “bad” LDL cholesterol. Steinberg needed Endo's statin; Endo needed Steinberg's stature.

Undaunted by Sankyo's decision to stop developing *his* statin, Endo found another believer named Mabuchi who agreed to test ML-236B on his FH patients. In 1981, they reported that ML-236B had no effect on the “homozygous” FH patients who had 100% genetically defective LDL receptors. It did, however, lower cholesterol in “heterozygous” FH patients with half the normal LDL receptors.

Effects of ML-236B (Compactin) on Sterol Synthesis and Low Density Lipoprotein Receptor Activities in Fibroblasts of Patients with Homozygous Familial Hypercholesterolemia

Toshihiro Hara, Hiroshi Mabuchi, Akira Yoshimura, Akira Watanabe, Takanobu Wakasugi, Ryozo Tatami, Kohei Ueda, Ryoshi Ueda, Tomio Kametani, Junji Koizumi, Susumu Miyamoto, and Ryoyu Takeda

J. Clin. Invest. © *The American Society for Clinical Investigation, Inc.* Volume 67 May 1981

That was an early “clue” that statins' worked via the LDL-receptors and not by blocking cholesterol synthesis.

After it was clear that statin studies in FH patients had resumed in Japan, former NIH chief Daniel Steinberg advised Vagelos to get back into the “knock-down, drag-out race”. He insisted that there were people, like FH patients, who were dying for Merck's statins. “Even if there were risks, even life-threatening risks, those had to be balanced against the potential life-saving benefits of treatment. Dropping the program might deny some patients a chance to prolong their lives,” he advised (reference 5). He could get the job done at the FDA.

People with FH lived as long as anyone else until the turn of the 20th century when CVD rates began to rise in the U.S. (references 6 and 7). But the self-declared hero also had a lipid theory to defend. He had already spent a half a billion taxpayers' dollars trying to prove it. The premise that lowering cholesterol would reduce CVD was repeatedly tested, but the results were abysmal and generated nothing but skepticism among cardiologists. It drove Steinberg mad.

Steinberg was sick of the naysayers. The lipid theory skeptics stuck in his craw like cholestyramine. He would make believers out of them soon enough. They would learn to conform to NIH-endorsed national cholesterol policy rather than risk losing their medical licenses.

Having shoved sandy bile-acid resins down thousands of subjects' throats, all Steinberg had was relative statistics to wave for banners and no absolute numbers or hard science to back him up. He still had a cholesterol war to wage and opponents to crush. Like the captain of an elite guard, he had the drive, tax money and position to foist a cholesterol-lowering drug on the public again. And, there was "no proof," said he, that statins were dangerous – only rumors.

An interpretive history of the cholesterol controversy, part V: The discovery of the statins and the end of the controversy[1]

Journal of Lipid Research Volume 47, 2006

Daniel Steinberg[2]

Department of Medicine, University of California-San Diego, La Jolla, CA

Steinberg

Dropping the program might deny some patients a chance to prolong their lives. Moreover, there was still no hard evidence that compactin would be toxic in humans, only rumors about toxicity in dogs given very high doses.

He lied. Greed listened. He led the fungal war. The FDA trusted Steinberg and gave Merck a green light.

Statins came to market because of two mad men. Endo was seeking vindication at all costs. Steinberg had to be right at all costs. Statins were the answer to uphold them both.

Steinberg credits himself and a handful of his comrades for encouraging Merck to start human statin trials in Dallas when the two captains in the East and West, Sankyo and Merck, had already called a stop to the madness.

In short nothing was going to stop Endo – not even cell mutations, cancer in dogs and the crippling results on his first patient. Nothing was going to stop Steinberg – not even life-threatening risks.

Endo had succeeded. He became westernized.

Steinberg already was.

Chapter 8: Mimicry

Mimicry is pretending to be something that you are not. Men do it, butterflies do it and lactone-ring-making toxic fungi do it. The lactone ring in statins is an example of lethal fungal "mimicry".

Merck consultant Daniel Steinberg claims that Beecham dropped out of the statin race in 1980 because they failed to recognize what a treasure they had. This, he says (lies), is because they missed that the "lactone" portion of their compactin was what interrupted reductase's function.

An interpretive history of the cholesterol controversy, part V: The discovery of the statins and the end of the controversy[1]

Journal of Lipid Research Volume 47, 2006

Daniel Steinberg[2]

Department of Medicine, University of California-San Diego, La Jolla, CA

Steinberg

Their initial report did not mention the close homology between the lactone ring in compactin and that of 3-hydroxymethylglutarate. [1]

A scientist with an agenda cannot be trusted to tell us the truth. Let us take a closer look at this "lactone ring" that Steinberg implies Beecham "missed".

Upon closer look, it is the lactone ring of statins that makes them poisons. Reductase confuses this lactone ring with "good food" to make mevalonate. It is a deadly mistake.

Fungi make primary metabolites to live and replicate – hence the word "primary". In the toxic world of fungi, poisonous secondary metabolites mimic primary metabolites. If you're a fungus among us looking for something to quickly rot (and eat – remember fungi cannot make food; they decay/digest it and absorb it), you make a toxic secondary metabolite that looks, smells and tastes like a primary metabolite. If the enemy is fooled and ingests the deadly toxin, you keep the real estate. In this light, fungi do not only digest dead matter; they can kill living matter too – and feast upon the spoils.

Statins are secondary fungal metabolites made to kill competing microbes. Statins look like the precursor to mevalonate; reductase is "tricked" to bond with the statin. Reductase in turn is blocked (disabled, inhibited, neutralized – pick a word). It is lethal for the single-celled microbes that take the bait.

Endo reasoned fungi might make secondary metabolites that block reductase; cholesterol and isoprenoids are, after all, life-essential. Sankyo was replete with toxic fungi, test animals and bosses with stockholders to appease.

The discovery and development of HMG-CoA reductase inhibitors

Akira Endo

Department of Applied Biological Science, Tokyo Noko University, Fuchu, Tokyo, 183 Japan

Endo

I began in 1971, with Dr. Masao Kuroda, to search for HMG-CoA reductase inhibitors of microbial origin. We hoped that certain microorganisms would produce such compounds as a weapon in the fight against other microbes that required sterols or other isoprenoids for growth. Inhibition of HMG-CoA reductase would thus be lethal to these microbes.

Journal of Lipid Research Volume 33, 1992

Secondary metabolites were and are to this day potential mycotoxin gold for any drug company. Many drugs are fungal toxins. Penicillin serves as one example – which explains why some people die from just a single dose (in some cases this is due to massive destruction of red blood cells). Drug companies call a lethal or potentially lethal reaction to a fungal toxin an "allergy".

Isoprenoids make over 25,000 different types of primary metabolites found in nature. Vital to supporting life, including fungi, isoprenoids support cell functions such as metabolism, replication and membrane stability. Isoprenoids – as primary metabolites – are pro-life.

Isoprenoids also form the largest group of secondary metabolites found in nature. These are anti-life. ***Fungi make them to mimic primary metabolites and kill competing organisms.*** If the competing organism is single-celled, it dies quickly. If the competing organism is multi-celled, it dies one cell at a time.

Isoprenoids give membranes strength (dolichol), make energy (CoQ10) and promote cell cycles (isopentenyl adenine). By blocking isoprenoid synthesis, statins cause cells to:

- Lose their shape and "round up" (i.e., loss of dolichol)
- Stop replicating (i.e., loss of isopentenyl adenine)
- Die (i.e., loss of CoQ10)

Adding cholesterol ***does not*** rescue cells from statin toxicity. Adding mevalonate does. The statin blockade of making isoprenoids (not cholesterol) from mevalonate is what kills cells.

> **The discovery and development of HMG-CoA reductase inhibitors** — Akira Endo
>
> Subsequently, studies by other investigators showed that in cultured fibroblasts high concentrations of mevastatin block passage through the cell cycle (45–47) and alter cell morphology (48). Both effects could be prevented by the addition of mevalonate but not by the addition of cholesterol, which suggested that either mevalonate or one (or more) of its nonsterol products was involved.
>
> Journal of Lipid Research Volume 33, 1992

The lactone ring of statins mimics a portion of HMG-CoA that reductase converts into mevalonate. By confusing the statin for HMG-CoA, reductase's normal active site (below) is blocked by the statin (following page).

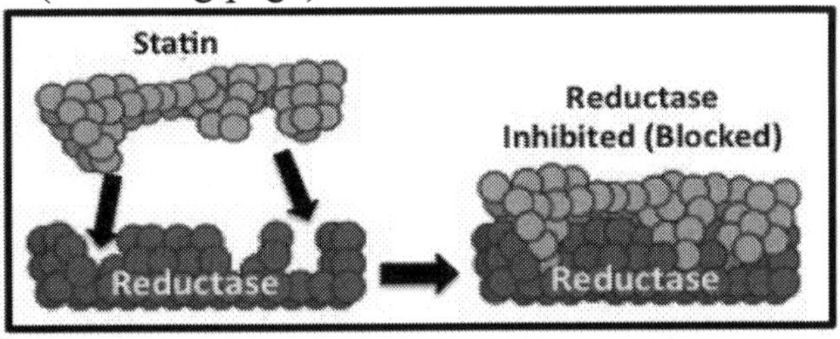

Steinberg is correct. In the callous world of statin-making fungi, it is indeed the lactone ring of statins that stuffs up reductase and kills enemy “bugs” – dead. Or, if you're a human and ingest a statin, you, too, experience the toxic effects of reductase blockade and mevalonate deprivation – albeit slowly (except the Baycol victims who died rather quickly).

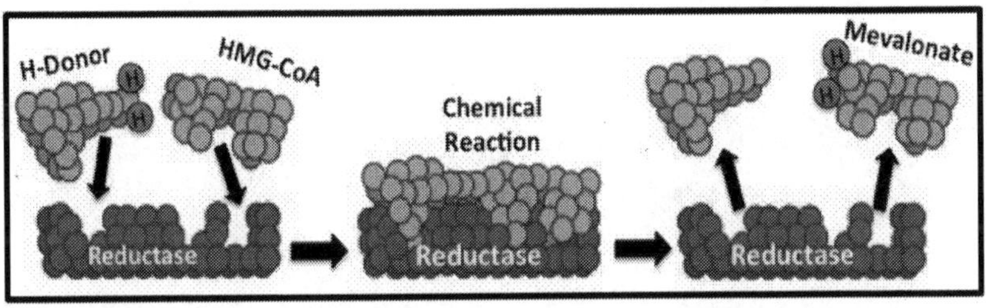

One cell or ten thousand cells at once, the process remains the same: reductase is blocked then cells make more reductase which stimulates LDL receptors to be made at the same time. Cells ultimately get their fill of LDL cholesterol (via the receptors) but they remain deprived of isoprenoids so reductase is again increased in an attempt to make isoprenoids. Blood cholesterol is lowered again.

When it's time for the cells to cycle they are blocked. Some cells make enough reductase to overcome the statin blockade and cell cycles are restored...until another statin is ingested and then blocked again. Round and round it goes like Russian roulette.

The truth of statin toxicity was buried long ago.

But statins *do* lower cholesterol! So does snake venom – another secondary metabolite made by poisonous snakes to kill.

What secondary fungal metabolites like statins all have in common is a lactone ring – thank you Dr. Steinberg. It's easy to find lactone rings under UV light because they fluoresce. Statins (fluorescent molds) are like an alien contaminant engineered by

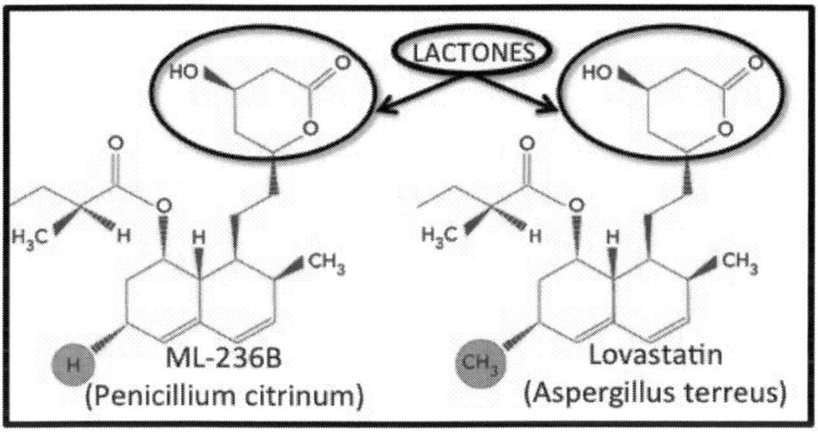

sci-fi movie antagonists to destroy an entire race.
Even more outlandish is where the robber barons persuade an entire planet to gladly pay for a fungal toxin that creates a slew of new diseases to sell them even more drugs, bankrupt third-party payers, escalate medical costs, destroy whole nations and collapse world economies.

And so it goes until "poof!" it all implodes. Black screen, rolling credits, "The End".

"Man, could you believe *that* story? Terrifying!"

It is, indeed, the lactone ring that attaches to and disables reductase. Beecham got it. Endo and Merck did not.

Contrary to Steinberg's implication, this artful mimicry by disease-causing fungi is not a good thing. Many lactone ring-bearing secondary metabolites induce cancer, destroy organs, disable nerves and cause muscles to tremble.

Many of these lactone ring-containing mycotoxins are made by the fungi *Aspergillus* and *Penicillium* – as are, respectively, Merck's lovastatin and Endo's ML-236B/mevastatin. Scientists are not entirely sure just how these toxins work but Endo has made some sense of it for us:

> **The discovery and development of HMG-CoA reductase inhibitors**
>
> 
>
> Endo
>
> **Akira Endo**
>
> Department of Applied Biological Science, Tokyo Noko University, Fuchu, Tokyo, 183 Japan
>
> **These results suggested that the lactone portion of the mevastatin molecule is the active center and binds to the HMG binding site of the reductase molecule. The structural similarity between the lactone and HMG portions supports this conclusion.**
>
> Journal of Lipid Research Volume 33, 1992

Some antibiotics are secondary fungal metabolites with specific deadly effects on disease-causing microbes but do not kill human cells. Even so, some people have potentially deadly "allergic" reactions to fungal antibiotics like penicillin.

Statins – secondary fungal metabolites – are anti-life or anti-bios. Statins are *antibiotics.* Because antibiotics are anti-bios and kill "good" vitamin-producing bacteria in the gut, most are prescribed for as short a term as possible. Statins, on the other hand, are often prescribed for life. Most antibiotics also have specific action on specific microbes. Not so with statins. ***Statins indiscriminately kill any cell including human cells***.

On August 1, 1997, an FDA memo from Drs. Ramsey through

Dempsey through Freeman finally found its way to Dr. Lumpkin's desk. This memo was in response to a June 9, 1997 request by Lumpkin for FDA staff to review the published literature to see if lovastatin is an antibiotic (reference 8).

When Merck did the dog-and-pony show for the FDA on February 19, 1987 that cleared the way for lovastatin's approval, they ignored Merck's biochemist Eve Slater who told them that lovastatin is a "fungal metabolite" (maybe they were eyeing the doughnuts and coffee). They had in their possession Merck's NDA (New Drug Application) and toxicology data – making it indisputably clear that lovastatin is a fungal metabolite.
No one objected when they heard and/or read the words "fungal metabolite". Those words were disregarded.

"Primary fungal metabolites" are pro-life and not used as dangerous drugs that would require FDA approval in the first place. If its radar were intact and fully functional, the FDA would automatically interpret "fungal metabolite" as ***"secondary fungal metabolite".***

On August 1, 1997 Lumpkin got his answer. Yes, lovastatin is an antibiotic. It kills all kinds of fungi and bacteria. Furthermore, he learned that dying microbes are restored to life with mevalonate.

The statin developers knew that statins are lethal to microbes (antibiotics). They also knew that statins are lethal (antibiotic) to human cells unless the cells successfully mutate.

The discovery and development of HMG-CoA reductase inhibitors

Endo

Akira Endo
Department of Applied Biological Science, Tokyo Noko University, Fuchu, Tokyo, 183 Japan

I began in 1971, with Dr. Masao Kuroda, to search for HMG-CoA reductase inhibitors of microbial origin. We hoped that certain microorganisms would produce such compounds as a weapon in the fight against other microbes that required sterols or other isoprenoids for growth. Inhibition of HMG-CoA reductase would thus be lethal to these microbes.

Journal of Lipid Research Volume 33, 1992

Here are more answers for Dr. Lumpkin who wants to know if lovastatin is an antibiotic.

We, too, will send him a response.

Chapter 9: Dear Dr. Lumpkin

Dear Dr. Lumpkin,

This letter is in regard to your inquiry on June 9, 1997 as to possible antibiotic activity of lovastatin.

Lovastatin – all statins – are indisputably antibiotics.

Statins block mevalonate synthesis. Mevalonate makes cholesterol and isoprenoids. While not all antibiotic drugs block isoprenoids, drugs that block isoprenoids are antibiotics.

When isoprenoid synthesis is blocked, cells die. Antibiotics kill cells.

Isoprenoids include thousands of life-essential molecules such as vitamins A and E. Nearly all plants, animals and microbes make them. (A few microbes, such as rickettsia and mycoplasma, have lost the ability to make isoprenoids; they enter into cells and cause disease and/or death by stealing isoprenoids from host cells.)

Two unrelated biochemical pathways make isoprenoids:

1. NMP: Non-Mevalonate Pathway (gram-negative and tuberculosis bacteria, malarial parasites and plants)

2. MP: Mevalonate Pathway (fungi, gram-positive bacteria, animals and humans)

Drugs that target the NMP have antibacterial (gram-negative), anti-malarial and anti-tuberculosis effects; these are antibiotics without known toxic effects on human cells.

Drugs that target the MP have anti-fungal and anti-bacterial (gram-positive) antibiotic effects with potentially deadly toxic effects on human cells – especially if used long-term.

In your files, please review NDA #20-702. You will find there that the manufacturer warned the FDA that cellular depletion of isoprenoids with a statin could be "theoretically deleterious".

Lipitor New Drug Application (NDA)

Orloff

Medical Reviewer: Dr. David G. Orloff

NDA #20-702 submission date: 6-17-1996

Review completed: 10-28-96

Parke Davis to the FDA: "Mevalonate is an intermediate not only in the pathway to cholesterol, but also in the synthesis of the prenyl, geranyl and farnesyl pyrophosphates (used in post-translational modifications of proteins), ubiquinones (compounds of the electric transport chain and critical in energy metabolism, dolichols (used in the maturation of glycoproteins), and isopentenyladenine (a compound of tRNA). ***Cellular depletion of any or all of these metabolic products could theoretically be deleterious"*** (emphasis added).

Absolute scientific convention mandates that the deadly effect of depleting cells of isoprenoids is not theoretical. It kills. Please inform all your statin drug companies and Dr. Orloff.

Isoprenoids are "primary metabolites" vital for several core cell functions. Dolichols, for example, are required for cell wall and cell membrane synthesis. Antibiotics that block isoprenoids and thus dolichol synthesis cause spheroplast formation (swollen, round cells) and death in single-celled microbes.

Statins induce the same effect in human cells. Cells "round up" and die. Humans are multi-celled organisms. It takes time for the antibiotic effect on human cells and organs to manifest. **We do not have a diagnosis for antibiosis to human cells.** The diagnosis is missed and instead called multiple sclerosis, global amnesia, impotence, diverticulosis, pancreatitis, myositis, acute renal failure, etc.

Inhibitory Effects on Lipid Metabolism in Cultured Cells of ML-236B, a Potent Inhibitor of 3-Hydroxy-3-methylglutaryl-Coenzyme-A Reductase

Endo

Isao KANEKO, Yoko HAZAMA-SHIMADA, and Akira ENDO
Fermentation Research Laboratories, Sankyo Co. Ltd, Tokyo

(Received January 4, 1978)

Cell growth in the presence of 5 μg/ml of ML-236B was not detectably affected until after 48 h but most cells became round within 24 h.

Synthesis of Δ^2-Isopentenyl tRNA from Mevalonate in Cultured Human Fibroblasts*

(Received for publication, April 14, 1980, and in revised form, May 21, 1980)

Jerry R. Faust, Michael S. Brown, and Joseph L. Goldstein

When HMG CoA reductase[1] is inhibited by compactin, mevalonate formation is blocked and cultured cells die.

The Journal of Biological Chemistry
Vol. 254, No. 12, Issue of June 25, pp. 5403-5409, 1979
Printed in U.S.A.

Inhibition of Cholesterol Synthesis with Compactin Renders Growth of Cultured Cells Dependent on the Low Density Lipoprotein Receptor*

(Received for publication, January 5, 1979)

Joseph L. Goldstein, Jean A. S. Helgeson, and Michael S. Brown
From the Departments of Molecular Genetics and Internal Medicine, The University of Texas Health Science Center at Dallas, Dallas, Texas 75235

Mevalonate, the product of HMG-CoA reductase, also supported growth, confirming that compactin was exerting its killing effect by a specific inhibition of HMG-CoA reductase.

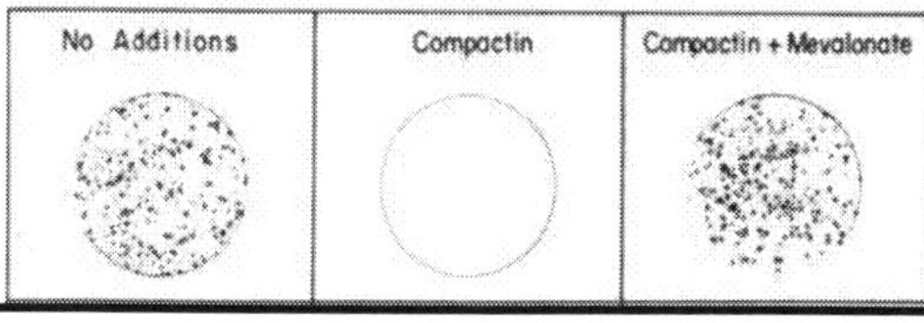

THE JOURNAL OF BIOLOGICAL CHEMISTRY
Vol. 256, No. 13, Issue of July 10, pp. 6762-6768, 1981
Printed in U.S.A.

Isolation and Characterization of Cells Resistant to ML236B (Compactin) with Increased Levels of 3-Hydroxy-3-methylglutaryl Coenzyme A Reductase*

(Received for publication, December 22, 1980, and in revised form, March 16, 1981)

Judith Ryan‡, Edna C. Hardeman§, Akira Endo¶, and Robert D. Simoni‖

From the Department of Biological Science, Stanford University, Stanford, California 94305 and the ¶Department of Agricultural and Biological Chemistry, Tokyo Noko University, Tokyo 183, Japan

At a concentration of 50 μg/ml of ML236B in the culture medium, cholesterol alone is ineffective in preventing cell death; however, mevalonate remains effective.

While not all antibiotic drugs are secondary fungal metabolites, most secondary fungal metabolites are antibiotic mycotoxins. *Aspergillus*, *Penicillium*, *Monascus* and *Proteus* fungi make these antibiotic mycotoxins to kill competing microbes. Statins are secondary metabolites extracted from these four fungi.

Bonn 2010

Analysis of the genetic potential of the sponge-derived fungus *Penicillium chrysogenum* E01-10/3 for polyketide production

Fungal mycotoxins

Mycotoxins are known as low-molecular-weight natural products (i.e. small molecules) produced as secondary metabolites in filamentous fungi. These metabolites represent a chemically heterogeneous group, but they all exhibit high toxicity. By definition mycotoxins are synthesised in filamentous fungi and are toxic to vertebrates and other animal groups in extremely low (i.e. microgram) concentrations [15]. When present in food, these fungal metabolites can have toxic effects with acute (e.g. liver or kidney deterioration) and chronic (e.g. liver cancer) symptoms. Due to their mutagenic and teratogenic profile, exposure to fungal metabolites may result in skin irritation, immunosuppression, birth defects, neurotoxicity and death [16]

The members of the statin family of secondary metabolites are potent inhibitors of 3-hydroxy-3-methylglutaryl-coenzyme A (HMG-CoA) reductase, the key enzyme in cholesterol biosynthesis in humans [87].

If the FDA is to preserve its mandate to ensure safety in drugs, secondary fungal metabolites for use in humans, for long-term, should have action on the NMP and not the MP.

Statins block the MP and are thus "antibiotic" to human cells. Statins are often prescribed indefinitely.

As with most antibiotics, mutations and resistance can be induced in human cells. By 1985, this was proven in three independent laboratories.

More specifically, statins are a class of secondary metabolites called "polyketides".

Chem Biol. 1999 Jul;6(7):429-39.

Lovastatin biosynthesis in Aspergillus terreus: characterization of blocked mutants, enzyme activities and a multifunctional polyketide synthase gene.

Hendrickson L, Davis CR, Roach C, Nguyen DK, Aldrich T, McAda PC, Reeves CD.

ICOS Corporation, 22021 20th Ave SE, Bothell, WA 98021, USA.

Abstract

BACKGROUND: Lovastatin, an HMG-CoA reductase inhibitor produced by the fungus Aspergillus terreus, is composed of two polyketide chains. One is a nonaketide that undergoes cyclization to a hexahydronaphthalene ring system and the other is a simple diketide, 2-methylbutyrate.

Many polyketides are also potent mycotoxins. These include aflatoxin, fumonisins, ochratoxins, and zearalenone. All have structural similarities to statins.

Recent Advancements in the Biosynthetic Mechanisms for Polyketide-Derived Mycotoxins

Justin Huffman, Ryan Gerber, and Liangcheng Du

Department of Chemistry, University of Nebraska-Lincoln, Nebraska, USA 68588

Biopolymers. 2010 September ; 93(9): 764–776. doi:10.1002/bip.21483.

Abstract

Polyketides are a large group of natural products produced by microorganisms and plants. They are biopolymers of acetate and other short carboxylates and are biosynthesized by multifunctional enzymes called polyketide synthases (PKSs). This review focuses on advances in molecular mechanisms of biosynthesis of four toxic polyketide, aflatoxins, fumonisins, ochratoxins, and zearalenone. These metabolites are structurally diverse and differ in their mechanisms of toxicity. However, they are all of concern in food safety and agriculture because of their toxic properties and their frequent accumulation in crops used for food and feed.

Furthermore, statins are polyketides with a lactone ring. Some polyketide secondary metabolites with lactone rings are very potent fluorescent blue-green toxins that lower cholesterol. The *Aspergillus*, *Penicillium*, *Monascus* and *Proteus* fungi make them. These are also the fungi from which statins are extracted.

Aflatoxin, from *Aspergillus flavus,* is a highly carcinogenic lactone-ring-containing polyketide mycotoxin found as a common food contaminant. Merck's lovastatin, from *Aspergillus terreus*, is also a polyketide mycotoxin with a lactone ring.

The lactone ring of polyketides renders these mycotoxins potent cholesterol-lowering antibiotics as well as cancer-causing and organ-toxic agents. Aflatoxin, like lovastatin, lowers cholesterol.

FURTHER STUDIES ON THE CARCINOGENIC ACTION OF CERTAIN LACTONES AND RELATED SUBSTANCES IN THE RAT AND MOUSE

F. DICKENS AND H. E. H. JONES

From the Courtauld Institute of Biochemistry, Middlesex Hospital Medical School, London, W.1

Received for publication January 12, 1965

The lactone ring of polyketide mycotoxins is seen with UV light because it has a FGP (Fluorescent Green Protein). Aflatoxin's cancer-causing effect is decreased 450-fold when the lactone ring is cleaved (and made no longer fluorescent):

CELLULAR AND MOLECULAR LIFE SCIENCES
Volume 37, Number 1, 16-17, DOI: 10.1007/BF01965543

Role of lactone ring of aflatoxin B1 in toxicity and mutagenicity

L. S. Lee, J. J. Dunn, A. J. DeLucca and A. Ciegler

Abstract: Cleavage of the lactone ring of aflatoxin B1 results in a nonfluorescent compound that has greatly reduced biological activity. Mutagenicity, as measured by the Ames test, is reduced 450-fold compared to that of aflatoxin B1, and toxicity, as measured by the chick embryo test, is reduced 18-fold.

Similarly, lactones are associated with statin toxicity.

The Role of Statin Lactones in Statin Toxicity

Principal Investigator Uwe Christians

Recipient Organization UNIVERSITY OF COLORADO DENVER/HSC AURORA

It is our hypothesis that the statin lactones play a key role in statin pharmacokinetics and toxicity.

Lactone ring-containing statins partially react with water into acid forms (some remains in lactone form). Statin-induced muscle toxicity is associated with the lactone form.

Eur J Pharm Sci. 2008 Apr 23;33(4-5):317-25. Epub 2008 Jan 18.

Statin induced myotoxicity: the lactone forms are more potent than the acid forms in human skeletal muscle cells in vitro.

Skottheim IB, Gedde-Dahl A, Hejazifar S, Hoel K, Asberg A.

School of Pharmacy, University of Oslo, Norway. i.b.skottheim@farmasi.uio.no

Abstract

Statins exist in both acid and lactone forms in vivo. High plasma levels of the lactone forms have been observed in patients with statin induced myopathy...Atorvastatin lactone showed a 14-fold, fluvastatin lactone a 26-fold, pravastatin lactone a 23-fold, and simvastatin lactone a 37-fold higher potency to induce myotoxicity compared to their corresponding acid forms.

There is imminent danger to any cell when a lactone ring disables the MP-dependent reductase.

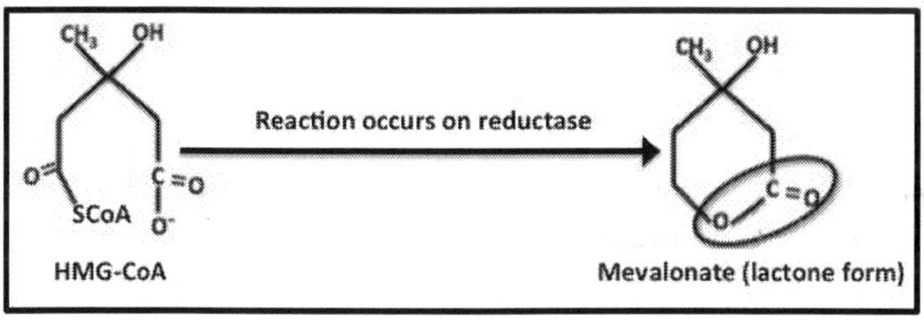

The lactone ring reacts with reductase and disables it from reacting with the normal food-derived primary metabolite HMG-CoA that is normally converted to mevalonate.

The lactone ring of secondary metabolites such as monocolin-K (lovastatin), compactin (pravastatin), aflatoxin and ochratoxin-A attaches to reductase, blocking the mevalonate pathway. All are cholesterol-lowering antibiotics that kill MP-dependent cells or MP-dependent microorganisms. (The lactone portion is circled.)

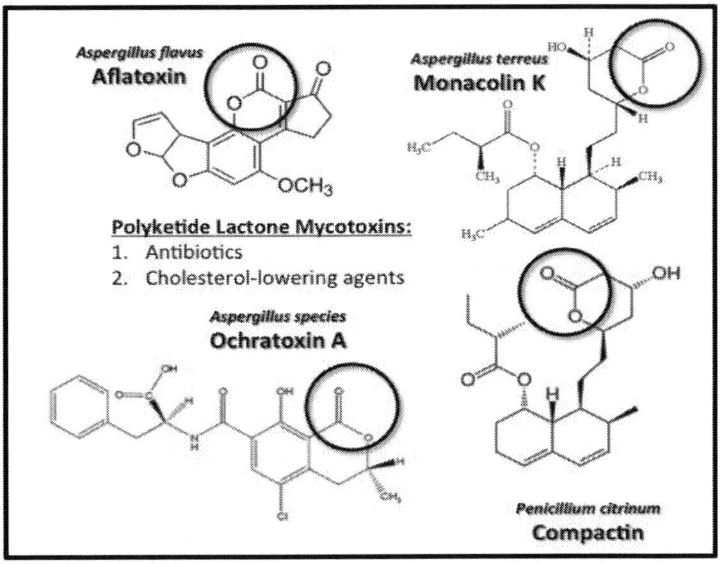

Mevalonate is required for normal cell function and replication. Cholesterol is made from mevalonate. All of these mycotoxins lower cholesterol. Because mevalonate is required for normal cell function and replication, all of these mycotoxins have antibiotic activity against single-celled and multi-celled microbes.

A gift from nature: the birth of the statins

Akira Endo

Discovering compactin from blue-green mold

In 1971, I speculated that microbes would produce antibiotics that inhibited HMG-CoA reductase as a defense mechanism against other microbes that require sterols and/or other mevalonate-derived isoprenoids for their growth, and we created a research unit to isolate such products, focusing on fungi as a source of these metabolites.

Isoprenoids are required for DNA replication; therefore, all of these mycotoxins are clearly genotoxic (toxic to the DNA/genes).

[CANCER RESEARCH 51, 3602–3609, July 1, 1991]

Synchronization of Tumor and Normal Cells from G_1 to Multiple Cell Cycles by Lovastatin[1]

Khandan Keyomarsi,[2] Larue Sandoval, Vimla Band, and Arthur B. Pardee

Divisions of Cell Growth and Regulation [K. K., L. S., A. B. P.] and Cancer Genetics [V. B.], Dana Farber Cancer Institute, Boston, Massachusetts 02115

In this paper, we report that these criteria for synchronization are met using Lovastatin to arrest normal and tumor cells of epithelial as well as fibroblast origin reversibly in the G_1 phase of the cell cycle. Lovastatin, an antihyperlipodemic agent, is widely used for the treatment of hypercholesterolemia. This agent competitively inhibits HMG-CoA[3] reductase, the enzyme required for conversion of HMG-CoA to mevalonic acid (8). In addition, inhibition of mevalonate synthesis by Lovastatin or compactin, a related fungal toxin (9), also inhibits DNA replication (10–15). DNA replication is restored by the addition of mevalonate, the product of the reaction catalyzed by HMG-CoA reductase.

(3) A. Endo, *J. Antibiot.*, 32, 852 (1979).
(4) A. Endo, *J. Antibiot.*, 33, 334 (1980).
(5) A. W. Alberts, J. Chen, G. Kuron, V. Hunt, J. Huff, C. Hoffman, J. Rothrock, J. Lopez, H. Joshua, E. Harris, A. Pachett, R. Monaghan, S. Currie, E. Stapley, G. Albers-Schönberg, O. Hensen, J. Hirshfield, K. Hoogsteen, J. Liesch, and J. Springer, *Proc. Natl. Acad. Sci. U.S.A.*, 77, 3957 (1980).
(6) T. Y. K. Lam, V. P. Gullo, R. T. Goegelman, D. Jorn, L. Huang, C. DeRiso, R. L. Monaghan, and L. Putter, *J. Antibiot.*, 34, 614 (1981).
(7) G. Albers-Schönberg, H. Joshua, M. B. Lopez, O. D. Hensens, J. P. Springer, J. Chen, S. Ostrove, C. H. Hoffman, A. W. Alberts, and A. A. Pachett, *J. Antibiot.*, 34, 507 (1981).
(8) A. Endo, K. Hasumi, and S. Negishi, *J. Antibiot.*, in press.
(9) A. Endo, K. Hasumi, T. Nakamura, M. Kunishima, and M. Masuda, *J. Antibiot.*, in press.
(10) N. Serizawa, K. Nakagawa, K. Hamano, Y. Tsujita, A. Terahara, and H. Kuwano, *J. Antibiot.*, 36, 604 (1983).
(11) N. Serizawa, K. Nakagawa, K. Hamano, Y. Tsujita, A. Terahara, and H. Kuwano, *J. Antibiot.*, 36, 608 (1983).
(12) N. Serizawa, K. Nakagawa, Y. Tsujita, A. Terahara, H. Kuwano, and M. Tanaka, *J. Antibiot.*, 36, 918 (1983).
(13) H. Yamashita, S. Tsubokawa, and A. Endo, *J. Antibiot.*, in press.

To sum: statins are lactone ring-bearing polyketide antibiotic mycotoxins that block life-essential isoprenoids.

The father of statins, Japan's Akira Endo, discovered a new mycotoxin – a new antibiotic – during the busy drug development decade known as "the mycotoxin gold rush". Expediently, he chose to publish his early finds in the "Journal of Antibiotics". Alternatively, he could have published them in the "World Mycotoxin Journal".

For an excellent review on the above, see "Five Questions About Non-Mevalonate Isoprenoid Biosynthesis" by Odom.

Finally, here are 13 references for the synthesis of the first statin (mycotoxin antibiotic) called compactin. Please note that these "recipes" are published in the "Chemistry and Biology of Mycotoxins and Related Fungal Metabolites".

Chem. Rev. **2009**, *109*, 3903–3990

Chemistry and Biology of Mycotoxins and Related Fungal Metabolites

Stefan Bräse,* Arantxa Encinas,† Julia Keck,‡ and Carl F. Nising§

Institut für Organische Chemie, Karlsruhe Institute of Technology, Fritz-Haber-Weg 6, D-76131 Karlsruhe, Germany

References for Compactin (Mevastatin) Synthesis:

(a) Hagiwara, H.; Nakano, T.; Kon-no, M.; Uda, H. *J. Chem. Soc., Perkin Trans. 1* **1995**, 777. (b) Clive, D. L. J.; Murthy, K. S. K.; Wee, A. G. H.; Prasad, J. S.; Da Silva, G. V. J.; Majewski, M.; Anderson, P. C. *Stud. Nat. Prod. Chem.* **1992**, *11*, 335. (c) Burke, S. D.; Deaton, D. N. *Tetrahedron Lett.* **1991**, *32*, 4651. (d) Clive, D. L. J.; Murthy, K. S. K.; Wee, A. G. H.; Prasad, J. S.; Da Silva, G. V. J.; Majewski, M.; Anderson, P. C.; Evans, C. F.; Haugen, R. D.; Heerze, L. D.; Barrie, J. R. *J. Am. Chem. Soc.* **1990**, *112*, 3018. (e) Danishefsky, S. J.; Simoneau, B. *J. Am. Chem. Soc.* **1989**, *111*, 2599. (f) Clive, D. L. J.; Murthy, K. S. K.; Wee, A. G. H.; Prasad, J. S.; Da Silva, G. V. J.; Majewski, M.; Anderson, P. C.; Haugen, R. D.; Heerze, L. D. *J. Am. Chem. Soc.* **1988**, *110*, 6914. (g) Grieco, P. A.; Lis, R.; Zelle, R. E.; Finn, J. *J. Am. Chem. Soc.* **1986**, *108*, 5908. (h) Keck, G. E.; Kachensky, D. F. *J. Org. Chem.* **1986**, *51*, 2487. (i) Rosen, T.; Heathcock, C. H. *J. Am. Chem. Soc.* **1985**, *107*, 3731. (j) Girotra, N. N.; Wendler, N. L. *Tetrahedron Lett.* **1982**, *23*, 5501. (k) Hsu, C. T.; Wang, N. Y.; Latimer, L. H.; Sih, C. J. *J. Am. Chem. Soc.* **1983**, *105*, 593. (l) Hirama, M.; Uei, M. *J. Am. Chem. Soc.* **1982**, *104*, 4251. (m) Wang, N. Y.; Hsu, C. T.; Sih, C. J. *J. Am. Chem. Soc.* **1981**, *103*, 6538.

Before reading the above, you should take leave from your very important job of protecting us all, go back to school and take the class you obviously missed: Basic Biochemistry 101. Before leaving, however, please update your staff.

Yours truly,

James B. and Hannah Yoseph

Chapter 10: The Cancer-Cholesterol Connection

We had wanted to include in our letter to Dr. Lumpkin an explanation as to how statins and related lactone ring-bearing mycotoxins induce cancer. We decided not to overwhelm him. And, anyway, he didn't ask if statins caused cancer – he only wanted to know if they killed microbes.

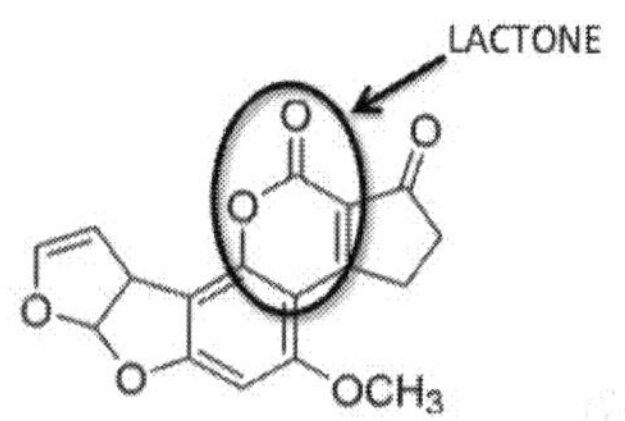

Aflatoxin
(Aspergillus flavus)

In 1960, outbreaks of liver cancer almost decimated the farm-raised rainbow trout population in the U.S. and farm-raised turkey population in the U.K. A toxin from the fungus *Aspergillus flavus* was found in commercial feed and given the name "aflatoxin" (named after the fungus that makes the toxin). Like lovastatin, aflatoxin is a polyketide secondary metabolite from *Aspergillus* with a lactone ring. Like statins, aflatoxins are antibiotics that lower cholesterol.

Nothing good ever came from *Aspergillus terreus*, a common disease-causing food mold, including Merck's lovastatin. It is a pathogenic fungus causing aspergillosis, otomycosis, onchomycosis, abscesses of the aorta and various skin infections. Ingestion causes death in rodents and abortions in cattle. Single-celled organisms are simple-fare: it is antibiotic, antifungal and even antiviral against herpes.

Aspergillus terreus makes a dozen secondary metabolite mycotoxins – all of which are antibiotic. This includes monacolin-K (Merck's lovastatin) as follows:

- Citreoviridin (antibiotic)
- Citrinin (antibiotic)
- Clavacin (antibiotic)
- Ferrichrysin (antibiotic)
- Geodin (antibiotic)
- Monacolin-K (antibiotic)
- Patulin (antibiotic)
- Terrecine (antibiotic)
- Terreine (antibiotic)
- Terretonine (antibiotic)
- Territrem-A (antibiotic)
- Territrem-B (antibiotic)

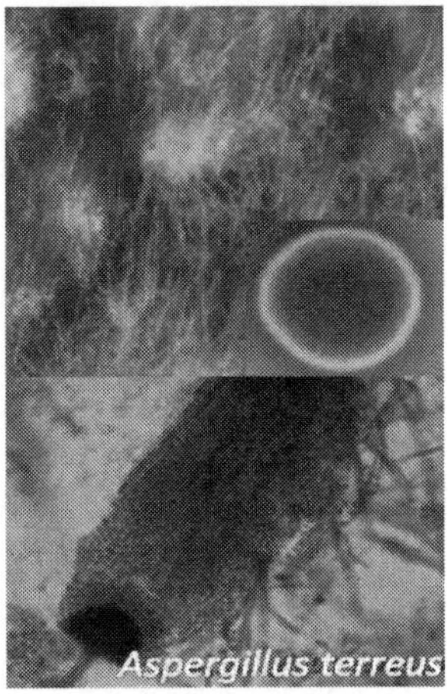

Territrem A and B are so named because of the terrible "tremors" they cause. They are lactone polyketides with structural similarities to lovastatin/monacolin-K. They are potent inhibitors, not of reductase, but of an enzyme called acetylcholinesterase that is essential for normal neuromuscular function:

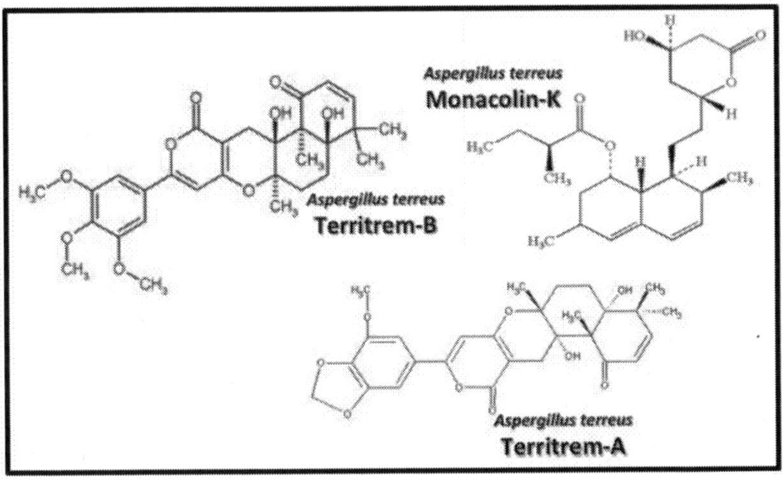

Most physicians would diagnose territrem-induced spasms and shakes as myasthenia gravis, multiple sclerosis or a neurodegenerative disease such as Parkinson's or Lou Gehrig's disease. The disease would be attributed to a "genetic proclivity" rather than possible food poisoning by a common grain mold.

Citreoviridin and lovastatin, both made by *Aspergillus terreus*, have almost identical molecular weights and formulas. Like lovastatin, citreoviridin weakens heart muscle and lowers blood pressure (some prescribers use statins to lower blood pressure). *Aspergillus terreus* mycotoxins are also toxic to the kidneys, liver and nervous systems and cause birth defects and cancer.

Chem. Rev. **2009**, 109, 3909-3990

Chemistry and Biology of Mycotoxins and Related Fungal Metabolites

Table 2. Mycotoxins Produced by *Aspergillus* sp.

fungus	mycotoxin produced
Aspergillus terreus	Territrem A,[25] Citreoviridin, Citrinin (2), Gliotoxin (527), Patulin (3), Terrein, Terreic acid, Terretonin, Itaconic acid, Aspulvinone, Asterric acid, Asterriquinone, butyrolactone I, Emodin (573), Geodin, Itaconate, Lovastatin,[26] Questin, Sulochrin, Terrecyclic acid.

Our story of cancer-causing cholesterol-lowering toxic food molds inevitably returns to Dallas and the marvelous work of Marvin Siperstein.

Siperstein discovered that cholesterol is a moving target. Because it is so vital to life, cells need an instant source. LDL receptors provide cells with a means to quickly absorb cholesterol from the blood. If blood cholesterol drops, then cholesterol production inside cells increases. If blood cholesterol increases, then cholesterol production inside cells decreases. Because cholesterol is such a moving target, dietary changes do not significantly lower blood cholesterol (0 to 4%).

To support this, Siperstein showed that dietary blood cholesterol actually decreases cholesterol synthesis inside cells. Cholesterol in the diet lowers cholesterol produced in cells from mevalonate.

TABLE I

Effect on Varying Amounts of Dietary Cholesterol on Cholesterol Synthesis

Cholesterol in Diet	Cholesterol Synthesis (mμmoles added acetate-2-^{14}C)
0	67
0.1	36
0.25	28
0.5	1.8
1.0	2.4
2.5	1.8

Siperstein also discovered a connection between low blood cholesterol, elevated cholesterol synthesis and cancer. In every type of cancer cell he studied, the mevalonate pathway that controls cell cycles was out-of-control. Predictably, reductase was elevated; resultantly, cells replicated at an escalated rate. Adding cholesterol to the diet did not decrease cholesterol synthesis from mevalonate inside cancer cells like normal cells.

- **Normal cells:** Increased cholesterol in diet, decreased reductase and decreased cholesterol synthesis in cells

- **Cancer cells:** Increased cholesterol in diet, increased reductase and increased cholesterol synthesis in cells

Loss of Feedback Control of Hydroxymethylglutaryl Coenzyme A Reductase in Hepatomas

MARVIN D. SIPERSTEIN, ANN M. GYDE, AND HAROLD P. MORRIS

Proceedings of the National Academy of Sciences
Vol. 68, No. 2, pp. 315-317, February 1971

Hungry for cholesterol to replicate, cancer cells turn on the mevalonate pathway and, in time, lower the supply in the blood.

Eur J Cancer. 2010 Jun;46(9):1735-43. Epub 2010 Apr 29.

Severe hypocholesterolaemia is often neglected in haematalogical malignancies

Cholesterol plays a key role in cell proliferation, hence it has been suggested that low cholesterol levels are probably linked to the high cholesterol demands from neoplastic cells.

Brown, working at Siperstein's side, knew of the connection between elevated reductase, low blood cholesterol and cancer:

> **Feedback Control of Cholesterol Synthesis in Circulating Granulocytes and Deletion of Feedback Control in a Granulocytic Leukemia.** FRED I. POLSKY,* MICHAEL S. BROWN,* AND MARIVIN D. SIPERSTEIN,** Dallas, Tex.
>
> **This finding suggests that loss of the cholesterol feedback system may be a more general characteristic of malignant change than was generally believed.**
>
> *J. Clin. Invest.* (1973) 52:65a

No longer Siperstein's right-hand man, 24 years later Brown was Merck's hired hand. Fully knowing that statins, aflatoxin and cancer cells all elevate reductase, he unscrupulously suggested that the FDA approve lovastatin for anyone with "sluggish" cholesterol receptors" – a phrase he coined from thin air as part of the sales pitch. There is no evidence to support that anything like "sluggish cholesterol receptors" even exists.

Statins increase reductase – which mimics the condition of out-of-control cell cycles in cancer cells. It was a simple matter of time that the link between statins and cancer would surface.

> **JAMA®**
> The Journal of the American Medical Association
>
> **Carcinogenicity of Lipid-Lowering Drugs**
>
> **EXCERPT**
>
> **To the Editor.** —The article by Drs Newman and Hulley[1] on carcinogenicity of lipid-lowering drugs has created a concern among patients and physicians that currently used lipid-lowering drugs may cause cancer. This concern almost certainly has led some patients to discontinue their drugs and others to avoid initiation of therapy.

The statin-low cholesterol-cancer conundrum

U. Ravnskov[1], K.S. McCully[2] and P.J. Rosch[3,4]

Introduction

Hundreds of millions of people all over the globe are currently being administered statins because it is believed that their lipid lowering actions provide cardioprotective benefits. Adverse effects are considered uncommon and mild, and authors of numerous case-control studies of patients on statin treatment and matched, untreated individuals have even suggested a protective effect against numerous non-cardiovascular diseases, including cancer. In contrast, four controlled, randomized statin trials have resulted in a statistically significant increase of cancer in the treatment group; and several case-control and cohort studies have also shown a significant risk of cancer associated with statins.

Merck knew that cancer cells and elevated reductase were connected. Dallas did too. In time, independent studies showed that statin-treated patients had significantly more cancer.

Low cholesterol and cancer.

H Kritz, C Zielinski and H Sinzinger

Abstract

PURPOSE The relation between plasma cholesterol (CH) concentration and mortality is complex. The plasma CH concentration correlates positively with mortality from coronary heart disease, but some studies have shown a negative relation with death from cancer. If these two relations reflect causal mechanisms that are reversible by changing the plasma CH concentration, the benefits of lipid reduction for heart disease might be offset by an increased mortality from cancer. Different aspects between lipid metabolism and cancer, as well as new insights into this interesting field, are discussed.

JCO Nov 1, 1996:3043-8

Siperstein found that the mechanism that normally suppresses reductase was broken in all the cancer cells he studied. In some cancer cells, the "off" feedback mechanism was so broken that more cholesterol rather than less was made when dietary blood cholesterol was elevated:

TABLE II

Loss of Cholesterol Feedback System in Mouse Hepatoma BW 7756

Tissue	Diet	Cholesterol Synthesis mμmoles acetate-2-^{14}C
Normal Liver	Low Cholesterol 5% Cholesterol	5.2 0.2
Hepatoma BW 7756	Low Cholesterol 5% Cholesterol	17.6 19.3

These findings were reported in two of Siperstein's papers entitled "Cholesterol and Cancer" and "The Relationship of Cholesterol Biosynthesis to Cancer". Both Nobel-worthy papers are available in the electronic public record and remain largely ignored with the rest of his marvelous work.

THE RELATIONSHIP OF CHOLESTEROL BIOSYNTHESIS TO CANCER

BY MARVIN D. SIPERSTEIN, M.D., PH.D.

DALLAS

Two of Siperstein's colleagues, Brown and Goldstein, joined him in 1972 and collaborated on further investigating the cholesterol and cancer connection:

Fed Proc. 1973 Dec;32(12):2168-73.

Regulation of cholesterol synthesis in normal and malignant tissue.

Brown MS, Goldstein JL, Siperstein MD.

A method was developed to measure reductase – the "on/off and increase/decrease switch" of the mevalonate pathway. They reported on how the normal controls of the mevalonate pathway were broken in the liver cancer cells and leukemia cells they studied.

In every cancer cell Siperstein studied from 1968 to 1972, and then studied with Brown and Goldstein from 1972 to 1973, the mevalonate pathway and thus cholesterol regulation was broken. This included white blood cells that have a high demand for cholesterol. The predictable cancer in Sankyo's dogs was a cancer of white blood cells in the organ first exposed to an ingested statin (small intestinal lymphomas). The mevalonate pathway controls went haywire; cells replicated uncontrollably.

Siperstein wanted to know if a broken mevalonate pathway was at the root of cancer. If it was, ***he reasoned that a known cancer-causing agent might disrupt the mevalonate pathway before any sign of cancer***. He recalled the rapid cancer outbreak in 1960 when a mycotoxin from the food mold *Aspergillus flavus* was discovered as the cancer cause and given the name "aflatoxin" ("a" for *Aspergillus* and "fla" for *flavus*).

Siperstein fed aflatoxin to normal cells to see if the mevalonate pathway would show signs of trouble *before* the cells became malignant. ***Within one week of giving aflatoxin to normal liver cells, the mevalonate pathway was disrupted, demonstrating that this was not an incidental finding in cancer cells.***

CHOLESTEROL AND CANCER

BY MARVIN D. SIPERSTEIN, M.D., PH.D.

DALLAS

"Those sterols! Dr. Obisopo frowned ... Longbotham had even suggested a connexion between fatty alcohols and neoplasms. In other words, cancer might be regarded, in a final analysis, as a symptom of sterol-poisoning".

Aldous Huxley, 1939, *After Many a Summer Dies the Swan*, Page 52—Harper and Row

What proved to connect cancer and cholesterol was the mevalonate pathway of life. Mevalonate is required to make both cholesterol and isoprenoids for cell replication. In some types of cancer cells, the replication rate is out-of-control.

Because statins block cell cycles, early statin investigators thought statins might have clinical use as anti-cancer agents:

Cholesterol and Mevalonic Acid Are Independent Requirements for the In Vitro Proliferation of Human Bone Marrow Granulocyte Progenitor Cells: Studies Using ML-236B

By Philip C. Hoffman, Carol M. Richman, Richard A. Larson, and Stanley Yachnin

Blood, Vol. 61, No. 4 (April), 1983

Our hope is that ML-236B or similar compounds may ultimately prove useful in the pharmacologic suppression of malignant cell growth.

[CANCER RESEARCH 51, 3602–3609, July 1, 1991]

Synchronization of Tumor and Normal Cells from G_1 to Multiple Cell Cycles by Lovastatin[1]

Khandan Keyomarsi,[2] Larue Sandoval, Vimla Band, and Arthur B. Pardee

Divisions of Cell Growth and Regulation [K. K., L. S., A. B. P.] and Cancer Genetics [V. B.], Dana Farber Cancer Institute, Boston, Massachusetts 02115

In this paper, we report that these criteria for synchronization are met using Lovastatin to arrest normal and tumor cells of epithelial as well as fibroblast origin reversibly in the G_1 phase of the cell cycle. Lovastatin, an antihyperlipodemic agent, is widely used for the treatment of hypercholesterolemia. This agent competitively inhibits HMG-CoA[3] reductase, the enzyme required for conversion of HMG-CoA to mevalonic acid (8). In addition, inhibition of mevalonate synthesis by Lovastatin or compactin, a related fungal toxin (9), also inhibits DNA replication (10–15). DNA replication is restored by the addition of mevalonate, the product of the reaction catalyzed by HMG-CoA reductase.

Effects of mevinolin and mevalonate on cell growth in several transformed cell lines

Kathy P. Fairbanks, Veronique D. Barbu, Larry D. Witte, I. Bernard Weinstein, DeWitt S. Goodman

Journal of Cellular Physiology
Volume 127, Issue 2, pages 216–222, May 1986

Studies were conducted to explore the effects of mevinolin (lovastatin), a competitive inhibitor of HMG CoA reductase, on the growth and morphology of normal and transformed murine fibroblasts. Mevinolin is known to block DNA synthesis and cell growth in a number of kinds of non-transformed cells. Eight cell lines were studied, including two normal fibroblast cell lines and derivatives of these cell lines transformed by chemical carcinogens, X-irradiation or the H-ras oncogene. All of the eight cell lines displayed appreciable growth inhibition by 5 uM mevinolin and marked inhibition by 30uM mevinolin. Mevinolin also induced a marked rounding in the morphology of all the cell lines…Thus mevinolin might be useful as an anti-tumor agent for specific tumors.

While blocking cell reproduction of cancer cells with a statin might seem like a good idea, ***blocking isoprenoid production with a statin can induce cancer.*** To understand this requires a short visit to the "ras" family.

"Ras" is a famous family of proteins in human cells. They are famous because they are implicated in cancer.

The Ras proteins are molecular switches that activate and deactivate other cell proteins that control communication, growth and replication.

For ras proteins to function, isoprenoids are added to them. This is called "prenylation". Mutations that inhibit ras prenylation cause death or defective growth of cells that can become cancer.

Statins block prenylation of ras (also called p21^{ras}) proteins. Endo again tells the truth when a lie would probably better serve him. He explains clearly how blocking ras prenylation with a statin can cause "uncontrolled cell division" – or, in a word, "cancer".

The discovery and development of HMG-CoA reductase inhibitors

Akira Endo

Department of Applied Biological Science, Tokyo Noko University, Fuchu, Tokyo, 183 Japan

The prenyl proteins include growth-regulating p21^{ras} proteins, a family of GTP-binding and hydrolyzing proteins that regulate cell growth (50, 51), and lamin B (52, 53), a structural component of the nuclear lamina that is associated with the inner nuclear membrane. Overproduction of p21^{ras} proteins or mutations that abolish their GTPase activity lead to uncontrolled cell division (54).

Journal of Lipid Research Volume 33, 1992

Endo reports that both "overproduction of p21^{ras} proteins" or "mutations that abolish their (GTPase) activity" lead to cancer. Because statins induce an increase in reductase, this can potentially lead to overproduction of ras proteins – leading to cancer. On the other hand, complete blockade of prenylation of ras proteins can abolish their GTPase activity – causing cancer.

Statins are not anti-cancer drugs. They are a bad idea no matter how you look at them.

Do NOT block the mevalonate pathway.

Siperstein and others have repeatedly demonstrated a connection between disruption of the mevalonate pathway, an increase in reductase and cancer (reference 9). Out-of-control reductase in cancer cells has been widely reported for five decades:

- Siperstein and Fagan (1964)
- Goldstein *et al.* (1973)
- Brown *et al.* (1974)
- Chen, Kandutsch, Heineiger (1978)
- George and Goldfarb (1980)
- Gregg *et al.* (1982)
- Yachnin, Toub, Mannickarottu (1984)
- Bruscalalupi, Leoni, Mangiantini *et al.* (1985)
- Engstrom and Schofield (1987)
- Erickson *et al.* (1988)
- Azrolan and Coleman (1989)
- Kawata *et al.* (1990)
- Bennis, Favre, LeGuillard, Soula (1993)
- Parker *et al.* (1993, 1994)
- Elson and Yu (1994)
- Elson (1995)
- Elson, Peffley, Hentosh, Mo (1999)
- Hentosh *et al.* (2001)
- Peffley and Gayen (2003)

Statins (a mycotoxin) disrupt the mevalonate pathway, increase reductase, lower cholesterol and increase cancer risk.

Aflatoxin (a mycotoxin) disrupts the mevalonate pathway, increases reductase, lowers cholesterol and causes cancer.

Citrinin (a mycotoxin) disrupts the mevalonate pathway, increases reductase, lowers cholesterol and increases cancer risk.

All of the cancer-causing mycotoxins, including statins, have lactone rings. They all "inhibit" reductase and induce a reflexive increase in reductase.

Could there be a connection between mycotoxins – common food mold contaminants – and some types of cancer? Could it really be that simple? Food grains, after all, are stored long term; improper drying increases the risk of toxic mold contamination. That possibility could collapse whole empires profiting from current cancer paradigms – including the media that receives huge profits from drug advertisements and in so doing trades their children's inheritances for bowls of stew.

Perhaps Tullio Simoncini, MD, who cures some cancers with baking soda (same remedy to kill common mold on house plants), knows it's that simple. He routinely records his

successful results with laparoscopic video cameras and openly shares that his remedy was found by entreating God for plain-sense answers.

Simoncini practices medicine in Italy. His work is shunned in the U.S. where state authorities revoke physicians' licenses for curing cancer with a simple therapy rather than treating it with FDA-approved and financially lucrative noxious regimes.

"Cure" is a four-letter word in for-profit medicine. "Treatment", on the other hand, can last forever and often does.

Chapter 11: Mycotoxin Mayhem

"Poison" called by any other name is still poison. Call it hemlock, arsenic, cyanide or secondary metabolite. "Secondary metabolite" is the euphemism that agenda-driven scientists and drug companies use for toxic statins.

There are many ways to lower cholesterol. There are a few poisonous food mold toxins that will do the trick if you're willing to take the risk:

- **Aflatoxin** (lactone/UV-fluorescent)
- **Citrinin** (inverted lactone/UV-fluorescent)
- **Fumonisins** (lactone/UV-fluorescent)
- **Luteoskyrin** (lactone/UV-fluorescent)
- **Monocolin-K/Statin** (lactone/UV-fluorescent)
- **Ochratoxin-A** (lactone/UV-fluorescent)
- **Patulin** (lactone/UV-fluorescent)
- **Rubratoxin-B** (lactone/UV-fluorescent)
- **Zearalenone** (lactone/UV-fluorescent)

All of the above mycotoxins from *Aspergillus* and *Penicillium* lower blood cholesterol and cause cancer in animals.

Breast and prostate are common cancer types caused by mycotoxins. An enormous body of science that connects mycotoxins to breast cancer were reported decades before statin approval:

- Dickens and Jones (1965, 1967) used patulin to produce breast adenomas in mice and rats.

- Saito (1971) and Corrado (1971) both induced breast cancer in mice with moldy rice extracts. (Endo extracted the first statin from moldy rice.)

- Schoental *et al.* (1979) reported that breast cancers were induced in rats dosed with T-2 toxin.

- Boorman found breast fibroadenomas in over 50% of ochratoxin-fed female mice (1988). Fibroadenomas increase risk for breast cancer in humans (Dupont, 1994).

There are connections that have also been made with human cancers and mycotoxins.

Many mycotoxins, including statins, suppress the immune system. The drug cyclosporine, a fungal mycotoxin-antibiotic, is prescribed long-term to suppress the immune system in organ transplant patients. In 1986, First and Penn reported that cancer developed in 87 out of 88 patients given cyclosporine after an organ transplant; most of the malignant cancers were breast, ovarian and testicular. (These tissues are highly dependent upon a balance of hormones made from cholesterol.)

Cyclosporine-induced cancer, including breast cancer, has been reported by Vogt (1990) and Escribano-Patino (1995). Harrison and his team (1993) found aflatoxin DNA in a sampling of breast cancer tissue. A 1986 French study by Lé found an association between breast cancer and mold-fermented cheese consumption.

Oxalic acid is made by various fungal species and is found in breast cancer calcifications. Taylor and Georgian-Smith (1994) found a regression of breast cancer malignancy and calcifications with the antifungal drug Tamoxifen.

Cancer clusters in mold-contaminated buildings have also been reported.

In 2006, 28 of 102 staff members and two students at a New Richmond, Wisconsin elementary school were diagnosed with cancer (contaminated air filters were found). In 2004, 20 teachers at a Swedish high school, where toxic black mold was found, developed cancer.

The relationship between aflatoxin from *Aspergillus flavus* and hepatocellular carcinoma is now well known. Nevertheless, throughout the Far East, *Aspergillus flavus* is still used instead of yeast to ferment beverages. Saki and soy sauce are both made, respectively, by fermenting rice and soybeans in the presence of *Aspergillus flavus*. ***Hepatocellular carcinoma remains the leading cancer in Asia.***

The EPA web site posts information on mycotoxin-related diseases and cancer:

> **EPA Mold Remediation in Schools and Commercial Buildings**
>
> **Mold Toxins (Mycotoxins)**
>
> * Many symptoms and human health effects attributed to inhalation of mycotoxins have been reported including: mucous membrane irritation, skin rash, nausea, immune system suppression, acute or chronic liver damage, acute or chronic central nervous system damage, endocrine effects, and cancer. More studies are needed to get a clear picture of the health effects related to most mycotoxins. However, it is clearly prudent to avoid exposure to molds and mycotoxins.

While these mycotoxins lower blood cholesterol, they also increase cholesterol in cells of tissues with LDL receptors (reference 10). Statins do the same. This is the pattern that Siperstein found in cancer cells; it is the opposite of normal cells:

- **Cancer cells:** Increased dietary cholesterol, increased reductase and increased cholesterol inside cells (leading to below-normal or low blood cholesterol)

- **Statin-fed cells:** Increased dietary cholesterol, increased reductase and increased cholesterol inside cells (leading to below-normal or low blood cholesterol)

- **Normal cells:** Increased dietary cholesterol, decreased reductase and decreased cholesterol synthesis

Remember Endo's "nontoxic cholesterol crystals" that Sankyo's toxicologists insisted were a sign of drug toxicity? Despite Endo threw caution to the wind, the toxicologists were correct. Elevated cholesterol in cells is toxic and can cause apoptosis – programmed cell death. When this happens in muscle cells (as seen with metastatic cancer and statin myopathy) it causes muscle wasting. Statin-injured muscle has been described as "mush" (reference 11). There is no such thing as "nontoxic cholesterol crystals".

Statin-Associated Myopathy with Normal Creatine Kinase Levels

Paul S. Phillips, MD; Richard H. Haas, MD; Sergei Bannykh, MD, PhD; Stephanie Hathaway, RN; Nancy L. Gray, RN; Bruce J. Kimura, MD; Georgirene D. Vladutiu, PhD; John D.F. England, MD; and the Scripps Mercy Clinical Research Center*

A muscle biopsy performed during atorvastatin therapy revealed increased lipid droplets, ragged red fibers, and cytochrome oxidase-negative muscle fibers, all consistent with lipid myopathy.

Ann Intern Med 2002;136:501-505

Effects of lipoprotein lipase and statins on cholesterol uptake into heart and skeletal muscle*

Masayoshi Yokoyama,* Toru Seo,† Taesik Park,* Hiroaki Yagyu,* Yunying Hu,* Ni Huiping Son,* Ayanna S. Augustus,* Reeba K. Vikramadithyan,* Rajasekhar Ramakrishnan,† Leslie K. Pulawa,§ Robert H. Eckel,§ and Ira J. Goldberg[1,*]

In mice with greater LDL uptake resulting from muscle overexpression of LPL, statin therapy increased LDL uptake and tissue cholesterol content and caused muscle damage. Increased cellular cholesterol can lead to dysfunction or even apoptosis (8).

March 2007 The Journal of Lipid Research, 48, 646-655.

Siperstein thought that the increased cholesterol inside cancer cells was due to increased cholesterol synthesis from mevalonate. Lactone-bearing cancer-causing mycotoxins like aflatoxin work like statins. They inhibit reductase, which increases reductase and LDL receptor synthesis; the increased cholesterol found inside cancer cells is due to the elevated LDL receptors that pull cholesterol from the blood into cells. It is bad, *not* good.

Statins lower blood cholesterol and increase tissue cell cholesterol like other cancer-causing mycotoxins. Increased cancer risk with statins is therefore predictable. The following studies have demonstrated an increase in cancer risk with statin use:

- PROSPER
- SEAS
- Chang *et al.* 2011 (Taiwan prostate cancer study)
- CARE (breast cancer)

In the PROSPER trial, there was a 25% increase in newly diagnosed cancers in older people after four years of statin use. In the CARE trial, 12 women in the statin group developed breast cancer, compared to only one in the placebo group. A 2011 study in Taiwan found more prostate cancer in male statin users.

There are at least two mechanisms to account for statin-induced cancer:

1. Statins indirectly reproduce the state of cancer cells by inducing an increase in reductase.

2. Statins directly induce cancer via the same mechanism as other cancer-causing mycotoxins.

The elevated reductase seen in many cancer cells is either a symptom or cause of some cancers. Since most cancer cells have elevated turnover rates, it makes sense that reductase would be elevated.

Many (if not all) cancer cells have elevated reductase. Statins are, at the very least, fuel to the fire.

Brown, Goldstein, Endo, Merck scientists and others repeatedly demonstrated that the reflexive increase in reductase with statins is due to isoprenoid deprivation. If the reflexive increase in reductase lies at the root cause of some cancers and is not just a symptom, we would expect that feeding statin-fed cells isoprenoids might prevent and reverse cancer.

And it does.

Dietary isoprenoids suppress reductase and the resultant fire of runaway cell cycles. Table 1, below, includes the type and amount of isoprenoid for the type of cancer.

Suppression of Mevalonate Pathway Activities by Dietary Isoprenoids: Protective Roles in Cancer and Cardiovascular Disease[1,2]

CHARLES E. ELSON[3]

Isoprenoids differ from most food-borne xenobiotics in having a potent tumor-suppressing action. The growth of established tumors is suppressed by dietary isoprenoids (see review by Elson and Yu 1994a).

TABLE 1

IC_{50} values for the suppression of cell proliferation by assorted isoprenoids

Cell type	Isoprenoid	(mmol/l)	Source
HT-29 human colon carcinoma	d-Limonene	5.00	Crowell et al. 1994
HT-29 human colon carcinoma	Perillic acid	0.90	Crowell et al. 1994
HT-29 human colon carcinoma	Perillaldehyde	0.35	Crowell et al. 1994
HT-29 human colon carcinoma	Perillyl alcohol	0.05	Crowell et al. 1994
HT-29 human colon carcinoma	Perillic acid methyl ester	0.05	Crowell et al. 1994
NIH/3T3 mouse embryo	Perillic acid	1.20	Crowell et al. 1994
NIH/3T3 mouse embryo	Perillyl alcohol	0.80	Crowell et al. 1994
WB-ras rat liver epithelial cells	Cineole	2.50	Ruch and Sigler 1994
WB-ras rat liver epithelial cells	Pinene	2.00	Ruch and Sigler 1994
WB-ras rat liver epithelial cells	Limonene	1.00	Ruch and Sigler 1994
WB-ras rat liver epithelial cells	Menthol	0.75	Ruch and Sigler 1994
WB-ras rat liver epithelial cells	Perillic acid	0.40	Ruch and Sigler 1994
WB-ras rat liver epithelial cells	Perillyl alcohol	0.25	Ruch and Sigler 1994
PHA-stimulated lymphocytes	d-Limonene	5.00	Schulz et al. 1994
PHA-stimulated lymphocytes	Perillic acid	1.50	Schulz et al. 1994
PHA-stimulated lymphocytes	Perillyl alcohol	0.60	Schulz et al. 1994
P388 mouse lymphoid	Geraniol	0.50	Shoff et al. 1991
B16 mouse melanoma	Geraniol	0.10	Shoff et al. 1991
MIA PaCa2 human pancreatic	Perillyl alcohol	0.30	Bronfen et al. 1994
MCF-7 human breast cancer	β-Ionone	0.01	Sheffield[4]
MDA-MB-231 human breast cancer	β-Ionone	0.10	Sheffield[4]
MDA-MB-435 human breast cancer	δ-Tocotrienol	0.23	Guthrie et al. 1994
MDA-MB-435 human breast cancer	α-Tocotrienol	0.23	Guthrie et al. 1994
MDA-MB-435 human breast cancer	γ-Tocotrienol	0.07	Guthrie et al. 1994
H69 human small cell lung carcinoma	α-Tocotrienol	0.10	Komiyama et al. 1989
H69 human small cell lung carcinoma	γ-Tocotrienol	0.10	Komiyama et al. 1989
HeLa human cervix carcinoma	α-Tocotrienol	0.10	Komiyama et al. 1989
HeLa human cervix carcinoma	γ-Tocotrienol	0.10	Komiyama et al. 1989
P388 mouse lymphoid	α-Tocotrienol	0.10	Komiyama et al. 1989
P388 mouse lymphoid	γ-Tocotrienol	0.05	Komiyama et al. 1989

Elevated reductase in statins is attributed to isoprenoid starvation. Plant isoprenoids suppress cancer.

To make the connection between statins and cancer does not require a PhD (Piled Higher and Deeper) degree. Connect the dots for yourself because the drug companies won't do it for you; neither will the American Cancer Society who has no incentive to ever work themselves out of their jobs.

Plant isoprenoids that reduce cancer risk are a class called "phytoalexins" that include plant isoflavanoids. ***Phytoalexins are made by plants to surround, isolate and kill invading fungi.***

Merck knew what they were doing. Merck sells a mycotoxin falsely implied to decrease the incidence of CVD by increasing the rate of more-deadly diseases such as cancer. They advertise that consumers' cups will become half-full, knowing full well they will instead become half-empty.

Merck caused mycotoxin mayhem.

It's been said that past behavior determines future behavior. Let's take a look at some of Merck's past behavior – from the public record. (God only knows what goes on behind closed doors.)

Chapter 12: The Not-So-Moral Corporation

It is the pattern of a serial killer always on the prowl for a new victim: he connives, contrives and plans so he will not be caught and revealed as the monster he is.

Merck's history of concealing drug-related hazards, demonstrates Merck's pattern for:

1. Misleading the public about foreknown hazards to their products.

2. Minimizing or concealing adverse effects that result in its liability for injury or death.

On February 8, 2005, the Los Angeles Times reported that a 1991 Merck seven-page memo released by a whistleblower and obtained by attorney James Moody, provided the first hard evidence that Merck knew that babies were getting 87 times the mercury allowance considered safe for adults. For eight years Merck took no action until September 1999, when amidst rising public concern about the risk of mercury (thimerosal) in childhood vaccines, Merck released the news, "Now Merck's infant vaccine line is free of all preservatives". Then, according to an FDA letter sent in response to a congressional inquiry, Merck continued to distribute vaccines containing mercury for more than two more years until October 2001.

According to page 61 of Merck's SEC Form 10-Q filed in 2010, about 200 thimerosal-related lawsuits were pending for which Merck is a defendant (as of December 31, 2009).

A lawsuit filed in September, 2008 under the Racketeering Influenced and Corrupt Organizations (RICO) Act, was settled by Merck out of court (Master Docket No. 08-0825). The lawsuit claims that an internal study showed that Merck's Vytorin, a combination statin-based drug for lowering cholesterol, posed serious safety concerns. Plaintiffs claimed the drug makers did not disclose the results of this study and instead sought to delay and conceal the negative results. A $41.5 million dollar settlement was agreed upon while more RICO suits remain in the queue. To date Merck denies any fault.

In April 2008, the Journal of the American Medical Association published two studies analyzing Merck documents that had surfaced during Vioxx litigation, which the public now knows caused serious cardiovascular side effects. Collectively, they concluded that Merck had "violated scientific-publishing ethics by ghostwriting_dozens of academic articles, and minimized the impact of patient deaths in its analyses of some human trials."

One study found that medical papers on Vioxx "were often prepared by unacknowledged authors and subsequently attributed authorship to academically affiliated investigators who often did not disclose financial support."

Another study concluded that Merck "neither provided to the FDA nor made public in a timely fashion" evidence that Vioxx use was linked to increased risk of death. Merck paid $4.85 billion to 44,000 Americans injured by Vioxx with strokes and heart attacks, however to date they deny any fault (Wall Street Journal, March 3, 2008).

As reported in "The Australian", in April 2009 evidence surfaced in the Federal Court in Melbourne that exposed the criminal intent of Merck staffers who admitted they intended to "stop funding to institutions" and "interfere with academic appointments". Emails between staff members at Merck included a list of doctors who were critical of the company or of the drug Vioxx and that contained words "neutralize", "neutralized" and "discredit" next to the names of various doctors.

"We may need to seek them out and destroy them where they live," said one email from a Merck employee.

The court was told that James Fries, professor of medicine at Stanford University, wrote to Merck head Ray Gilmartin in October 2000 to complain about the treatment of some of his researchers who had criticized the drug. "Even worse were allegations of Merck damage control by intimidation," he wrote, …"This has happened to at least eight (clinical) investigators … I was mildly threatened myself but I never have spoken or written on these issues."

The same trial in Melbourne revealed that Merck created a fake medical journal, "The Australasian Journal of Bone and Joint Medicine", in which they paid the publisher (Elsevier) to circulate studies about Vioxx written by paid ghostwriters to draft positive articles about the drug. In a formal statement electronically published at the Elsevier web site entitled, "Statement from Michael Hansen Regarding Australia Based Sponsored Journal Practices Between 2000 and 2005", the CEO of Elsevier's Health Sciences Division, Michael Hansen, admitted that the practice was "unacceptable", and expressed regret for the publications (reference 12).

Merck's Vioxx scandal surfaced as the result of one man: Dr. David Graham, associate director for science in the FDA Drug Center's Office of Drug Safety. Graham had to find help outside the FDA when he discovered serious problems with Vioxx. He told Senate investigators that he had been subjected to veiled threats and intimidation when he informed the FDA of his findings. A Grand Jury probe followed, and Vioxx was finally removed from the market in 2004. ***The FDA study headed by Graham had estimated that the defective drug could have contributed to 27,785 heart attacks and sudden cardiac deaths between 1999 and 2003.***

After Vioxx was recalled, it was revealed that the FDA had tried to silence Graham.

Perhaps Dr. Graham is one of the group of anonymous FDA scientists who appealed to President Obama by letter in 2009 to investigate rampant FDA corruption. This letter, authenticated by the FDA (reference 13), includes concerns about the FDA's Center for Drug Evaluation and Research (CDER). This letter has been coined "The FDA Corruption Letter".

The scientists explain how a federal court found that a drug had been approved because CDER's top personnel "didn't have a choice" and had to "ignore the science and the law" to approve it or they would "be removed from their positions of authority". As if written for a mafiosa-movie script, the following excerpt from page two implies the FDA is now acting according to higher-level instructions outside the public interest:

> **DEPARTMENT OF HEALTH AND HUMAN SERVICES**
>
> Food and Drug Administration
> Office of Device Evaluation
> 9200 Corporate Boulevard
> Rockville, MD 20850
>
> The Honorable Barack H. Obama
> President of the United States
> 1600 Pennsylvania Avenue NW
> Washington, DC 20500
>
> April 2, 2009
>
> On January 7, 2009, FDA physicians and scientists wrote to Mr. John Podesta[4]: "Through this letter and your action, we hope that future FDA employees will not experience the same frustration and anxiety that we have experienced for more than a year at the hands of FDA managers because we are committed to public integrity and were willing to speak out. Currently, there is an atmosphere at FDA in which the honest employee fears the dishonest employee, and not the other way around. Disturbingly, the atmosphere does not yet exist at FDA where honest employees committed to integrity and the FDA mission can act without fear of reprisal. ... America urgently needs change at FDA because FDA is fundamentally broken, failing to fulfill its mission, and because re-establishing a proper and effectively functioning FDA is vital to the physical and economic health of the nation."[5]

The attempt to silence Graham within the FDA and the lack of response from the White House makes one wonder what the hell is going on.

If you kill someone in an automobile accident, you are subject to charges of manslaughter. If you kill someone as the result of momentary rage, you are subject to charges of second-degree murder. If you deliberately and maliciously plan to kill someone and follow through with that plan, you are subject to charges of first-degree murder. Merck and its employees knowingly kill their victims with impunity and are unutterably malicious with anyone who tries to stop them.

The final trump for the likes of Merck would be sweeping legislation to protect them from litigation after a drug has been FDA-approved. That bold move, called "pre-emption", has already been tabled; if ever passed, Merck would finally hold a bona-fide license to kill with impunity by the Federal Death Agency.

P. Roy Vagelos, after retiring in 1994 as Merck's CEO, set himself to the task of persuading the public on just how "moral" Merck was during its statin development days.

Moral restraint may have appeared to be Merck's motive when Vagelos stopped statin research in 1980. Rather than waste stockholder money on a sinking ship, Vagelos called a halt and plugged the hole.

Work soon resumed. Morality was not an issue.

PART TWO: THE STATINIC SCIENTISTS

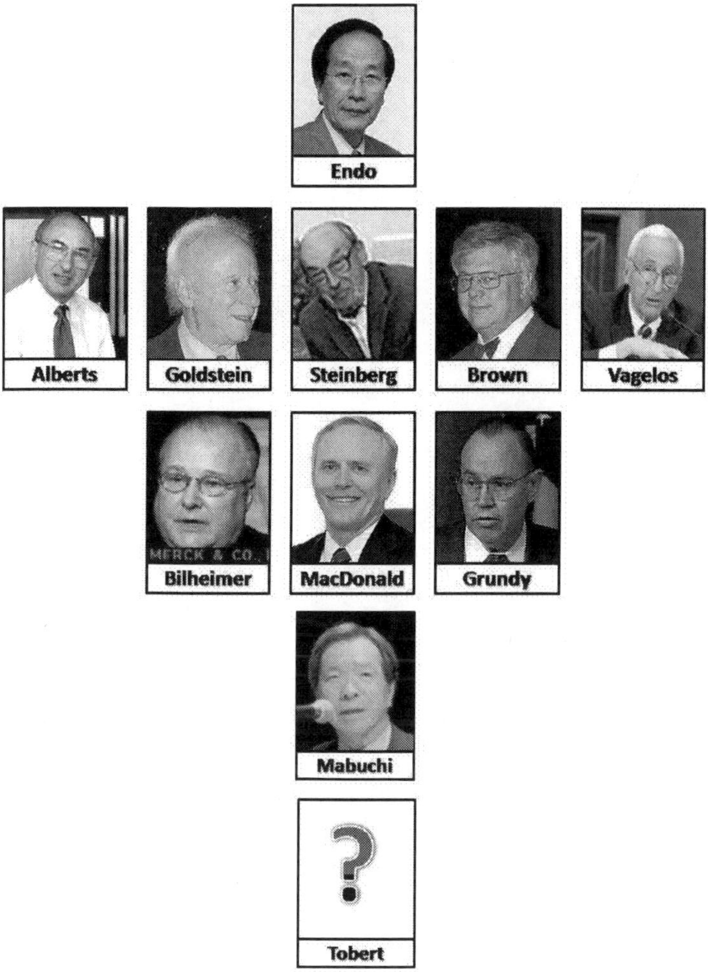

Chapter 13: Guilty!

LDL cholesterol is good. Without it we die. LDL cholesterol is so good that our cells make LDL receptors as a second way to quickly obtain the stuff of life. There is no such thing as bad cholesterol. LDL cholesterol is not guilty of anything.

Merck scientists and statin developers Brown, Goldstein, Endo and Steinberg clearly understood the risks of using a pathogenic fungal mycotoxin to lower what they call our "bad" cholesterol. They hid nothing from us. The health hazards recorded in this book were gleaned from the public record – mostly from them.

Decades of planning went into effect by the statinic scientists before delivering a literal poison to market that prescribers and consumers would swallow whole. The decorated statin inventor, however, knew better than that. When asked why he wouldn't take statins for his own high cholesterol, Endo quoted a strange Japanese proverb: "The indigo dyer wears white trousers."

How One Scientist Intrigued by Molds Found First Statin

Akira Endo is at Biopharm Research Laboratories, Inc., 3-41-3 501 Shimorenjaku, Mitaka, Tokyo 181-0013, Japan. e-mail: aendo@biopharm.co.jp

By PETER LANDERS
Staff Reporter of THE WALL STREET JOURNAL
January 9, 2006; Page A1

Akira Endo

At his checkup in 2004, his LDL, or "bad" cholesterol, was 155, a level at which many U.S. doctors would prescribe a statin. Dr. Endo says he didn't take anything and brought the number down to 130 last year by exercising more. Why would the inventor of statins bypass his own invention? Dr. Endo can only cite a Japanese proverb, "The indigo dyer wears white trousers."

Indigo dye is extremely toxic to human cells. Endo was, rather circuitously, sending out a warning. Like the indigo dyer who knows the same, the mycotoxin gold rush digger knew that statins were poison. Smart indigo dyers don't wear indigo pants. Smart statin inventors don't take statins.

Multiple hurdles had to be overcome to push toxic statins through the approval process. Every leap needed to look clean and on the up-and-up. Daniel Steinberg filled the shoes. Indifferent to the core, he believed that LDL cholesterol was "bad" for us and he would fix it. His influence at the NIH and the AHA provided the funds and policy. His relationships to Brown and Goldstein provided the scientists. As Merck's advisor, he brought his credibility to influence the FDA.

The mantra for setting national policy on a new disease is: "NIH, NIH, NIH". As judge, jury, prosecutor and enforcer, the former NIH chief declared cholesterol "guilty" – end of report. There was no room for dispute with him.

An interpretive history of the cholesterol controversy: part I[1]

Journal of Lipid Research Volume 47, 2006

Daniel Steinberg[2]

Department of Medicine, University of California-San Diego, La Jolla, CA

Steinberg

This is not a general review of atherogenesis nor a history of lipid research per se. Rather, it is an inquiry into how, after much controversy, cholesterol and lipoproteins were implicated, indicted, and ultimately found guilty.

Lipid theorists like Steinberg blame LDL cholesterol for CVD because some CVD "plaques" contain oxidized LDL cholesterol, dead microbes and dead white blood cells. Ruptured plaques that block blood flow to the heart or brain can cause a heart attack or stroke. Found at the scene of the crime, LDL cholesterol is "guilty" – even though it is ***oxidized*** LDL cholesterol that is found in plaques.

Lipid theorists reason that the lower the blood LDL cholesterol, the better. ***They ignore the process of cholesterol oxidation.***

Cholesterol, oxidation and CVD go hand-in-hand. Consequently, ANTIoxidants such as vitamins C and E prevent CVD because ***antioxidants prevent and neutralize oxidation by lipid oxidizers***.

The causal relationship between oxidizers and CVD has been known for a long time but has been suppressed. This way, the perpetual parasitic feast on public funds to search for a cure goes on ad infinitum. It remains the great cholesterol con-job from the 20th century.

Oxidizers are electron thieves. Lipids (such as cholesterol) that have double bonds are electron-rich and therefore easily oxidize (lose electrons). This creates a chain reaction of robbing more electrons from surrounding lipids. The result is damaged cell membranes that line arteries and oxidized blood lipids like LDL cholesterol.

If LDL cholesterol is damaged by oxidation, the liver must make more. Levels rise. Antioxidant supplements help prevent lipid oxidation. Levels decrease. Polyunsaturated dietary fats such as fish oil help repair damage by lipid oxidation. Levels decrease.

Avoiding lipid-damaging oxidizers prevents the vicious cycle in the first place. There is no money in that recommendation.

CVD happen to arteries, not veins. Arteries are lined with lipid-rich electron-rich cell membranes and the blood contains lipid-rich LDL cholesterol. Oxidizers that directly enter the arteries through the lungs (such as in cigarette smoke) and stomach (such hypochlorous acid from chlorinated city water) have been associated with lipid oxidation. Fat-soluble weak acids like hypochlorous acid, aspirin, alcohol and caffeine are quickly absorbed through the stomach wall into the bloodstream.

Unsaturated lipids and LDL cholesterol are more electron-rich than saturated lipids; they are therefore more easily oxidized. It follows that highly unsaturated lipids such as fish and flax oils replace damaged oxidized lipids and lower cholesterol levels.

This is a long-known and simple explanation for why antioxidants and polyunsaturated oils lower cholesterol. It also lines up with CVD-related medical finds and statistics.

Chlorine is a *very* strong oxidizer. It instantly reacts with water to form hypochlorous acid that kills microbes in seconds by oxidizing (destroying) their lipids. CVD plaques are full of oxidized cholesterol and dead mycoplasmas that normally circulate in arterial blood. White blood cells that ingest oxidized cholesterol in attempt to clean up the mess are killed by apoptosis; these are called "foam cells".

Arteries are our "pipes". Boiler engineers know that water must be completely chlorine-free before passing through metal pipes. If not, chlorine will oxidize (corrode) the inside of pipes over years or decades – even stainless steel and titanium.

If chlorine destroys the walls of metal pipes, what does it do to the lipid-rich cell membranes that line the walls of arteries and the lipid-rich LDL cholesterol dissolved in the blood? If chlorine corrodes metal, what does it do to dissolved metals in blood that are particularly important for normal heart and muscle function?

Want to kill some marine life? Put them in a tank of chlorinated tap water and watch them slowly die. Chlorinated water is made safe for fish by adding enough vitamin C (a potent antioxidant) to neutralize the chlorine. While Steinberg and his friends bilk the public for billions of research dollars by blaming cholesterol for CVD, the verdict on chlorine was out long ago.

Chlorinated Drinking Water on Myocardial Structure and Functions

Revis, N.W., Osborne, T.R., and Holdsworth, G. "Effect of Chlorinated Drinking Water on Myocardial Structure and Functions in Pigeons and Rabbits," 5th Conf. on Water Chlorination. Eds R. J. Jolly et al. 1985 page 365 373

Chlorine reacts with the double bond in fatty acids and cholesterol producing chlorinated derivatives. These derivatives are absorbed from the gastrointestinal tract and metabolized by a variety of organs. Significant increases in heart weight occur in rats given chlorinated fatty acids. Furthermore, we observed hypercholesterolemia in pigeons and rabbits exposed to chlorinated water. Collectively these results suggest that chlorine or chlorination by-products may adversely affect the cardiovascular system through the well-known association of plasma cholesterol levels with the onset of atherosclerosis and of cardiac hypertrophy with hypertension.

Chlorinated water has been shown to:

- Harden arteries (atherosclerosis)
- Raise blood pressure (hypertension)
- Enlarge the heart (cardiac hypertrophy)
- Raise cholesterol (hypercholesterolemia)
- Kill fish and other aquatic life

Clin Lipidol. Author manuscript; available in PMC 2011 October 1.
Published in final edited form as:
Clin Lipidol. 2010 December 1; 5(6): 835–852.
doi: 10.2217/clp.10.68
PMCID: PMC3041592
NIHMSID: NIHMS269308

Lipid oxidation by hypochlorous acid: chlorinated lipids in atherosclerosis and myocardial ischemia

David A Ford

David A Ford, Department of Biochemistry & Molecular Biology, Center for Cardiovascular Research, Saint Louis University School of Medicine, Room 325, Doisy Research Center, 1100 South Grand Blvd, St Louis, MO 63104, USA, Tel.: +1 314 977 9264, Fax: +1 314 977 9205;
David A Ford: fordda@slu.edu

Our understanding of the role of chlorinated lipids in physiological and pathophysiological conditions is at the early stages, and these molecules may prove to be extremely important in the pathophysiological sequelae of diseases, including atherosclerosis and ischemic heart disease. Recent studies demonstrated that these chlorinated lipids accumulate in these diseases, yet the family of chlorinated lipid metabolites needs to be elucidated and the role of these metabolites as mediators of disease remains to be understood.

Effect of Drinking Water Containing Chlorine on Cholesterol Metabolism

Revis, N.W., Osborne, T.R., McCauley, P., Bull, R., and Holdsworth, G.

The U.S. Department of Energy (DOE) at Oak Ridge and the U.S. Environmental Protection Agency (EPA) performed a study on chlorine's effect on raising blood LDL cholesterol levels:

Proc. Natl. Acad. Sci. USA
Vol. 83, pp. 1485–1489, March 1986
Medical Sciences

Relationship of drinking water disinfectants to plasma cholesterol and thyroid hormone levels in experimental studies

N. W. Revis*†, P. McCauley‡, R. Bull‡, and G. Holdsworth*

*Oak Ridge Research Institute, 113 Union Valley Road, Oak Ridge, TN 37830; and ‡United States Environmental Protection Agency, 26 West St. Clair Street, Cincinnati, Ohio 45219

Both LDL and HDL cholesterol increased in response to these drinking water disinfectants (Fig. 2*a*). However, significant increases were only observed in the LDL cholesterol.

The World Health Organization (WHO) has also reported on a study of 46 communities in central Wisconsin that demonstrated total cholesterol and LDL cholesterol levels were higher in communities drinking chlorinated water:

Chlorine in Drinking-water

Background document for development of
WHO *Guidelines for Drinking-water Quality*

In a study of 46 communities in central Wisconsin where chlorine levels in water ranged from 0.2 to 1 mg/litre, serum cholesterol and low-density lipoprotein levels were higher in communities using chlorinated water. Levels of high-density lipoprotein (HDL) and the cholesterol/HDL ratio were significantly elevated in relation to the level of calcium in the drinking-water, but only in communities using chlorinated water. The authors speculated that chlorine and calcium in drinking-water may interact in some way that affects lipid levels (*31*)

31. Zeighami EA, Watson AP, Craun GF. Serum lipid levels in neighboring communities with chlorinated and nonchlorinated drinking water. *Fundamental and applied toxicology*, 1990, 6:421-432.

Originally published in **Guidelines for drinking-water quality**, 2nd ed. Vol.2. *Health criteria and other supporting information. World Health Organization, Geneva, 1996.*

Despite the DOE, EPA and WHO have acknowledged the destructive effects of chlorine on the heart and blood, to date chlorination of water remains business as usual. The NIH and AHA are strangely silent on the matter.

With this explanation in mind to account for a three-fold increase in CVD since 1908 when chlorination of public water supplies and ingestion of phosphoric acid-containing soda pops became increasingly popular, let's review the "preponderance of evidence" against LDL cholesterol with which Steinberg inspired FDA approval and national policy for statin use.

In 2006, Steinberg published a five-part article in the "Journal of Lipid Research" – a journal he continues to shape as former Editor-in-Chief. Since this journal was started with NIH taxpayer funds and Steinberg is a former NIH chief, he enjoys an open forum to mold cholesterol policy. In this article, he boasts that by 1987 the evidence against cholesterol was so compelling that Sol Sobel of the FDA approved lovastatin without any trials to prove that it even lowered CVD risk (reference 14). All that Merck needed to show the FDA was that statins lowered cholesterol.

Here are five points for his "guilty" charge against cholesterol (with the authors' counterpoints to follow each indictment):

Point One: Steinberg begins his case against LDL cholesterol with the Russian scientist Nikolai Anitschkow who produced atherosclerosis in rabbits by feeding them an all-cholesterol diet. This could not be reproduced in other animal species until normal thyroid function was disrupted.

An interpretive history of the cholesterol controversy, part V: The discovery of the statins and the end of the controversy[1]

Journal of Lipid Research Volume 47, 2006

Daniel Steinberg[2]
Department of Medicine, University of California-San Diego, La Jolla, CA

Steinberg

In 1913, a young experimental pathologist named Anitschkow,[2] working at the Military Medical Academy in St. Petersburg, showed that simply feeding rabbits purified cholesterol dissolved in sunflower oil induced vascular lesions closely resembling those of human atherosclerosis...
Steiner and Kendall, 33 years later, would show that inhibiting thyroid function in dogs and then feeding them cholesterol does increase blood cholesterol and then does induce lesions (21).

Counterpoint:

1.) Rabbits eat mostly greens, not cholesterol.

2.) Even Anitschkow reported that the "colossal doses" of cholesterol he fed rabbits did not represent what happens in man and that he did not believe that this was the cause of CVD (reference 15). Animals fed chlorinated water also lose normal thyroid function and get CVD-like lesions (reference 16).

3.) In 1953, Siperstein fed cholesterol to birds, which lowered their cholesterol and even reversed CVD – just the opposite of what Anitschkow did to rabbits in 1913.

Prevention of Plasma Cholesterol Elevation and Atheromatosis in the Cholesterol-Fed Bird by the Administration of Dihydrocholesterol
M. D. SIPERSTEIN, C. W. NICHOLS, JR. and I. L. CHAIKOFF
Circulation 1953;7;37-41

Point Two: Steinberg continues his inquest on cholesterol by claiming that people with a genetic form of high cholesterol have more CVD – like Anitschkow's rabbits.

An interpretive history of the cholesterol controversy: part II: the early evidence linking hypercholesterolemia to coronary disease in humans[1]

Journal of Lipid Research Volume 47, 2006

Daniel Steinberg[2]
Department of Medicine, University of California-San Diego, La Jolla, CA

Steinberg

Their work established familial hypercholesterolemia as a monogenic defect, implying that the arterial disease was secondary to the elevated blood cholesterol, i.e., that the pathogenesis was analogous to the pathogenesis in Anitschkow's cholesterol-fed rabbits.

Counterpoint:

1.) LDL cholesterol is easily oxidized therefore people with higher levels of circulating LDL cholesterol may be more susceptible to lipid oxidation by chlorinated water.

2.) People with FH have led long healthy lives without CVD, especially prior to chlorination of public water supplies at the turn of the 20th century (references 6 and 7).

3.) People with FH have elevated reductase (due to defective LDL receptors). No studies have been performed to rule out the potential deleterious effects of this condition.

Point Three: Steinberg cites evidence of CVD in one-third of autopsied Korean War casualties. Since the average age of these soldiers was 22, he implies that cholesterol treatment should begin in childhood. (National guidelines originally spearheaded by Steinberg now recommend treatment by age nine.)

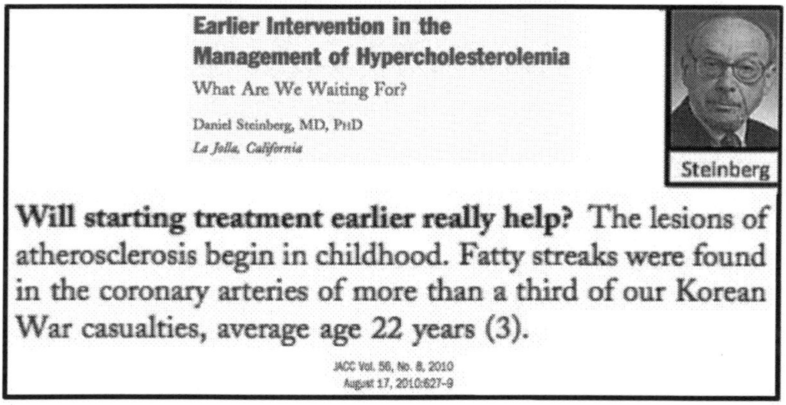

Earlier Intervention in the Management of Hypercholesterolemia

What Are We Waiting For?

Daniel Steinberg, MD, PhD

La Jolla, California

Steinberg

Will starting treatment earlier really help? The lesions of atherosclerosis begin in childhood. Fatty streaks were found in the coronary arteries of more than a third of our Korean War casualties, average age 22 years (3).

JACC Vol. 56, No. 8, 2010
August 17, 2010:627-9

Counterpoint: William Enos and a team of physicians autopsied 300 U.S. soldiers killed in the Korean War. Over 77% (not one-third as per Steinberg) had CVD (reference 17). During the Korean War, the potable water was so heavily chlorinated that it was said to be barely drinkable. Similar results were found in dead soldiers from Vietnam where water was also heavily chlorinated (reference 18). In 1969, Joseph Price, MD, published scientific proof for the chlorine-CVD connection in "Coronaries Cholesterol Chlorine".

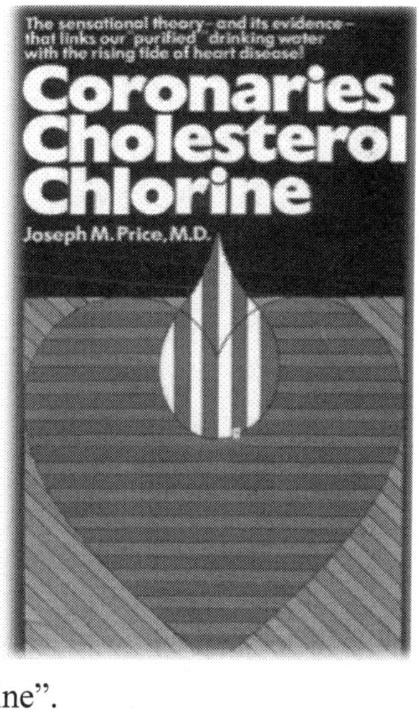

Point Four: Steinberg again implicates dietary cholesterol as the cause of elevated cholesterol in two Japanese migration studies.

An interpretive history of the cholesterol controversy: part II: the early evidence linking hypercholesterolemia to coronary disease in humans[1]

Steinberg

Journal of Lipid Research Volume 47, 2006

Daniel Steinberg[2]
Department of Medicine, University of California-San Diego, La Jolla, CA

The Japanese who had moved to Hawaii had higher blood cholesterol levels and higher heart attack rates than the Japanese on Honshu who had not migrated. The difference was even more striking in those who had settled in San Francisco.

Counterpoint:

1.) Water, not food, can again account for this difference. The U.S. began to chlorinate public water supplies in 1908 when CVD rates began to rise; Japan did not begin the practice until the U.S. occupied Japan after WWII (reference 19).

2.) Phosphoric acid, a strong oxidizer commonly used in soda pop and popular in the U.S at the time of the Japanese immigration, has also been linked with CVD (reference 20).

3.) Toxins from common molds have also been linked with higher cholesterol and heart attack rates (reference 21-22); exposure to toxic molds in the U.S. was not explored.

The Internet Journal of Toxicology ISSN: 1559-3916

High Cholesterol Levels And Chronic Exposure To Toxigenic Molds In Damp Buildings: A High Risk For Cardiovascular Diseases And Stroke

J. E. Ehiri
E. C. Anyanwu

Proposed mechanism of mycotoxin effects on cholesterol metabolism

Already, it is known that the rate-limiting step of cholesterol biosynthesis is catalyzed by HMG-CoA reductase that is responsible for most of the complex regulatory controls.[7,8,9] It is most likely that mycotoxins are capable of disrupting the action of this rate-limiting HMG-CoA enzyme (reductase) because, the reactions of mycotoxins fit into, have affinity for, and are very similar to those of cholesterol biosynthesis.

Point Five: Steinberg cites more studies that support his theory that high cholesterol is due to diet. He includes a 1966 study that demonstrated a diet higher in polyunsaturated fat lowered cholesterol and decreased risk of a second heart attack.

Counterpoint: Cell membranes are made of lipids (fats) that include saturated fats, unsaturated fats and cholesterol (an unsaturated fat). Unsaturated lipids and LDL cholesterol are easily oxidized. Unsaturated dietary fats replenish damaged oxidized lipids, reducing the need for the liver to make new lipids (lowering blood levels) and reducing the risk of CVD.

The preponderance of evidence is that LDL cholesterol is good and that oxidizers that oxidize LDL cholesterol are bad.

For cholesterol to be made dissolvable in blood, it attaches to a protein to make a lipoprotein. Different proteins have different densities such as LDL (low density lipoprotein) and HDL (high density lipoprotein). LDL cholesterol is more easily oxidized than HDL cholesterol. Lipid theorists like Steinberg then call LDL cholesterol "bad" because it obeys universal chemical laws.

Much to-do has been made in regard to the anti-cancer and heart-protective effects of antioxidants such as vitamin C, vitamin E, selenium, grape seed extract, etc.

Little to-do, on the other hand, is made about the oxidizers that damage LDL cholesterol in the first place by the following chain reaction:

- Oxidizers steal electrons from electron-rich cell membrane lipids.

- Oxygen radicals are formed.

- Oxygen radicals steal more electrons from more electron-rich cell membrane lipids.

The damage spreads until the fire burns out.

When cells are injured for any reason, lipid hormones called prostaglandins are quickly made from cholesterol in an effort to respond to the damage. By convention, cholesterol production must rise.

Prostaglandins regulate important functions such as blood pressure, inflammation and clotting. Over a dozen types of prostaglandins are grouped into three "series" that balance various opposing reactions in cells.

Series 1 (Omega 6) & Series 3 (Omega 3)	Series 2 (Omega 6)
Decreases blood pressure	Increases blood pressure
Increases airway dilation	Increases airway constriction
Increases oxygen flow	Decreases oxygen flow
Decreases pain and inflammation	Increases pain and inflammation
Decreases body temperature	Increases body temperature
Suppresses immune system	Activates immune system
Inhibits platelet clotting	Promotes platelet clotting

Series 1 and 2 prostaglandins are made from omega-6 type fats (such as olive and sesame oils), and Series 3 is made from omega-3 type fats (such as fish and flax oils). Omega-3 type fats are more unsaturated and therefore more electron-rich than omega-6 type fats. Therefore, Series 3 prostaglandins are more quickly damaged by oxidation. This can result in an imbalance of prostaglandins (excess Series 2). This causes high blood pressure, inflammation, pain, clotting, an activated immune system and other serious problems associated with CVD.

When a fat-soluble oxidizing acid is drunk on an empty stomach without food, it can be absorbed through the stomach wall into the bloodstream. The lipid cell membranes that line the arteries and the dissolved lipids in arterial blood take the blunt of oxidation. This provides an explanation for why CVD happens in arteries and not veins.

How could such an obvious hazard to our "pipes" have been so ignored that not one study by the AHA or NIH can be found in the public record?

Steinberg misses the connection either in ignorance or by design.

None of this is rocket science despite all the cholesterol chicanery. Follow the money. Cures are not profitable.

Lying and ignoring, on the other hand, can be hugely profitable if the end result is a popular drug "treatment".

Chapter 14: What a racket!

Want to get filthy rich? First create a problem real or imagined. Then create a solution and sell it to everyone. Be advised: that, by definition, is racketeering.

Steinberg sits atop the heap of the greatest protection racket of all time. First, he created the problem. Then he personally forged the solution. Lastly, he jammed it down the throats of doctors and patients in perpetuity.

No man has enjoyed more leverage in shaping and policing national cholesterol policy than Daniel Steinberg. Like some multi-tentacle system-sapping leviathan, Steinberg slipped into the pockets of most every statin-related taxpayer-funded government agency and for-profit drug behemoth.

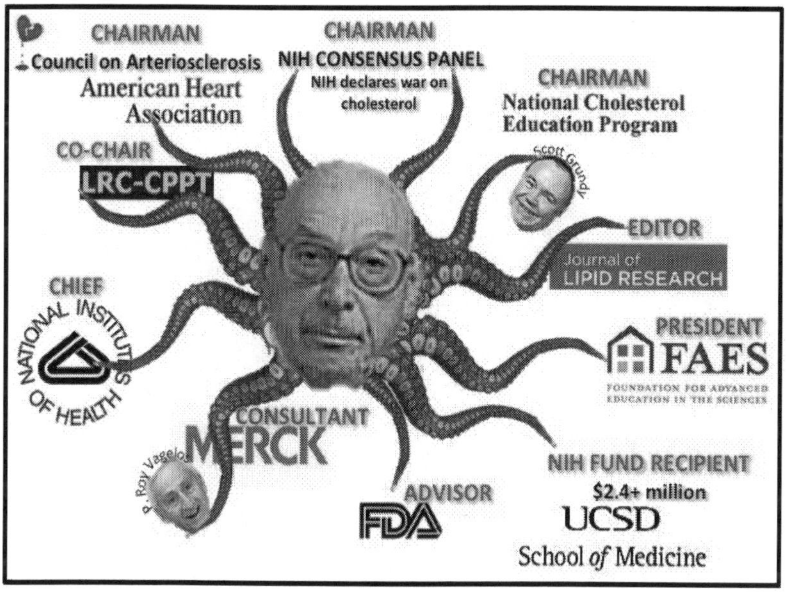

Almost single-handedly he paved the way for FDA statin approval and then filled Merck's coffers by setting national cholesterol guidelines. One can't help but wonder if even the

FDA knew that it was the same man behind the curtain pulling all the multiple strings and swinging wide open hell's gates.

The advantage of perpetuating a false lipid theory and ensuring its enforcement is that the drug company honoraria and research monies never end. The benefit of backing drugs like statins that treat symptoms and not cause of a so-called disease is that the cash cow never dries. The advantage of setting one's feet on high places at the NIH with access to hundreds of millions of taxpayer funds is that if friends like Grundy aren't already strategically placed like Vagelos, you can make sure they become so.

Like a card game with a stacked deck, the drug development and grant monies game is controlled from most every angle.

It is racket of unbelievable scope done in full public view and completely legal. Legality, however, does not define morality. It is simply the American way of for-profit medicine.

Steinberg's hats are so varied that he can even write a third-person account of the statin success story as if he's an outsider. When the masks are removed, the tale is in fact almost entirely his to tell – first person from the inside. For example, in his "Cholesterol War" essays, Steinberg lends credibility to various authorities such as "the Chairman of the Council on Arteriosclerosis" and the "NIH Consensus Panel" who decided this or that. All along, it was he who chaired the post or panel and decided this or that.

Winners write history. Steinberg isn't shy to record for the world the sequence of events that led to statin approval – but he is clever to not always drop his name but instead use titles. A little research quickly unveils that the titles he drops belong to him.

Here's how one man laid the strategic groundwork for ultimate FDA approval of statins:

- In 1969, the chairman of the Council on Arteriosclerosis of the American Heart Association declared, "It is now good medical practice to treat – and I use the word advisedly – people who have definite hyperlipoproteinemia (high cholesterol)" (reference 23).

  The chairman was Daniel Steinberg.

- In January 1984, the results of the Lipid Research Clinics Coronary Primary Prevention Trial (LRC-CPPT) were released to the world. The NIH-led, taxpayer-paid, thirteen-year-long and $150-million-dollar trial demonstrated that lowering blood cholesterol lowers absolute heart disease risk by less than two percent. Despite the worthless results, Steinberg claimed that the study provided the long-sought, definitive evidence that lowering cholesterol reduces heart disease risk.

  The LRC-CPPT was co-chaired by Daniel Steinberg.

- In May 1984, a new drug application (NDA) for human testing was approved for Merck's lovastatin in nine months – one of the shortest approval times for the FDA.

  Daniel Steinberg was Merck's scientific advisor whom the FDA trusted.

- In December 1984, the NIH consensus panel agreed, as one voice with their chairman who delivered the consensus statement, that LDL cholesterol was the cause of CVD. The panel recommended that the NCEP (National Cholesterol Education Program) be adopted.

  Daniel Steinberg chaired the NIH consensus panel and provided the documents for approval.

- In 1985, Scott Grundy led the NIH-backed National Cholesterol Education Program (NCEP) that set national policy for lowering cholesterol with statins.

  Daniel Steinberg chaired the panel that placed Grundy in charge of the NCEP.

Steinberg reports that Solomon Sobel of the FDA did not even require Merck to prove that lovastatin lowered CVD risk; the fact that statins lowered cholesterol was good enough. He boasts that the conclusions of Steinberg's three-day Consensus Conference at the NIH in 1984 and the results of the LRC-CPPT in 1984 "smoothed the way" for statin approval in 1987:

An interpretive history of the cholesterol controversy, part IV: The 1984 Coronary Primary Prevention Trial ends it—almost[1]

Daniel Steinberg[2]
Department of Medicine, University of California-San Diego, La Jolla, CA

Steinberg

According to Dr. Solomon Sobel, head of the Division of Metabolic and Endocrine Drugs at the time Merck's lovastatin came up for review, the results of the Lipid Research Clinics CPPT and the conclusions of the 1984 Consensus Conference figured very large in the adoption of such a policy and smoothed the way for the later approval of the statins.

The NCEP continues to meet and revise cholesterol policy with ever-decreasing target LDL cholesterol levels. The recommended age for statin use for life is now age nine.

Conflicts of interest also continue to run amuck with the NCEP so-called "experts". All of the doctors who wrote the new 2004 NCEP guidelines under Dr. Cleeman's direction had received payments or research money from statin manufacturers as follows (reference 24):

Dr. Grundy: Payments from Merck, Pfizer, Sankyo, Bayer, Kos, Abbott, Bristol-Myers Squibb and AstraZeneca; grant funds from Merck, Abbott, and Glaxo Smith Kline.

Dr. Bairey: Payments from Pfizer, Merck, Kos and Bayer; grant funds from Merck, Pfizer, Procter & Gamble, Novartis, Wyeth, AstraZeneca and Bristol-Myers Squibb.

Dr. Brewer: Payments AstraZeneca, Pfizer, Sankyo, Lipid Sciences, Merck, Fournier, Tularik, Esperion, and Novartis.

Dr. Clark: Payments from Abbott, AstraZeneca, Bristol-Myers Squibb, Merck, and Pfizer; grant funds from Abbott, AstraZeneca, Bristol-Myers Squibb, Merck and Pfizer.

Dr. Hunninghake: Payments from AstraZeneca, Merck, Pfizer, and Kos; research funds from AstraZeneca, Bristol-Myers Squibb, Kos, Merck, Novartis and Pfizer.

Dr. Pasternak: Payments from Pfizer, Merck, Takeda, Kos, BMS-Sanofi, Johnson & Johnson-Merck, AstraZeneca and Novartis.

Dr. Smith: Grant funds from Merck.

Dr. Stone: Payments from Abbott, AstraZeneca, Bristol-Myers Squibb, Kos, Merck, Novartis, Pfizer, Reliant, and Sankyo.

Steinberg loathes lipid theory resistance and bemoans opponents like Thomas J. Moore who imply that conflicting fiscal interests like his with Merck have clouded his science:

An interpretive history of the cholesterol controversy, part IV: The 1984 Coronary Primary Prevention Trial ends it—almost[1]

Daniel Steinberg[2]

Fig. 6. *Cover of The Atlantic, September 1989, featuring an attack by journalist Thomas J. Moore on the Consensus Conference, its members, and the proposition that decreasing high cholesterol levels would reduce cardiac morbidity and mortality. See text for details. (From The Atlantic, September 1989, with permission.)*

Things got even worse. A few years after the Consensus Conference, *The Atlantic* published and featured on its cover (**Fig. 6**) an article by Thomas J. Moore entitled "The cholesterol myth" (37). Moore, a journalist covering science, wrote: "...the dissenters have been overwhelmed by the extravaganza put on not just by the heart institute but by a growing coalition that resembles a medical version of the military-industrial complex. This coalition includes...the 'authorities'...the heart institute [The National Heart, Lung and Blood Institute] itself...and the American Heart Association." Moore then went on to name explicitly five investigators very active in the lipid field at the time who had offered to make themselves available to answer questions about the statins, which had just been introduced by Merck for clinical use (Antonio Gotto, Scott M. Grundy, John LaRosa, Robert I. Levy, and Daniel Steinberg). There followed a series of short paragraphs about this "Gang of Five" (my term) and the arguably actionable conclusion that "It is likely that one reason these physicians consented to such an arrangement is that their laboratories were heavily involved in research funded by Merck." Finally, borrowing from Marc Antony, "There is no reason to doubt the honesty, sincerity, and expertise of any of these men." Yes, the cholesterol controversy has seen its share of vitriol.

When someone with political standing like Steinberg shouts long and loud enough, ears inevitably bend. He insists to this day that the "cholesterol wars" are over for good, the debate is finished and statins are here to stay. He shouted repeatedly enough using our money until we finally bought the lie and became afraid of the stuff that life is made of.

As Merck's advisor, Steinberg systematically cleared every roadblock that might hinder statins' delivery to the market. The biggest hurdle was getting Merck back in the statin saddle after stopping trials in 1980.

Sankyo had to be discredited, and Steinberg had some ideas on how to do it. By advising Merck and the FDA to resume human trials and dismiss Sankyo's dog lymphomas as that of conservative over-reaction by the Japanese, he invented a slew of reasons to discredit Sankyo:

An interpretive history of the cholesterol controversy, part V: The discovery of the statins and the end of the controversy[1]

Daniel Steinberg[2]

Sankyo was strongly tilted toward conservatism in the 1960s, partly because of several serious instances of post-marketing toxicity, including the tragic experience with thalidomide. This conservatism tended to be shared generally by the medical profession in Japan at the time. One prominent Japanese clinician warned that "powerful drugs, like a sharp knife, should be considered dangerous." Another warned students not to prescribe drugs at full dosage, thereby running the risk of toxicity, but whenever possible to use half the normal dosage. Another factor may have been the somewhat parochial approach of the pharmaceutical companies in Japan at that time, an unwillingness to openly exchange information with and seek advice from those outside the company "family" (Akira Yamamoto, personal communication). In any case, Sankyo dropped compactin and continued to hunt for other fungal inhibitors.

How could something so life threatening have been so callously trivialized? Why would Merck and the FDA trust such heartless dismissals for reported cancer? Sanko certainly wouldn't have dropped the golden egg after investing millions of dollars unless something was seriously wrong with their statin-fed dogs. The type of cancer Sankyo reported (lymphomas) should have even been foreseen because lymphocytes have a high demand for circulating blood cholesterol. Based on statins' mechanism of action, apoptosis of lymphocytes is predictable.

Steinberg is a master at exacting a strategy that doctors sometimes joke about amongst themselves: "Baffle 'em with BS." Having convinced himself that statins do not cause cancer, the American Cancer Society fellow praises Merck scientific advisor Jean Wilson, Dallas-based scientists Brown, Goldstein, Bilheimer, and Grundy and Merck employees MacDonald, Alber-Schonberg, Hoffman, Monaghan, Patchett and Chen for pressing Merck and the FDA forward with government approval and resuming human statin experiments:

An interpretive history of the cholesterol controversy, part V: The discovery of the statins and the end of the controversy[1]

Daniel Steinberg[2]

Department of Medicine, University of California-San Diego, La

Dropping the program might deny some patients a chance to prolong their lives. Moreover, there was still no hard evidence that compactin would be toxic in humans, only rumors about toxicity in dogs given very high doses. There was no way to be certain about the extent of risk, but the potential ben-

This line of argument was urged on Vagelos by a number of clinicians who had used lovastatin in early safety and efficacy trials, including Roger Illingworth of Portland and Scott M. Grundy, David Bilheimer, Joseph L. Goldstein, and Michael S. Brown of Dallas. Two members of Vagelos' Scientific Advisory Board, Jean Wilson from Dallas and Daniel Steinberg from La Jolla, made the same case. In his memoir, Vagelos remembers that "we needed advice from the type of authorities in their field whom the FDA would consult." After these meetings, Merck presented all of its data to the FDA and got a green light for additional clinical trials in high-risk patients. Merck was on its way to putting the first statin drug into the hands of clinicians (the outstanding team at Merck that saw this project to completion included Drs. Georg Alber-Schonberg, Carl Hoffman, James MacDonald, Richard Monaghan, and Arthur Patchett and Ms. Julie Chen).

Prior to the time of this advice by Steinberg and his accomplices to revive Merck's statin trials on humans, the main toxic effect of statins as reported by the experts was not that statins slowly induce cancer, but that statins quickly block the cell cycle and kill cells within 48 hours. Steinberg knew this.

What kind of scientist could so easily turn a blind eye to multiple warning signs of pending destruction to cells? Did Merck's money corrupt Steinberg's reasoning? Not likely. He is either a lousy scientist or a liar. What is evident by his own disclosure is that he is an intellectual with an agenda. Merck's interest in him was most likely based on his misguided passion for the lipid theory and political clout that he holds to this day.

In Steinberg's own words, he was both a scientific advisor to Merck as well as an authority in a specialized field "whom the FDA would consult." From his own bio, that "specialized field" includes: "Biosynthesis, secretion and catabolism of the plasma lipoproteins; physiologic and pharmacologic regulation of plasma cholesterol levels". The FDA seeks out such specialists, when reviewing a new drug application, to join an "Advisory Committee":

FindArticles / Health / FDA Consumer / Dec-Jan, 1987

Getting outside advice for the 'close calls.'

by Dixie Farley

MEMBERSHIP

FDA pays its drug advisory committee members $100 a day while the committee meets and also reimburses costs for travel, food and lodging.

Most members are physicians whose medical specialties involve prescribing drugs under the purview of their committees. Others are registered nurses, statisticians, epidemiologists (who study disease occurrence), and pharmacologists (who study drug effects in the body).

NEW DRUGS

On Feb. 19, 1987, FDA asked its Endocrinologic and Metabolic Drugs Advisory Committee whether a new cholesterol-lowering drug called lovastatin should be approved. One question was, "What precautions, if any, do you recommend to ensure safe use of lovastatin?"

The FDA seeks outside advice for approval of new drugs in spite of inviting conflicts-of-interest! Despite this issue remains controversial, the FDA found a way out. Advisory Committee members with conflicting interests must request a waiver. During the year of lovastatin's approval, the FDA granted 14 conflict-of-interest waivers.

When it came time to review lovastatin for approval the entire process was so corrupted the FDA existed for only one purpose: to lend credibility to Merck's application and drug approval.

With the FDA and the NIH support, Merck was guaranteed success and enormous profits. Sure enough, they beat the "Japs" to market. They were the first to sell death in the form of a compressed statin tablet.

In hindsight, Steinberg had gained both his credibility and influence as a result of his part in unraveling the MER/29 fiasco:

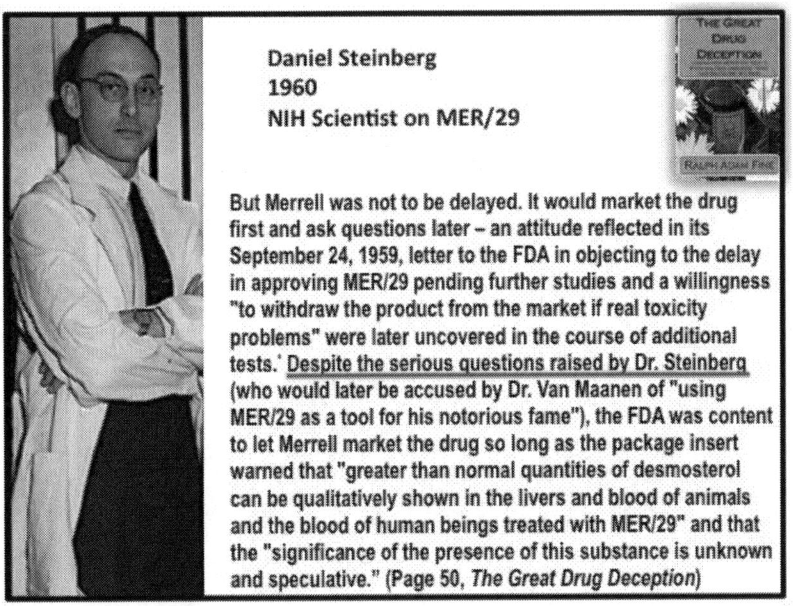

MER/29 blocked the conversion of desmosterol to cholesterol and Steinberg was concerned about the build-up of desmosterol in cells. He stood his ground and resisted the tide of Merrell physicians such as McMaster who pushed hard for FDA approval (from "The Great Drug Deception" by Judge Ralph A. Fine).

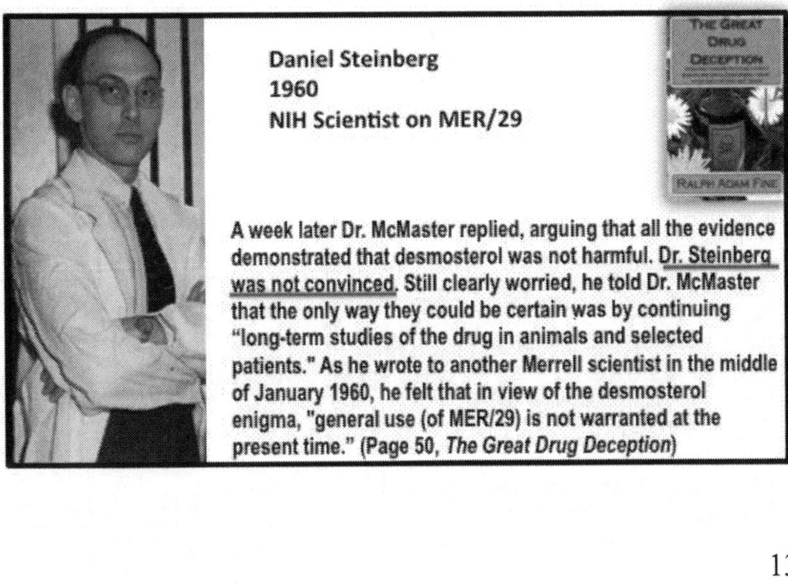

Merrell's Robert McMaster was, like Merck's Jonathan Tobert, responsible for overseeing the testing of MER/29 on humans. It is ironic that during the MER/29 standoff, Steinberg told McMaster that there was no proof for the lipid theory and that acceptable toxicity of MER/29 must be "as near to zero as possible":

Daniel Steinberg
1960
NIH Scientist on MER/29

Dr. Steinberg, the physician with the National Heart Institute who had reported on the accumulation of desmosterol in MER/29-treated patients, objected to this optimistic interpretation of what he felt was a very serious situation. In a letter to Dr. McMaster, he pointed out that since there was "no assurance" that drugs which lower cholesterol levels actually benefit the patient, "the acceptable incidence of toxic effects must be as near to zero as possible." As this was not true with MER/29, he argued that "it is not justifiable to expose the patient to potentially damaging effects." (Page 103, *The Great Drug Deception*)

After MER/29, the FDA suffered loss of public trust. Dr. John Nestor, the medical officer in charge of MER/29, was so disgusted by FDA's operations that in 1963 he reported to Senator Humphrey that bureaucrats were overruling FDA scientists so that drugs were approved without proof of safety. FDA commissioner John L. Harvey publicly admitted, "The drug should not have gone to market in the first place."

Steinberg was not the only MER/29 voice of reason. Oddly enough, the other was Merck. After testing MER/29, Merck warned Merrell of cataracts in rats. Twenty-five years later, it was Merck, the ostensibly "moral company", that brandished Steinberg's full support and spurious explanations as to why lovastatin would not repeat MER/29's wrongs. In the backdrop of Merck and Steinberg's reliable history with MER/29, the FDA felt safe about trusting them.

Shift happens. No longer an NIH public servant and now working for Merck, Steinberg invented multiple bogus claims touting lovastatin's safety such as:

1.) Statins are non-toxic.

2.) Statins do not cause cataracts.

3.) Lymphomas were not likely found in Sankyo's dogs.

4.) Statins did not work on Merck's rats because rats have high HDL ("good") cholesterol levels.

In his five-part series, "An Interpretive History of the Cholesterol Controversy", Steinberg parrots his advice that Merck and the FDA would have heard from him regarding lovastatin's safety:

> "The toxic effects might be unique to triparanol (MER/29) which turned out to be the case, so that other inhibitors (statins) might be free of such effects."
>
> "Fortunately, some drug companies did not completely shut down their research programs on inhibitors of cholesterol biosynthesis. However, most of them decided to steer clear of inhibitors that blocked synthesis at the later stages, hoping that inhibitors working at earlier steps (statins) would not share with triparanol (MER/29) the disastrous effects on the eye and on hair growth."
>
> "They also showed that the drug worked in rabbits, hens, and monkeys. In retrospect, the reason for the initial "failure" in rats is clear. The drug does actually inhibit cholesterol synthesis in vivo in the rat, just as effectively as it does in other species, even though there is a compensatory increase in the amount of reductase enzyme. However, rats have extremely low

LDL levels. Most of their plasma cholesterol is in the HDL fraction."

Steinberg lies. Statins failed to lower cholesterol in rats, hamsters and mice because these animals make cholesterol mainly in the kidneys and not the liver – the "target organ" of statins; the reflexive increase in reductase took effect in the largely spared kidneys. Other than *rapid death*, there were no adverse effects of lovastatin on rabbits. Finally, MER/29 proved less toxic than statins because it blocked the final step of the mevalonate pathway and therefore did not block cell cycles. Good liars at least remember their lies.

The advisory committee was so stacked in Merck's favor that they could have taken a vote and saved the time of listening to all the phony evidence and bogus claims.

In an interview with Solomon Sobel, the head of the FDA division that approved lovastatin, Dr. Sobel reports that after Merck terminated lovastatin's trials in 1980, the FDA became "actively involved" in statin development (this interview is posted at the FDA web site):

From the FDA Web site:

http://www.fda.gov/AboutFDA/WhatWeDo/History/ProductRegulation/SelectionsFromFDLIUpdateSeriesonFDAHistory/ucm082054.htm

Statins: A Success Story Involving FDA, Academia and Industry

This article originally appeared in the "History Corner" column of the March-April 2007 issue of Update magazine, the bimonthly publication of the Food and Drug Law Institute

Suzanne White Junod, Ph.D,
FDA Historian

Following Merck's decision to terminate clinical trials, FDA became actively involved in maintaining interest in the development of the "statins."

How did the FDA ever become "actively involved in maintaining interest" in the development of a for-profit prescription drug, especially in light of the MER/29 disaster? The FDA did not take a skeptical stance about another cholesterol-lowering drug affecting the same biochemical pathway. Who pressed the FDA to stir this toxic fungal brew that was killing rabbits in days, causing cataracts in rats within weeks and reportedly inducing intestinal cancer in dogs within months?

Only one man fits those shoes: Daniel Steinberg.

Sobel and Steinberg croon in concert. FDA's Solomon Sobel confirms what Steinberg brags – that the FDA did not even require Merck to prove that lovastatin lowered CVD risk. Based on what Sobel calls the "surrogate lowering of LDL cholesterol", lovastatin was approved in record time without any clinical evidence that it did anything but lower cholesterol. Other secondary metabolites such as citrinin, aflatoxin and watered-down snake venom might have even qualified as FDA-approved drugs for Sobel's so-called suitable "surrogate lowering of LDL cholesterol".

From the FDA Web site:

http://www.fda.gov/AboutFDA/WhatWeDo/History/ProductRegulation/SelectionsFromFDLIUpdateSerieson FDAHistory/ucm082054.htm

Statins: A Success Story Involving FDA, Academia and Industry

Suzanne White Junod, Ph.D.
FDA Historian

Cholesterol Study Changes Thinking

On March 23, 1984, Merck submitted a company sponsored IND for lovastatin and the approval work proceeded apace.[4] The new drug application for lovastatin was approved nine months after its submission to FDA, which was one of the shortest approval times for an NDA by FDA up to that time. The decision by the Division of Metabolic and Endocrine Drug Products to approve agents for marketing based on the surrogate of lowering LDL cholesterol was a key component in shortening the review time for lovastatin. Lovastatin was released for marketing in 1987.

Sol Sobel, with Steinberg's self-aggrandizing style, sings praises of the FDA's interest in pushing statin development across the finish line. He is clear that FDA's fast tracking of the statins ensured Merck's lovastatin hit the streets ahead of MER/29's record ten-month delivery time in 1960.

In the same interview, Sobel jokes about how some pharmacists think that statins, in being so effective, should even be added to public drinking-water supplies.

Are they trying to kill us? Not likely, although it's a slow death anyway. At 1/100th the dose that kills animals in weeks or months it takes years or decades for the same injuries to kill humans so that a connection is never made. They are the James Bonds of the drug cartels with FDA licenses to kill with impunity, but they are shooting at the wrong target. They need to put statins in *their* water supplies, not ours!

Statins aren't working. In 1900, CVD accounted for only 10% of worldwide deaths. In 2005, 29% of all deaths in the world were caused by CVD and the numbers are still rising. In 2010, CVD became the leading cause of death in developing countries where public water supplies are becoming modernized. By 2015, the WHO estimates CVD will continue to rise to 30% of all worldwide deaths.

The statin market continues to expand.

Statins have been shown to weaken skeletal and heart muscle and induce dementia by a variety of mechanisms. Figures from the National Center for Health Statistics show that, since the early '90s when statins became increasingly popular, the incidence of heart muscle failure and Alzheimer's disease has risen sharply.

There is no cure for heart failure short of a heart transplant. Statin-induced dementia improves by discontinuing the drug. In the meantime, research monies forever flow from the taxpayers' treasury to find the elusive cures for Alzheimer's and CVD.

What a racket!

Chapter 15: Dallas Needs an Enema

For over sixty years, the Southwestern Medical Center at Dallas has received countless millions in taxpayer funds in the form of NIH grants. Like former NIH Chief Steinberg, Southwestern's Brown, Goldstein and Dietschy – all with former ties to the NIH and involved in cholesterol research – regularly receive generous NIH grants for their work.

Lovastatin's development and approval was in large part due to NIH funded research by Brown, Goldstein and their colleagues. In 1982, the FDA expedited arrangements for Merck to give lovastatin to Dallas-based medical doctors Grundy, Bilheimer and Brown for experimentation on people with a genetically defective form of high cholesterol. An FDA-backed Investigational New Drug (IND) was granted for this work – two years before an IND was even given to Merck to start human trials.

In 1982, the statin ball was in Dallas' court. The body of evidence first established in Siperstein's Dallas-based lab on the deadly effect of statins on cells was ultimately altered. Merck commandeered the evidence so that statins could be approved and Dallas would ultimately need an enormous enema.

Steinberg, as former Editor-in-Chief of the "Journal of Lipid Research", ensured players Brown, Goldstein, Bilheimer and Grundy had open access to publish their results in his journal. Tony Gotto, president of the Dallas-based American Heart Association with strong ties to Merck's purse strings, did the same with AHA's popular "Circulation" magazine. Brown, as AHA's representative investigator, kept Gotto in the circle.

And so the stage was set for human statin experiments to begin in the U.S. and the results to be immediately published, fully endorsed by the NIH and AHA and widely circulated to physicians. In Japan, Endo had already completed the first tests on Yamamoto and Mabuchi's FH patients, so the Dallas boys were a bit behind. That would change soon enough.

The great race to be first to market a mycotoxin to the masses was in full swing and the Southwestern Medical Center at Dallas had a small population of FH patients to test. In two short years, Steinberg would call the NIH cholesterol consensus panel and have them endorse his consensus statement; he would then set Grundy as both chair and AHA representative of the NCEP. Grundy would lead the NCEP and set standards that would instantly qualify 25% of the adult population for statin treatment.

By 1990, physicians would, in mass, fear loss of licensure by not complying with the NCEP/AHA-endorsed protocols.

It was a task of master-level manipulations in the making. Steinberg kept out of the spotlight and directed from the sidelines in concert with Gotto at the AHA, Vagelos at Merck, Sobel at the FDA and the Dallas docs at Southwestern.

By 1982 when statin testing on FH patients began, there were two known problems that Dallas needed to repair:

1. The statin-induced increase in reductase had to be corrected. It was a serious design flaw.

2. Statins did not work on the homozygous FH patients who suffer from painful cholesterol deposits in tissues and could benefit the most from cholesterol lowering treatment. This would have to be reported to the FDA.

"Fix it," came the order. Money was not an issue. Funds from Merck, the AHA and the NIH freely flowed into the Brown and Goldstein lab. ***They never fixed it.***

In 1978, Brown and Goldstein discovered with Endo that statins (compactin) increased reductase. The following year, they reported on the "killing effect" of statins. This would later change, but by 1982 when human tests began at Dallas, the cat was already out of the bag. By this time they had published that:

- Compactin killed cells.
- Mevalonate prevented statin-induced cell death.
- Cholesterol did not prevent statin-induced cell death.

THE JOURNAL OF BIOLOGICAL CHEMISTRY
Vol. 254, No. 12, Issue of June 25, pp. 5403-5409, 1979
Printed in U.S.A.

Inhibition of Cholesterol Synthesis with Compactin Renders Growth of Cultured Cells Dependent on the Low Density Lipoprotein Receptor*

(Received for publication, January 5, 1979)

Joseph L. Goldstein, Jean A. S. Helgeson, and Michael S. Brown
From the Departments of Molecular Genetics and Internal Medicine, The University of Texas Health Science Center at Dallas, Dallas, Texas 75235

Mevalonate, the product of HMG-CoA reductase, also supported growth, confirming that compactin was exerting its killing effect by a specific inhibition of HMG-CoA reductase.

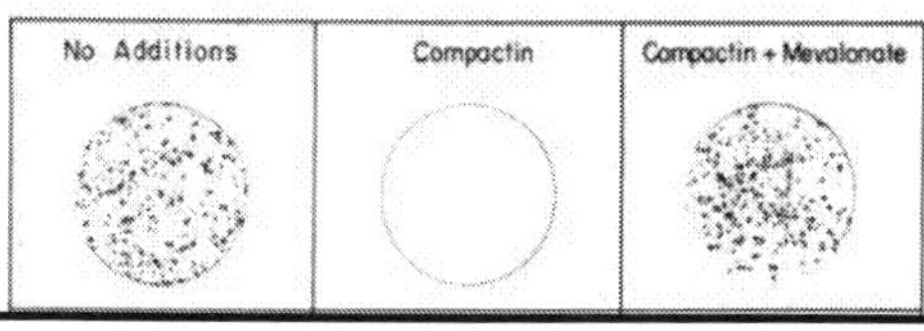

They concluded the obvious. Cells need to make something from mevalonate other than cholesterol to live. If cells increased reductase sufficiently to make it, they lived. If not, they died:

Proc. Natl. Acad. Sci. USA
Vol. 79, pp. 1185–1189, February 1982
Cell Biology

Appearance of crystalloid endoplasmic reticulum in compactin-resistant Chinese hamster cells with a 500-fold increase in 3-hydroxy-3-methylglutaryl-coenzyme A reductase

(inhibitors of cholesterol synthesis/membrane biogenesis/enzyme regulation/low density lipoprotein/drug resistance)

DANIEL J. CHIN, KENNETH L. LUSKEY, RICHARD G. W. ANDERSON, JERRY R. FAUST, JOSEPH L. GOLDSTEIN*, AND MICHAEL S. BROWN

Departments of Molecular Genetics, Cell Biology, and Internal Medicine, University of Texas Health Science Center at Dallas, 5323 Harry Hines Boulevard, Dallas, Texas 75235

Contributed by Joseph L. Goldstein, December 2, 1981

If reductase cannot increase sufficiently to overcome the inhibition by compactin, the cells die (1, 3, 4).

By 1980, Brown and Goldstein thought that adding mevalonate to statins to prevent the increase in reductase would fix the problem of cells dying. At the time, they didn't know that without the increase in reductase statins would not work:

Feedback Regulation of 3-Hydroxy-3-Methylglutaryl Coenzyme A Reductase in Livers of Mice Treated with Mevinolin, a Competitive Inhibitor of the Reductase

TORU KITA, MICHAEL S. BROWN, and JOSEPH L. GOLDSTEIN, *Departments of Molecular Genetics and Internal Medicine, University of Texas Health Science Center at Dallas, Texas 75235*

The ability to suppress the elevated HMG CoA reductase with mevalonate may prove useful in potentiating the effectiveness of mevinolin as a hypocholesterolemic agent.

*J. Clin. Invest. © The American Society for Clinical Investigation, Inc. · 0021-9738/80/11/1094/07 $1.00
Volume 66 November 1980 1094–1100*

In order to make statins safe for animals, Brown and Goldstein would have to uncover the isoprenoid ("putative nonsterol regulator") that caused the increased reductase. Then – and only then – would the “killing effect” of statins be prevented and perhaps made possible for use in animals or humans.

> **Multivalent feedback regulation of HMG CoA reductase, a control mechanism coordinating isoprenoid synthesis and cell growth**
>
> **Journal of Lipid Research** Volume 21, 1980
>
> **Michael S. Brown**[1] **and Joseph L. Goldstein**
>
> Departments of Molecular Genetics and Internal Medicine, University of Texas Health Science Center at Dallas, Dallas, TX 75235
>
> When the putative nonsterol regulator of HMG CoA reductase is identified, it may be possible to administer this compound to animals and perhaps to patients, preventing the compensatory rise in HMG CoA reductase and thus enhancing the effectiveness of compactin and other cholesterol synthesis inhibitors as well.

One or more of the isoprenoids from mevalonate (“nonsterol regulator”) was the source of the elevated reductase. This non-cholesterol isoprenoid was obviously a “regulator” or controller of reductase. When blocked, reductase remains elevated like an unsatisfied hungry appetite. Was it CoQ10…or something else?

With statins added to cultured cells, Brown and Goldstein could measure the increase in reductase. They discovered that adding cholesterol back these cells would decrease reductase by 90-95% but still not prevent cell death. They then sequentially added back the isoprenoids from mevalonate (CoQ10, dolichol, etc.) to see if they could return reductase, and cell function, back to normal.

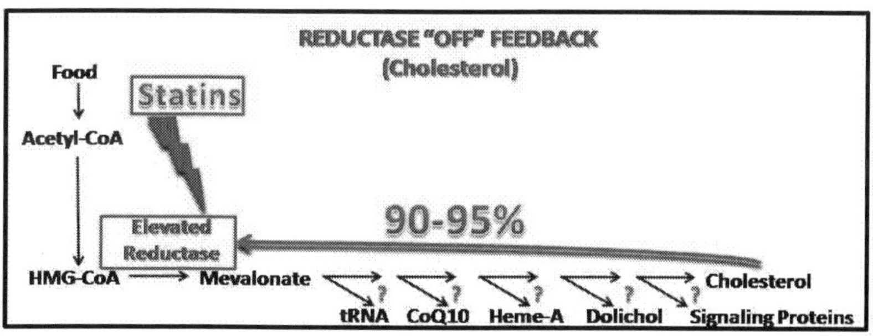

Nothing worked. They theorized that isoprenoids from mevalonate might have to be *made* by cells to control reductase and prevent statin toxicity. Endo reported similar results in 1980:

THE JOURNAL OF BIOLOGICAL CHEMISTRY
Vol. 256, No. 13, Issue of July 10, pp. 6762-6768, 1981
Printed in U.S.A.

Isolation and Characterization of Cells Resistant to ML236B (Compactin) with Increased Levels of 3-Hydroxy-3-methylglutaryl Coenzyme A Reductase*

(Received for publication, December 22, 1980, and in revised form, March 16, 1981)

Judith Ryan‡, Edna C. Hardeman§, Akira Endo¶, and Robert D. Simoni||

We demonstrate that the cytotoxicity of ML236B to CHO-K1 cells at a concentration of 8 μg/ml in the culture medium can be prevented by the addition of either mevalonate or cholesterol (Fig. 1). At a concentration of 50 μg/ml of ML236B in the culture medium, cholesterol alone is ineffective in preventing cell death; however, mevalonate remains effective. Addition of other mevalonate-derived metabolites to the culture medium along with cholesterol including ubiquinone, dolichol, and isopentenyladenine, did not prevent the toxic effect of ML236B. It is not clear, however, that the addition of these hydrophobic compounds to the culture medium leads to their proper entry or targeting.

The above paper, and others, demonstrates that during this time after Endo had left Sankyo, Dallas and Japan were closely watching one another's work. As early as 1980, Brown, Goldstein and Endo all knew that if they could discover how to fully suppress reductase, they would also discover how to prevent the toxic effects of statins and, in so doing, stop statin injury and cell death. ***They never accomplished this feat.***

At the time, the work by Brown, Goldstein and Endo reflects a wrong belief that all of the isoprenoids made by mevalonate had been identified. Siperstein largely discovered the short list that they knew about; but they were mistaken. Many more mevalonate-derived isoprenoids essential to normal cell function have since been found.

The problem with lovastatin was not just that it killed cells. In addition to stopping normal cell cycles, the fungal toxin also blocked DNA replication (chapter one):

[CANCER RESEARCH 51, 3602–3609, July 1, 1991]

Synchronization of Tumor and Normal Cells from G_1 to Multiple Cell Cycles by Lovastatin[1]

Khandan Keyomarsi,[2] Larue Sandoval, Vimla Band, and Arthur B. Pardee

Divisions of Cell Growth and Regulation [K. K., L. S., A. B. P.] and Cancer Genetics [V. B.], Dana Farber Cancer Institute, Boston, Massachusetts 02115

In this paper, we report that these criteria for synchronization are met using Lovastatin to arrest normal and tumor cells of epithelial as well as fibroblast origin reversibly in the G_1 phase of the cell cycle. Lovastatin, an antihyperlipodemic agent, is widely used for the treatment of hypercholesterolemia. This agent competitively inhibits HMG-CoA[3] reductase, the enzyme required for conversion of HMG-CoA to mevalonic acid (8). In addition, inhibition of mevalonate synthesis by Lovastatin or compactin, a related fungal toxin (9), also inhibits DNA replication (10–15). DNA replication is restored by the addition of mevalonate, the product of the reaction catalyzed by HMG-CoA reductase.

It was during this time that Brown and Goldstein were trying to figure out how to prevent statins from killing cells that Siperstein went to work in his San Francisco lab to help solve the problem. Using samples of compactin from Beecham, he discovered that statins blocked DNA replication by blocking cells from making the isoprenoid called isopentenyladenine:

Isopentenyladenine as a mediator of mevalonate-regulated DNA replication*

Proc. Natl. Acad. Sci. USA
Vol. 77, No. 10, pp. 5842–5846, October 1980
Biochemistry

VALERIA QUESNEY HUNEEUS, MILLIE HUGHES WILEY, AND MARVIN D. SIPERSTEIN†

Nonetheless, the finding that a specific mevalonate derivative can control DNA synthesis—coupled with the previous observation that the feedback control of mevalonate production is consistently and uniquely lost in malignant (7–14) and in premalignant cells (7)—further supports our earlier suggestion (7) that derangements in the control of mevalonic acid production may play a role in the transformation of normal cells into cancer cells.

Note Added in Proof. After we submitted this manuscript, Habenicht *et al.* (31) confirmed our earlier finding (16) that mevalonate is required for DNA synthesis.

Had Siperstein's discovery been made widely known, Watson would have been horrified to learn that statin research continued. Crick would have turned over in his grave. Siperstein further demonstrated that not just one isoprenoid from mevalonate is needed for DNA replication and normal cell cycles; cholesterol is just as vital for cell membrane growth and cell cycles:

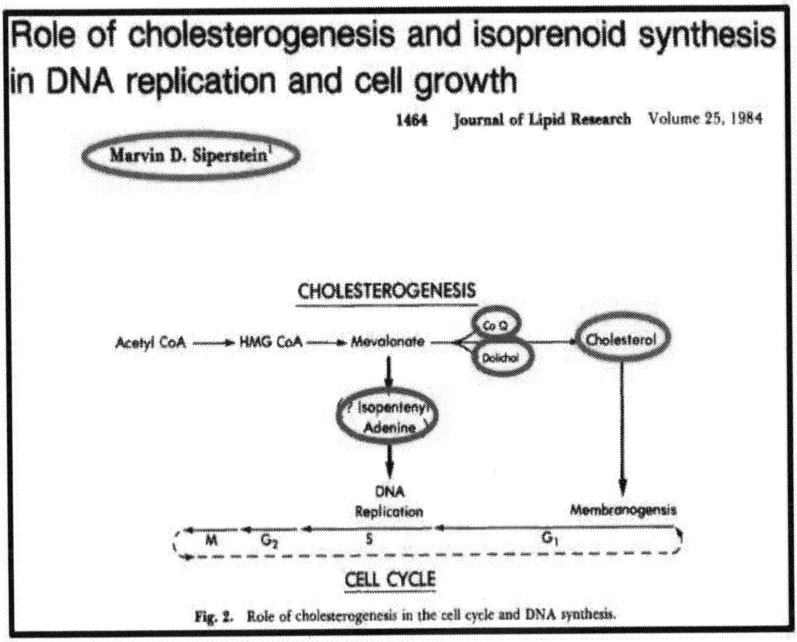

Fig. 2. Role of cholesterogenesis in the cell cycle and DNA synthesis.

Before testing on humans at Dallas, the docs at Dallas and the scientists at Merck diligently tried to figure out how to make lovastatin safe. They failed.

To sum, they all knew that:

1. Statins block mevalonate synthesis.
2. This blockade kills cells.
3. Mevalonate reverses this killing effect on cells.
4. Mevalonate reverses this killing effect on animals.

Before their story "changed", here is what Brown/Goldstein, Endo and Merck clearly reported on the above four effects:

1. Statins block cell synthesis of BOTH cholesterol and isoprenoids from mevalonate. This elevates reductase (Brown and Goldstein):

Proc. Natl. Acad. Sci. USA
Vol. 79, pp. 1185–1189, February 1982
Cell Biology

Appearance of crystalloid endoplasmic reticulum in compactin-resistant Chinese hamster cells with a 500-fold increase in 3-hydroxy-3-methylglutaryl-coenzyme A reductase

(inhibitors of cholesterol synthesis/membrane biogenesis/enzyme regulation/low density lipoprotein/drug resistance)

DANIEL J. CHIN, KENNETH L. LUSKEY, RICHARD G. W. ANDERSON, JERRY R. FAUST, JOSEPH L. GOLDSTEIN*, AND MICHAEL S. BROWN

Departments of Molecular Genetics, Cell Biology, and Internal Medicine, University of Texas Health Science Center at Dallas, 5323 Harry Hines Boulevard, Dallas, Texas 75235

Contributed by Joseph L. Goldstein, December 2, 1981

In the presence of compactin, a competitive inhibitor of reductase, cells develop a compensatory increase in reductase activity (2). This regulatory response is triggered by a deficiency of cholesterol and other mevalonate-derived products.

2. This blockade of cholesterol and isoprenoids from mevalonate kills cells (Brown, Goldstein and Endo):

Feedback Regulation of 3-Hydroxy-3-Methylglutaryl Coenzyme A Reductase in Livers of Mice Treated with Mevinolin, a Competitive Inhibitor of the Reductase

TORU KITA, MICHAEL S. BROWN, and JOSEPH L. GOLDSTEIN, *Departments of Molecular Genetics and Internal Medicine, University of Texas Health Science Center at Dallas, Texas 75235*

The fibroblast experiments have been interpreted to indicate the existence of a multivalent feedback mechanism in which cholesterol and a nonsterol product derived from mevalonate are both required for maximal suppression of HMG CoA reductase activity. By inhibiting the synthesis of mevalonate, compactin blocks the synthesis of both regulators and thus produces a compensatory increase in HMG CoA reductase that is reversed only when the cells can synthesize or take up sufficient amounts of both substances (5, 10).

*J. Clin. Invest. © The American Society for Clinical Investigation, Inc. · 0021-9738/80/11/1094/07 $1.00
Volume 66 November 1980 1094–1100*

THE JOURNAL OF BIOLOGICAL CHEMISTRY
Vol. 255, No. 14, Issue of July 25, pp. 6546-6548, 1980

Synthesis of Δ^2-Isopentenyl tRNA from Mevalonate in Cultured Human Fibroblasts*

(Received for publication, April 14, 1980, and in revised form, May 21, 1980)

Jerry R. Faust, Michael S. Brown, and Joseph L. Goldstein

When HMG CoA reductase[1] is inhibited by compactin, mevalonate formation is blocked and cultured cells die.

THE JOURNAL OF BIOLOGICAL CHEMISTRY
Vol. 254, No. 12, Issue of June 25, pp. 5403-5409, 1979
Printed in U.S.A.

Inhibition of Cholesterol Synthesis with Compactin Renders Growth of Cultured Cells Dependent on the Low Density Lipoprotein Receptor*

(Received for publication, January 5, 1979)

Joseph L. Goldstein, Jean A. S. Helgeson, and Michael S. Brown
From the Departments of Molecular Genetics and Internal Medicine, The University of Texas Health Science Center at Dallas, Dallas, Texas 75235

Mevalonate, the product of HMG-CoA reductase, also supported growth, confirming that compactin was exerting its killing effect by a specific inhibition of HMG-CoA reductase.

Inhibitory Effects on Lipid Metabolism in Cultured Cells of ML-236B, a Potent Inhibitor of 3-Hydroxy-3-methylglutaryl-Coenzyme-A Reductase

Isao KANEKO, Yoko HAZAMA-SHIMADA, and Akira ENDO Eur. J. Biochem. *87*, 313 – 321 (1978)

The results shown in Fig. 7 and Table 4 indicate that the complete inhibition of endogenous sterol synthesis by ML-236B resulted in the death of cells and further a slight activity of endogenous sterol synthesis (from mevalonate) was essential to the normal growth of cells even when sufficient amounts of cholesterol were provided exogenously.

3. Mevalonate reverses the killing effect of statins on cells (Endo, Brown and Goldstein):

The discovery and development of HMG-CoA reductase inhibitors

Journal of Lipid Research Volume 33, 1992

Akira Endo

Subsequently, studies by other investigators showed that in cultured fibroblasts high concentrations of mevastatin block passage through the cell cycle (45–47) and alter cell morphology (48). Both effects could be prevented by the addition of mevalonate but not by the addition of cholesterol, which suggested that either mevalonate or one (or more) of its nonsterol products was involved.

The Journal of Biological Chemistry
Vol. 256, No. 13, Issue of July 10, pp. 6762–6768, 1981
Printed in U.S.A.

Isolation and Characterization of Cells Resistant to ML236B (Compactin) with Increased Levels of 3-Hydroxy-3-methylglutaryl Coenzyme A Reductase*

(Received for publication, December 22, 1980, and in revised form, March 16, 1981)

Judith Ryan‡, Edna C. Hardeman§, Akira Endo¶, and Robert D. Simoni||

We have examined the ability of mevalonate and a number of mevalonic acid-derived products to prevent death of the parental cell line in the presence of 8 or 50 μg/ml of ML236B. At 8 μg/ml of ML236B, cell death was prevented in the CHO-K1 cell line by the addition of mevalonate (data not shown)

Feedback Regulation of 3-Hydroxy-3-Methylglutaryl Coenzyme A Reductase in Livers of Mice Treated with Mevinolin, a Competitive Inhibitor of the Reductase

Toru Kita, Michael S. Brown, and Joseph L. Goldstein, *Departments of Molecular Genetics and Internal Medicine, University of Texas Health Science Center at Dallas, Texas 75235*

The ability to suppress the elevated HMG CoA reductase with mevalonate may prove useful in potentiating the effectiveness of mevinolin as a hypocholesterolemic agent.

J. Clin. Invest. © The American Society for Clinical Investigation, Inc. · 0021-9738/80/11/1094/07 $1.00
Volume 66 November 1980 1094–1100

4. Mevalonate reverses the killing effect of statins on mammals (Merck):

0022-3565/89/2482-0496$02.00/0
THE JOURNAL OF PHARMACOLOGY AND EXPERIMENTAL THERAPEUTICS

Vol. 248, No. 2
Printed in U.S.A.

Toxicity of the HMG-Coenzyme A Reductase Inhibitor, Lovastatin, to Rabbits

DOUGLAS J. KORNBRUST, JAMES S. MACDONALD, CHENNEKATU P. PETER, DONALD M. DUCHAI, R. JOHN STUBBS, JOHN I. GERMERSHAUSEN and ALFRED W. ALBERTS
Department of Safety Assessment, WP 44-1, Merck Sharp and Dohme Research Laboratories, West Point, Pennsylvania
Accepted for publication October 7, 1988

During the extensive preclinical safety evaluation of lovastatin, it was observed that female New Zealand albino rabbits were unusually sensitive to the potential toxicity of the drug compared with other animal species. Some rabbits died within 2 wk of repetitive daily administration of lovastatin at dose levels that were well tolerated for much longer periods by rats, mice, dogs and monkeys.

The ability of mevalonate to prevent or reverse lovastatin-induced hepatotoxicity and to protect against kidney and gallbladder toxicity indicated that these changes were a consequence of the pharmacologic action of lovastatin in inhibiting HMG-CoA reductase and blocking mevalonate formation.

By 1980, statin researchers still didn't know exactly how compactin lowered blood cholesterol; what they knew, for sure, was that it was lethal to cells and animals. They wanted to fix it. By 1982 when human tests began on FH patients in Dallas, they still did not know how to prevent statin toxicity.

When considering the potential benefits versus risks of lowering cholesterol with statins, the FDA first approved statins only for use on FH patients. Because of extremely high cholesterol levels due to genetically defective LDL cholesterol receptors, these people are considered at "high risk" for CVD. Steinberg advised Merck and the FDA to resume statin trials on these patients and assured them, "***Even if there were risks, even life-threatening risks***, those had to be balanced against the potential life-saving benefits of treatment. Dropping the program might deny some patients a chance to prolong their lives" (reference 25).

Steinberg was wrong. Statins had no effect on patients with the homozygous form of this disease (no normal cholesterol receptors) but had some effect on patients with the heterozygous type (half-normal amount of cholesterol receptors). With this find, statin's effect on LDL receptors finally made sense.

Effects of ML-236B (Compactin) on Sterol Synthesis and Low Density Lipoprotein Receptor Activities in Fibroblasts of Patients with Homozygous Familial Hypercholesterolemia

Toshihiro Hara, Hiroshi Mabuchi, Akira Yoshimura, Akira Watanabe, Takanobu Wakasugi, Ryoyo Tatami, Koshi Ueda, Ryosei Ueda, Tomio Kametani, Junji Koizumi, Susumu Miyamoto, and Ryoyu Takeda

ML-236B was shown to lower serum cholesterol level in patients with FH (15). Mabuchi et al. showed that this drug is effective in lowering serum cholesterol levels in heterozygous patients with FH, but not in the homozygotes.[2] Thus, the present data of LDL receptor activity in vitro may provide a reasonable basis for the clinical evaluation of this drug in FH.

J. Clin. Invest. © The American Society for Clinical Investigation, Inc. Volume 67 May 1981

Serendipity. Or was it?

In 1984, three years before FDA approval of lovastatin and two years after they had begun testing on humans, Brown and Goldstein reported on the elevated reductase/elevated LDL receptor link.

Other laboratories confirmed the conclusion that a statin-induced increase in reductase "tricks" cells into making more LDL cholesterol receptors; this, in turn, lowers blood cholesterol (references 26-30).

Proc. Natl. Acad. Sci. USA
Vol. 83, pp. 8370–8374, November 1986
Medical Sciences

Mevinolin, an inhibitor of cholesterol synthesis, induces mRNA for low density lipoprotein receptor in livers of hamsters and rabbits

(3-hydroxy-3-methylglutaryl CoA reductase/S1-nuclease assay/regulation of cell surface receptors/Watanabe-heritable hyperlipidemic rabbits)

Patrick T. S. Ma, Gregorio Gil, Thomas C. Südhof, David W. Bilheimer, Joseph L. Goldstein, and Michael S. Brown

Departments of Molecular Genetics and Internal Medicine, University of Texas Health Science Center, Southwestern Medical School, 5323 Harry Hines Boulevard, Dallas, TX 75235

Lipoprotein Receptors in the Liver

CONTROL SIGNALS FOR PLASMA CHOLESTEROL TRAFFIC

MICHAEL S. BROWN and JOSEPH L. GOLDSTEIN

Whenever hepatic LDL receptors are suppressed, the plasma LDL level rises; conversely, whenever these receptors are induced, the plasma LDL level falls.

J. Clin. Invest. © The American Society for Clinical Investigation, Inc. Volume 72 September 1983 743–747

Statin toxicity (blockade of isoprenoids) caused the increase in reductase. The increase in reductase also caused an increase in LDL cholesterol receptors that lowered blood cholesterol. What caused toxicity also made the drug "work".

224 THE NEW ENGLAND JOURNAL OF MEDICINE July 26, 1990

INFLUENCE OF PRAVASTATIN, A SPECIFIC INHIBITOR OF HMG-CoA REDUCTASE, ON HEPATIC METABOLISM OF CHOLESTEROL

EVA REIHNÉR, M.D., MATS RUDLING, M.D., DAGNY STÅHLBERG, M.D., LARS BERGLUND, M.D., STAFFAN EWERTH, M.D., INGEMAR BJÖRKHEM, M.D., KURT EINARSSON, M.D., AND BO ANGELIN, M.D.

Conclusions. **Inhibition of hepatic HMG-CoA reductase by pravastatin results in an increased expression of hepatic LDL receptors, which explains the lowered plasma levels of LDL cholesterol. (N Engl J Med 1990; 323: 224-8.)**

Merck could not have it both ways. Finding the cure to prevent statin toxicity would also prevent the drug from working.

Biochem. J. (1989) **260**, 731–736 (Printed in Great Britain) 731

Co-ordinate regulation of low-density-lipoprotein receptor and 3-hydroxy-3-methylglutaryl-CoA reductase and synthase gene expression in HepG2 cells

David T. MOLOWA and George M. CIMIS
Department of Molecular Pharmacology and Biochemistry, Merck Sharp & Dohme Research Laboratories, Rahway, NJ 07065, U.S.A.

We conclude that the expression of the LDL receptor, HMG-CoA reductase and HMG-CoA synthase is co-ordinately regulated in HepG2 cells.

Chapter 16: The NIH-Merck-Dallas Hole

In the deep recesses of space there are black holes that cannot be seen. Their gravitational pull is so strong that everything is captured, including light.

Corruption is like that. It cannot exist in the light of truth. But leave out the light of truth and it gobbles up everything.

The statin "success" story inevitably points to strong influence by the NIH and an agenda led by Steinberg to criminalize cholesterol. Brown and Goldstein were from the NIH and the NIH supported most of their work.

Bilheimer, who received with Grundy and Brown the FDA's approval to test lovastatin on FH patients, was an NIH grant recipient and colleague of Brown and Goldstein from the Massachusetts General Hospital. Like Brown and Grundy, Bilheimer was also an AHA investigator with direct access to publish in AHA's "Circulation" magazine.

The NIH black hole ran infinitely deeper. Grundy, who held the FDA IND for human experimentation with lovastatin in Dallas, was a former Phoenix-based NIH director. His associate and former research partner, Daniel Steinberg (NIH Chief from 1951-1968) positioned Grundy to lead the NIH's National Cholesterol Education Program (NCEP) that would establish national guidelines for lowering cholesterol with statins.

Despite the then-known dangers, by 1982 it was full-speed ahead for testing lovastatin. The NIH anti-cholesterol scientists Grundy, Bilheimer and Brown led the way with NIH's Steinberg in the wings. Grundy, with ties to Texas, the NIH, AHA and Merck, was another kingpin who could adjoin all the spokes of the statin-wheel and sway the FDA to endorse the NIH-bandwagon.

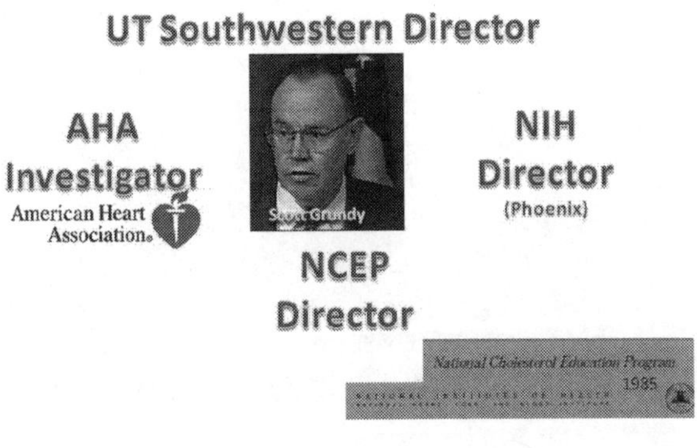

1985 proved to be a banner year for the Dallas anti-cholesterol docs. Grundy had completed the NCEP national guidelines for lowering cholesterol; this included policy for prescribing statins to the general public and was influenced by his statin experiments with Bilheimer on FH patients. Timed two years before the February 19, 1987 FDA advisory meeting, three key political events helped secure a successful outcome for Merck:

1. The NIH-funded Steinberg-led CPPT trial results were published that claimed a barely statistically significant reduction in CVD with the lowering of blood cholesterol.

2. Former NIH fellows Brown and Goldstein shared a Nobel Prize for their statin-related work on cholesterol.

3. Former NIH director Grundy set the cholesterol guidelines for prescribers and consumers. This was taxpayer-paid, government-backed and right on time for FDA's approval of Merck's lovastatin.

Notably, it was the NIH boys who supported Merck not only as paid advisors but, more importantly, by setting national medical policy on the treatment of cholesterol via the Steinberg/Grundy-inspired NCEP. To that end, the February 19, 1987 FDA meeting was strategically held – not at the FDA – but at the NIH Lister Hill Auditorium in Bethesda.

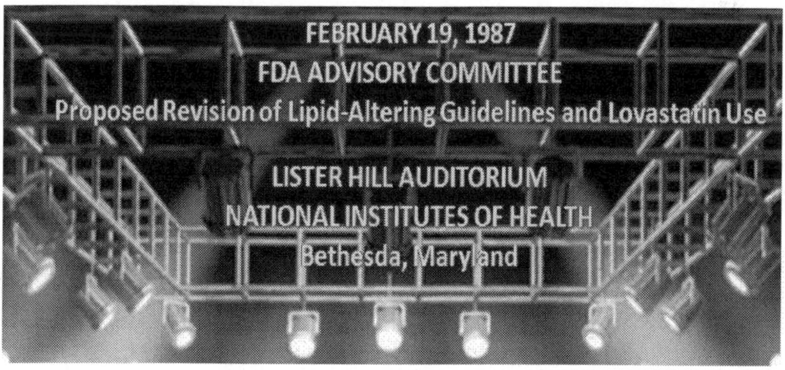

Merck had the home-team advantage; the FDA employees, after all, were guests at this NIH-hosted event – and the NIH boys backed Merck. As important, Merck backed them.

Many of the FDA, Dallas and Merck attendees were former NIH employees and fellows. Inescapably, the atmosphere was one of a celebratory good-old-boys' club reunion. And, as icing is sweet on cake, Merck's pitch on lovastatin was preceded by a review of the NCEP-approved national cholesterol-altering guidelines. With the NIH, NCEP, two Nobel laureates (Brown and Goldstein) to back them and Merck consultant Frederick Singer to chair the meeting Merck couldn't lose.

NIH fellow P. Roy Vagelos
Earl Stadtman's lab
NIH Bethesda, 1961

Deeper into the black hole is the trail of NIH-issued research performed for Merck's Vagelos via Dallas and the U.S. taxpayers. Here's how it works:

First, you graduate from medical school and obtain a PhD fellowship by working at Earl Stadtman's prestigious NIH lab.

Now that you have NIH connections, next, market yourself to a major pharmaceutical company like Merck. Once hired, scour the NIH-funded research laboratories for discoveries that may serve your drug company's interests:

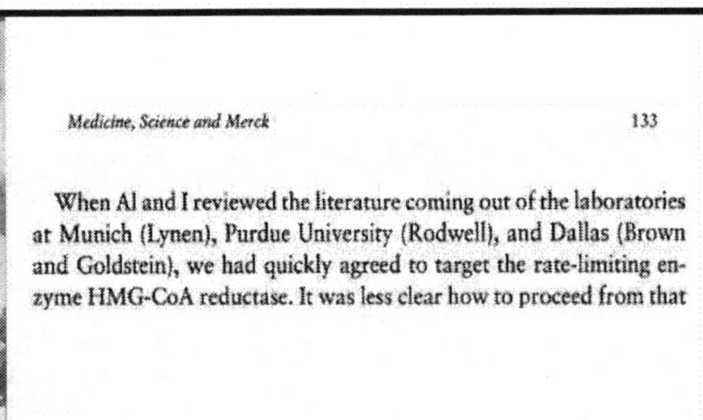

Medicine, Science and Merck 133

When Al and I reviewed the literature coming out of the laboratories at Munich (Lynen), Purdue University (Rodwell), and Dallas (Brown and Goldstein), we had quickly agreed to target the rate-limiting enzyme HMG-CoA reductase. It was less clear how to proceed from that

When you find a match, contact your friends at a NIH grant-financed university, send a sample of your new drug as a "gift" to ostensibly further their research and advance your company's interests for free on the taxpayer-paid gravy train. Express your heartfelt gratitude in writing.

Proc. Natl. Acad. Sci. USA
Vol. 80, pp. 4124–4128, July 1983
Medical Sciences

Mevinolin and colestipol stimulate receptor-mediated clearance of low density lipoprotein from plasma in familial hypercholesterolemia heterozygotes

(low density lipoprotein receptors/3-hydroxy-3-methylglutaryl-CoA reductase/compactin/bile acid metabolism)

DAVID W. BILHEIMER*, SCOTT M. GRUNDY*†, MICHAEL S. BROWN*‡, AND JOSEPH L. GOLDSTEIN*‡

Michael Funk, Sylvia Ettefagh, Marjorie Whelan provided excellent technical assistance. We thank Dr. Jonathan Tobert of Merck Sharp and Dohme for making mevinolin available. This research was supported by grants from the National Institutes of Health (HL-20948, HL-15949, and HL-29252).

Then, enjoin NIH alumni employed by the FDA such as Gloria Troendle (present at the lovastatin advisory committee meeting) who will assuredly support your cholesterol-lowering drug:

The Washington Post

Monday, October 22, 2007

Gloria Troendle; Metabolic and Endocrine Disease Expert at FDA

At NIH, she worked for the originators of the classification of elevated lipid levels in the human vascular system, Donald Fredrickson and Robert Levy, whose pioneering work made possible the current family of cholesterol-controlling drugs.

Finally, cheer on your colleagues at the NIH and AHA who establish national cholesterol-altering policy via the NCEP and ATP (Adult Treatment Panel). Over time, they will increasingly expand the number of patients who are candidates for your drug. Again, with taxpayer funds and AHA's "Circulation" magazine at their fingertips, this free pro-statin press will reach the world and obligate physicians to prescribe your cell-killing drug. Because it kills humans *v e r y   s l o w l y*, you will sell many other symptom-treating drugs as long as the connection is never made.

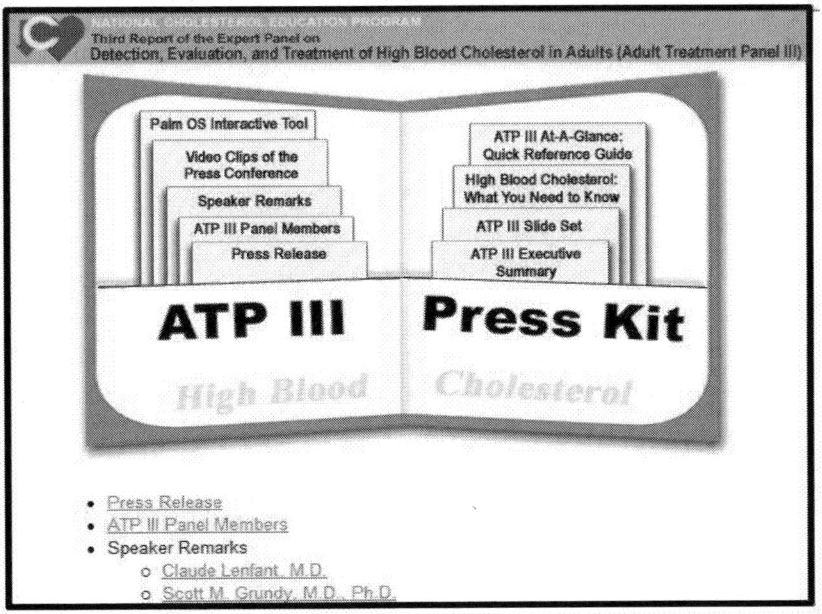

And so it was that the NIH-AMA-Merck team of Grundy, Bilheimer, Brown and Goldstein set to testing lovastatin on FH patients – subjects who they reasoned did not have a long life to lose anyway despite evidence to the contrary. It was a "go" with a green light from the FDA via taxpayer money routed to Dallas through multiple NIH grants.

They confirmed "in vivo" on humans what they had already seen "in vitro" on cell cultures – that lovastatin blocks mevalonate which increases reductase and, since the genes that make reductase and LDL receptors are co-regulated, increases the number of LDL receptors. By this time, however, Dallas did not report the complete mechanics of lovastatin (not a word on mevalonate deprivation and cell death):

Proc. Natl. Acad. Sci. USA
Vol. 80, pp. 4124–4128, July 1983
Medical Sciences

Mevinolin and colestipol stimulate receptor-mediated clearance of low density lipoprotein from plasma in familial hypercholesterolemia heterozygotes

(low density lipoprotein receptors/3-hydroxy-3-methylglutaryl-CoA reductase/compactin/bile acid metabolism)

DAVID W. BILHEIMER*, SCOTT M. GRUNDY*†, MICHAEL S. BROWN*‡, AND JOSEPH L. GOLDSTEIN*‡

The current data suggest that mevinolin alone or mevinolin plus bile acid depletion (i.e., ileal bypass or colestipol therapy) decreases plasma LDL levels primarily by raising the number of LDL receptors and, thus, enhancing the removal of LDL from plasma.

At the FDA Advisory Committee meeting, Brown explained a whole new way for how lovastatin worked; after 1985, lovastatin blocked only cholesterol (not isoprenoid) synthesis:

> **"It turns out that lovastatin is an effective therapy in lowering the blood cholesterol level in these FH heterozygotes, *in part* because, by inhibiting cholesterol synthesis, it stimulates the normal gene to produce more LDL receptors" (Michael Brown to the FDA, Feb. 19, 1987 FDA Advisory Committee Transcript, page 119).**

Take note of two carefully chosen words (above): "in part".

The market for lovastatin to high-risk FH patients was only one in 500 people. But with the NCEP in Grundy's grasp and endorsement by Nobel laureates, the AHA and the NIH, Brown boldly recommended to the FDA that lovastatin be approved for use on the general public:

> **"The interesting thing, and the important thing for our discussion today is that this mechanism not only applies to FH heterozygotes, who have one normal gene and one mutant gene, but it also applies to the vast majority of people with high blood cholesterol**

levels who have two normal-functioning genes, but whose genes appear to be working in a sluggish fashion" (Michael Brown to the FDA, Feb. 19, 1987 FDA Advisory Committee Transcript, p. 119-120).

Brown didn't have a shred of evidence for "sluggish cholesterol receptors" – a phrase he pulled out of thin air. If a Nobel laureate says so then that must have been good enough because eight months later lovastatin was on the shelves. Based upon how statins *really* lower cholesterol, however, Brown could have said something more forthright such as:

"Mevalonate is the molecule that every cell makes to grow and divide. Just as the slowest worker in an assembly line is the "bottle neck" of the process, reductase is the rate-limiting (slowest) enzyme in the mevalonate pathway. Statins are like dragon-fire under the ass of a sluggish worker forcing him to work at a harder, faster pace. This will also fire up cholesterol receptors – because it just so happens to be that reductase genes and LDL receptor genes are turned on together and so statins can lower *anyone's* LDL cholesterol! Any questions?

Statins would have been approved anyway. The problem that Brown would have created by telling the truth was not that the FDA wouldn't approve lovastatin but that the drug would have been difficult to sell. He had been well coached by Steinberg and Tobert. He lied the worst of all lies: he lied the lie of omission.

At least Grundy publicly admitted that by the early 1980's there was no proof that lowering cholesterol would lower the risk of CVD; there was only conjecture. In fact, the only medical claim that Merck can make today is that lovastatin lowers cholesterol (without any proof of safety):

> **Statins: A Success Story Involving FDA, Academia and Industry**
>
> *Suzanne White Junod, Ph.D., FDA Historian*
>
> *This article originally appeared in the "History Corner" column of the March-April 2007 issue of* Update *magazine, the bimonthly publication of the Food and Drug Law Institute*
>
> Scott Grundy recalled that in 1982, the climate for lipid-altering drug development was not particularly good. Treatment for elevated LDL was based, he said, on "a conjecture known as the lipid hypothesis." Namely, that pharmacologic or dietary reduction of the "harmful" cholesterol would benefit the patient by arresting atherosclerosis. There was no proof at that time that drugs or diet used to lower cholesterol would be the clinical equivalent of patients with "spontaneously occurring" low cholesterol.

Brown, as one of Merck's many paid mouthpieces, echoed Merck's whole new story: Statins don't block mevalonate synthesis which deprives cells of life-essential isoprenoids; ***statins only block cholesterol synthesis, which increases cholesterol receptors and lowers cholesterol.***

So they said – after 1985 that is – after Nobel and the NCEP.

God only knows just how deep the NIH-Merck-Dallas black hole went. Predictably, multiple statin-related lawsuits have been filed against Merck for racketeering activity (RICO violations), state Consumer Anti-Fraud offenses, unjust enrichment and common law fraud. One example is RICO case number 2:08-cv-00285-DMC-MF that quickly and quietly settled out-of-court in 2009 for $41.5 million – a pittance in terms of total statin revenues (reportedly $100 billion by 2006).

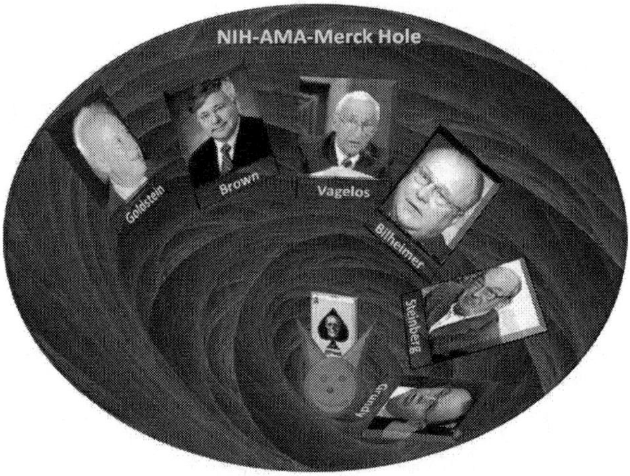

Merck continues to line Grundy's pockets with honoraria; Grundy continues to update NCEP's cholesterol guidelines for prescribers so as to ever-increase the population of lifetime statin users – children no longer excluded.

Today, Bilheimer sits secure as Merck's global medical director.

Chapter 17: Merck Knew

When a child tiptoes into the kitchen to steal another handful of cookies, he sneaks because he does not have permission to eat all he wants. He hides because he knows he is doing wrong. If statins were so good for us, then Merck would have nothing to hide.

To reiterate: Statins disable the enzyme reductase, causing cells to make more reductase to overcome the mevalonate blockade – or die. Merck knew it from the start because Brown and Goldstein knew it from their first collaboration with Endo at Dallas.

In the presence of a statin, cells make more reductase by making more endoplasmic reticulum (ER) factories, which appear like ***whorls and microcrystals instead of the normal pancake-shape***. These abnormal structures were found in rat statin-fed liver cells and photographed by Merck in 1984 (below).

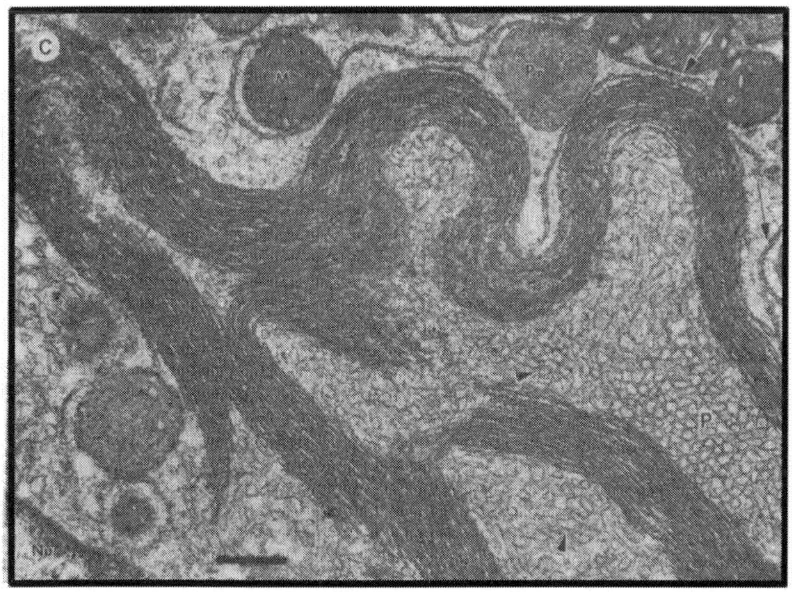

(So much for Steinberg's claim that statins worked on rats.)

In 1977, during development of Endo's statin, Sankyo also discovered abnormal crystalline structures in cells of rats fed high-dose compactin for five weeks. Akira Endo explains how Sankyo's toxicologists thought these ER "crystals" were toxic substances, but later downgraded the crystals to just "non-toxic cholesterol".

> A gift from nature: the birth of the statins
>
> Akira Endo
>
> We encountered a second challenge in April 1977. The issue was the detection of microcrystalline structures in the liver cells of rats that had been fed extremely large amounts of compactin (more than 500 milligrams per kilogram body weight per day (mg/kg/d)) for 5 weeks. The toxicologists insisted that these structures were toxic substances. It took us 9 months to identify these microcrystalline structures as nontoxic cholesterol.

The problem of accumulated cholesterol was not investigated. ***Statins do foist cholesterol from the blood onto LDL receptors of various organs, especially the liver.*** There is a problem with liver cells internalizing and processing all the extra cholesterol forced onto their receptors causing "non-toxic cholesterol" to accumulate inside cells. This causes apoptosis.

This liver cell demise is detected as elevated liver enzymes.

Knowing today how statins *really* work, it is likely that Sankyo's toxicologists found both ER crystals and an accumulation of LDL cholesterol inside cells. In fact, an early study in Japan demonstrated that "mutant" cells (that survive statin-induced cell death) are rendered defective in internalizing LDL cholesterol (endocytosis) that has accumulated on their membranes:

MOLECULAR AND CELLULAR BIOLOGY, Nov. 1982, p. 1354–1361 Vol. 2, No. 11
0270-7306/82/111354-08$02.00/0

Chinese Hamster Cell Mutant Resistant to ML236B (Compactin) Is Defective in Endocytosis of Low-Density Lipoprotein

AKINORI MASUDA, SHIN-ICHI AKIYAMA, AND MICHIHIKO KUWANO*
Department of Biochemistry, Oita Medical School, Hazama-cho, Oita 879-56, Japan

Once in the running for a major drug exploit, the temptation ever loomed to minimize abnormalities without further investigation. "Oh; it was just cholesterol accumulating and crystalizing inside the cells. But look at how the blood cholesterol keeps dropping! Blood tests will look so good, no one will ever know! Press on!"

Yet the question begged to be asked: "What are ALL those abnormal-looking structures inside the rat liver cells doing there...is that toxic?"

Prescribers of statins believe that statins work by inhibiting reductase, and in so doing, lower the production of cholesterol inside cells…when in fact cholesterol is accumulating inside cells through the LDL receptors. If you don't believe it, ask your doctor how statins work. A chemical inhibitor after all, by definition, slows down or stops a chemical reaction:

Chemistry-dictionary.com:
"Inhibitor: A catalyst that decreases the rate of reaction."

Dictionary.reference.com:
"Inhibitor: A substance that decreases the rate of or stops completely a chemical reaction."

Since statins are a drug-class called "reductase inhibitors", physicians are fooled into thinking that statins slow down or stop the mevalonate pathway. They know that the mevalonate pathway makes cholesterol. If mevalonate is blocked, cells make less cholesterol. Simple enough. No questions.

The increase in reductase in statin-fed cells disqualifies the classification of statins as reductase "inhibitors". Cells reflexively increase reductase to replace the inhibited reductase. ***If reductase was truly "inhibited" by statins (without the increase), cells would die sooner than later.*** Even though Brown, Goldstein and Endo were surprised that ML-236B increased reductase, statins were never reclassified as "reductase stimulators". Later, when Brown and Goldstein discovered that elevated reductase was what made statins work, statins were never reclassified as "LDL receptor stimulators".

Either way, cells die anyway.

None of this was reported to the FDA advisory committee on lovastatin's approval in 1987. ***A full disclosure on how statins really work would have required a full disclosure on statin toxicity.*** Toxic drugs do not sell very well; doctors rarely prescribe them.

Proc. Natl. Acad. Sci. USA
Vol. 79, pp. 1185–1189, February 1982
Cell Biology

Appearance of crystalloid endoplasmic reticulum in compactin-resistant Chinese hamster cells with a 500-fold increase in 3-hydroxy-3-methylglutaryl-coenzyme A reductase

DANIEL J. CHIN, KENNETH L. LUSKEY, RICHARD G. W. ANDERSON, JERRY R. FAUST, JOSEPH L. GOLDSTEIN*, AND MICHAEL S. BROWN

In the presence of compactin, a competitive inhibitor of reductase, cells develop a compensatory increase in reductase activity (2). This regulatory response is triggered by a deficiency of cholesterol and other mevalonate-derived products. If reductase cannot increase sufficiently to overcome the inhibition by compactin, the cells die (1, 3, 4).

Certainly most physicians, once informed that statins either kill cells or induce a reflexive increase in reductase to survive – at any dose – would take exception to the classification of statins as reductase "inhibitors" which is a half-truth.

It is a twisted obfuscation akin to classifying a serial killer as a "restrainer" or "inhibitor" who binds and cripples his victims before they try to run away for their lives and then, when exhausted, shoots them in the back. He is anything but an inhibitor: he is a binder, a disabler, an inducer of frenzied mayhem, a destroyer – but certainly *not* an inhibitor.

Just as a nutrient-starved person requires more and more food, a mevalonate-starved cell is induced to make more and more reductase. For this reason, ***Endo reported how statins such as his ML-236B are not really inhibitors of reductase synthesis:***

> Eur. J. Biochem. 87, 313–321 (1978)
>
> Inhibitory Effects on Lipid Metabolism in Cultured Cells of ML-236B, a Potent Inhibitor of 3-Hydroxy-3-methylglutaryl-Coenzyme-A Reductase
>
> Isao KANEKO, Yoko HAZAMA-SHIMADA, and Akira ENDO
> Fermentation Research Laboratories, Sankyo Co. Ltd, Tokyo
> (Received January 4, 1978)
>
> Thus, the mode of action of ML-236B is clearly different from that of cholesterol derivatives [7] and clofibrate-related drugs [15] which cause an inhibition of the synthesis of 3-hydroxy-3-methylglutaryl-CoA reductase or an enhancement in the rate of degradation of the enzyme within intact cells or a combination of both of these effects [7].

Endo had a rethink after his work in Dallas. Brown and Goldstein later reported that cells increase reductase up to 200 times or more the normal amount:

> **Regulation of the mevalonate pathway**
>
> **Joseph L. Goldstein & Michael S. Brown** NATURE · VOL 343 · 1 FEBRUARY 1990
>
> **Post-transcriptional control of HMG CoA reductase**
>
> HMG-CoA reductase is among the most highly regulated enzymes in nature. The complexity of this regulation was first revealed through the use of potent reductase inhibitors from fungi. These agents, which include compactin and lovastatin (mevinolin), competitively inhibit the enzyme at concentrations of less than 10^{-8} M (ref. 25). In cultured cells, they block the synthesis of mevalonate and trigger adaptive reactions that yield a 200-fold increase in reductase protein within a few hours[26,27].

Statins, then, are not reductase inhibitors at all; rather, they are reductase stimulators at any dose. ***Statins do not inhibit the production of reductase one iota, although that is what most prescribers think.*** Instead, statins deactivate already-made reductase; this, in turn, stimulates cells to make more.

If prescribers knew that statins are really reductase stimulators, they might have raised a few eyebrows upon their introduction and asked a few right questions. After all, inducing cells to perpetually kick out reductase or die is like throwing captives into the deep end of a pool with their wrists tied. They survive as long as they keep kicking; if they succumb to fatigue, they drown. That is what statins do to cells. Common sense dictates that if the medical community knew the truth of the matter, they might not have bought on to their classification as "reductase inhibitors" – the supreme lie of omission propagated by the statin promoters.

Lying about and withholding the fact of stimulated rather than inhibited reductase allowed statins to become the most prescribed drug on earth.

What happens in the human body when reductase is stimulated? What are the side effects of elevated reductase? What are the side effects of elevated reductase in the presence of a reductase deactivator? What is the biological consequence of deactivated reductase? These questions have not been asked and the answers have not been investigated.

Classifying statins as "reductase inhibitors" misleads prescribers to think that statins inhibit cholesterol synthesis by inhibiting reductase synthesis. The truth of the matter is that it is the reflexive increase in reductase that lowers cholesterol. More specifically, it is the increase in LDL cholesterol receptors due to the increase in reductase that lowers cholesterol. Inhibition of cholesterol synthesis inside cells is not what lowers cholesterol – but that is what most doctors think.

> Biochem Biophys Res Commun. 1978 May 15;82(1):247-54.
>
> **Lack of correlation between the rate of cholesterol biosynthesis and the activity of 3-hydroxy-3-methylgutaryl coenzyme A reductase in rats and in fibroblasts treated with ML-236B.**
>
> Bensch W.R., Ingebritsen T.S., Diller E.R.,

Within a year before the FDA's approval of Merck's lovastatin in 1987, Brown and Goldstein shared a Nobel Prize worth over $1.4M for their work on statins. In Brown's acceptance speech, no mention is made of the isoprenoid blockade by statins that arrests cell cycles, elevates reductase and kills cells.

What Brown reveals in this speech is a half-truth – that statins block cholesterol which increases reductase and LDL receptors. It was the beginning of a concerted campaign to conceal the whole truth of how statins *really* lower cholesterol. Furthermore, what Brown calls a "new steady state" is an obfuscation for "reset reductase elevation due to isoprenoid synthesis blockade".

> A Receptor-Mediated Pathway for Cholesterol Homeostasis
> Author(s): Michael S. Brown and Joseph L. Goldstein
> Source: *Science*, New Series, Vol. 232, No. 4746 (Apr. 4, 1986), pp. 34-47
> Published by: American Association for the Advancement of Science
> Stable URL: http://www.jstor.org/stable/1697034
>
> When given to experimental animals, compactin or mevinolin initially inhibit cholesterol synthesis in the liver, and this triggers a complex regulatory mechanism that lowers the plasma LDL-cholesterol level. With Kovanen and Kita, we showed that the inhibition of cholesterol synthesis elicits a dual compensatory re- ? sponse: (i) hepatocytes synthesize increased amounts of HMG CoA reductase; and (ii) they synthesize increased numbers of LDL receptors (*110*). When a new steady state is attained, the increase in HMG CoA reductase is almost sufficient to overcome the inhibitory effects of compactin. Total body cholesterol synthesis is only slightly reduced (*111*). Meanwhile, the plasma LDL level has decreased as a result of the increase in LDL receptors.

In 1980, Brown and Goldstein clearly reported statins block mevalonate and not just cholesterol. This mutates cells into what they called "mevalonate auxotrophs" (mutant cells deficient in mevalonate):

Multivalent feedback regulation of HMG CoA reductase, a control mechanism coordinating isoprenoid synthesis and cell growth

Journal of Lipid Research Volume 21, 1980 505

Michael S. Brown[1] and Joseph L. Goldstein

Departments of Molecular Genetics and Internal Medicine, University of Texas Health Science Center at Dallas, Dallas, TX 75235

Incubation of cultured cells with compactin blocks mevalonate production (4, 5) and converts the cells into mevalonate auxotrophs.

In a 1984 paper, Merck reported that ***the higher the statin dose, the more reductase is elevated to overcome the potentially lethal effects of blocking mevalonate***. They even photographed the resultant structural damage to cells:

Hydroxymethylglutaryl-coenzyme A reductase-containing hepatocytes are distributed periportally in normal and mevinolin-treated rat livers

Vagelos | Alberts

Medical Sciences: Singer *et al.* *Proc. Natl. Acad. Sci. USA 81 (1984)* 5559

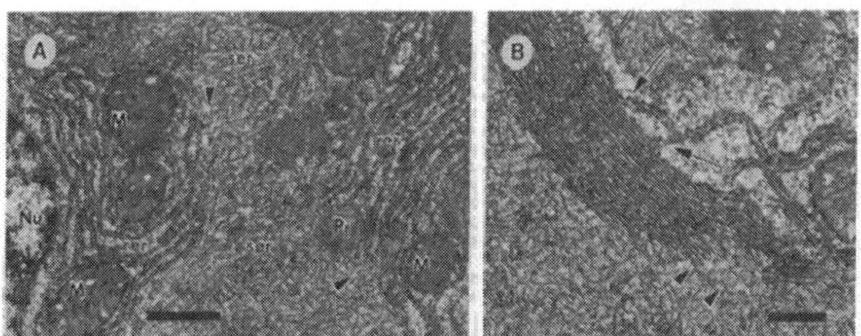

M = mitochondrion; Pr = peroxisome. (*A*) Rats treated with 0.075% mevinolin for 12 days exhibited hepatocytes with many SER tubules merging (at arrowheads) with RER profiles. The corresponding IF distribution of HMG-CoA reductase of this tissue is seen in Fig. 2*B*. (Bar = 1 μm.) (*B*) Same material as *A*. Stacks of parallel endoplasmic reticulum cysternae were frequently found in these hepatocytes. Profiles of RER appeared to be coalescing into these stacks (arrows), and SER vesicles (arrowheads) seemed to be budding from their ends. (Bar = 250 nm.) (*C*)

Proc. Natl. Acad. Sci. USA
Vol. 81, pp. 5556–5560, September 1984

Is this a toxic effect of lovastatin on cells? Yes, this is a toxic effect of lovastatin. It is not normal for cells to product a bunch of whorls and crystals of ER. Merck knew better and reported so:

Lovastatin, an inhibitor of cholesterol synthesis, induces hydroxymethylglutaryl-coenzyme A reductase directly on membranes of expanded smooth endoplasmic reticulum in rat hepatocytes

IRWIN I. SINGER*†, SOLOMON SCOTT*, DIANA M. KAZAZIS*, AND JESSE W. HUFF‡
Departments of *Biochemical and Molecular Pathology and ‡Biochemical Regulation, Merck Sharp and Dohme Research Laboratories, Rahway, NJ 07065

Because it is widely recognized that proliferation of SER membranes and accompanying induction of microsomal enzymes occurs in hepatocytes after exposure to various toxins or phenobarbital (12, 13, 19), the appearance of SER whorls after lovastatin administration might imply that this compound exerts <u>a toxic subcellular side effect in hepatocytes</u>.

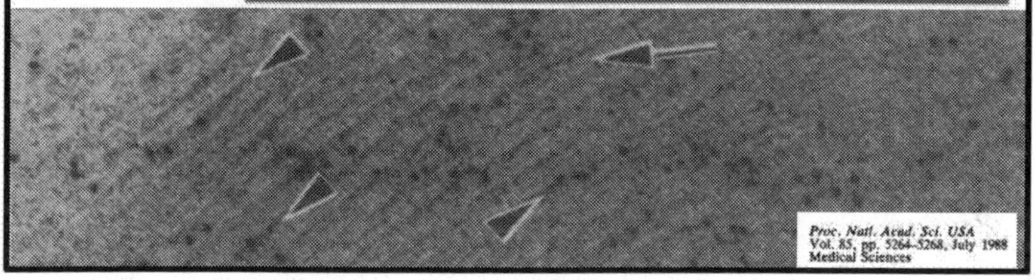

Like Endo insisting that what Sankyo's toxicologists thought were toxic crystals were instead "nontoxic cholesterol", Merck dresses up the toxic proliferation of ER as a "mechanism-based effect of lovastatin".

Of course it is mechanism-based; that is stating the obvious. Is carbon monoxide from car exhaust toxic? According to Merck, the answer to that question would be, "It is mechanism-based."

Many questions remain unanswered such as: How long can a cell keep manufacturing more ER factories to make more reductase before running out of resources? How long can a cell run away from its assailant before it dies of exhaustion? Why is the proliferated ER not the normal pancake-shape? Since cholesterol and dolichol lends strength to membranes, are the abnormally shaped ER membranes due to mevalonate deprivation?

Others have asked the same sort of questions about the whorls and crystals of ER in statin treated rat liver cells. One team discovered that adding mevalonate restored the cells to normal:

Localization of 3-hydroxy-3-methylglutaryl CoA reductase and 3-hydroxy-3-methylglutaryl CoA synthase in the rat liver and intestine is affected by cholestyramine and mevinolin

Andrew C. Li,* Richard D. Tanaka,†* Kimberly Callaway,† Alan M. Fogelman,* and Peter A. Edwards*,**

Effect of mevalonolactone on both the stability of the whorls and on the distribution of hepatic HMG-CoA reductase

No whorls were apparent 45 min after treatment (Table 2). At this time the cells could not be distinguished from the cells of a normal liver when studied by electron microscopy.

We conclude that the whorls are present in the livers of rats fed cholestyramine and mevinolin because the cells are deprived of a cellular product normally synthesized from mevalonate.

Journal of Lipid Research Volume 29, 1988

Like Brown, Goldstein, Endo and others, Merck knew that mevalonate prevents or reverses statin-induced liver toxicity:

Toxicity of the HMG-Coenzyme A Reductase Inhibitor, Lovastatin, to Rabbits

DOUGLAS J. KORNBRUST, JAMES S. MacDONALD, CHENNEKATU P. PETER, DONALD M. DUCHAI, JOHN I. GERMERSHAUSEN and ALFRED W. ALBERTS
Department of Safety Assessment, WP 44-1, Merck Sharp and Dohme Research Laboratories, West Point, Pennsylvania
Accepted for publication October 7, 1988

Alberts

The prevention or reversal of lovastatin-induced hepatotoxicity in rabbits by coadministration of mevalonic acid is strong support for this mechanism. However, the potentiation of lovastatin hepatotoxicity by cholesterol supplementation indicates that depletion of cholesterol is not the basis of the toxicity. The reason why cholesterol administration exacerbated lovastatin toxicity in rabbits is unclear at present, but one possibility is that a deficiency in another, possibly nonsterol, product of mevalonate may be the ultimate biochemical defect responsible for the liver (kidney or gallbladder) damage.

Mevalonate restores statin-fed liver cells to their normal appearance after making whorls and stacks and crystals of ER. Mevalonate also prevents or reverses liver damage. This confirms that the ER alterations are either the cause or symptom of the mechanism of cell damage, organ damage and animal death with statins.

Merck is correct: Statin cell toxicity, organ demise and host death is mechanism-based.

In 1984, Merck also discovered a way to accelerate mechanism-based cell alterations by a statin – by giving rats a second cholesterol-lowering drug called a "bile resin". ***The combination lowered cholesterol better than lovastatin alone (great!), it elevated reductase more than lovastatin alone and it made more abnormal-appearing ER than lovastatin alone.***

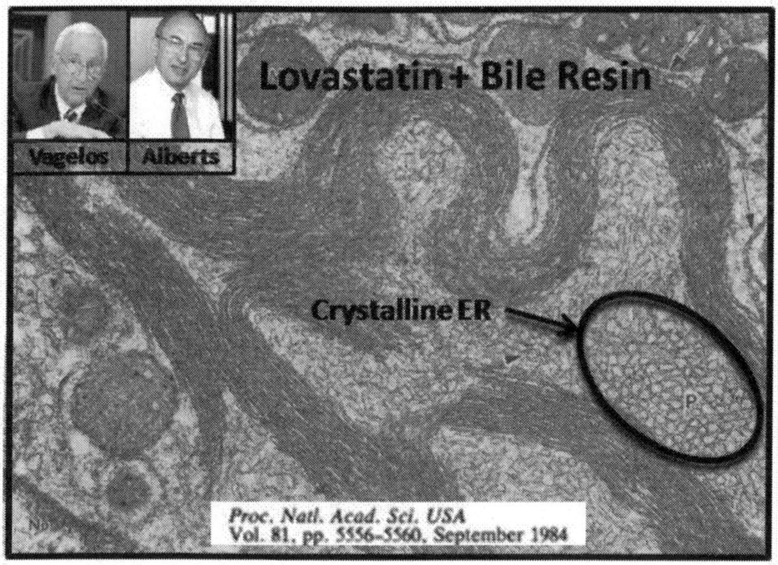

This drug combination is what reportedly killed the majority of Baycol users.

The liver has a very high-demand for cholesterol to make bile that is made in the liver and then stored in the gall bladder for digestion of fat; the bile is then recycled back to the liver from the intestines for reuse.

Bile acid resins block the recycling of bile (cholesterol) back to the liver. Adding a bile resin to a statin is like stealing a back-up life-preserver from a drowning victim; ***liver cells now have to increase reductase more than with just a statin alone*** to not die from mevalonate-deprivation compounded by accelerated cholesterol deprivation.

Actually, Merck had not discovered anything new with the statin induced crystals. They simply copied Dallas who copied Tokyo:

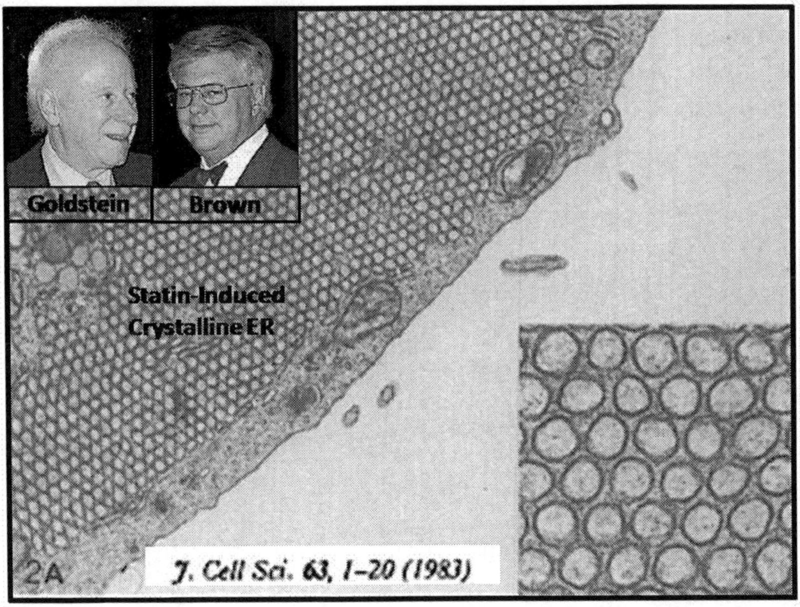

The combination of a statin and bile resin made the most ER crystals – ER with fragile membranes sorely deficient in mevalonate (dolichol). This helps account for why most of the rapid deaths caused by Baycol and other statins happened mainly to victims who were prescribed a statin with a bile resin. With statins alone those people would have been relegated to a slower death – with the association of the drug-induced death less likely of ever having been made.

In Merck's statin information sheets, the toxicity of combining bile resins with a statin is mentioned, but not explained – and not because Merck is ignorant.

Merck knew. Merck knows. That is why the information was and is withheld.

Chapter 18: Merck Knew Better

From the earliest days of development, Merck toxicologist James MacDonald and co-workers anticipated statin-induced toxicity to cells – which are not "side effects" at all as implied in Merck's literature, but are direct "mechanism based" effects of blocking reductase.

The Toxicology of HMG—CoA Reductase Inhibitors: Prediction of Human Risk

James S. MacDonald and Margaretann M. Halleck

Toxicol Pathol 2004 32: 26

Fetal Effects: In addition to cholesterol, HMG-CoA reductase is responsible for the synthesis of nonsterol intermediates essential for cellular function (Figure 1). Thus, it was not surprising when decreased body weights and skeletal malformations were first observed in fetuses of rats and mice given lovastatin during pregnancy (MacDonald et al., 1988).

Deprivation of mevalonate is the underlying cause of statin-induced injury and why rabbits die more quickly than other species. Like Brown, Goldstein and Endo, Merck knew that mevalonate deprivation is the source of cell injury and animal demise because mevalonate saved dying animals:

Toxicity of the HMG-Coenzyme A Reductase Inhibitor, Lovastatin, to Rabbits

Alberts

DOUGLAS J. KORNBRUST, JAMES S. MACDONALD, CHENNEKATU P. PETER, DONALD M. DUCHAI, JOHN I. GERMERSHAUSEN and ALFRED W. ALBERTS

Department of Safety Assessment, WP 44-1, Merck Sharp and Dohme Research Laboratories, West Point, Pennsylvania

Accepted for publication October 7, 1988

It is known that cholesterol given as a dietary supplement to rabbits will cause a feedback down-regulation of hepatic HMG-CoA reductase (White *et al.*, 1981). Thus, the administration of cholesterol along with lovastatin may have reduced the stimulus for reductase enzyme induction and accelerated the depletion of nonsterol mevalonate metabolites. Additional studies are planned ...

... depletion of cholesterol is not the basis of the toxicity. The reason why cholesterol administration exacerbated lovastatin toxicity in rabbits is unclear at present, but one possibility is that a deficiency in another, possibly nonsterol, product of mevalonate may be the ultimate biochemical defect responsible for the liver (kidney or gallbladder) damage.

If mevalonate reversed or prevented statin toxicity and death in rabbits, perhaps only one of the non-cholesterol isoprenoids would do the same (CoQ10, dolichol, etc.). ***This idea surfaced because giving cholesterol to statin-fed rabbits actually killed them faster.*** Merck's statin inventor Alfred Alberts likewise reasoned that depletion of one or more isoprenoids by statins was the cause of statin toxicity.

Do statins lower blood cholesterol? Yes, they do! Do nuclear power plants make power? Yes, they do – as well as make toxic nuclear waste. Even Endo admits that loss of normal cell function is the inherent price to pay for lowering cholesterol with a statin.

> **The discovery and development of HMG-CoA reductase inhibitors** — Akira Endo
>
> Subsequently, studies by other investigators showed that in cultured fibroblasts high concentrations of mevastatin block passage through the cell cycle (45–47) and alter cell morphology (48). Both effects could be prevented by the addition of mevalonate but not by the addition of cholesterol, which suggested that either mevalonate or one (or more) of its nonsterol products was involved.
>
> Journal of Lipid Research Volume 33, 1992

At some point the statin developers reasoned that CoQ10 deprivation was the most likely statin-blocked that was killing animals. CoQ10 is essential to the energy-making mechanism of all cells (a process called aerobic metabolism); any poison that blocks metabolism (such as cyanide, arsenic or carbon monoxide) can cause rapid death.

Metabolism is how cells "breathe." We breathe air into our lungs so that oxygen is delivered to our cells for metabolism; anything that obstructs this process "suffocates" the cells – and CoQ10 is as essential to metabolism as oxygen.

Skeletal and heart muscle cells have a very high demand for CoQ10. Muscle cell damage (myopathy) and muscle cell death (rhabdomyolysis) are the most commonly reported statin injuries. Three years after FDA approval of lovastatin, Merck decided that statin-blockade of CoQ10 synthesis was causing statin myopathy.

Michael Brown wrote a patent for adding CoQ10 to Merck's statins to prevent statin myopathy. ***In the body of this patent, he explains how CoQ10 should both prevent and/or cure statin-induced myopathy.***

United States Patent **4,933,165**
Brown **June 12, 1990**

Coenzyme Q.sub.10 with HMG-CoA reductase inhibitors

Inventors: **Brown; Michael S.** (Dallas, TX)
Assignee: **Merck & Co., Inc.** (Rahway, NJ)
Appl. No.: **07/298,535**
Filed: **January 18, 1989**

1. A pharmaceutical composition comprising a pharmaceutical carrier and an effective antihypercholesterolemic amount of an HMG-CoA reductase inhibitor and an amount of Coenzyme Q.sub.10 effective to counteract HMG-CoA reductase inhibitor-associated skeletal muscle myopathy.

3. A method of counteracting HMG-CoA reductase inhibitor-associated skeletal muscle myopathy in a subject in need of such treatment which comprises the adjunct administration of a therapeutically effective amount of an HMG-CoA reductase inhibitor and an effective amount of Coenzyme Q.sub.10 to counteract said myopathy.

In its application to the counteraction of myopathy the present invention is accordingly to be understood as providing for the avoidance of myopathy where this may otherwise occur as well as the amelioration of myopathy. The term counteracting is accordingly to be understood as connecting both a precautionary or prophylactic as well as curative or treatmental function.

CoQ10 was never added to Merck's statins.

Merck statin developers finally reasoned a CoQ10 deficit was the likely cause of statin toxicity and were so sure of themselves that Jonathan Tobert wrote another patent for Merck to add CoQ10 to lovastatin for the purpose of reversing and preventing liver cell injury. But, again, CoQ10 was never added.

There's another explanation for Merck's reservation to add CoQ10 to their statins: CoQ10 is one of the over-the-counter antioxidant nutrients that lowers cholesterol on its own. So, while CoQ10 may have made lovastatin safer, it would have lowered cholesterol, with or without the statin.

In Canada, statin information sheets include a warning on the unknown effects of CoQ10 depletion. This warning, however seemingly protective of its citizenry, is like warning consumers of the unknown effects of a dose of rat poison without taking an arsenic antidote. Furthermore, it's simply bad science to violate the moral precept to "do no harm" by recommending supplementation of a nutrient that's normally made by cells in the first place – ***and which is so vital to life***.

Blocking CoQ10 production, which hinders aerobic metabolism, is as potentially deadly as arsenic, cyanide and carbon monoxide that likewise block aerobic metabolism in cells.

> **"We are now in a position to witness the unfolding of the greatest medical tragedy of all time. Never before in history has the medical establishment knowingly created a life threatening nutrient deficiency in millions of otherwise healthy people."**
>
> ***- Peter H. Langsjoen, MD*** *(statins and CoQ10 depletion)*

Here's why CoQ10 is so vital to life and why its production via the mevalonate pathway should never be blocked: ATP is the energy source that every cell makes from hydrogen. Dietary carbo***hydrates*** are metabolized into ***hydrogen*** atoms. Hydrogen is then delivered to the ATP-making factory by a form of niacin (vitamin B3) abbreviated as "NAD". A hydrogen atom is comprised of one electron and one proton.

NAD delivers hydrogen atoms to the ATP-making factory where electrons and protons are separated from hydrogen. The hydrogen protons are pumped into a "proton energy dam" that makes ATP (cellular energy). ***ALL cells need ATP to live.***

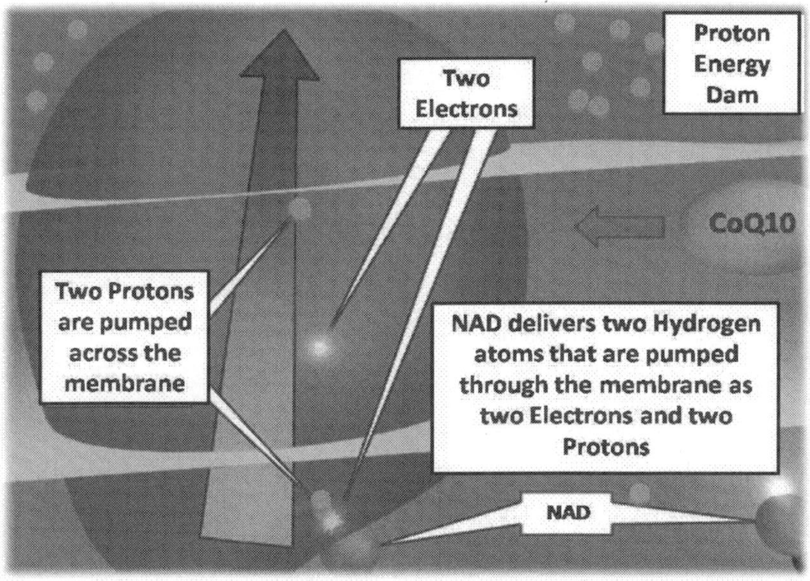

CoQ10 transports the electrons (from hydrogen) so that the process doesn't back up, slow down or stop – hence giving rise to the term "electron transport chain". ***Without this process of electrons being transported by CoQ10, metabolism can slow down or stop.*** By blocking CoQ10 synthesis, statins are like cyanide, arsenic and carbon monoxide that likewise slow down or completely stop electron transport. ***If electron transport stops, so do organs and the organism. Death quickly follows.***

Do NOT block the mevalonate pathway.

Do NOT block CoQ10.

In the final analysis, statins lower cholesterol by inducing cells to make cholesterol receptors. There are much safer natural alternatives such as selenium and linoleic acid (safflower oil) that, like statins, lower blood cholesterol by increasing LDL receptor production, only without the inherent dangers of blocking mevalonate, arresting cell cycles and choking cells to death by blocking CoQ10:

BIOMETALS

Volume 19, Number 5, 493-501, DOI: 10.1007/s10534-005-5393-z

Hypercholesterolemia and LDL receptor mRNA expression: Modulation by selenium supplementation

Sanjiv Dhingra and Mohinder P. Bansal

Conjugated Linoleic Acid Upregulates LDL Receptor Gene Expression in HepG2 Cells

(Manuscript received 10 July 2003. Initial review completed 25 August 2003. Revision accepted 17 October 2003.)

Shaomei Yu-Poth,* Dezhong Yin,** Guixiang Zhao,* Penny M. Kris-Etherton[†1] and Terry D. Etherton* **

*Graduate Program in Nutrition, [†]Department of Nutritional Sciences, and **Department of Dairy and Animal Science, The Pennsylvania State University, University Park, PA 16802*

A final reason why adding CoQ10 to Merck's statin was a "bad" idea for business: ***It would have been an open acknowledgment of a very serious design defect – an admission of guilt.***

Merck knew better.

Chapter 19: The Players

On Thursday, February 19, 1987 at 9:00 a.m., the FDA held an advisory committee meeting to review the NIH clinical guidelines for altering cholesterol with Merck's new cholesterol-altering drug, lovastatin. The NIH hosted the event at their facility in Bethesda, Maryland.

Remarkably, an FDA employee did not chair this meeting. Dr. Frederick Singer, a Merck consultant, chaired it.

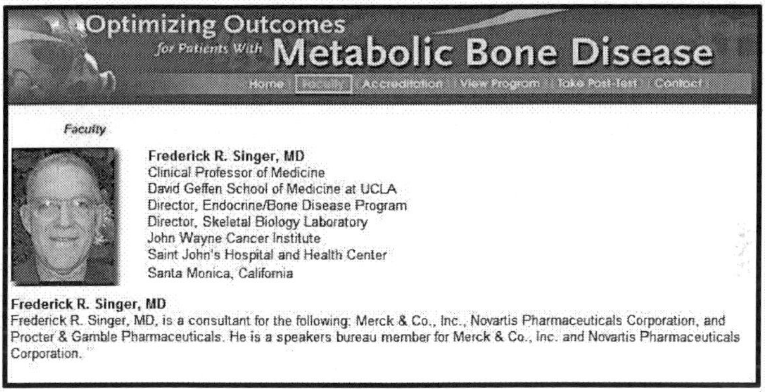

If this was a boxing match, Merck was weighted to win. In one corner of the ring representing Merck was former heavyweight superstar Mike Brown with his 1985 Nobel Prize for cholesterol research (shared with Joe Goldstein in the audience), flanked by NIH heavyweight Daniel Steinberg, the champion watchdog of MER/29. In the opposite corner as an FDA-paid advisor was Merck consultant John LaRosa. Center-stage, chairing the committee for the FDA, stood Merck consultant Fred Singer.

Merck interest was also equally weighted in the guest audience; half were Merck consultants. But with the Brown, Goldstein and Steinberg dynamic trio on their side, who would rival any of those contenders? If anything, the FDA employees must have felt honored to congregate with the in-crowd of the drug industry.

The FDA advisory committee roster included four FDA employees, 8 paid FDA advisors (two were Merck consultants) and 11 Merck speakers and guests as follows:

FDA employees: John Short; Gloria Troendle, MD; Solomon Sobel, MD; Alexander Fleming, MD.
FDA advisers: Frederick Singer, MD (chairman and Merck consultant); John LaRosa, MD (Merck consultant); Nancy Sajben, MD; Philip Troen, MD; John M. Karon, PhD; James R. Gavin, MD; Andrew P. Goldberg, MD; Susan Ratzan, MD.
Merck employees: Daniel Steinberg, MD; Michael Brown, MD; James MacDonald, PhD; Jonathan Tobert, MD; Kenneth Given, MD; Hyman Zimmerman, MD; Leo Chylack, MD; Eve Slater, MD.

Invited guests and speakers at this meeting included:

Guests: Joe Goldstein, MD (Merck consultant); Roger Illingsworth, MD (Merck speaker); William Insull (Merck consultant), MD; David Blankenhorn, MD; Peter Kador, PhD; John Galambos, MD.

The total-voting members on the FDA advisory committee: ***twelve*** (two with Merck interest). Merck representatives (including voting members and guests): ***thirteen***.

Another whole book could be written on how Merck had systematically subverted the process enough to essentially approve their own drug. The question is, why subvert the process in the first place if there is nothing wrong with the drug?

No serious detractors were in the room to make them lie and become civilly and criminally liable. They did it anyway.

After Dr. Steinberg made his case on why cholesterol must be stamped out at all cost, here is Dr. Brown's explanation to the FDA (representing Merck) on how lovastatin lowers cholesterol:

> **"As you have heard, lovastatin is an inhibitor of HMG CoA reductase. It cuts off this limb of the cholesterol supply cycle, or at least it diminishes the ability of cells to make cholesterol. One response that cells make, in response to that inhibition, is to increase their production of LDL receptors so as to replenish that cholesterol and take up more LDL. This, in turn, contributes to the lowering of LDL in the blood" (page 117).**

To say that Brown's overview of "lovastatin biochemistry" was a gross over-simplification would be a gross over-simplification. ***It was, rather, a gross series of omissions pertinent to human safety.*** For example, lovastatin does not cut off any limb of the cholesterol supply cycle; ***it cuts off the entire mevalonate pathway*** – of which cholesterol is only one limb. ***He also failed to explain his, Goldstein's and Endo's discovery of the vital***

response that cells must make in response to that inhibition – that of making more reductase – or die like a Merck lab rabbit.

A similar short-circuited explanation was presented next by Merck's Eve Slater, MD on the biochemistry of lovastatin. Like Brown, she accentuated the positive such as the specificity of lovastatin's action on reductase:

> **"A highly potent inhibitor is frequently a highly specific inhibitor as well...We know of no enzyme other than HMG CoA reductase which is subject to meaningful inhibition by lovastatin" (page 124).**

Slater's explanation is clearly lacking; ***she failed to include just how specific reductase is for cell life*** – and just how specifically mevalonate rescues cells and animals from certain statin-elicited death. She may as well have said, "We have discovered a new bullet that is specific for the center of the heart; no matter where you aim it, the bullet will always pierce the center of the heart." A key player in FDA's approval of lovastatin, she would soon be honorifically seated in Washington, D.C., directing the nation's drug and immunization policies.

Dr. MacDonald, Merck toxicologist, presented an overview of Merck's animal studies. Endo's early studies explained how statins failed to lower cholesterol in rats, mice and hamsters due to a high reflexive increase in reductase (and smooth ER). This response reopened the mevalonate pathway and saved the animals. MacDonald lied to the committee about this:

> **"This represents proliferation of the smooth endoplasmic reticulum, the membrane to which HMG CoA reductase is bound, and is a unique effect in the rat. We have demonstrated this both with electron microscopy and with fluorescent-labeled antibodies**

against the enzyme. These changes are not observed in dogs or primates, and represent the unique mechanism of regulation of cholesterol synthesis in rodents" (page 131).

Unlike rats, rabbit cells have low normal levels of reductase and, when fed statins, did *not* produce a strong life-saving elevation in reductase. Rabbits, therefore quickly died. MacDonald attributed the mortality of rabbits to "elevated blood levels" – but elevated blood levels of *what* was never explained (and no one asked):

> **"Similar observations of this have been seen in the case of rabbits. In this species, frank extracellular necrosis is observed after administration of relatively high doses. This species is significantly more sensitive to the toxicity in a shorter period of time. We do not, as I mentioned, understand the reason for this, but it may be related to the markedly elevated blood levels that we see in this species compared to others" (pages 131-132).**

Unlike rats that could overcome the mevalonate blockade and rabbits that could not, dogs fell somewhere in-between with signs of liver cell damage. MacDonald doesn't understand this effect in dogs either:

> **"This finding in dogs (liver cell damage) is a characteristic with HMG CoA reductase inhibitors, in our laboratory, and the prevention by mevalonate suggests that this change may be related to alteration in lipid metabolism. We clearly do not understand the mechanism of that however" (page 133).**

After reporting to the committee that cataracts were never observed in any of their dead rats (albeit a few cases with dogs), questions were opened to the floor. Dr. Rifkin – who had been asked to replace a passionate and rather argumentative LaRosa who made various pro-statin appeals during the first half of the day – asked:

> **"Can you say anything about the cataracts that occurred in the MER/29 situation that bears on interpreting your data?" (page 144).**

After various convolutions MacDonald boldly claimed there was no similarity – and then chairman Singer was quick to the rescue:

> **"Okay, we can go on. Thank you" (page 145).**

And that was that – as if an impertinent question had disrupted progress. The subject of MER/29 was held fast at bay for the rest of the day.

The 240-page meeting minutes contains such a convoluted web of omissions and obfuscations that volumes could be written on the mess. For example, Merck scientists repeatedly warned that their animals had normal cholesterol and so their toxicity data was compromised; that is more than ludicrous because lab animals can easily be fed high-cholesterol diets. Also, Merck claimed to have no explanation as to why some species were more sensitive to lovastatin than others. Papers published within a year of FDA approval made it clear they understood the mechanism of mevalonate deprivation.

Merck glossed over liver cell damage in animals and humans by declaring the cause of the effect was unknown and even went so far to say that cataracts reported in humans were inaccurate because of a bias in using an older population with baseline cataracts. All that – and much, more – and not one of the four FDA scientists or FDA-paid advisors required an accounting for the missing pieces. Everyone was clearly well sold (or bought) before the meeting commenced.

An exceptional moment, however, presented itself when Philip Troen commented on how blood cholesterol is vital for making steroid hormones – and then asked Dr. Goldstein why Merck had not observed deficiencies in cholesterol-derived molecules such as adrenal steroids:

> **"I have three observations. Does the company (Merck) or any of its consultants have any data or hypothesis as to why, with such a ubiquitous process as cholesterol biosynthesis, there is so little clinical or laboratory effect on any other vital functions? At first when I thought about this, I thought, well, gee, all the stuff goes to the liver, and that is really not involved with adrenal steroidogenesis et cetera. But, clearly, we hear about the eye, we hear about some other kind of effects. The question is, why does it happen like that? Dr. Goldstein?" (page 218).**

Goldstein responded:

> **"Dr. Troen, I think one cannot answer that question. As I observe the animal toxicology, different species have different sensitivities to the effect of the drug in different organs, because of the fact that different organs synthesize cholesterol and the end products of the pathway at different rates – get some of it from the plasma, some of it from their cells – and have a different kind of exposure in the blood in those organs to blocking the pathway. (Say *what*? – comment added). I think the important point is that, wherever we have been able to study it technically, it is related to mevalonate deficiency in the target organ" (page 218).**

After a bit of do-si-do with Dr. Troen, Dr. Goldstein finally gave way to conscience: ***The mixed bag of statin toxicity symptoms was due to mevalonate blockade.*** Thank you, Doctor Goldstein.

Merck *et al.* held their breaths. Did Goldstein blow it for them? Interestingly, Goldstein didn't really answer Troen's question. He asked why Merck didn't comment on the predictable effects of blocking cholesterol (not mevalonate), such as depletion of the adrenal steroid hormones (cortisol and aldosterone) that cells make from cholesterol. But Goldstein disclosed a whole separate problem of statin toxicity – that of blocking mevalonate.

No one asked Goldstein for an elaboration. Whew!

Chairman Singer closed the meeting with the following decision for everybody:

> **"I think our recommendation is to approve this drug and hope that it does as much as we think it might, but that it should be used carefully. We are finished. Thank you" (page 240).**

Five months later, what may yet prove to be the most dangerous drug ever made would be available for public ingestion and, like MER/29, prescribed like candy.

Had the FDA behaved as champions of public safety rather than the champions of American ingenuity and business they might have asked:

1. Merck, your company has repeatedly claimed today that lovastatin is not genotoxic and that cancer has not been observed in any of your studies. DNA replication is blocked by statins and the genes are located on DNA. Isn't blocking DNA and gene replication genotoxic?

2. Statins should never be taken by any woman of reproductive age...right?

3. Rumors have circulated that Sankyo stopped human trials with their statin in Japan due to lymphomas in their lab dogs. Lymphocytes have an unusually high demand for cholesterol to make a complexity of membranes. Since lymphocytes circulate in the blood and originate from the

blood-rich bone marrow, do you think that the lowering of blood cholesterol could account for the lymphomas? Also, did you anticipate any changes in white or red blood cells due to the lowering of blood cholesterol? Did you perform any electron microscopic studies of statin-exposed blood cells?

4. We have heard today how lovastatin lowers blood cholesterol. Cholesterol is obtained from the blood by various organs for conversion into sex hormones, vitamin D, thyroid hormone, cortisol and aldosterone – to name a few vital molecules. Have you performed any studies to determine, therefore, if your drug negatively affects libido, erectile function, fertility, sperm formation, immune function, thyroid function, glucose levels, salt balance, blood pressure, etc.?

5. Lovastatin blocks CoQ10 production, which is necessary to make energy for human cells. Heart cells, in particular, have a very high demand for CoQ10, which is why it is widely prescribed in Japan for heart health. While your studies demonstrated a lower risk for CVD with lovastatin use, did you evaluate your patients for any loss of heart function, in other words, cardiomyopathy? Or, put another way: Does lovastatin trade hardening of the arteries for a weak heart – and if so – how does that benefit outweigh the risks of CVD?

6. You claim that in all of your studies, lovastatin decreased the risk of CVD. Did your scientists fully understand the risk of blocking CoQ10 and other mevalonate-derived molecules and evaluate the patients for possible negative outcomes?

7. Lovastatin blocks formation of heme-A from mevalonate. The liver P450 enzymes that metabolize drugs like statins and thus clear them from the blood are heme-dependent. Have you performed any studies to determine if blocking

heme-A production increases the risk of statin toxicity over time, especially if taken with other drugs that also require P450 enzymes for drug clearance?

8. Dr. MacDonald, you maintain that statins are safe for human use because the human statin dose is more like $1/100^{th}$ the toxic doses given to your animals. So, if a hundred-fold human dose can kill a rabbit in 9 days by a mechanism you say is not understood, does that mean that the human dose, in a person that does not tolerate the drug like rabbits, can kill such a person with a rabbit-like reaction in 900 days?

9. Dr. Tobert, as Clinical Director of the Merck statin trials, did you ensure that the scientists involved in gathering the data understood the complete action of the drug being tested – in other words, were they informed that statins block CoQ10, dolichol, heme-A and the signaling proteins involved in DNA and cell replication – so that they could look for signs of any related problems of deficiency of those metabolites – such as fatigue, weakness, advanced aging, memory loss, pancreatic dysfunction, diabetes, mood changes and cognition difficulties? ***And, if full disclosure of the drug's action was not made, would that not render all of your study results null and void?***

10. Dr. Tobert, as Clinical Director of all the Merck statin trials, did you fully inform the human subjects of the complete action of the drug being tested – in other words, were they informed that statins block CoQ10, dolichol, heme-A and the signaling proteins involved in DNA and cell replication – so as to obtain from them a thorough informed consent to all known risks? ***And, if full disclosure was not given to your study subjects, would that not render all of your study results null and void?***

Merck scientists withheld knowledge they had that the mevalonate blockade is deadly. They said the side effects were due to an unknown mechanism. Furthermore, Merck had inserted so many of their own people into the process that no willing and knowledgeable FDA employee was even there to challenge them.

And still they lied.

With Merck employees and advisors in the majority on the FDA committee, Merck could have told the whole truth and lovastatin would have been approved anyway.

The team players all knew this was all about beating "the Japs" to the market. The lies were not meant to acquire easy and quick approval. That was a forgone conclusion. The lies were about concealing the evidence from the general public before going to market *after* approval.

Bureaucrats love to challenge high-powered business interests more than judges love to overrule the objections of high-powered attorneys. The fix was in. No one was there to object.

No one even took a swing at Merck – not even when Jonathan Tobert failed to account for twelve lovastatin study related deaths.

Chapter 20: What the Bleep?

By the time the FDA advisory committee met, Merck had spent millions to develop statins, do double blind studies and develop a sales pitch. Now only one thing remained; it was to get statins approved. There was only one agenda and it was not a scientific one. It was to finish the job.

Merck's Jonathan Tobert was charged with the dog and pony show on the lovastatin trial results. He had the spotlight and the slide presentation. He was a natural for it. He had directed the human studies for Merck.

He, Steinberg, Singer and others had strategized for this day for years. They had planned the study so that it would give positive results. It would parallel Steinberg's CPPT study using cholestyramine in half the subjects and diet in all the subjects. Like the CPPT, they included dieticians and training.

They had discussed how to limit portions of the study to cast the results their way. First, the problem of liver cell toxicity was now known. They would need to limit the liver study to the known time for liver cells to recycle in 300 to 500 days. To play it safe, all the patients in the liver study were limited to the short end of that cell cycle: 10 months. There was the exception of one man; his liver function was monitored for 16 months, just short of the maximum liver cell cycle of 500 days.

They made decisions on what to say and not to say to the FDA. Omitting the topic of dead and dying rats would allow them to say no cataracts were seen in living rats.

The dog cataracts had to be excused. That was simple with 50 times the human dosage given to the dogs.

Some things they just decided to avoid discussing. The castrating effects of statins on men simply could not be revealed - until Dr. Philip Troen just had to bring it up:

"Were studies of sperm morphology carried out?" (page 166).

Tobert responded:

"Morphology was examined, and there was no appreciable difference in sperm morphology" (page 167).

Whatever that means.

There were three problems to explain from Merck's human studies that Tobert had to address. These had to be white washed.

Liver enzymes were elevated 1.5 to 3 times normal in the test subjects. Every word was carefully chosen to defuse the issue.

Second, they were well aware of MER/29 and the cataract effect. They sent 600 people to ophthalmologists for pre-cataract screening. That would change the baseline and make any new cataract findings minimal. It did not work. More new cataracts were found than could be explained by age or minimized by the baseline. Again, every word to explain it was selected one word at a time.

Third, a serious problem developed during the study that they had to avoid. Twelve of 750 patients died the first year. That number, compared to Steinberg's work in the CPPT study, would extrapolate to 60 deaths *the first year.* The CPPT had 63 deaths *over five years* with five times more people (3800 patients). An enormous number of statin users had died during the lovastatin study. As a relative (Steinbergian) statistic, that is 500% more deaths. OOPS!!

Tobert and Singer slipped it by the committee like a pair of snakes covered in cooking oil.

Singer choked, stammered and paused, then apologetically asked the dreaded question:

> **"One of the members of our committee, unfortunately, could not be here today, but he wrote a review, which will, at least partially, be read. But I guess I should ask a question that he asked. That is simply about the mortality, the comment being that it is probably not significant or not above what you would expect. The question is, was there an attempt to try to come to grips with the 12 deaths? Is that within the range of mortality rates for a given cholesterol?" (page 168).**

What the bleep?

Tobert responded:

> **"We did not do any formal analysis of that. This is a very high-risk population. The mean plasma cholesterol of all our patients taken together was over 350. Half of them already have coronary disease. Two-thirds of them are male. Actually, almost all the deaths occurred within the first year of treatment. After the first year, there has been very little (page 168-169).**

Very little…WHAT?

After Tobert sidestepped another question about CVD in the twelve people who died, Singer closed the deal:

> **"I do not think we need to belabor that point" (page 169).**

Tobert excused himself:

> **"The next speaker will be Dr. Zimmerman, who will address the liver findings" (page 169).**

And that was that. To this day no study has been done that tracks and records the death rate in first-year statin users.

In layman's terms, these guys are the BS artists of all time. They had just run the biggest con ever.

All of the above is derived from Tobert's presentation to the FDA advisory committee (pages 145-169).

The elusive Jonathan Tobert MD, PhD has finished his work with Merck and is now available to lead other drug companies, for a small fee, through the snares, foibles and thorns of the FDA approval process to successfully deliver more toxic drugs to the streets. Simply call him at Tobert Medical Consulting, LLC. He knows the way and has earned the tee.

Today, Tobert is still slippery as a snake. He has a near fascinating anonymity. The only thing that surfaces from the public record for a photo or veritable credential is a big question mark.

Tobert is shrouded in almost desperate mystery. Why? Who checked into his background? How did he rise to such a position of power and influence? He worked his way into the good old boy network as an outsider. How did he do that?

Could Tobert be the bad apple that spoiled the whole barrel? Is he like the nefarious Dr. King of the MER/29 mass disaster who ***proved not to be a real medical doctor***?

Nothing can be found on the Brit, except that he is a professed unbeliever and Director of the Center for Inquiry (CFI).

Skeptical Inquirer

CENTER FOR INQUIRY

Richard Schroeder, Chair of the Center for Inquiry's (CFI) Board of Directors, is pleased to announce that Jonathan Tobert, MD, PhD, has joined CFI as the organization's newest director.

Fostering a secular society requires attention to many specific goals, but three goals in particular represent the focus of our activities:

1. an end to the influence that religion and pseudoscience have on public policy
2. an end to the privileged position that religion and pseudoscience continue to enjoy in many societies
3. an end to the stigma attached to being a nonbeliever, whether the nonbeliever describes her/himself as an atheist, agnostic, humanist, freethinker or skeptic.

In signing his name, Jonathan seems to have a hard time distinguishing between a "B" and a "D". The CFI hails him as an "MD" as does the 1987 sign-in roster from the FDA lovastatin advisory committee meeting. In other places, an "MB" flanks his name, which is a British bachelor's degree:

Inhibitors of Cholesterol Synthesis and Cataracts-Reply

Donald B. Hunninghake, MD; Valery T. Miller, MD; Robert H. Palmer, MD; Gustav Schonfeld, MD; Evan A. Stein, MD, PhD; Jonathan A. Tobert, MB, PhD
The Lovastatin Study Group II

JAMA, 1987;(12):1602.

According to the CFI web site, Jonathan worked for the FDA's advisory committee for reproductive health drugs from 2004 to 2007. Again, no picture, bio or résumé is found at the FDA web site on him, and, rather interestingly, neither does his name include any degree titles. Most well educated high-profile people acquire more initials over time to put behind their names and proudly display them. In the January 23 and 24, 2007 meeting of the committee, Tobert seemed to have lost his.

He is listed as "Jonathan Tobert - Industry Representative":

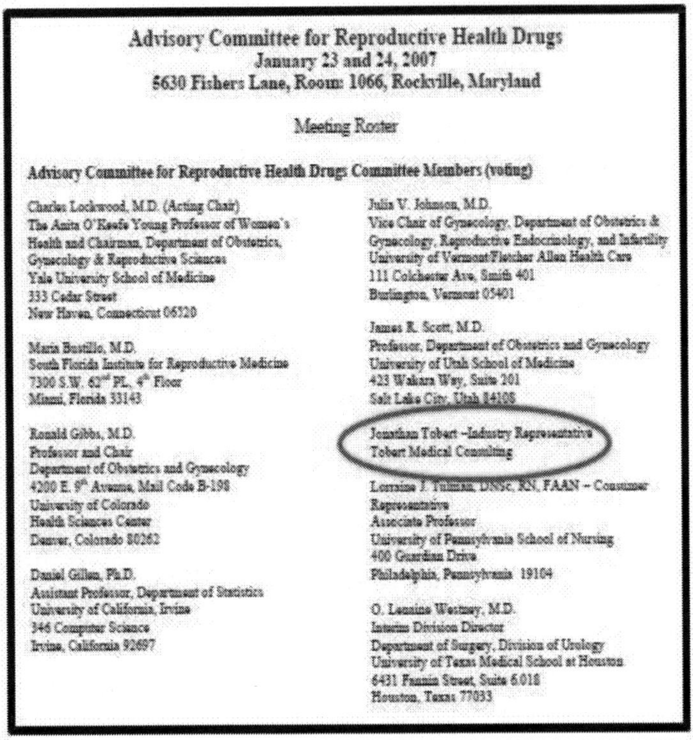

Advisory Committee for Reproductive Health Drugs
January 23 and 24, 2007
5630 Fishers Lane, Room 1066, Rockville, Maryland

Meeting Roster

Advisory Committee for Reproductive Health Drugs Committee Members (voting)

Charles Lockwood, M.D. (Acting Chair)
The Anita O'Keefe Young Professor of Women's Health and Chairman, Department of Obstetrics, Gynecology & Reproductive Sciences
Yale University School of Medicine
333 Cedar Street
New Haven, Connecticut 06520

Maria Bustillo, M.D.
South Florida Institute for Reproductive Medicine
7300 S.W. 62nd PL, 4th Floor
Miami, Florida 33143

Ronald Gibbs, M.D.
Professor and Chair
Department of Obstetrics and Gynecology
4200 E. 9th Avenue, Mail Code B-198
University of Colorado
Health Sciences Center
Denver, Colorado 80262

Daniel Gillen, Ph.D.
Assistant Professor, Department of Statistics
University of California, Irvine
346 Computer Science
Irvine, California 92697

Julia V. Johnson, M.D.
Vice Chair of Gynecology, Department of Obstetrics & Gynecology, Reproductive Endocrinology, and Infertility
University of Vermont/Fletcher Allen Health Care
111 Colchester Ave, Smith 401
Burlington, Vermont 05401

James R. Scott, M.D.
Professor, Department of Obstetrics and Gynecology
University of Utah School of Medicine
423 Wakara Way, Suite 201
Salt Lake City, Utah 84108

Jonathan Tobert –Industry Representative
Tobert Medical Consulting

Lorraine J. Tulman, DNSc, RN, FAAN – Consumer Representative
Associate Professor
University of Pennsylvania School of Nursing
400 Guardian Drive
Philadelphia, Pennsylvania 19104

O. Lenaine Westney, M.D.
Interim Division Director
Department of Surgery, Division of Urology
University of Texas Medical School at Houston
6431 Fannin Street, Suite 6.018
Houston, Texas 77033

What the bleep is a former Merck employee sitting on an FDA drug approval committee as a paid advisor? That is like inviting a known bank robber into your bank in the hope he will case the joint and then truthfully tell you how to prevent him from robbing it.

How does Jonathan Tobert retire from Merck in 2004, file a Limited Liability Corporation with a mission to help drug companies with "regulatory agency interactions" and then walk straight into the FDA and receive payment to vote on approval of drugs for the companies he is paid to represent – like Merck?

Who thought that one up? If this is a typical example of how our protective agencies work then we are in a lot of trouble.

What the bleep is wrong with this picture?

While Tobert's face may have eluded the public domain, his name repeatedly surfaces wherever there is a so-called scientific study or report hailing the safety and benefits of Merck's statins. The second human trial with lovastatin – the "4S" Study – is replete with Scandinavian-sounding names of scientists. And then there is the Englishman Tobert, in the shadows as Merck's director of human trials to ensure the study stayed "on track."
And why was Tobert's statin study performed in Scandinavia? Was the 4S Study – short for the "Scandinavian Simvastatin Survival Study" – a word play to see who would survive simvastatin toxicity?

Nowhere is there a record to be found that the 4S scientists and study subjects received full disclosure on the inherent risks of blocking mevalonate. Nor does that track include a full disclosure of the remedy to reverse statin-induced toxicity.

But is it wrong to withhold knowledge to do good? Shouldn't the 4S study physicians have known the inherent dangers of blocking mevalonate? Not likely. Ask any physician what biochemical products are made via the mevalonate pathway and he or she will likely only mention cholesterol and nothing else. That is, after all, what doctors are taught in medical school: mevalonate makes cholesterol – period.

Once a faulty theory or drug is in place, it is near impossible to shift the tide. The researchers and drug companies have convinced the entire medical community that the world is flat. That has become accepted reality, and now there is no need to review the evidence. The world is flat.

The drug companies that financially back medical schools with ongoing research funds are clever enough to have influenced physicians' curriculum on the mevalonate pathway. Who develops curriculum and protocols for medical students? Notably, the NIH controls the "Federation for Advanced Education of the Sciences" (FAES) and Steinberg was its former president. Physicians are taught cholesterol metabolism via the work of Brown and Goldstein, who, after 1985, began to mum the word on how blocking mevalonate (isoprenoids) with statins kills cells.

If Steinberg has his way, medical schools will one day call the LDL cholesterol receptor the "Brown and Goldstein receptor" – a catchphrase he dropped in a recent public interview.

What has happened is now accepted ignorance. The world is *not* flat. Mevalonate is essential for numerous isoprenoids that are as vital to the life of a cell as LDL cholesterol. Tobert and Steinberg are the fathers of a wrongful doctrine in medicine: that statins are pro-life.

For decades scientists will be adding to the hundreds of case reports already published on multi-organ failure and fatalities in statin users. They will continue to debate over whether or not death or disability from statin use is due to oxidative stress, mitochondrial dysfunction, CoQ10 depletion, cholesterol deprivation or bad genes. Case reports will pile as lives are destroyed because physicians remain ignorant that mevalonate is required for cell cycles.

Hundreds to thousands more toxic and fatal drug-drug interactions with statins will be reported without the connection that statins block heme-A production (cells use heme to make cytochrome P450 liver enzymes to metabolize many drugs including statins). Even more cases will go unnoticed as head scratching continues and graves are dug while more billions of dollars are raked.

There is no need to debate the verity of any of the statin studies on humans, including 4S led by Tobert, as long as a full disclosure of the risks of blocking mevalonate was not given to the scientists and study subjects. ***4S and all of the drug company studies that followed are worthless***. Furthermore, there are consumer protection laws to protect people from such harm.

Any statute of limitations for civil complaints is suspended by Merck's active concealment of statin-related hazards.

Merck kills their consumers and bullies anyone who tries to stop them. Merck's Vioxx scandal serves as a single example.

There are still a few good men at the FDA. Dr. David Graham is one of them. As associate director for science in the FDA Drug Center's Office of Drug Safety, Graham had to find help outside the FDA when he discovered serious problems with Merck's Vioxx. He told Senate investigators that he had been subjected to veiled threats and intimidation when he informed the FDA of his findings.

A Grand Jury probe followed, and Vioxx was finally removed from the market in 2004. The FDA study headed by Graham had estimated that the defective drug could have contributed to 27,785 heart attacks and sudden cardiac deaths between 1999 and 2003. One can only wonder how much harm would have been done without one good man to have sounded the alarm.
After Vioxx was recalled, it was revealed that the FDA had tried to silence Graham. Perhaps Dr. Graham is one of the group of

FDA scientists (names redacted) who appealed to President Obama by letter in 2009 to investigate rampant FDA corruption. This letter, authenticated by the FDA (reference 31), includes concerns about the FDA's Center for Drug Evaluation and Research (CDER). The scientists explain as a single example how a federal court found that a drug had been approved because CDER's top personnel "didn't have a choice" and had to "ignore the science and the law" to approve it or they would "be removed from their positions of authority".

The scientists state that the FDA is fundamentally broken – but any organization that is fundamentally broken can be fundamentally repaired. As if written for a mafiosa-movie script, the following excerpt from page two implies that the FDA is more than broken and, rather, directed by forces outside the public interest:

DEPARTMENT OF HEALTH AND HUMAN SERVICES

Food and Drug Administration
Office of Device Evaluation
9200 Corporate Boulevard
Rockville, MD 20850

The Honorable Barack H. Obama
President of the United States
1600 Pennsylvania Avenue NW
Washington, DC 20500

April 2, 2009

On January 7, 2009, FDA physicians and scientists wrote to Mr. John Podesta[4]: "Through this letter and your action, we hope that future FDA employees will not experience the same frustration and anxiety that we have experienced for more than a year at the hands of FDA managers because we are committed to public integrity and were willing to speak out. Currently, there is an atmosphere at FDA in which the honest employee fears the dishonest employee, and not the other way around. Disturbingly, the atmosphere does not yet exist at FDA where honest employees committed to integrity and the FDA mission can act without fear of reprisal. ... America urgently needs change at FDA because FDA is fundamentally broken, failing to fulfill its mission, and because re-establishing a proper and effectively functioning FDA is vital to the physical and economic health of the nation."[5]

Not so much as a whisper in response to the above letter makes one wonder what the bleep is going on.
Merck has unequivocally proven themselves master manipulators, liars, cheats and worse. They have discredited their

detractors, made hit lists, provided and generated falsified data and hired ghost writers to write phony papers supporting their deadly drugs. And our FDA invites them and theirs to sit on vital drug approval and planning committees.

How many other dangerous drugs have been approved under this faulty process? There is a long list to include MER/29, Baycol, Phen-Fen and Vioxx. But those are just the ones that have come to light.

The same good old boy network manages the AHA, the FDA and the NIH. By infiltrating those agencies, the drug companies have managed to set the standards for cholesterol levels.

The lower the standard acceptable level, the more drugs they sell. The more diseases caused or exacerbated by the drugs, the more drugs they sell.

It is virtually a license to print money.

Bribes and corruption are not necessarily cash money passed under the table. Merck used high-paying jobs, consulting fees, power and prestige to buy approval for statins. Eve Slater, for example, was a spokesperson for Merck on the FDA committee for the statin approval process. She later became Assistant Secretary of Health, setting national health care guidelines.

Imagine the celebration at Merck when one of their own was appointed to such a position of power. More protocols and policy could be set to save marketing expenses.

Again, it is the American way.

FDA's Dr. Graham describes in his own words the hellhole he stepped into for blowing the whistle on Merck's Vioxx. It also provides a peek into the depth of FDA corruption and clout:

The FDA Exposed: An Interview With Dr. David Graham, the Vioxx Whistleblower

Tuesday, August 30, 2005 by Manette Loudon

MANETTE: Has anyone tried to silence you and stop you from becoming a whistleblower?

DR. GRAHAM: Prior to my Senate testimony in mid-November of 2004, there was an orchestrated campaign by senior level FDA managers to intimidate me so that I would not testify before Congress. This intimidation took several forms. One attack came from our acting Center Director who contacted the editor of the Lancet, the prestigious medical journal in the United Kingdom, and intimated to the editor that I had committed scientific misconduct and that they shouldn't publish a paper that I had written showing that Vioxx increases the risks of heart attack. This high-level FDA official never talked to me about this allegation. He just went directly to the Lancet.

The second attack was from other high level FDA officials who contacted Senator Grassley's office and attempted to prevent Senator Grassley and his staff from supporting me and calling me as a witness. They knew that if they could disarm Senator Grassley that would neutralize me.

The third attack came from senior FDA officials who contacted Tom Devine, my attorney at the Government Accountability Project, and attempted to convince him that he should not represent me because I was guilty of scientific misconduct; I was a bully; a demigod; and a terrible person that couldn't be trusted. These people were posing as whistleblowers themselves ratting on another whistleblower. Some of these senior level FDA officials were in my supervisory chain and are people I work for. They were involved in a coordinated attempt to discredit me and to smear my name and to prevent me from giving testimony.

There's one other thing that happened the week before I testified. The Acting Commissioner of the FDA invited me to his office and offered me a job in the Commissioner's Office to oversee the revitalization of drug safety for the FDA if I would just leave the Office of Drug Safety and come to the Commissioner's Office. Obviously he had been tipped off by people in the Senate Finance Committee who are sympathetic to the FDA's status quo that I was going to be called as a witness. To preempt that, he offers me this job, which basically would have been exile to a fancy title with no real ability to have an impact. This was a conspiracy and it was coordinated and there was collaboration among senior level FDA officials. What a mess!

It is impossible to legislate morality and ethicality especially when hundreds of billions of dollars are at stake.

Nevertheless, it is still possible to pursue criminal and civil remedies.

Chapter 21: Déjà Vu, Merck and MER/29

The MER/29 grand jury indictment included evidence that Merrell Company scientists had withheld information from the FDA regarding cataracts in rats.

Déjà vu. Merck's Jonathan Tobert denied ever having seen cataracts in rats, citing only personal conversation with Merck's James MacDonald as his support.

In the wake of MER/29, Tobert should have cited at least one written report by Merck with hard scientific data ruling out cataracts. Instead, within weeks of FDA approval, Tobert claims he did not observe cataracts in lab rats because James MacDonald "told him so". Smells like a rat. Looks like a rat. Sounds like a rat. Probably is a rat.

Perhaps that communication went something like this: "Hi, James, Jonathan Tobert here. Hey, mate; lovastatin's about to be FDA approved and I'm writing an article to muster up some early press. By the way, did you ever see any cataracts in our rats? No? Mind if I quote you on that? Oh, jolly good. Thanks, chap!"

Dr. Richard Cenedella, a respected pharmaceutical consultant for decades, reports that all cholesterol-lowering drugs produce cataracts in rats as an early observation.

"I have consulted for many drug companies over the years. All of the hyper-lipidemic drugs induce cataracts in mice; it's an early observation that holds up."

Not unlike Merck's warning to Merrell in 1961, Cenedella issued an urgent appeal to Merck, warning them of pending catastrophe with statin-induced cataracts that he produced in rats within only two weeks:

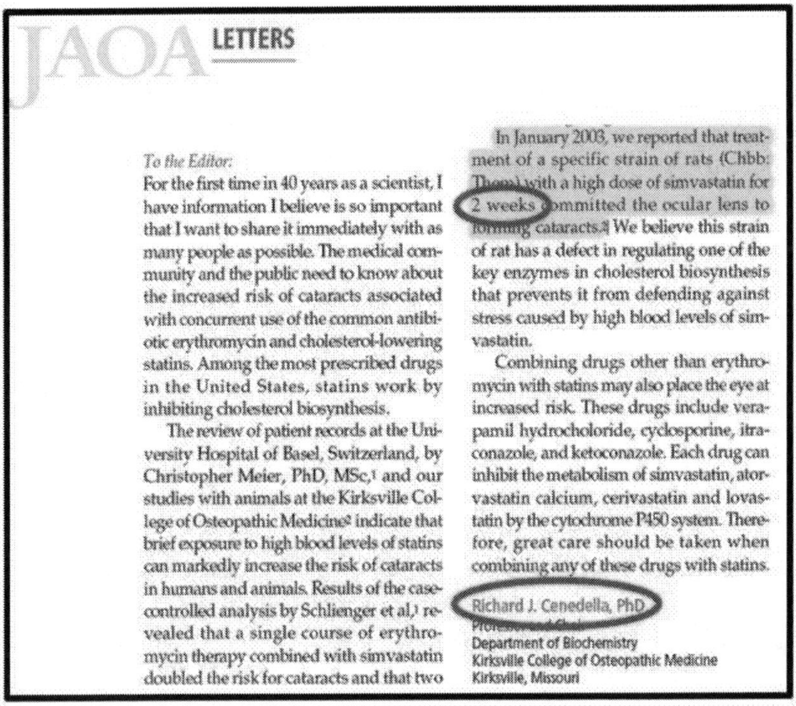

JAOA LETTERS

To the Editor:

For the first time in 40 years as a scientist, I have information I believe is so important that I want to share it immediately with as many people as possible. The medical community and the public need to know about the increased risk of cataracts associated with concurrent use of the common antibiotic erythromycin and cholesterol-lowering statins. Among the most prescribed drugs in the United States, statins work by inhibiting cholesterol biosynthesis.

The review of patient records at the University Hospital of Basel, Switzerland, by Christopher Meier, PhD, MSc,[1] and our studies with animals at the Kirksville College of Osteopathic Medicine[2] indicate that brief exposure to high blood levels of statins can markedly increase the risk of cataracts in humans and animals. Results of the case-controlled analysis by Schlienger et al,[1] revealed that a single course of erythromycin therapy combined with simvastatin doubled the risk for cataracts and that two

In January 2003, we reported that treatment of a specific strain of rats (Chbb: Thom) with a high dose of simvastatin for 2 weeks committed the ocular lens to forming cataracts.[2] We believe this strain of rat has a defect in regulating one of the key enzymes in cholesterol biosynthesis that prevents it from defending against stress caused by high blood levels of simvastatin.

Combining drugs other than erythromycin with statins may also place the eye at increased risk. These drugs include verapamil hydrocholoride, cyclosporine, itraconazole, and ketoconazole. Each drug can inhibit the metabolism of simvastatin, atorvastatin calcium, cerivastatin and lovastatin by the cytochrome P450 system. Therefore, great care should be taken when combining any of these drugs with statins.

Richard J. Cenedella, PhD
Department of Biochemistry
Kirksville College of Osteopathic Medicine
Kirksville, Missouri

Another lab, independent of Merck financial interests, reproduced Cenedella's find; instead of producing cataracts in two weeks, however, it took them only seven days:

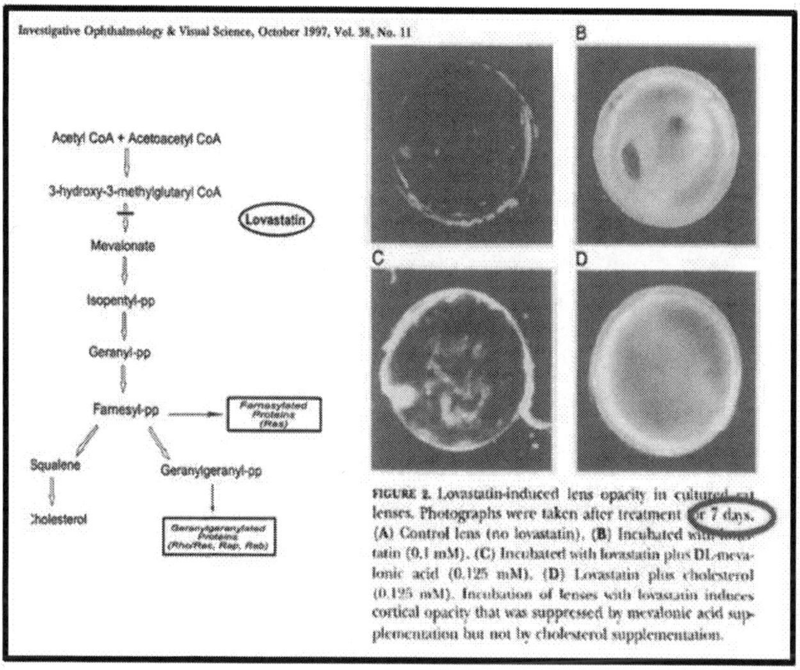

FIGURE 2. Lovastatin-induced lens opacity in cultured rat lenses. Photographs were taken after treatment for 7 days. (A) Control lens (no lovastatin). (B) Incubated with lovastatin (0.1 mM). (C) Incubated with lovastatin plus DL-mevalonic acid (0.125 mM). (D) Lovastatin plus cholesterol (0.125 mM). Incubation of lenses with lovastatin induces cortical opacity that was suppressed by mevalonic acid supplementation but not by cholesterol supplementation.

In 1961, Merrell scientists didn't see the same cataracts that the Merck scientists saw. Twenty-seven years later, Merck scientists didn't see the same cataracts that scientists like Cenedella found.

Tobert lies. In March of 1988, he boldly announced that to date there had been no cataracts seen in humans taking lovastatin – when the year before he had co-authored a paper documenting an increase in lens opacities in 101 lovastatin consumers.

You can tell when Tobert is lying. He is either writing or his lips are moving.

Merck's J. F. Walker kept it simple. He simply wrote that lens opacities in statin consumers were of no "significant" cataract-inducing potential – whatever that means.

Drugs. 1988;36 Suppl 3:83-6.

HMG CoA reductase inhibitors. Current clinical experience.

Walker JF.

Merck Sharp & Dohme Research Laboratories, Rahway, New Jersey.

Ophthalmological examinations in over 1100 patients treated with one or the other agent have revealed no evidence of significant short term (up to 2 years) cataractogenic potential.

?

In responding to the 1987-published claim by Tobert that cataracts had not been observed in human test subjects given statins for 18 weeks, Cenedella again diligently warned about cataracts in the following letter to the editor of JAMA:

Inhibitors of Cholesterol Synthesis and Cataracts

Richard J. Cenedella, PhD

To the Editor.— The results presented in the article entitled "Therapeutic Response to Lovastatin (Mevinolin) in Nonfamilial Hypercholoesterolemia"[1] clearly indicate that lovastatin (a potent inhibitor of the rate-limiting step in cholesterol biosynthesis) could be a useful agent for the management of an elevated low-density lipoprotein cholesterol level. The purpose of this letter is to caution against the possible complication of cataract development that might result from long-term use of this agent. Although the authors reported no apparent increases in lens opacities in adult subjects treated for 18 weeks with lovastatin, they should be aware that serious consequences could result from long-term inhibition of cholesterol synthesis by the ocular lens, especially in children and young adults.

JAMA, 1987;257(12):1602.

In his response, Tobert listed excuses: cataract screens were compromised because the patients were elders with complicated medical histories and pre-existent lens opacities

> **Inhibitors of Cholesterol Synthesis and Cataracts-Reply**
>
> Donald B. Hunninghake, MD; Valery T. Miller, MD; Robert H. Palmer, MD; Gustav Schonfeld, MD; Evan A. Stein, MD, PhD; Jonathan A. Tobert, MB, PhD
> The Lovastatin Study Group II
>
> *JAMA*, 1987;(12):1602.
>
> **In Reply.**—
>
> Dr Cenedella is correct in pointing out the potential for inhibitors of cholesterol synthesis to induce cataracts, particularly in young individuals. Pediatric use of lovastatin has been limited to patients with serious genetic disorders, mainly children with homozygous familial hypercholesterolemia. One of us (J. A.T.) has analyzed results of all the ophthalmologic examinations in patients taking lovastatin. Slit-lamp examination of the lens was performed at the baseline examination and during treatment in over 500 patients. The mean age of the patients studied was 50 years; 60% of them had heterozygous familial hypercholesterolemia and 50% had ischemic heart disease. The prevalence of lens opacities in these patients was 27% at the baseline examination and 31% at the last available examination during treatment with lovastatin. Interpretation of these data is complicated by the subjective nature of slit-lamp examination, uncertainty regarding the natural incidence of lens opacities in patients with severe...

At the FDA advisory committee meeting on lovastatin, Tobert had already admitted an increase in lens opacities. Six hundred of the patients had been pre-screened before the study began. The ophthalmologists had discovered a definitive increase in opacities. He dismissed the findings in his presentation as prejudice because the finding of cataracts in dogs was released in the middle of the study. He brought two Merck paid ophthalmologists to the committee meeting to offer testimony that contradicted the findings of all the other physicians.

They were not asked to testify.

The FDA only required Merck to screen for cataracts for one year. Was a detailed record made of these unthinkable so-called complications of the cataract exams? How can something so important as human sight be so trivialized in light of the historical record of the MER/29 travesty?

Then again, Tobert *is* the avowed skeptic and director of the Center For Inquiry. It is easy to heedlessly dismiss incriminating evidence when the cash is stacked on your side.

Tobert's response to Cenedella (page 213) includes Donald Hunninghake's name. Hunninghake helped write the Grundy/Steinberg NCEP that made billions for Merck and other companies that regularly reward them with "honoraria" (lots of money). Hunninghake earned at least $420,000 from drug makers between 1997 and 2003; in 2004, he left his job at the University of Minnesota to become a full-time consultant (reference 32).

After 25 years of widespread use, the stats are finally in: statin users have more cataracts than decreased risk of heart disease:

Statins may raise cataract, kidney risk **2010**

LONDON — Drugs to lower cholesterol and prevent heart disease, taken by millions of people worldwide, increase the risk of cataracts, kidney failure, muscle pain, and liver dysfunction, a study of more than 2 million Britons found.

The study, released today by the British Medical Journal, did not validate a range of potential benefits, other than lowering cholesterol, attributed to statins. The drugs generated $35.3 billion worldwide in 2009.

For every 10,000 people taking a statin, there were about **271 fewer cases of heart disease**, 8 fewer cases of esophageal cancer, **307 extra patients with cataracts**, 23 additional patients with acute kidney failure, and 74 extra patients with liver dysfunction, researchers estimated.

Should any of these statistics be a surprise? No. Cholesterol is vital to normal sight.

In the end, the MER/29 debacle proved a success – from how the FDA handled the drug, how the United States Congress investigated it and how the Federal Government successfully prosecuted the manufacturer for submitting false data. The swift action taken by authorities in the MER/29 catastrophe is unlikely today with so much commercial infiltration into "watchdog" agencies like the FDA. None of these history-repeating events are possible without cooperation by FDA insiders.

In her book "Confessions of an Rx Drug Pusher", former pharmaceutical rep Gwen Olsen exposes how she learned that an unprecedented number of lethal drugs are unleashed onto an unsuspecting public in record time. She saw first-hand how the minimizing of side effects or misinforming of physicians resulted in patients being injured or killed. On more than one occasion, she heard co-workers boast confidence in "our people in the FDA" or "our friends in the FDA".

Chapter 22: Nothing but the Truth

The heartbeat may speed up and slow down but it is always detectable because it is so vital to life. Similarly, reductase is always "on" at a detectable level to make isoprenoids needed for continual cell cycles.

Reductase does not always need to be on to make cholesterol because cells can obtain cholesterol from the blood through LDL receptors. Unlike cholesterol, some isoprenoids do not circulate in the blood and so reductase is always "on" to produce them.

An important discovery by Brown, Goldstein and Endo in 1977 was that ***reductase activity was markedly increased even when an ample cholesterol supply was available to statin-fed cells:***

Induction of HMG-CoA Reductase by Compactin

The relative increase in HMG-CoA reductase activity elicited by compactin was especially pronounced when the fibroblasts were growing in the presence of LDL, which ordinarily supplies sufficient cholesterol to the cells to suppress HMG-CoA reductase almost completely.

One possible explanation is that fibroblasts require small amounts of mevalonate for the synthesis of an essential substance other than a sterol.

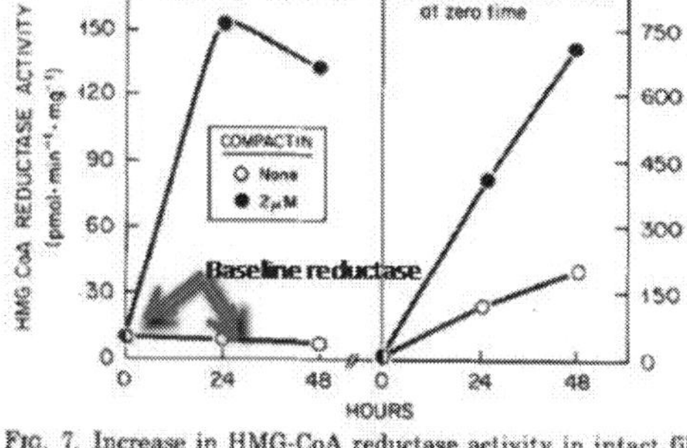

FIG. 7. Increase in HMG-CoA reductase activity in intact fibroblasts incubated with compactin in the presence (*A*) or absence (*B*) of lipoproteins.

From the very first statin experiment in Dallas, it was known that statins elevate reductase not by blocking cholesterol synthesis alone – but largely by blocking isoprenoid synthesis.

This "whole truth" was completely omitted in Brown and Goldstein's Nobel speech and recorded as a half-truth at the FDA meeting with three simple words – "in part because":

> **"It turns out that lovastatin is an effective therapy in lowering the blood cholesterol level in these FH heterozygotes, in part because, by inhibiting cholesterol synthesis, it stimulates the normal gene to produce more LDL receptors" (Michael Brown to the FDA, Feb. 19, 1987 FDA Advisory Committee Transcript, page 119).**

Again, statins block mevalonate synthesis. By blocking mevalonate, Brown and Goldstein were able to use statins to further their studies on the LDL receptor – something for which they have earned much applause. By blocking mevalonate, statins allowed them to more clearly "see" how cells obtain cholesterol from the blood through LDL cholesterol receptors:

The Journal of Biological Chemistry
Printed in U.S.A.

Inhibition of Cholesterol Synthesis with Compactin Renders Growth of Cultured Cells Dependent on the Low Density Lipoprotein Receptor*

(Received for publication, January 5, 1979)

Joseph L. Goldstein, Jean A. S. Helgeson, and Michael S. Brown

From the Departments of Molecular Genetics and Internal Medicine, The University of Texas Health Science Center at Dallas, Dallas, Texas 75235

Studies of the genetics of the LDL receptor would be facilitated by having culture conditions in which the growth of cells is dependent on LDL uptake through the receptor pathway. In order to establish such conditions, it is necessary to block the compensatory increase in cholesterol synthesis that occurs when cells are grown in lipoprotein-deficient serum so that they become dependent on an external source of cholesterol.

The recent discovery by Endo and collaborators (13) of a specific nonsteroidal inhibitor of cholesterol synthesis has made it possible to examine the question of the LDL receptor-dependent growth of cells.

Brown and Goldstein studied the defective genetics of the LDL receptor in people with FH who have extremely high cholesterol. It was for these patients that the FDA gave Dallas an IND to test lovastatin ***and not the general public.*** A complication of FH is painful deposits of oxidized cholesterol called "xanthomas"; it was believed that lowering blood cholesterol would improve this condition. Notably, two of these six FH patients with cholesterol levels over 500 didn't even have CVD. If cholesterol was the enemy, an opportunity was missed to investigate why one-third of Dallas' first FH patients did not have CVD despite they had three times the normal blood cholesterol level.

In 1981, Mabuchi reported that ML-236B had actually caused an increase in cholesterol in FH patients with the most severe form of the disease (homozygous FH).

> Effects of ML-236B (Compactin) on Sterol Synthesis and Low Density Lipoprotein Receptor Activities in Fibroblasts of Patients with Homozygous Familial Hypercholesterolemia
>
> Toshihiro Haba, Hiroshi Mabuchi, Akira Yoshimura, Akira Watanabe, Takanobu Wakasugi, Ryozo Tatami, Kosei Ueda, Ryosei Ueda, Tomio Kametani, Junji Koizumi, Susumu Miyamoto, and Ryoyu Takeda
>
> **When ML-236B was removed from the culture medium, the rate of cholesterol synthesis in homozygous cells that had been exposed to the drug was 1.5-fold higher than it was in the cells that were never exposed to the drug. This increase in sterol synthesis of homozygous cells in probably due to the increased intra-cellular HMG-CoA reductase activity.**
>
> *J. Clin. Invest.* © *The American Society for Clinical Investigation, Inc.* *Volume 67 May 1981*

Because people with homozygous FH have no functional LDL cholesterol receptors, ***statins increased blood cholesterol in the people who might have enjoyed some clinical benefit by reduction of painful xanthomas.*** These are the people who Steinberg said, "Dropping the statin program might deny them a chance to improve their lives, even if there were life-threatening risks" (reference 5). Steinberg knew there were "life threatening risks", but the FH patients were never Steinberg and Merck's target market. They completely ignored the contra-indicators in the very patients Steinberg said needed life-saving statins.

Statins had worsened blood cholesterol in homozygous FH patients. To overcome this, Mabuchi gave a combination of Endo's statin plus a second cholesterol-lowering drug to his "heterozygous" FH patients. In this more common form of FH, half of the LDL receptors are normal. The combination worked.

Reduction of Serum Cholesterol in Heterozygous Patients with Familial Hypercholesterolemia — Additive Effects of Compactin and Cholestyramine

Hiroshi Mabuchi, M.D., Takeshi Sakai, M.D., Yasuyuki Sakai, M.D., Akira Yoshimura, M.D., Akira Watanabe, M.D., Takanobu Wakasugi, M.D., Junji Koizumi, M.D., Ryoyu Takeda, M.D.

N Engl J Med 1983; 308:609-613 March 17, 1983

Brown, Goldstein, Bilheimer and Grundy in the West copied Mabuchi's work in the East, using Merck's statin in combination with colestipol (another bile resin drug like cholestyramine):

Mevinolin and colestipol stimulate receptor-mediated clearance of low density lipoprotein from plasma in familial hypercholesterolemia heterozygotes

Proc. Natl. Acad. Sci. USA
Vol. 80, pp. 4124–4128, July 1983
Medical Sciences

DAVID W. BILHEIMER*, SCOTT M. GRUNDY*†, MICHAEL S. BROWN*‡, AND JOSEPH L. GOLDSTEIN*‡

It was that same combination of a bile resin with Baycol that killed people.

The public record shows how easily the statinic scientists were incited by Japan's human experiments with Endo's statin two years before Dallas began testing lovastatin on FH patients (references 33-36). All of these men grew up in an era where "beating the Japs" was as American as apple pie. Add a little dash of, "If we don't do it, they will!" and you have a recipe for poisoning the whole world.

Now that statins are FDA-approved and the number-one-selling prescription drug in the world, Mabuchi has retracted on the safety of statins. In 2007, he published a remarkable paper carefully explaining the problems with statins and blocking CoQ10 and the other isoprenoids from mevalonate:

Current Drug Therapy, 2007, 2, 39-51

Coenzyme Q10 Reduction with Statins: Another Pleiotropic Effect

Hiroshi Mabuchi[1,*], Atsusi Nohara[1], Junji Kobayashi[1], Masa-aki Kawashiri[2] and Akihiro Inazu[3]

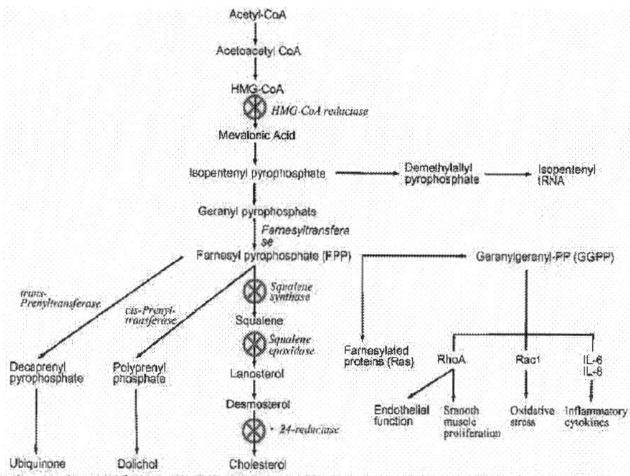

Fig. (1). Mevalonate pathway. Inhibition of HMG-CoA reductase by statins reduces the downstream products of mevalonate.

In this report, Mabuchi describes the development of a new drug that blocks squalene synthase – just two steps above the site of MER/29's action and at a level that does not block cell cycles. Squalene synthase blockers cause an *increase* in isoprenoids such as CoQ10. Mabuchi believes that this may help reverse statin-induced injuries.

In the above report, the phrase "pleiotropic effect" used by Mabuchi refers to the many effects caused by statins ("pleiotropic" means "more than one conversion"). Because statins block the normal function of every cell, including diseased and cancer cells, statins are thought to improve all kinds of illnesses by blocking normal function of diseased cells.

Physicians, uninformed of how statins *really* work, have coined this "phenomenon" the "pleiotropic effect" of statins rather than what it really is: poison from Pandora's box.

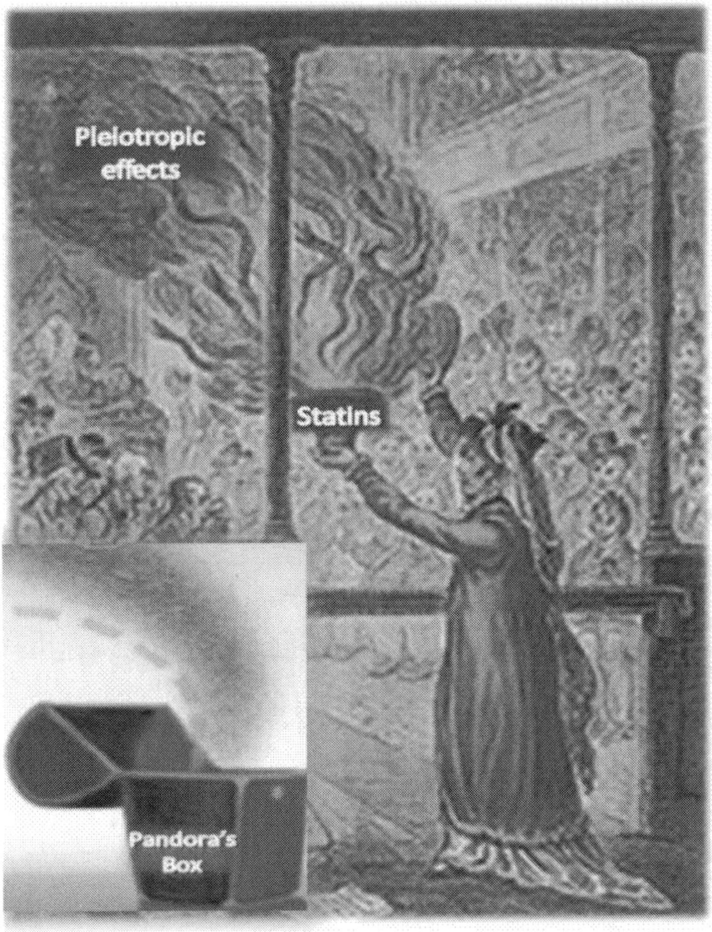

For example, statins suppress cell cycles of white blood cells. Patients with autoimmune diseases sometimes have immune "flare-ups" with elevated white blood cell counts. Because statins block white blood cell turnover, people with autoimmune diseases appear to be doing better because their white blood cell counts are down! Doctors wrongly conclude that statins have done some "good." Similarly, acute infections often elevate white blood cells; since statins block white blood cell cycles, statins "appear" to decrease infections!

Because replication of any type of diseased cell is blocked by statins, the list of the so-called pleiotropic positive effects of statins is ever growing.

Statins block the cell cycle of ***every cell*** in the body, so of course the effects are pleiotropic! And, while undoubtedly there are benefits to be measured by blocking the life cycle of diseased cells, the cost is at doing harm to ***every normal cell*** in the body.

No matter how you look at statins, the benefit-to-risk ratio is dreadful.

PART THREE: STATIN INJURIES

Chapter 23: Statin ADRs

Death, disease, fatigue and mental illness to name a few are the direct effect of statin ingestion. Thanks to Merck's scientists and consultants, there is no diagnosis for statin toxicity. Very little illness is reported as statin related. It comes on slowly in a group that regularly accepts the symptoms as part of aging.

However, a large body of evidence has mounted to prove a significant increase in chronic and deadly diseases among statin users. These are called Adverse Drug Reactions (ADRs). In spite that most of the ADRs are not reported as such, the evidence accumulates.

All cells, and not just liver and intestinal cells as once thought, make cholesterol from mevalonate. Statins first work on intestine and liver cells, eventually this drug passes through the entire body affecting every cell type. Statins even cross the blood-brain barrier and enter the central nervous system where they damage the brain and spinal cord.

Many of the early ADRs are due to intestinal problems and elevated liver enzymes (signaling liver cell damage). Common ADRs also include muscle pain and weakness and nerve/brain-related cognition problems, memory loss, emotional problems, personality changes, tremors, etc.

The web site "AskAPatient.com" provides an open forum for people to report their own ADRs. On a scale of satisfaction from low to high (1 to 5), as of November 2011, the average AskAPatient rating for lovastatin/Mevacor was only 1.6 (99 ratings) and 1.8 for simvastatin/Zocor (822 ratings). Before lovastatin's patent expired, Merck formulated Zocor (simvastatin) by making a chemical alteration to lovastatin.

Here is a small sample of ADRs and general comments posted by Mevacor and Zocor users at AskAPatient.com:

SIDE EFFECT FOR MEVACOR	SEX	AGE	DURATION DOSAGE	DATE ADDED
Sore neck and back, heart racing, left leg/left arm numb, light headed – in a fog all day, dizziness – feel like going to faint, can't concentrate, trouble forming words to speak, abnormal tiredness	M	36	2 months 10 mg 1XD	5/27/11
I started having shortness of breath about the same time as I started Lovastatin...thought it was just the weather but the problem has persisted to the point where I was having chest wall pain	F	69	3 months 10 mg 1XD	5/15/11
Had the sore muscle thing, but not severe. I am experiencing tremors (shaky hands, fingers, facial muscles – a "RARE" side effect of Lovastatin is "tremors". I have a friend who has extreme tremors and takes Lovastatin.	M	74	10 years 10 mg 1XD	3/18/11
At first no side effects, but after 2 weeks SEVERE muscle pain & burning in left shoulder then both shoulders. Couldn't sleep at all, pain felt like a burning sensation, hurt all the time. I had to stop exercising completely as that only aggravated symptoms.	F	46	20 days 10 mg 1XD	1/28/11
I have turned into a cripple. Massive arm pains, shoulder pains, knee pains, back pains. Can't sleep. I used to be very active and healthy. Now I feel like I am awaiting death any day now. Mine went from 220 to 198. I am going off of it tonight and will report back if I regain my life.	M	52	3 years 20 mg 1XD	1/11/11
The drug from hell. I felt like I was 200 years old. I could not move in the mornings I was so stiff. All my joints felt like they were swollen but they weren't. It was absolutely horrible. I took myself off the drugs and told my doctor I would NEVER consider taking a statin again. I would rather chance high cholesterol than feeling like that for the rest of my life.	F	50	60 days 30 mg 1XD	1/1/11
Severe muscle atrophy, pain everywhere, migraines frequent & horrible when I NEVER had them before, neck stiffness, unable to exercise effectively any longer. Have made the decision to go off them. Cholesterol was 204. Dr. said to go on them & it only dropped to 178. Not worth it. I am too young. I had had so many blood tests, MRI & Dr. visits with every specialty imaginable, trying to figure out what is wrong with me. I recently went on vacation & didn't have them & the difference was stunning!	F	32	2.5 years 10 mg 1XD	7/9/10
Left toe pain. At first, I blamed my new shoes. Yesterday, woke up with severe neck pain, stiff neck, soreness. Had a massage today, and some of the stiffness left. Some years ago, I took another statin at higher dose, and had continual muscle and joint pain until I figured out that it was caused by the drug.	M	52	3 months 20 mg 1XD	7/1/10
Thought I had the flu. Nausea, stomach ache, diarrhea, right side of my neck very sore shoulder joints ached constantly, could not sleep. Ached all over. I have never had any major problems with any drugs, but I will never take another statin. There was no warning from the doctor or pharmacist. Wish they could be in my skin tonight.	F	63	3 weeks 20 mg 1XD	3/25/10
Diarrhea, dehydration, stomach pain, muscle pain, cramps in toes and feet, trembling in arms and legs, dry eyes, belching, acid reflux, light headedness, high blood pressure, weakness. My blood pressure has always been 110/70. It went to 180. We were on vacation, got medical help on ship. Stopped taking it and improving. Still have gut pains. Easier to die then live this sick. All interest in life left. And it was my daughter's 40th party and I could not keep food. Change in personality.	F	66	20 days 40 mg 1XD	3/3/10
Hair loss/breakage and painful joints after taking 10 mg for 3 months. Doctor had doubled dose for 3 weeks because there was no improvement in my LDL when lab work was done. My hairdresser asked about new medications when we noticed my hair was breaking off and looked very "dull" not shiny. When I contacted my cardiologist I was told this was a side effect.	F	59	3 months 10 mg 1XD	12/29/07

SIDE EFFECT FOR ZOCOR	SEX	AGE	DURATION DOSAGE	DATE ADDED
Swollen glands, sciatica-like symptoms; excruciating pain on the left side of my body, feet, thigh, buttock and back, headache, depression fatigue, feelings of being very old – which I generally do not have, blurred vision in one eye, stomach upset, severe itching after I stopped taking the medicine. How do I make it stop without taking something else dangerous?	F	69	95 days 40 mg 1XD	6/5/11
Involuntary muscle twitching in both upper and lower extremities (mostly lower), tingling in hands and feet, cramping in legs and feet, muscle aches and random unexplained soreness in left elbow and other joints. Difficulty walking up or down stairs. Severe aggravation of pre-existing arthritic right knee.	M	38	10 months 40 mg 1XD	6/2/11
This is my 3rd, 4th, whatever time trying simvastatin. I have also tried lovastatin and atorvastatin. In all cases the symptoms are: after a week neck stiffens up like glass, is painful and causes headaches (every time I try this it takes less time), slight constipation, have noticed hair loss from top of head, loss of libido, loss of power in weight lifts, loss of endurance, dry eyes, sleep problems, tightness in back with general discomfort, loss of lust for life, my memory gets dull, little foggy headed, skin seems to age. All this because my cholesterol is 244 w/ HDL 65.	M	52	100 days 10 mg 1XD	5/5/11
This was a nightmare! Went into a very deep depression, craving sweets, chips, ice cream, etc., gained 10 lbs in 2 months. Hair loss, fuzzy thinking, plantar fasciitis in the extreme and would not get better no matter what I did. Once I stopped taking this horrible drug, within 7 days I was back and will never go there again!	F	57	3 months 40 mg 1XD	4/3/11
Terrible swelling in hands, went down after I discontinued meds but not totally. Now I have swelling and my fingers freeze up, also tingling and pain. This is still happening after being off the med for a month. Also my hair got very thin, my skin got very dry and had a lot of pain in my sides. This stuff is poison. I hope that my hands have not been ruined for life but it's starting to look that way.	M	42	1 month 40 mg 1XD	2/15/11
Where to begin. I initially had no idea this was causing my problems but as time went on...memory problems, blurred vision, complete muscle weakness, hip and knee joint pain and chest tightness and shortness of breath. I have been tested for MS, had an MRI, cat scan, pulmonary testing, an angiogram with all being OK...I am still addressing the blurred vision and my muscles are getting stronger every day. When I suggested to my Dr. that my symptoms for my heart could also be from the Zocor he said he didn't think so...Is the heart not a muscle??? He did have me go off it because of the muscle weakness. This was an awful drug. I was only on it for 23 days and it messed with my whole body. I am only 52. Be careful.	F	52	23 days 20 mg 1XD	1/31/10
Horrific joint/muscle pain, debilitating lassitude, imbalance, sleep problems burning sensations in legs digestive difficulties; all symptoms confusing to both Drs. Involved in the prescription and follow-up processes. I am still in pain and moderately incapacitated after nearly 5 yrs off this medication and it has aged me dramatically.	M	68	5 years 40 mg 1XD	11/18/1(
Took Baycol for several years back around 2000, then stopped when it was taken off market for causing the unpleasant side effect of death. Started on Zocor...started noticing side effects of erectile dysfunction...stopping again now, don't care what my doc says.	M	46	7 years 40 mg 1XD	7/17/10
Abdominal distress, low back pain, muscle weakness, some memory issues, lack of drive, constant chest pains and arm numbness but all "none cardiac related" hmmm, migraines, lack of libido, and general over all wastefulness. I have this constant feeling of imminent demise...too weak to exercise now so original health condition is worse than if I did nothing. Death does wonders for high pressure issues also!	M	47	4 months 40 mg 1XD	7/14/1(

Working at the same facility as Daniel Steinberg is Beatrice Golomb, MD, PhD of the Statin Effects Study Group at UCSD. She has accumulated a wealth of information on statin ADRs. Notably, she has found physicians often invalidate patients' complaints about statins.

Statin Effects Study

university.of.california.san.diego

Physician Response to Patient Reports of Adverse Drug Effects

Implications For Patient-Targeted Adverse Effect Surveillance

Beatrice A. Golomb,[1,2] John J. McGraw,[1,3] Marcella A. Evans[1] and Joel E. Dimsdale[4]

Golomb

Results: Eighty-seven percent of patients reportedly spoke to their physician about the possible connection between statin use and their symptom. Patients reported that they and not the doctor most commonly initiated the discussion regarding the possible connection of drug to symptom...

Because many statin users are middle age or older, their aches and pains are predictably attributed to the aging process instead of statin injury. The physicians are correct. Because statins block the rejuvenating cell cycle, they accelerate the aging and death process.

Occasionally, a statin-associated ADR is acknowledged by a health provider and reported through the "official" channels via the FDA's Adverse Events Reporting System. Even here, however, many of the ADRs are not made until the condition that prompted the report is grave – such as disability, near-death or death. Merck's Zocor serves as an example.

From late 1997 to April 2010, the consumer, the provider or both had reported over 10,000 Zocor-induced ADRs to the FDA. The connection between injury and statin use is usually not made; these numbers do not reflect the true extent of statin-induced injuries of which one-third caused death, near-death, or disability (source: Adverse Events Reporting System {AERS} - Zocor as Primary Suspect):

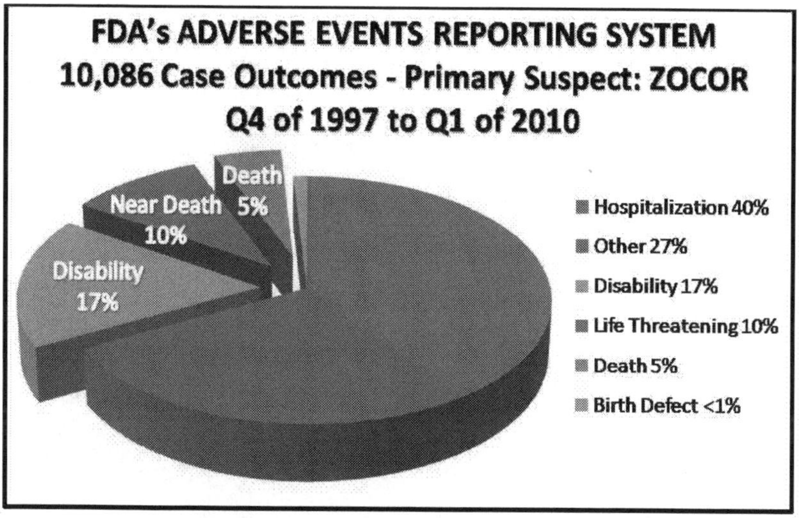

Unlike MER/29 that injured mainly skin and eyes, only 6% of Zocor ADRs have been eye and skin-related. The myriad of complaints is due to statins affecting all organs.

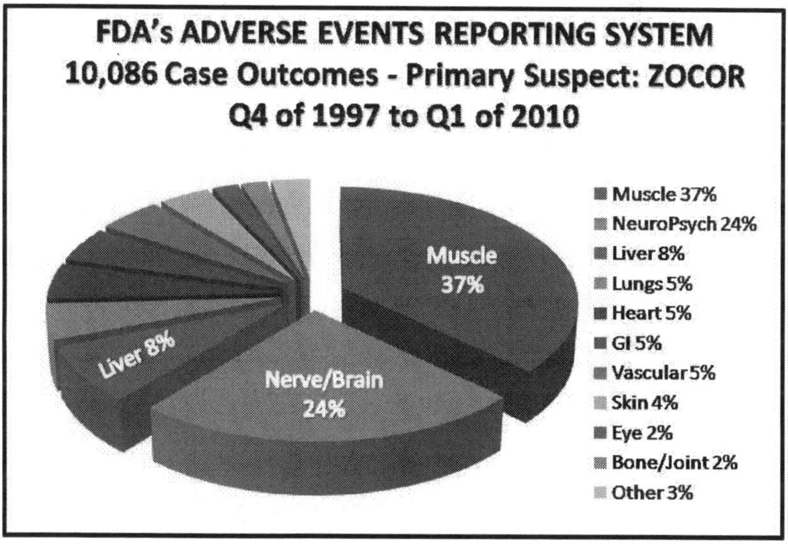

Merck categorizes statin-related injuries as "adverse reactions", not "direct effects" of statin use. This is recorded in consumer and prescriber information sheets:

Merck Sharp & Dohme Corp., a subsidiary of
MERCK & CO., INC.
Whitehouse Station, NJ 08889, USA

HIGHLIGHTS OF PRESCRIBING INFORMATION
These highlights do not include all the information needed to use ZOCOR safely and effectively. See full prescribing information for ZOCOR.

ZOCOR (simvastatin) Tablets
Initial U.S. Approval: 1991

6 ADVERSE REACTIONS

6.1 Clinical Trials Experience

Because clinical studies are conducted under widely varying conditions, adverse reaction rates observed in the clinical studies of a drug cannot be directly compared to rates in the clinical studies of another drug and may not reflect the rates observed in practice.

In the pre-marketing controlled clinical studies and their open extensions (2,423 patients with median duration of follow-up of approximately 18 months), 1.4% of patients were discontinued due to adverse reactions. The most common adverse reactions that led to treatment discontinuation were: gastrointestinal disorders (0.5%), myalgia (0.1%), and arthralgia (0.1%). The most commonly reported adverse reactions (incidence ≥5%) in simvastatin controlled clinical trials were: upper respiratory infections (9.0%), headache (7.4%), abdominal pain (7.3%), constipation (6.6%), and nausea (5.4%).

An adverse reaction is an unintended and unpredictable side effect of a drug due an unknown mechanism. As written in chapter 18, James MacDonald lied and told the FDA that "we clearly do not understand the mechanism" of lovastatin injury. By lying for the FDA record, ***the way was cleared for the direct and diverse negative effects of blocking mevalonate to be called "side effects" or "adverse reactions".***

Statin ADRs are a direct effect of blocking mevalonate; this was clear to Merck. Lovastatin developers knew that mevalonate rescued lab animals from certain injury and/or death, but did not publish this until *after* lovastatin was FDA approved:

Alfred Alberts: "All histopathological and serum biochemical change induced by lovastatin were completely prevented by co-administration of mevalonate...In addition, administration of mevalonate after the onset of lovastatin-induced hepatotoxicity effectively reversed the toxicity despite continued drug treatment" (reference 37).

Alberts

James MacDonald: "As with the effects on the liver described above, supplementation of rabbits with mevalonic acid prevents the nephrotoxicity observed...Similarly, necrosis of gallbladder epithelium was observed in rabbits receiving simvastatin and this change, too, was prevented by mevalonate co-administration (reference 38).

MacDonald

Merck's information sheets, to this day, describe statin injuries as "adverse reactions." To call the effects of blocking mevalonate "adverse reactions" is like choking someone and calling the predictable death by asphyxiation an "adverse reaction." Statin developers *clearly* understood the mechanism of statin-induced injury, and even how to reverse it, ***seven years before FDA's approval***:

Michael Brown (1980): "When HMG CoA reductase is inhibited by compactin, mevalonate formation is blocked and cultured cells die" (reference 39).

Brown

Akira Ando (1980): "At 8 ug/ml of ML236B, cell death was prevented in the CHO-K1 cell line by the addition of mevalonate" (reference 40).

Endo

Again, Merck's MacDonald admitted (after 1987) that it was clear to him from the start of lovastatin development that the direct effects of blocking mevalonate were predictable:

MacDonald

James MacDonald (2004): "As statins inhibit an enzyme that is essential not only for cholesterol biosynthesis but also for the synthesis of several other nonsterol precursors essential for normal cellular function, it was hypothesized early on that some or all of the toxicity seen at high exposure levels in animals could be related to an exaggeration of the desired biochemical effect...In addition to cholesterol, HMG-CoA reductase is responsible for the synthesis of nonsterol intermediates essential for cellular function. Thus it was not surprising when decreased body weights and skeletal malformations were first observed in fetuses of rats and mice given lovastatin during pregnancy" (reference 41).

A revisit of Merck's findings of statin-induced injuries in various animals serves as a basis for the wide array of human responses to statins. Some people fall ill with one dose while others experience no symptoms for years.

In rabbits, baseline levels of reductase are low. When fed statins, reductase did not increase as in other species and they quickly died. Adding cholesterol to the feed accelerated the poisoning effect of statins. The most likely explanation was that cholesterol served to further lower reductase:

Alfred Alberts (1988): "During the preclinical safety assessment of lovastatin, oral doses that were tolerated by dogs, rats and mice were found to be lethal to rabbits...the activity of HMG-CoA reductase in rabbit liver is less than that of other species, which may render the rabbit more susceptible to inhibitors of the enzyme...the administration of cholesterol along with lovastatin may have reduced the stimulus for reductase enzyme induction and accelerated the depletion of non-sterol metabolites" (reference 42).

Alberts

Rabbits make less cholesterol than other animal species; this provides an explanation for the low baseline level of reductase (references 43 and 44). Much of Merck's data on the rapid demise of statin-fed rabbits (and hastened by adding cholesterol to their diets) was left unrecorded. It was reported, only, as a general observation but without any numbers.

Testing that some human genotypes or even races might have similar reactions to statins was neither entertained nor investigated. However, it might explain the twelve deaths in Merck's first human trials.

Endo first tested his statin on rats. The problem with this species was not that they didn't make much cholesterol like rabbits, but that the increase in reductase was so strong that the blocking effect of statins had no effect in lowering cholesterol. These animals did not die as quickly as rabbits:

Akira Ando (1992; 2008): "Unexpectedly the feeding of rats with a diet supplemented with 0.1% mevastatin for 8 days caused no changes in plasma cholesterol levels...even at a dose as high as 500 mg/kg for 5 weeks. Furthermore, mevastatin was ineffective in mice...consistent with our findings, it strongly induced the HMG-CoA reductase of the liver" (references 45-46).

Endo

Like Goldilocks' three tries to find just the right mattress, statins proved "too hard" on rabbits and "too soft" on mice and rats. In what species would statins work "just right?"

The target was FH patients (until Brown suggested the make-believe "sluggish LDL receptors" to the FDA and now statins are good for everyone). To this end, Endo reasoned that the "just right" species would be one with high baseline levels of reductase:

> **Akira Ando (1992):** "We felt that mevastatin should be evaluated more pertinently in animal models comparable to FH in humans, since in patients with FH, regulation of HMG-CoA reductase is partially lost resulting in high reductase activity. At that time, however, such an animal model was not available" (references 47).

Endo

Alas, no such animal existed then or now. Then one of Endo's colleagues offered him some death-row hens. He tried his toxin on them and it worked. After a mere 30 days, he reported his "success" at lowering hen cholesterol without "significantly" decreasing their weight (reference 48).

Like Anitschkow and his rabbits, Endo failed to mention that hens do not die of cardiovascular disease.

Hens were just right and Merck's dogs proved to be just right too although there was a definite connection between the length of time of statin use and blindness in Merck's dogs (reference 49) and cancer in the Sankyo dogs.

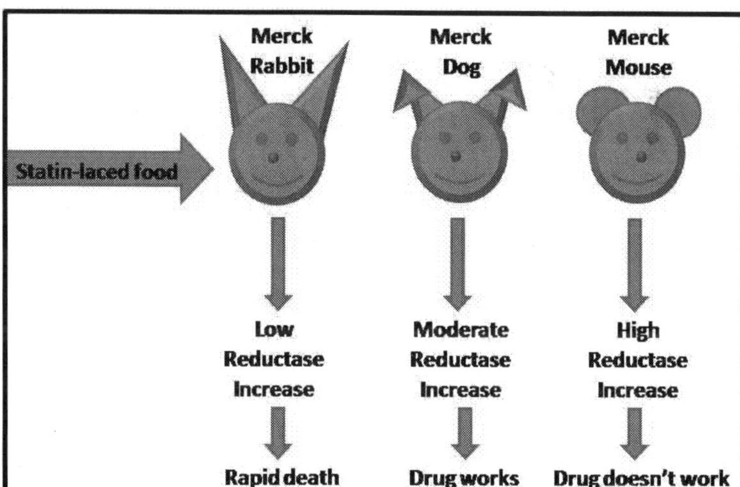

Humans were more like hens and dogs and less like rabbits or rats, or so the reasoning went because statins found their way into our medicine cabinets.

Another grand jury investigation, of the order of MER/29, could sort it all out – only this time the FDA would need to answer a few questions:

1. Dr. Solomon Sobel, you were the director of the Division of Metabolic and Endocrine Drugs in 1987. Did you read Dr. Endo's or Brown and Goldstein's research prior to the lovastatin advisory committee meeting on February 19, 1987? And, is it not true that meeting was held at the NIH, which had a clear agenda to change cholesterol policy?

2. Dr. Sobel, you are a well-educated well-qualified man to have arrived in your position. You did understand that statins caused an increase in reductase, that mevalonate is required for cells to replicate normally and that statins quickly arrested growth and killed human cells due to mevalonate deprivation – did you not?

3. Mr. Short and Drs. Sobel and Fleming, you are the surviving FDA employees to have attended the lovastatin FDA advisory committee meeting. Where was the coffee pot?

The recommended human dose for statins is 1 to 2 milligrams for every kilogram of body weight (1 to 2 mg/kg). In their toxicology reports (references 50 and 51), Merck repeatedly minimized animal deaths and injuries because the dose given statin-injured animals was 30 times or more the human dose.

Animal testing is a complex issue. If an adverse effect is seen in a test animal of any species, the default assumption is that the same effect could be seen in humans. A whole battery of inquiry excludes or includes the same result in humans, beginning with dosages that produce no observable adverse effects. Dosages are then increased to determine a margin of error; 100 times the human dose is often considered a safe margin.

No public record exists that these procedures were followed and documented by Merck. It is much less expensive to skip them or discredit negative results. That leaves the only scientifically valid assumption: that the same results will be seen in humans. It has proven correct. Dismissing side effects due to dosage levels in animals is just another way of lying. Either that, or the entire experimental process is a waste of time.

There is an animal species with an 88-97% genetic similarity to Homo sapiens that very accurately predicts the toxic effects of statins on humans: non-human primates.

Merck's toxicologist James MacDonald told the FDA advisory committee that lovastatin caused "no (negative) effect in the monkey" (reference 52). This claim stands in direct contrast to Glaxo's results from testing their statin on the marmoset:

Human & Experimental Toxicology (1994), **13**, 357–368

Toxicity of a Novel HMG-CoA Reductase Inhibitor in the Common Marmoset (*Callithrix jacchus*)

K. Owen, C.R. Pick, S.E. Libretto and M.J. Adams

Pathology and Toxicology Division, Glaxo Group Research Ltd, Ware, Hertfordshire, SG12 0DP, UK

At doses of 20 mg kg^{-1} day^{-1} or more some animals died or were killed for humane reasons. These animals had shown a range of clinical signs that included loss of weight, impaired balance, loss of muscle tone, unsteady movements, head nodding or shaking, hunched posture and signs of gastrointestinal disturbance. Alveolar capillary congestion and alveolar proteinosis was observed in some of these cases indicating that there may have been impairment of cardiac function.

Glaxo's statin given to primates resulted in weight loss, heart disease, muscle problems, balance difficulty, head shaking and intestinal problems – ***at only ten times the human dose***. The marmoset is one of the most reliable animal models for human toxicity studies.

The marmosets all died or were killed for humane reasons.

After their marmosets were sacrificed, Glaxo discontinued development of their statin.

Chapter 24: Muscle Damage

We all want to be strong and healthy. One of the most discouraging things we experience is becoming weak as we age. No one would take a pill that made him or her weak, at the expense of losing quality of life and becoming an invalid even if it did lengthen life.

As of April 2010, over 10,000 Zocor-induced ADRs had been reported to the FDA; a remarkable 42% of injuries involved skeletal and heart muscle. Also, because nerves innervate muscle, nerve injury and muscle injury are interrelated and together account for 66% of reported injuries.

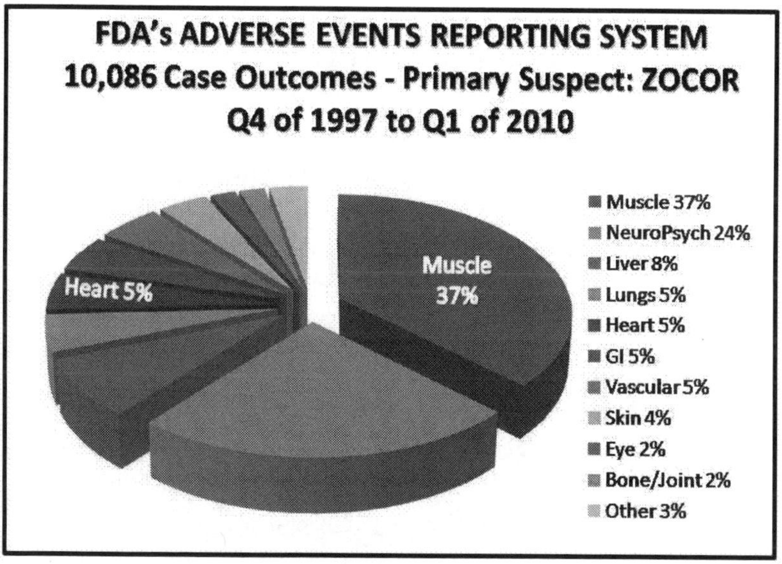

The skeletal muscle injuries were two forms: general myopathy (muscle pain and weakness) and rhabdomyolysis.

In rhabdomyolysis, muscles cells break down and block the kidney. This can result in permanent kidney damage and death from kidney failure.

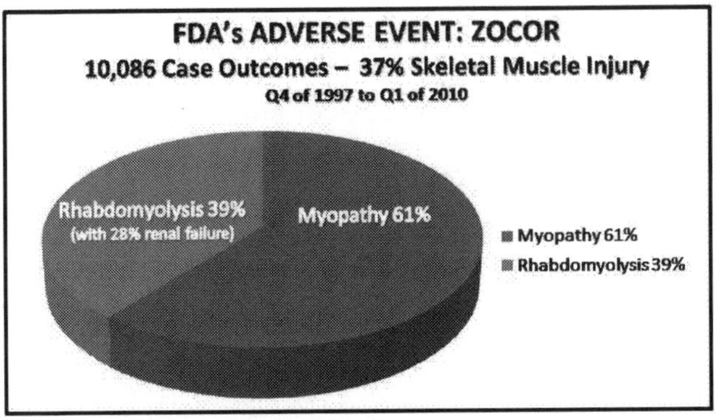

Rhabdomyolysis was the cause of multiple deaths from Bayer's "super powerful" statin Baycol. Ads boasted that Baycol was so potent that one could take it and pull tugboats. Bayer voluntarily

recalled their super-statin after people quickly died from kidney failure after taking Baycol. Injury suits have not been very successful, as the triggering mechanism for rhabdomyolysis has remained undisclosed.

Glaxo discontinued development of their statin after marmosets, given 10 times the human dose for one month, showed shrunken muscle filled with tiny "moth-eaten" holes:

Toxicity of a Novel HMG-CoA Reductase Inhibitor in the Common Marmoset (Callithrix jacchus)
K. Owen, C.R. Pick, S.E. Libretto and M.J. Adams
Hum Exp Toxicol 1994 13: 357
DOI: 10.1177/096032719401300512

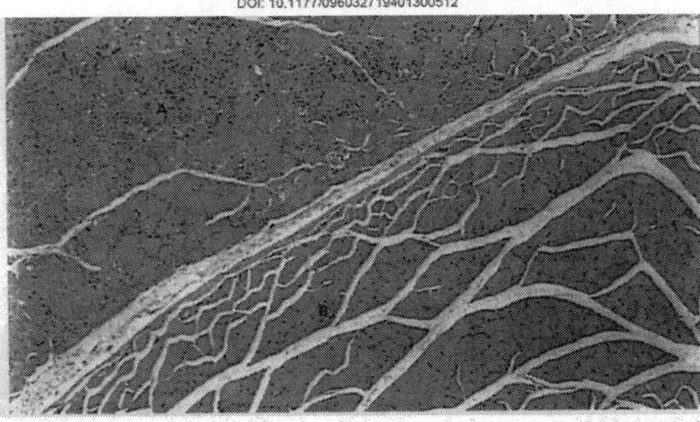

Figure 5 Light photomicrograph of affected (A) and non-affected (B) muscles from a marmoset that had received 20 mg GR95030X kg^{-1} day^{-1} for 32 days. ×125.

Injured muscle cells release a detectable enzyme (abbreviated as CPK) into blood. One point above normal is abnormal, but Merck successfully set the standard for determining muscle cell damage as ten times the upper limit of normal:

Merck Sharp & Dohme Corp., a subsidiary of
MERCK & CO., INC.
Whitehouse Station, NJ 08889, USA

HIGHLIGHTS OF PRESCRIBING INFORMATION
These highlights do not include all the information needed to use ZOCOR safely and effectively. See full prescribing information for ZOCOR.

ZOCOR (simvastatin) Tablets
Initial U.S. Approval: 1991

5 WARNINGS AND PRECAUTIONS

5.1 Myopathy/Rhabdomyolysis

Simvastatin, like other statins, occasionally causes myopathy manifested as muscle pain, tenderness or weakness with creatine kinase (CK) above ten times the upper limit of normal (ULN). Myopathy sometimes takes the form of rhabdomyolysis with or without acute renal failure secondary to myoglobinuria, and rare fatalities have occurred. The risk of myopathy is increased by high levels of statin activity in plasma. Predisposing factors for myopathy include advanced age (≥65 years), uncontrolled hypothyroidism, and renal impairment.

Merck came to this figure and convinced doctors it was a good idea. This has served to lower Merck's reported incidence of myopathy to less than .5% (reference 53) rather than the 10-15% incidence rate that is clinically observed (reference 54).

Merck's definition of "myopathy" as "ten times the upper limit of normal CPK levels" went unchallenged for 22 years, until a 2009 study published in the Canadian Medical Association Journal reported muscle damage in statin users who had normal CPK's. Muscle biopsies were performed on 44 people with statin-associated myopathy. Fifty-seven percent of patients with an abnormal biopsy had a *normal* CPK; only one patient had an abnormal biopsy and an elevated CPK. The severity of muscle damage was not correlated with length of statin therapy.

In this study, significant muscle damage was defined as 2% or more damaged muscle fibers per tissue sample. This was found in 16 of 29 patients with myopathy currently taking statins and 9 of 15 patients with myopathy who had discontinued statins. This disproves Merck's claim that myopathy resolves after statin discontinuation (reference 55). Severity of muscle damage also had no correlation with length of statin use.

Muscle damage appeared as tiny holes located inside muscle cells around tinier T-shaped tubes called T-Tubules (see light-colored "spots" in photo "A" and "G" below). T-tubules are part of the cholesterol-derived muscle cell membrane, which transmits signals for muscle contraction.

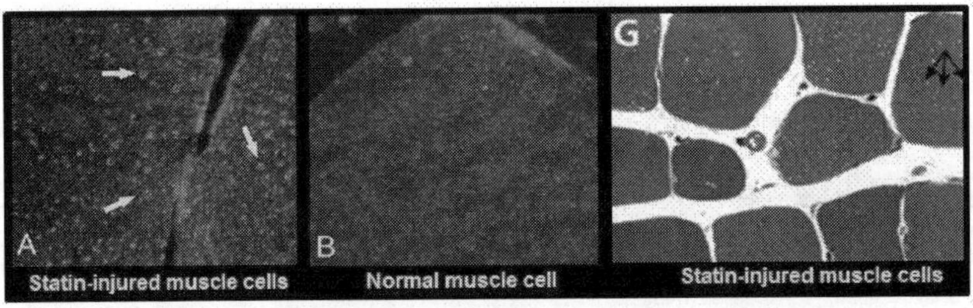

Statin therapy induces ultrastructural damage in skeletal muscle in patients without myalgia

A Draeger,[1]* K Monastyrskaya,[1] M Mohaupt,[2] H Hoppeler,[1] H Savolainen
[1] Institute of Anatomy, University of Bern, Switzerland

Journal of Pathology
J Pathol 2006; 210: 94–102
Published online 23 June 2006 in Wiley InterScience (www.interscience.wiley.com) DOI: 10.1002/path.2018

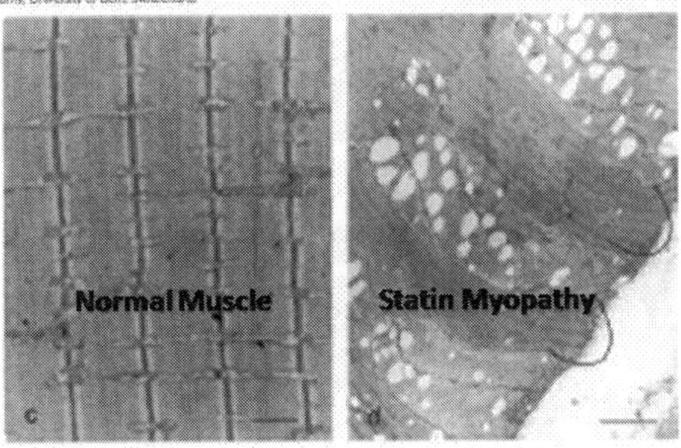

Figure 2. Myofibrillar changes in the skeletal muscle of statin-treated patients. (a–d) Electron micrographs of biopsies derived from two patients (b: patient 8; d: patient 5) and two controls (a, c). Slight Z-line deviations (white arrows in b) constitute an early sign of muscle damage (compare with the straight Z-line in a). The development of contraction bands (brackets in d) is indicative of regional, uncontrolled Ca^{2+} influx. Bars: (a) = 0.5 μm; (b) = 0.4 μm; (c) = 0.8 μm; (d) = 3.5 μm

Lowering cholesterol is not a good idea for anyone who wants intact T-tubules and to pull tugboats. The moth-eaten holes in photo “A” above are similar to the holes in the sarcolemma (T-tubules) found by Glaxo in their marmoset experiment:

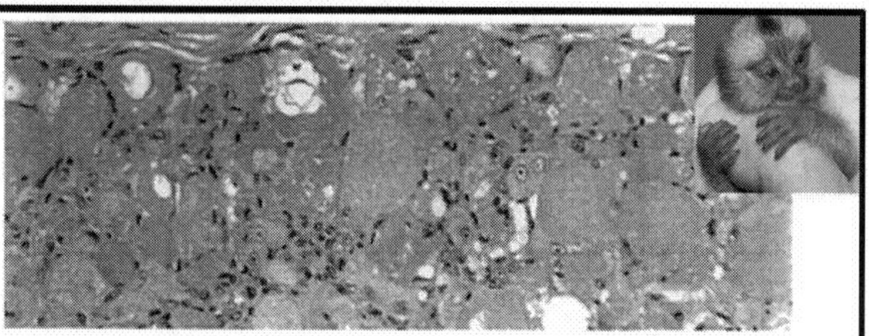

Figure 4 Light photomicrograph of motheaten and shrunken muscle fibres from a marmoset that had received 20 mg GR95030X kg^{-1} day^{-1} for 32 days. ×250.

Parke-Davis attributed muscle cell injury as due to either a decrease in mevalonate-derived CoQ10 or signaling proteins. Merck concluded the same (references 56-57). Skeletal muscle and heart muscle cells have very high demands for ATP – which is blocked by statins. ATP depletion by CoQ10 is a predictable direct effect of statins and not a side effect or adverse drug reaction.

In 1989, Merck was so sure that statin-induced myopathy must have something to do with CoQ10 depletion that Dr. Brown wrote a patent for adding CoQ10 to Merck's statins and correct the design defect. ***He is clear that adding CoQ10 will both prevent myopathy ("precautionary or prophylactic") and cure it ("curative or treatmental").***

United States Patent
Brown

4,933,165
June 12, 1990

Inventors: **Brown; Michael S.** (Dallas, TX)
Assignee: **Merck & Co., Inc.** (Rahway, NJ)
Appl. No.: **07/298,535**
Filed: **January 18, 1989**

Coenzyme Q.sub.10 with HMG-CoA reductase inhibitors

What is claimed is...A method of counteracting HMG-CoA reductase inhibitor-associated skeletal muscle myopathy in a subject in need of such treatment which comprises the adjunct administration of a therapeutically effective amount of an HMG-CoA reductase inhibitor and an effective amount of Coenzyme Q.sub.10 to counteract said myopathy.

In its application to the counteraction of myopathy the present invention is accordingly to be understood as providing for the avoidance of myopathy where this may otherwise occur as well as the amelioration of myopathy. The term counteracting is accordingly to be understood as connecting both a precautionary or prophylactic as well as curative or treatmental function.

Because CoQ10 blockade by statins is a predictable direct effect, the patent author is certain that adding CoQ10 will prevent and reverse myopathy.

In Merck's patent, Brown explains how adding CoQ10 to statins will prevent cardiomyopathy (heart muscle disease) as well as skeletal myopathy. Brown sites Mabuchi who reported in 1981 that lowering LDL with statins by 50% also lowers CoQ10 by 50%. This increases the risk of heart muscle failure in exchange for lowering LDL cholesterol in the blood:

Inventors: Brown; Michael S. (Dallas, TX)
Assignee: Merck & Co., Inc. (Rahway, NJ)
Appl. No.: 07/298,535
Filed: January 18, 1989

BACKGROUND OF THE INVENTION

Coenzyme Q.sub.10 is a redox component in the respiratory chain and is found in all cells having mitochondria. It is thus an essential co-factor in the generation of metabolic energy and is particularly important in muscle function. For example, Folkers et al., Proc. Natl. Acad. Sci., 82: 901 (1985) have measured the levels of Coenzyme Q.sub.10 (CoQ.sub.10) in endomyocardial biopsy samples taken from patients with varying stages of cardiomyopathy. Folkers et al. states that these data show decreasing tissue levels of CoQ.sub.10 with increasing severity of the symptoms of cardiac disease. ...Furthermore high levels of lovastatin can reduce CoQ.sub.10 in the liver (MK-803 NDA report) and reduces LDL-bound CoQ.sub.10 at doses employed in humans [H. Mabuch et al, N. E. J. Med., 478 (Aug. 1981].

In the above patent, Brown also sites a report by Karl Folkers who, in 1985, reported that lovastatin decreases CoQ10 in heart muscle causing a new risk of heart disease (cardiomyopathy):

Karl Folkers (1990): "The clinical use of lovastatin is to reduce a risk of cardiac disease, and if lovastatin were to reduce levels of CoQ_{10}, this reduction would constitute a new risk of cardiac disease, since it is established that CoQ_{10} is indispensable for cardiac function...All data from the three protocols revealed that lovastatin does indeed lower levels of CoQ_{10}" (reference 58).

Merck did not bring the new and improved statin to market.

Chapter 25: Nerve/Brain Damage

Of all the things folks miss, they usually miss their minds the most. Bad joke? Not if you are taking statins. Ask flight surgeon and former astronaut Dr. Duane Graveline who temporarily lost his memory (called global amnesia) after taking statins.

Graveline has categorized thousands of cases of statin injuries that are documented at his web site (SpaceDoc.com) and in his many books on what he calls the "dark side" of statins. He has written extensively on the importance of dolichols for normal brain function. Dolichols are isoprenoids made from the mevalonate pathway and thus blocked by statins.

Of some 10,000 Zocor related ADRs, about 2,400 involve the brain and nerves.

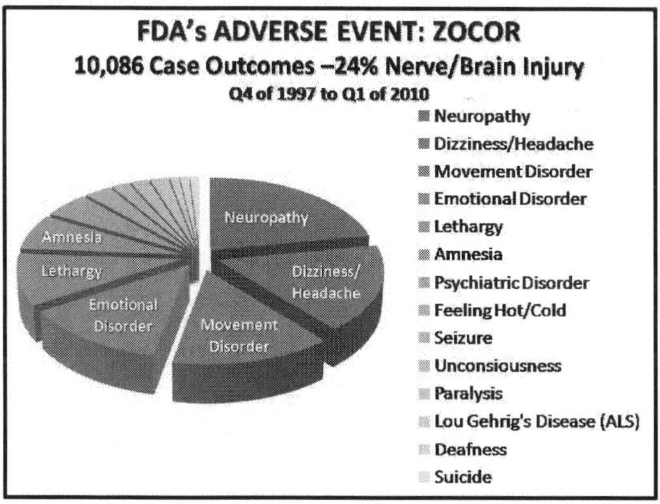

While the greatest percentage of ADRs is muscle-related (42%), what appears to be muscle dysfunction can instead be injury to the nerves that innervate muscles. In this light, nerve-related injury is the largest class of statin-induced injury.

Cholesterol provides structure and a protective barrier to all cell membranes. The central nervous system (brain and spinal cord) makes up 23% of the cholesterol pool (reference 59). This is because half of the brain matter is cholesterol and nerves are surrounded with a protective wrap called “myelin” that is mostly cholesterol. Myelin is essential for the normal "firing" of nerve signals – not unlike the plastic coating over copper wire that insulates so that electricity flows safely through the wire.

Experiments on baby rats with drugs that block the mevalonate pathway demonstrate that interruption of cholesterol metabolism alters normal myelination of nerves outside the central nervous system – called “peripheral nerves”. These are all the nerves that extend throughout the body from the spinal cord. A normal compact nerve-sheath (left below) degenerates into an abnormally loose arrangement (right below).

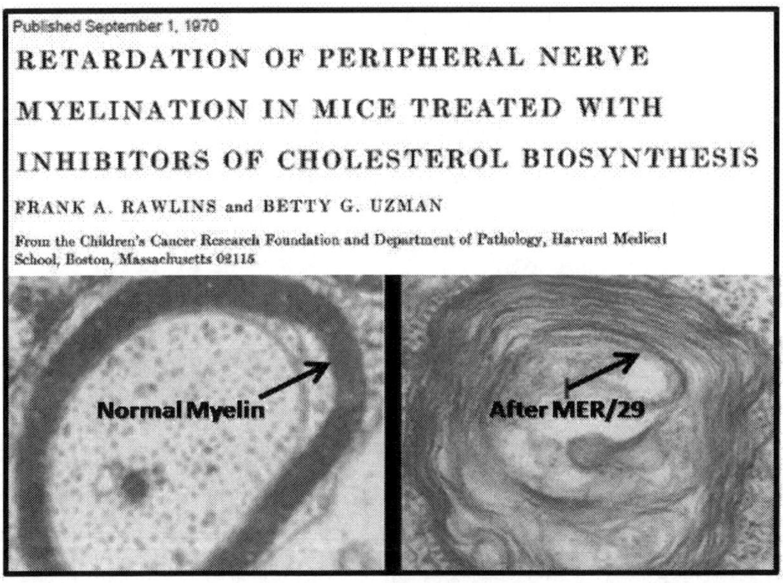
Published September 1, 1970

RETARDATION OF PERIPHERAL NERVE MYELINATION IN MICE TREATED WITH INHIBITORS OF CHOLESTEROL BIOSYNTHESIS

FRANK A. RAWLINS and BETTY G. UZMAN

From the Children's Cancer Research Foundation and Department of Pathology, Harvard Medical School, Boston, Massachusetts 02115

A 1999 study demonstrated that statins kill nerve cells:

Journal of Neurochemistry
Lippincott Williams & Wilkins, Inc., Philadelphia
© 1999 International Society for Neurochemistry

Inhibition of Cholesterol Production but Not of Nonsterol Isoprenoid Products Induces Neuronal Cell Death

Makoto Michikawa and Katsuhiko Yanagisawa

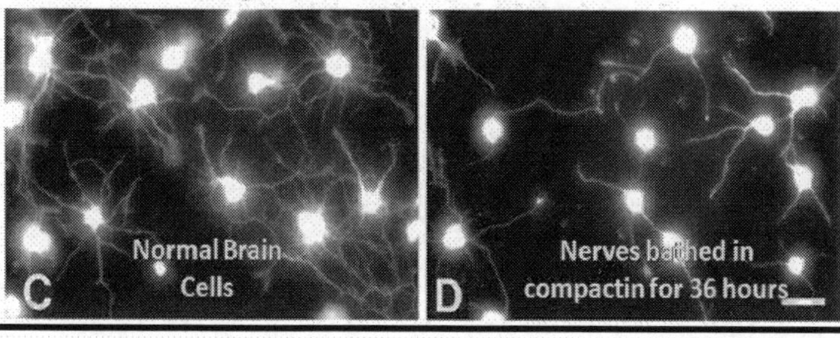

Physicians in Denmark found that people taking statins were more likely to develop peripheral neuropathy – characterized by weakness, tingling and pain in the hands and feet, and difficulty walking. Taking statins for two or more years raised the risk of nerve damage by 26 percent:

Statins and risk of polyneuropathy

NEUROLOGY 2002;58:1333–1337 **A case-control study**

D. Gaist, MD, PhD; U. Jeppesen, MD, PhD; M. Andersen, MD, PhD; L.A. García Rodríguez, MD, MSc; J. Hallas, MD, PhD; and S.H. Sindrup, MD, PhD

For patients treated with statins for 2 or more years the odds ration of definite idiopathic polyneuropathy was 26.4 (7.8 to 45.4). *Conclusions:* Long-term exposure to statins may substantially increase the risk of polyneuropathy.

The Danish study, published in 2002, was not the first to implicate statins in the development of nerve problems. Merck had already discovered the neurotoxic brain-bleeding effects of lovastatin in dogs – but did not publish this until 1988 (reference 60). Photo "B" on the following page is a sample from this report of a dog's brain after 12 days of ingesting lovastatin-laced feed:

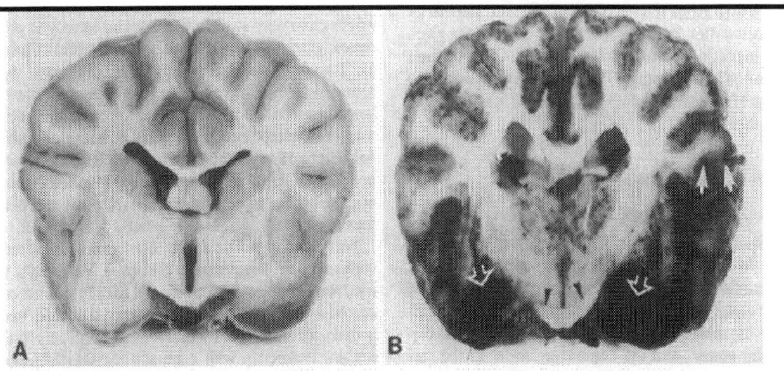

Figure 3—Coronal, 3 to 4 mm slices of perfusion-fixed brain after diaminobenzidine incubation, from dogs injected intravenously with HRP 55 to 65 minutes before anesthesia and perfusion. A—Control. There is no evidence of HRP leakage into neuropil. B—A dog killed with nervous signs after 12 days treatment with 180 mg/kg/day lovastatin, there is locally extensive leakage in the region of the amygdala (open arrows), and multifocal leakage in the cerebral cortex (closed arrows). White matter appears less affected. The optic chiasma and tract is free of extravasated HRP (arrowheads).

Merck's MacDonald and Alberts reported that the toxic effects of lovastatin on nerves and brain tissue also included injury to the optic nerve – the cranial nerve that transmits visual information to the brain (this was less than 100 times the human dose):

American Journal of Pathology, Vol 132, 427-443, Copyright © 1988 by American Society for Investigative Pathology

Brain and optic system pathology in hypocholesterolemic dogs treated with a competitive inhibitor of 3-hydroxy-3-methylglutaryl coenzyme A reductase

PH Berry, JS MacDonald, AW Alberts, S Molon-Noblot, JS Chen, CY Lo, MD Greenspan, H Allen, G Durand-Cavagna and R Jensen
Department of Safety Assessment, Merck Sharp & Dohme-Chibret, Riom, France.

The central nervous system (CNS) of affected dogs exhibited endothelial degeneration and hemorrhagic encephalopathy. Focal extravasation of horseradish peroxidase occurred frequently (6/8) in the retrolaminar optic nerve of asymptomatic or clinically affected dogs given 180 mg/kg/day lovastatin, with endothelial degeneration and discrete optic nerve degenerative lesions interpreted as ischemic.

In Merck's prescribing information sheets for Zocor, on the other hand, the nerve-toxic effects of memory loss and neuropathy (nerve disease) are reported as post-approval "adverse reactions" that were unobserved by Merck prior to FDA approval of Zocor in 1991:

Merck Sharp & Dohme Corp., a subsidiary of
MERCK & CO., INC.
Whitehouse Station, NJ 08889, USA

HIGHLIGHTS OF PRESCRIBING INFORMATION
These highlights do not include all the information needed to use ZOCOR safely and effectively. See full prescribing information for ZOCOR.

ZOCOR (simvastatin) Tablets
Initial U.S. Approval: 1991

6.2 Post-Marketing Experience
Because the below reactions are reported voluntarily from a population of uncertain size, it is generally not possible to reliably estimate their frequency or establish a causal relationship to drug exposure. The following additional adverse reactions have been identified during postapproval use of simvastatin: pruritus, alopecia, a variety of skin changes (e.g., nodules, discoloration, dryness of skin/mucous membranes, changes to hair/nails), dizziness, muscle cramps, myalgia, pancreatitis, memory impairment, paresthesia, peripheral neuropathy, vomiting, anemia, erectile dysfunction, interstitial lung disease, rhabdomyolysis, hepatitis/jaundice, hepatic failure, and depression.

Oh, *really*.

Studies on lowering cholesterol and resulting damage to the myelination process of the optic nerve (leading to blindness) and all nerves (leading to difficulty with hearing, touch, temperature control, balance, etc.) predated Merck's 1988 study on dogs by more than a decade.

Lipids. 1970 Aug;5(8):665-71.
Inhibitors of cholesterol synthesis and myelin formation.
Smith ME, Hasinoff CM.

Lab Invest. 1972 May;26(5):534-9.
Myelin degeneration in sciatic nerve of rats treated with hypocholesteremic drug AY9944.
Suzuki K, De Paul LD.

A Quantitative Electron Microscopic Analysis of Myelination in the Optic Nerve of Suckling Rats Treated with an Inhibitor of Cholesterol Biosynthesis
Frank A. Rawlins*
Z. Zellforsch. 140, 9—23 (1973)

Merck referenced these studies in their work.

There are yet some physicians who question the "evidence-based medicine" that is largely based on drug-company study results. One is Dr. Uffe Ravnskov, spokesman for the International Network of Cholesterol Skeptics.

Dr. Ravnskov began studying cholesterol in 1989 when Sweden launched an anti-cholesterol campaign, four years after America's NCEP. He discovered that drug trials involving statins produced negligible absolute reductions in heart disease rates and that lowering cholesterol increased the overall death rate from other causes.

If you find yourself losing your mind, first check your medicine cabinet.

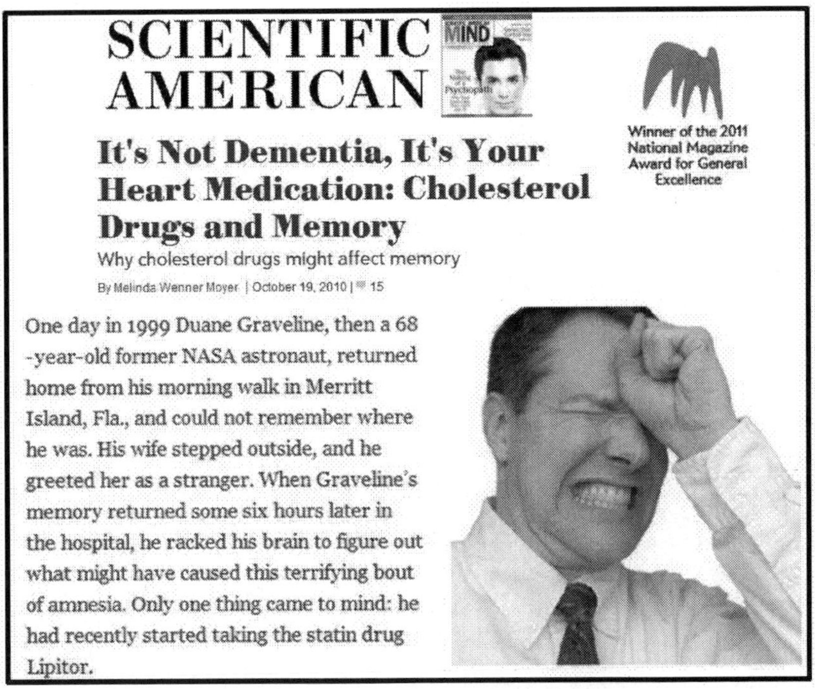

SCIENTIFIC AMERICAN

Winner of the 2011 National Magazine Award for General Excellence

It's Not Dementia, It's Your Heart Medication: Cholesterol Drugs and Memory

Why cholesterol drugs might affect memory

By Melinda Wenner Moyer | October 19, 2010 | 15

One day in 1999 Duane Graveline, then a 68-year-old former NASA astronaut, returned home from his morning walk in Merritt Island, Fla., and could not remember where he was. His wife stepped outside, and he greeted her as a stranger. When Graveline's memory returned some six hours later in the hospital, he racked his brain to figure out what might have caused this terrifying bout of amnesia. Only one thing came to mind: he had recently started taking the statin drug Lipitor.

Chapter 26: Liver Damage

Some people like liver. They eat it but do not want anything eating theirs.

Eight percent of all reported Zocor injuries are due to liver damage. Liver injury is a predictable direct effect of statins and not a side effect or adverse drug reaction.

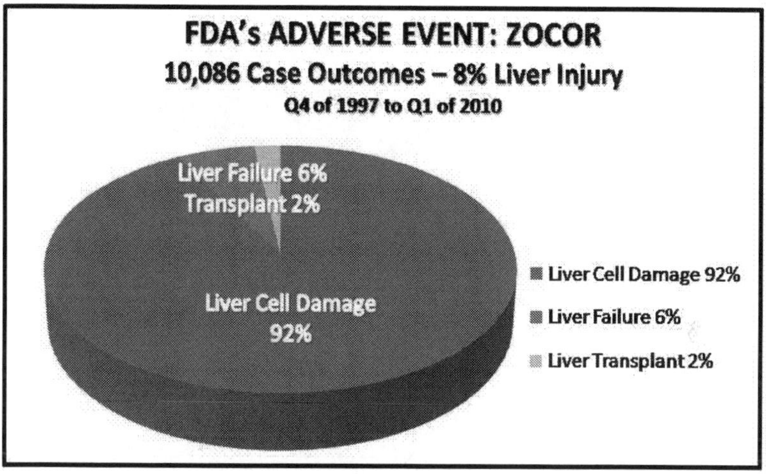

From the small intestines, statins are absorbed into the blood and pass through the liver. While all organs make cholesterol, the liver makes the most to make bile. Bile digests fat and is recycled to the liver.

That makes the liver the "target organ" of statins.

By blocking reductase, liver cells receive a false message that mevalonate levels are "low" and reflexively produce more reductase. Elevated reductase stimulates the liver cells to make more LDL receptors that attract LDL cholesterol from the dense blood tributaries that flow through the liver. LDL cholesterol is then used by liver cells for making bile that is stored in the gallbladder for release into the small intestine when needed for fat digestion.

Injured liver cells release detectable enzymes ("transaminases") into the blood. Those enzymes can be measured and those measurements are used to detect liver injury or demise.

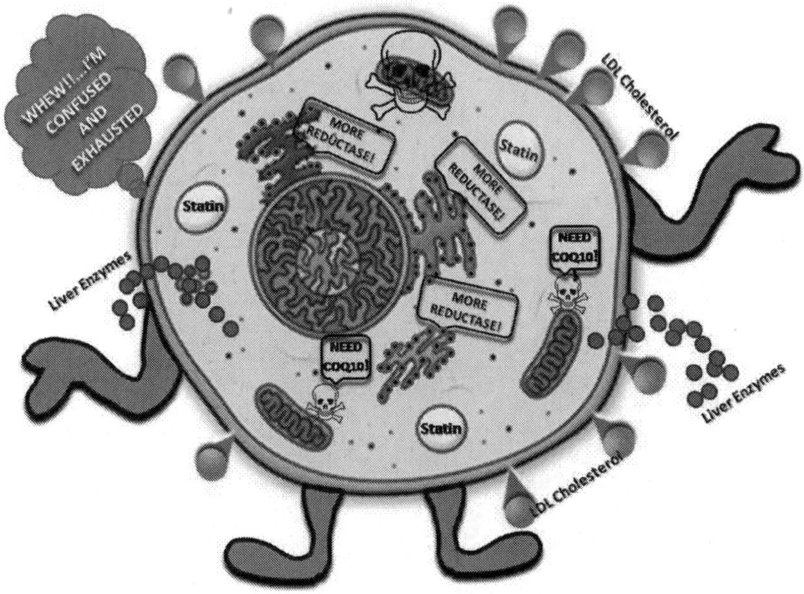

One point above normal is abnormal, but Merck successfully set the standard for liver cell injury or death as *three times* the upper limit of normal on two consecutive tests. Having raised this standard for statin-induced liver damage has lowered Merck's reported incidence of liver damage to less than 2% (in their prescribing information sheets).

Jonathan Tobert also prepared a patent for Merck. This time, to prevent liver damage, he again added CoQ10 to Merck's statins. In so doing, Merck hoped to correct the design defect of the drug. Because CoQ10 blockade by statins is a predictable result and not an adverse drug reaction, this patent demonstrates clear foreknowledge by Merck that CoQ10 depletion by statins was damaging to the liver and is a direct effect. Merck believed that CoQ10 supplements would both prevent and cure liver damage by their statins:

United States Patent **4,929,437**
Tobert **May 29, 1990**

Coenzyme Q.sub.10 with HMG-CoA reductase inhibitors

Inventors: **Tobert; Jonathan A.** (Maplewood, NJ)
Assignee: **Merck & Co., Inc.** (Rahway, NJ)
Appl. No.: **07/305,140**
Filed: **February 2, 1989**

In its application to the counteraction of liver damage and, in particular, elevated transaminase levels, the present invention is accordingly to be understood as providing for the avoidance of liver damage and elevated transaminase levels where this may otherwise occur as well as the amelioration of said damage and elevated transaminase. The term counteracting is accordingly to be understood as connecting both a precautionary or prophylactic as well as curative or treatmental function.

In Merck's prescribing information sheets, the "4S" study is referenced as the prime study that established lovastatin's liver injury rate as less than 2%. The same Jonathan Tobert who directed Merck's 4S study, and who claimed in patent 4,929,437 that CoQ10 would entirely prevent and cure liver injury, also omitted CoQ10 supplementation in 4S and every subsequent Merck clinical study.

Merck's patent contradicts Tobert's report to the FDA that Merck had no idea what caused elevated liver enzymes with their statins:

> **"We do not know the mechanism of these idiosyncratic increases in transaminases" (Jonathan Tobert to the FDA Advisory Committee on Lovastatin, February 19, 1987, transcript page 156).**

Blocking CoQ10 with a toxin and then adding CoQ10 back to the pill is like stabbing someone with a knife and then handing them a suture kit.

Every human cell, except red blood cells and fat cells, contains up to thousands of tiny energy-making batteries called mitochondria. The number of these in any cell depends on the energy needs of a cell. A skin cell, for example, has tens of them whereas a heart cell can have thousands of them. It is inside these peanut-shaped pools of water-like matrix that energy is made from hydrogen broken down from food.

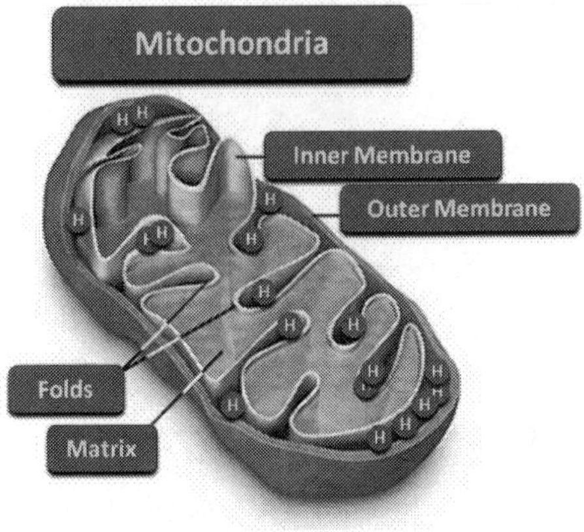

Mitochondria look like pools with a double-liner (inner and outer membranes). These peanut-shaped pools are batteries that accumulate hydrogen in the space between the membranes. As hydrogen builds up under "pressure", it flows into the matrix – and it is this movement of hydrogen that makes energy for every cell to perform its various functions (such as making cholesterol or contracting heart muscle).

This process is similar to how water is used to make electricity. In a hydroelectric dam, flowing water spins turbines that make electricity. In mitochondria, dammed-up hydrogen atoms flow to make energy.

The process is called aerobic metabolism and it cannot occur without oxygen. The reason we breathe oxygen is so metabolism within cells can occur. Without cellular metabolism, we die.

Death by asphyxiation can occur at the cellular level by choking metabolism. This is called "chemical asphyxiation". Poisons or drugs that block the process of making the hydrogen energy dam can be fatal.

Arsenic, cyanide and carbon monoxide all block the movement of hydrogen into the hydrogen energy dam by blocking one of the protein-based "cytochromes" that keep aerobic metabolism functioning. CoQ10 is just as vital as cytochromes for all of this to work.

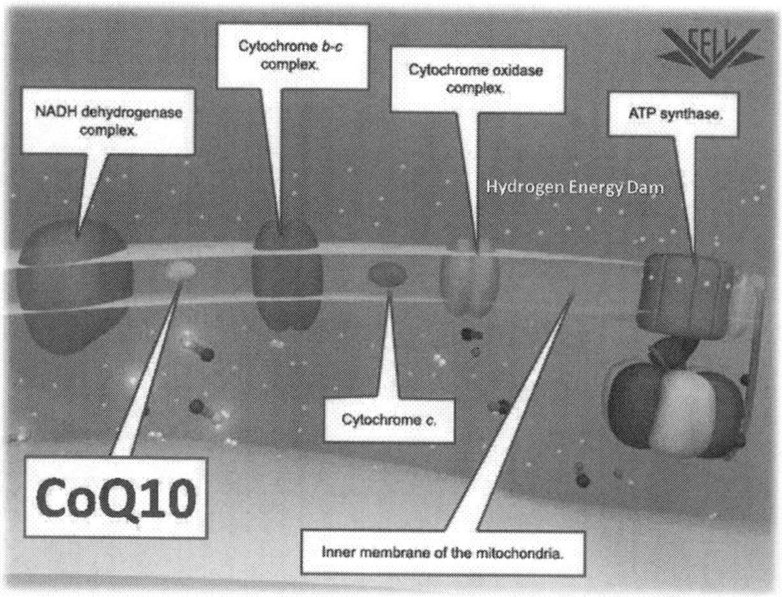

By restricting CoQ10 production by blocking mevalonate, cellular energy is hindered or stopped.

The cells most negatively affected by blocked CoQ10 synthesis are the ones that have the highest energy demand: heart cells, skeletal muscle cells, brain cells, nerve cells, liver cells, lung cells and pancreas cells.

CoQ10 is a nutrient and physicians receive little to no training in nutrition. As a result, they do not understand the importance of CoQ10 and how its production or depletion is a matter of cell life or death. Uninformed of the dangers involved in blocking cellular metabolism, some think it wise to advise, "Take one statin twice daily with 100 mg of CoQ10."

Good advice and blocking the mevalonate pathway do not mix, no matter what is added back to the mix.

Chapter 27: Lung Damage

Nothing is as frightening as not being able to breathe. Just thinking about it makes our hearts race. As of 2010, over 500 Zocor-induced lung-related ADRs have been reported to the FDA. Most of these complaints are for "difficulty breathing".

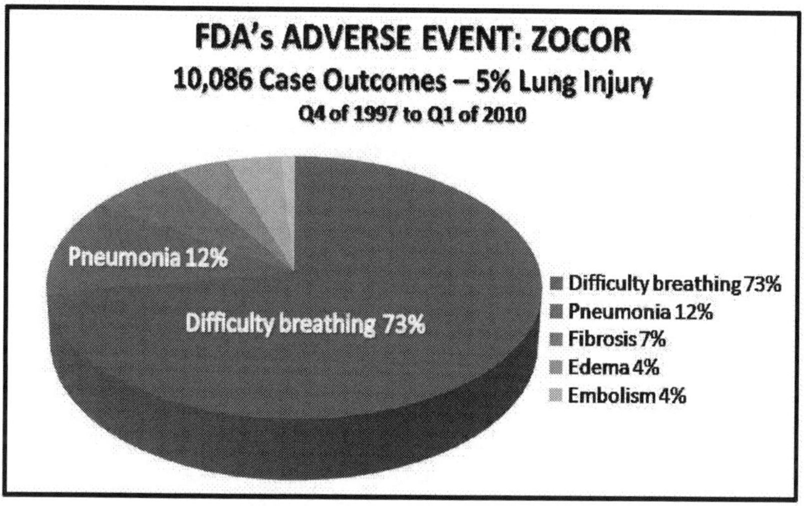

The symptom of "difficulty breathing" (73% of the above ADRs) can be a sign of lung fibrosis or interstitial lung disease (ILD) where the lungs no longer easily expand. On x-ray, ILD is more difficult to diagnose than edema (fluid in the lungs) and pneumonia. Complications with ILD, nevertheless, can also cause edema, pneumonia and fibrosis. Therefore, all of the above ADRs may be interrelated.

Physicians at a lung clinic in Australia began to notice an increase in ILD among patients taking a statin alone or with other drugs known to not cause lung problems. A common complaint was difficulty breathing and a dry cough. Seven of these cases were reported. Treatment for six of these seven patients included discontinuing statins; one died and five slowly improved without complete health restored. The patient whose statin was not stopped died of cardiac failure:

mja.com.au | The Medical Journal of Australia

Notable cases

Tim Walker, Joe McCaffery and Chris Steinfort

Potential link between HMG-CoA reductase inhibitor (statin) use and interstitial lung disease

Patient	Sex, age	Presentation	Medications at presentation	Treatment	Outcome
1	F, 78	Progressive dyspnoea, dry cough	Atorvastatin (10 mg, 1 year), fosinopril, sertraline	Colchicine, atorvastatin withdrawn	Slow progression; lung function deteriorated but clinical condition stable, little dyspnoea on 3-year follow-up
2	M, 78	Progressive dyspnoea (3 weeks), no cough or fever	Pravastatin (40 mg, 10 years), aspirin, frusemide, isosorbide mononitrate, perindopril, sertraline	Prednisolone (50 mg), pravastatin withdrawn	Progression, discharged with home oxygen, died 18 months later (respiratory failure)
3	F, 74	Cough and fever (3 days) (consistent with pneumonia) on background of worsening exertional dyspnoea	Simvastatin (10 mg for 2 years, then 20 mg for 1 year), aspirin, thyroxine, frusemide, diltiazem, nicorandil, long-acting nitrates	Prednisolone (50 mg), simvastatin withdrawn	Gradual reduction in infiltrative change on imaging, lung function stable at 9-month follow-up
4	M, 83	Progressive dyspnoea (6 months)	Pravastatin (40 mg, 1 year), aspirin, digoxin, frusemide, ramipril, ranitidine	Prednisolone (40 mg), azathioprine, pravastatin withdrawn	Slow progression
5	F, 67	Chronic mild dyspnoea (9 months), dry cough (6 months)	Simvastatin (40 mg, 5 years), aspirin	Prednisolone (25 mg, reduced to 10 mg after 3 months), simvastatin withdrawn	Marked improvement (TLCO: 51% after 1 month, then 65% after 1 year)
6	M, 68	Progressive dyspnoea and hypoxia	Simvastatin (10 mg, 2 years), atenolol, candesartan, esomeprazole, frusemide, warfarin	Prednisolone (37.5 mg), azathioprine, simvastatin continued	Progressive cardiac failure, died 9 months after presentation
7	M, 64	Progressive dyspnoea, dry cough	Atorvastatin (20 mg for 3 years, then 40 mg for 2 years), fosinopril	Prednisolone (initially 50 mg, then 10 mg maintenance), atorvastatin withdrawn	Slight initial improvement (TLCO: 52% at 2-month follow-up), then stable disease

A biopsy from patient six (above) showed an infiltration of white blood cells into the lungs, collapsed air sacs (alveoli) and thickened air sac walls. This makes it hard to breathe:

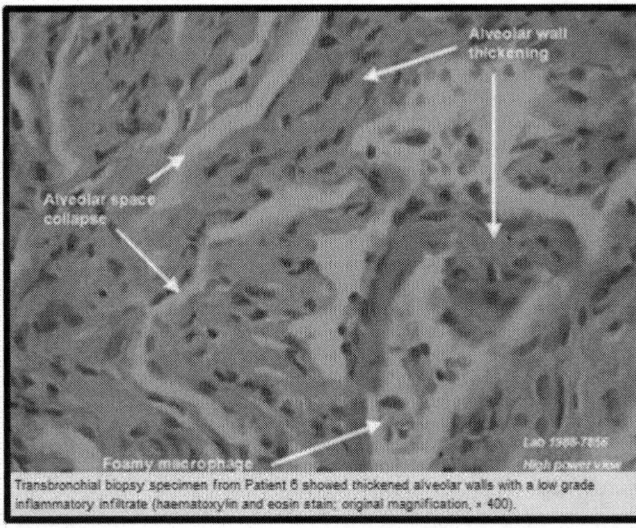

Transbronchial biopsy specimen from Patient 6 showed thickened alveolar walls with a low grade inflammatory infiltrate (haematoxylin and eosin stain; original magnification, × 400).

MER/29 also caused pulmonary fibrosis due to lipid deposits in the lungs. This was also seen with the diet drug chlorphentermine. Sample (1) shows that the lung sacs are filled with foamy-appearing white blood cells (as in patient 6 on page 260). A blow-up of one white blood cell (2) shows it is filled with lipid deposits.

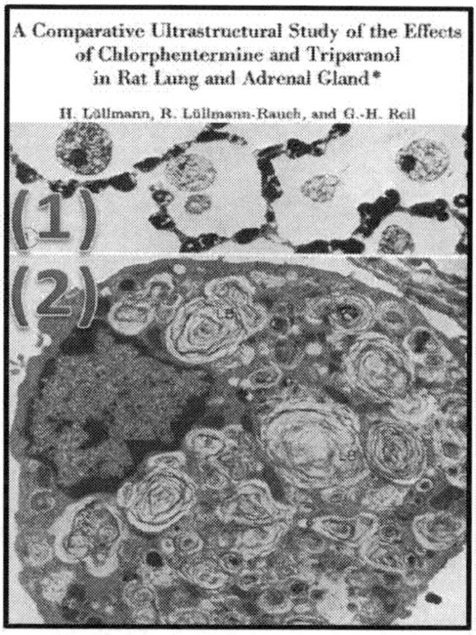

Build-up of lipids inside lung cells, called "hyperlipidosis", gives the lungs a "ground glass" appearance and makes it difficult to breathe. This has also been reported with statins like Zocor:

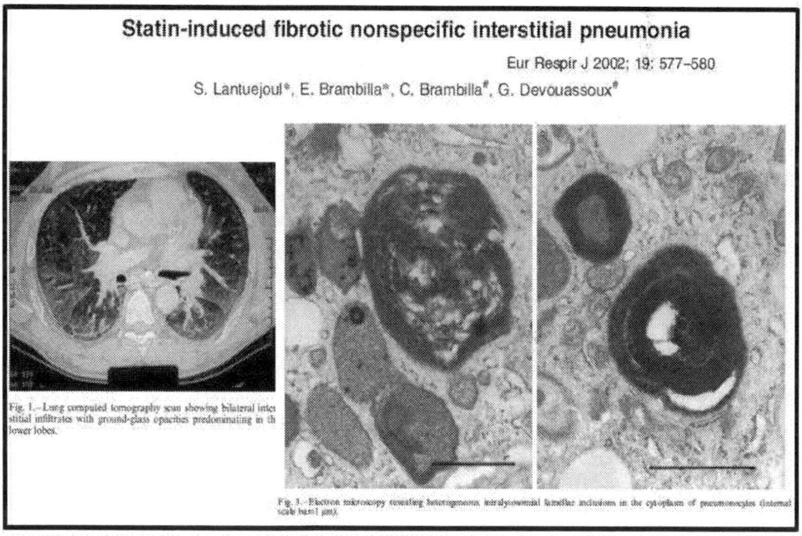

Whatever the exact mechanism proves to be for statin-induced lung damage, the stats are in and scientists have begun to gather the data and connect the dots. For example, a notable number of cases of pulmonary fibrosis associated with statin use have been reported to the WHO international pharmaco-vigilance system:

PULMONARY FIBROSIS REPORTED WITH STATINS

A. Kiuru[1], Q-Y Yue[2], R.H. Meyboom[1, 3]

1. Signal Detection and Analysis, Uppsala Monitoring Centre, UPPSALA, Sweden. 2. The Medical Products Agency, UPPSALA, Sweden.
3. Division of Pharmacoepidemiology and Pharmacotherapy, Utrecht University, UTRECHT, Netherlands

Results

Vigibase contains 59 reports (see table 1) on the preferred term PULMONARY FIBROSIS (total number: 3742) for different statins, reported from nine countries.

Table 1. Cases of pulmonary fibrosis reported with statins in Vigibase.

Drug	Total No. reports - any ADR	Total No. reports - of combination	No. of reporting countries	Fatal outcome
ATORVASTATIN	19464	12	6	1
CERIVASTATIN	14031	4	3	0
LOVASTATIN	12906	6	2	0
PRAVASTATIN	8459	12	4	0
ROSUVASTATIN	5270	2	2	0
SIMVASTATIN	22790	23	6	2
Total		59	9	3

Four of the reports (two cases each of cerivastatin and simvastatin) were removed from this assessment due to suspicion of duplication. In the 55 reports assessed, the time to onset was inconclusive or not stated in the majority of the reports (see table 2). Patient demographics can be seen in figure 1.

An independent search through the FDA's AERs also unmasked a pattern of statin-induced ILD/fibrosis. This report concluded that, while the exact mechanism of statin-caused lung damage remains unknown, ILD is likely a "class effect" of statins.

CHEST PAPERS IN PRESS

Statins and Interstitial Lung Disease: A Systematic Review of the Literature and of FDA Adverse Event Reports

Antonio B Fernández, Richard H Karas, Alawi A Alsheikh-Ali and Paul D Thompson

Chest; Prepublished online August 8, 2008;

Results: The literature search using Pub Med yielded 8 articles describing a total of 14 case reports of ILD in association with statin use. The FDA–AER system database contained 162 cases of reported statin-induced ILD, as of June 2007. For every 10,000 reports of a statin-associated adverse event, approximately 1 to 40 reports were for an ILD.

Conclusions: Statin-induced interstitial lung disease is a possible newly recognized side effect of statin therapy. The mechanism of lung injury is not defined. The current review provides novel information from the FDA-AER that supports a possible, although unusual, pulmonary class effect of statins.

Chapter 28: Birth Defects

We want babies, healthy babies. Nothing could be more reprehensible than knowingly selling a product that can hurt our babies.

Siperstein, Brown, Goldstein, Endo and others have proved that statins block cell cycles. This being so, it is right that the FDA has given statins a pregnancy category of "X" (risks involved in use of the drug by pregnant women clearly outweigh potential benefits).

On the other hand, the NCEP expert panel and the American Heart Association make no specific recommendations regarding precautions with statin use for women of childbearing age. The American College of Obstetrics and Gynecologists makes no distinction regarding statin use recommendations for women aged 20 to 45 years. The U.S. Preventive Services Task Force makes no recommendations whatsoever on treatment with statins (references 61-64).

All of the statin prescribing information sheets likewise skirts any clear warning on the danger of blocking the mevalonate pathway and cell replication in fetal development. No need for any "me-too" statin manufacturer to wake up any sleeping giants already lulled to sleep by Merck.

Nowhere is it indisputably clear to prescribers and consumers that women should avoid statin use before or during pregnancy. Nowhere is there a clear trumpet sounding that blocking the cell cycle and baby making do not mix.

Merck has performed its investigation and boldly declare that their statins do not cause a "notable increase" (again, whatever *that* means) in the risk of birth defects and that pregnant women should only take drugs when the benefits outweigh the risks – in a context that could be readily misunderstood by the reader to include statin use. Merck also attributes some negative retrospective cohort data on statin-caused birth defects to "reporting bias":

> **Pregnancy outcomes after maternal exposure to simvastatin and lovastatin.**
>
> **Authors**
>
> Pollack PS, Shields KE, Burnett DM, et al.
>
> **Institution**
>
> Merck & Co., Inc. Research Laboratories, West Point, Pennsylvania 19486-0004, USA.
>
> **CONCLUSIONS**
>
> Although the number of reports was relatively small, there was no evidence of a notable increase in congenital anomalies in women exposed to simvastatin or lovastatin versus the general population. Greater reporting of congenital abnormalities in the retrospective cohort is not unexpected and may reflect a reporting bias. Drugs should be used during pregnancy only if the benefits outweigh the risks. Simvastatin and lovastatin remain contraindicated during pregnancy.

The last sentence above, "simvastatin and lovastatin remain contraindicated during pregnancy", implies that perhaps they should *not* be contraindicated. This has been a sore spot for Merck after multiple failed attempts to convince the FDA that their statins are safe for over-the-counter (OTC) use. In 2007, Merck licensed the U.S. rights to OTC lovastatin to GlaxoSmithKline (GSK).

GSK hasn't given up yet, and in the meanwhile, Zocor has been long approved for OTC use in the U.K.

Dr. Allen A. Mitchell is a leader in the field of drug-related birth defects. He has co-authored over 70 studies sponsored by the Slone Epidemiology Center at Boston University. This includes a 2008 study on statin-associated birth defects.

> **Maternal exposure to statins and risk for birth defects: A case-series approach**[†‡§¶]
>
> Emily E. Petersen[1,2], Allen A. Mitchell[3], John C. Carey[4], Martha M. Werler[3], Carol Louik[3], Sonja A. Rasmussen[1,*]
>
> Article first published online: 15 SEP 2008
>
> DOI: 10.1002/ajmg.a.32493
>
> Copyright © 2008 Wiley-Liss, Inc.
>
> Issue
>
> 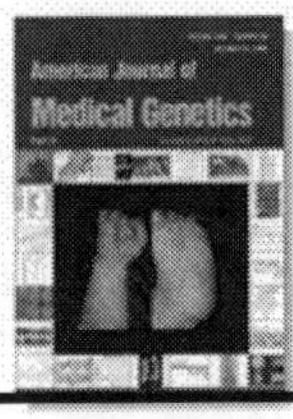
>
>
> American Journal of Medical Genetics Part A
>
> Volume 146A, Issue 20, pages 2701–2705, 15 October 2008

Following completion of this incriminating report, Dr. Mitchell was approached by Merck and then served as a consultant in a Merck assessment of statin safety in pregnancy. This transaction was disclosed in the fine print.

In the FDA's AERs from 1997 to 2010 with Zocor as the sole suspect, 92 cases of term-birth defects were reported. ***It is remarkable that even one uninformed physician or consumer even made the connection of mevalonate blockade and birth defects*** – never mind drug-induced abortions due to defects.

Life begins with one sperm cell and one egg cell that combine to make a new cell with 23 chromosome pairs. That cell then rapidly divides innumerable times to make an embryo. Depriving these cells of mevalonate is a predictable disaster in the making:

Proc. Natl. Acad. Sci. USA
Vol. 82, pp. 3257–3261, May 1985
Cell Biology

Defective macromolecule biosynthesis and cell-cycle progression in a mammalian cell starved for mevalonate

(restriction point)

MICHAEL SINENSKY AND JUDITH LOGEL

Eleanor Roosevelt Institute for Cancer Research, 4200 East Ninth Avenue, Box B129, Denver, CO 80262

LOVASTATIN INDUCES MITOTIC ABNORMALITIES IN VARIOUS CELL LINES

Jan Lamprecht[a], Cezary Wójcik[a, †], Marek Jakóbisiak[b], Micheal Stoehr[a], Dieter Schrorter[a], Neidhard Paweletz[a]

Cell Biology International
Volume 23, Issue 1, January 1999, Pages 51-60

After 24–48 h incubation...of cells in the presence of 1.0–60.0 μ lovastatin, diverse mitotic perturbations have been observed. The most noteworthy phenomena recorded were prometaphase retardation and chromosome lagging during metaphase and anaphase. After the recovery in lovastatin-free media, the cells continued mitosis without any disturbances. Mevalonic acid prevented the effects of lovastatin. We conclude that the effects were specific for lovastatin-induced inhibition of mevalonic acid synthesis.

The connection, however, was clear to Merck from the start and even anticipated in their animal experiments:

The Toxicology of HMG—CoA Reductase Inhibitors: Prediction of Human Risk
James S. MacDonald and Margaretann M. Halleck
Toxicol Pathol 2004 32: 26

Fetal Effects: A priori, it would seem logical that the developing fetus might be particularly sensitive to the pharmacological effect of statins. Cholesterol plays a central role in biosynthesis of hormones and is an essential lipid in cellular membranes. In addition to cholesterol, HMG-CoA reductase is responsible for the synthesis of nonsterol intermediates essential for cellular function (Figure 1). Thus, it was not surprising when decreased body weights and skeletal malformations were first observed in fetuses of rats and mice given lovastatin during pregnancy (MacDonald et al., 1988).

Merck's information sheets, on the other hand, do not warn about the statin-blocked isoprenoids required for DNA and cell replication; only cholesterol (and cholesterol derivatives) are mentioned. Merck is even so bold as to claim that there is no evidence that Zocor causes birth defects:

Merck Sharp & Dohme Corp., a subsidiary of
MERCK & CO., INC.
Whitehouse Station, NJ 08889, USA

ZOCOR (simvastatin) Tablets

Women who are pregnant or may become pregnant. Serum cholesterol and triglycerides increase during normal pregnancy, and cholesterol or cholesterol derivatives are essential for fetal development. Because HMG-CoA reductase inhibitors (statins) decrease cholesterol synthesis and possibly the synthesis of other biologically active substances derived from cholesterol, ZOCOR may cause fetal harm when administered to a pregnant woman. Atherosclerosis is a chronic process and the discontinuation of lipid-lowering drugs during pregnancy should have little impact on the outcome of long-term therapy of primary hypercholesterolemia. There are no adequate and well-controlled studies of use with ZOCOR during pregnancy; however, in rare reports congenital anomalies were observed following intrauterine exposure to statins. In rat and rabbit animal reproduction studies, simvastatin revealed no evidence of teratogenicity. **ZOCOR should be administered to women of childbearing age only when such patients are highly unlikely to conceive.** If the patient becomes pregnant while taking this drug, ZOCOR should be discontinued immediately and the patient should be apprised of the potential hazard to the fetus *[see Use in Specific Populations (8.1)]*.

This contrasts with Merck's MacDonald who reported that due to birth defects seen in animals given lovastatin that *all* statins are to be considered teratogenic (whether ever observed or not). Zocor is the same as lovastatin with a synthetic modification and lovastatin causes birth defects. Connect the dots because Merck won't.

The Toxicology of HMG—CoA Reductase Inhibitors: Prediction of Human Risk
James S. MacDonald and Margaretann M. Halleck
Toxicol Pathol 2004 32: 26

Given the fetal findings with lovastatin and fluvastatin, all HMG-CoA reductase inhibitors were considered teratogenic and, in the USA, are currently classified as pregnancy category X.

Zocor has also been shown to have deleterious effects on the placenta, contributing to birth defects and spontaneous abortion:

Simvastatin has deleterious effects on human first trimester placental explants

Human Reproduction Vol.20, No.10 pp. 2866–2872, 2005

I.Kenis[1], S.Tartakover-Matalon[1,4], N.Cherepnin[2], L.Drucker[1], A.Fishman[3], M.Pomeranz[1] and M.Lishner[1,4]

[1]Oncogenetic Laboratory, Department of Internal Medicine 'A', [2]Department of Internal Medicine 'F' and [3]Department of Obstetrics & Gynecology, Sapir Medical Center, Kfar-Saba and [4]Sackler Faculty of Medicine, Tel Aviv University, Tel Aviv, Israel

In 2004, two scientists (Muenke and Edison) reviewed 52 term cases of first-trimester statin exposure that were reported to the FDA from 1987 to 2001. ***Forty-two percent had serious structural defects at birth including:***

- 3 severe cases of central nervous system defects
- 2 cases of holoprosencephaly (undivided brain)
- 1 case of hydrocephalus (water-filled brain)
- 3 cases of a missing limb
- 2 cases of vertebral, cardiac, tracheal, esophageal, renal and limb defects (VACTERL)

Central Nervous System and Limb Anomalies in Case Reports of First-Trimester Statin Exposure

N Engl J Med 2004; 350:1579-1582 | April 8, 2004

Among these cases, there were 20 reports of malformation, including 5 severe defects of the central nervous system (2 of which were holoprosencephaly) and 5 unilateral limb deficiencies; one patient had both of these malformations. The two simvastatin-exposed cases of limb deficiency were complex lower-limb anomalies including both long-bone shortening and aplasia or hypoplasia of the foot structures. The infant in one of these cases and a lovastatin-exposed infant also had rare forms of the VACTERL association (i.e., three or more of the following findings: vertebral, anal, cardiac, tracheal, esophageal, renal, and limb defects).

TABLE 1

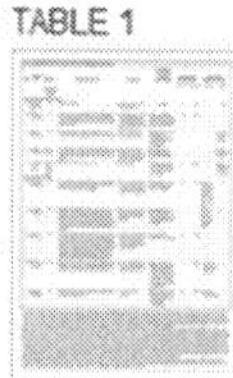

Congenital Anomalies Associated with First-Trimester Statin Exposure.

Similar limb defects and even holoprosencephaly were reported as early as 1964 (Roux) in animals fed MER/29 and other cholesterol inhibitors such as AY9944.

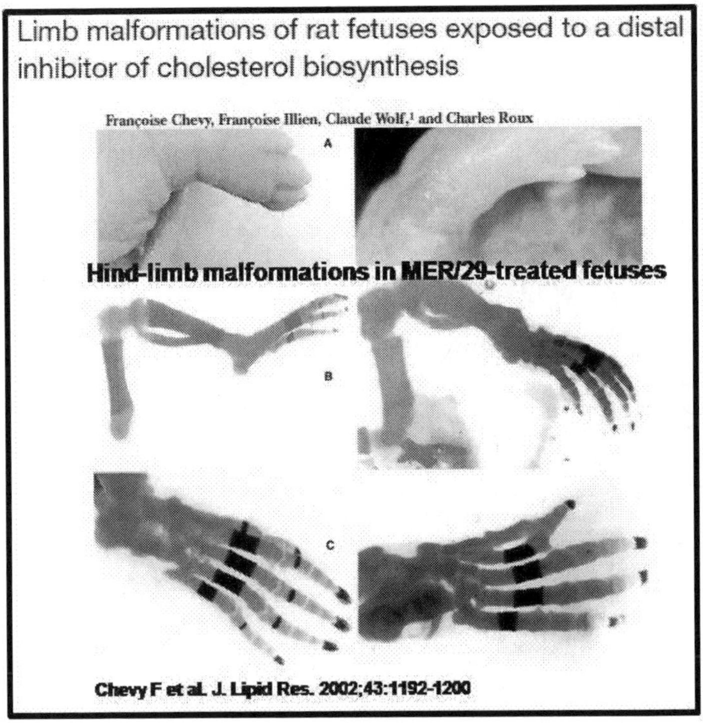

All of this horror is nothing new. The folks who made MER/29 also gave us thalidomide (chronicled by Judge Fine).

Chapter 29: Eye, Skin and Hair Damage

We spend billions on skin and hair treatments that promise to make us look younger and healthier. We wear safety glasses to protect our eyes and require auto manufacturers to install shatterproof windshields. If you take statins long enough, you might save all that money and not need a car. If you take statins long enough, you risk premature aging, hair loss and blindness.

Like the cholesterol-rich myelin that ensures normal operation of nerves and brain matter, the skin, hair and lens of the eye are cholesterol-rich. Cholesterol in the skin and hair provides a water-impermeable barrier; cholesterol in the lens of the eye provides a cement-like lubricating matrix for aligning lens molecules such as lipid-bound proteins.

From 1997 to 2010, over 1,300 Zocor injury cases involving the eye, skin and/or hair had been reported to the FDA:

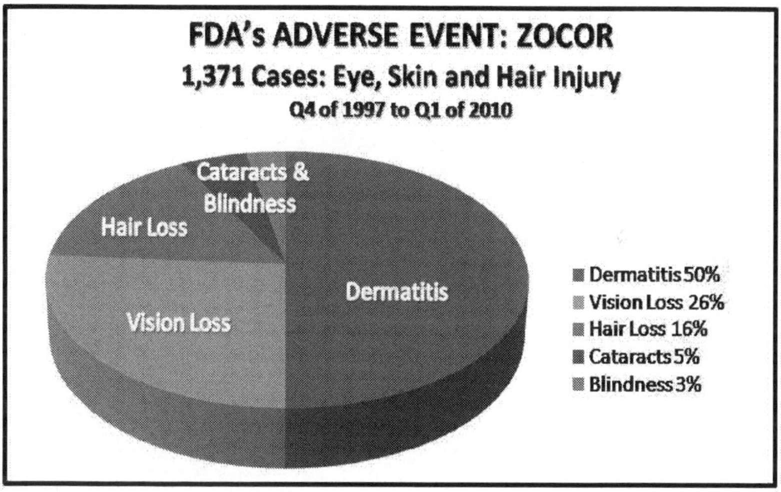

Some of the statin-related injuries to the eye, skin and hair are similar to MER/29 injuries that were attributed, at least in part, to loss of cholesterol in the cells of these tissues. Many of the injury claimants who suffered vision loss or blindness from cataracts also had skin and hair changes. In most cases, the skin and hair returned to normal after stopping MER/29, but the damage to the lens more often than not worsened over time. For example, a 23-year-old medical student who participated in a MER/29 drug trial lost hair within weeks but did not develop cataracts until six months after discontinuing the drug:

CATARACTS PRODUCED BY TRIPARANOL
(MER/29)

BY *Thomas J. Kirby*, M.D.

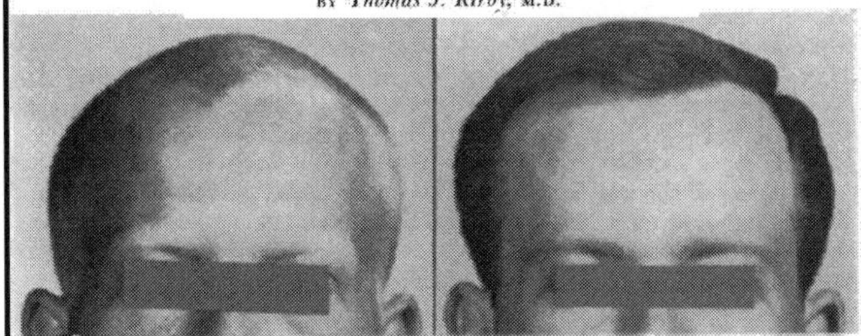

FIGURE 5. CASE 4.

Appearance of 23-year-old medical student who was a normal control in a clinical investigation of triparanol. *Left*, note loss of color of hair and eyebrows. *Right*, shows return of normal color of hair 8 months after drug was stopped and 2 months before cataracts developed.

TR. AM. OPHTH. SOC., vol. 65, 1967

In another case, cataracts began eight months after stopping the drug after hair and skin changes had normalized:

CATARACTS PRODUCED BY TRIPARANOL
(MER/29)

BY *Thomas J. Kirby*, M.D.

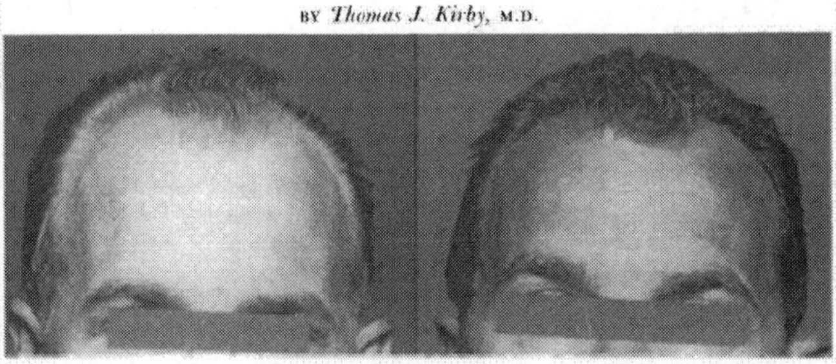

FIGURE 1. CASE 1.

Left, one month after triparanol therapy was discontinued because of loss of hair and ichthyosis. Note gray color at hairline and temples and thinness of forelock in mid-forehead. *Right*, seven months after triparanol therapy was discontinued. Natural color has returned and hair is thicker. Cataracts developed 1 month later.

TR. AM. OPHTH. SOC., vol. 65, 1967

In 1965, the courts began to debate whether cataracts, skin changes and hair loss were all due to MER/29:

Toole v. Richardson-Merrell Inc. / Civ. No. 23181. First Dist., Div. Three / June 12, 1967 Plaintiff developed cataracts in both eyes, hair loss over his entire body and dry, red and inflamed skin from taking MER/29.
Fleishman v. Richardson-Merrell Inc. / N.J. Appellate Court/ Jan. 23, 1967 Plaintiff developed "permanent eye damage" from taking MER/29.
Roginsky v. Richardson-Merrell Inc. / U.S. Appellate Court 2nd Circuit / Jan. 4, 1967 Plaintiff developed cataracts, scaling rash and hair loss from taking MER/29.
Ostopowitz v. Richardson-Merrell Inc. / N.Y.L.J./ Jan. 11, 1967 Plaintiff developed cataracts from taking MER/29.
Golden v. Richardson-Merrell Inc. / Civ. No. 5992, W.D.Wash. / April 7, 1966 Plaintiff developed cataracts, scaling rash and hair loss from taking MER/29.
Cudmore v. Richardson-Merrell Inc. / Appelate 5th District Dallas / Dec. 17, 1965 Plaintiff developed cataracts, flaking of skin and hair loss from taking MER/29.

In *Toole v. Richardson-Merrell*, the California Court of Appeals upheld that Richardson-Merrell was liable for punitive damages. The jury awarded Toole $500,000 in damages and the trial judge reduced it to $250,000. The court of appeals upheld the punitive award, and stated that the acts of the MER/29 manufacturer were performed without regard to injurious consequences.

The most common diagnosis for the MER/29-related skin diseases was "ichthyosis" (thin, dry, itchy and scaly skin). This same diagnosis was ascribed to statin-associated skin disease within the first year statins were stocked on the shelves (1987):

ARCHIVES OF
DERMATOLOGY

HOME | CURRENT ISSUE | PAST ISSUES | TOPIC COLLECTIONS | CME | PHYSICIAN JOBS | SUBMIT | SUBSCRIBE

Vol. 123 No. 11, November 1987

36TH ANNUAL SYMPOSIUM ON THE BIOLOGY OF SKIN

Ichthyosis Induced by Cholesterol-Lowering Drugs

Implications for Epidermal Cholesterol Homeostasis

Mary L. Williams, MD; Kenneth R. Feingold, MD; Gerhard Grubauer, MD; Peter M. Elias, MD

Arch Dermatol. 1987;123(11):1535-1538.

At the website forum "AskAPatient.com", many of the hair, skin and vision problems that consumers attribute to statins mirror the MER/29-related complaints recorded in public records:

AskAPatient.com / Dec. 29, 2007 / Lovastatin Complaint
Hair loss/breakage and painful joints after taking 10 mg of lovastastin for 3 months...my hairdresser asked about new medications when we noticed my hair was breaking off and looked very "dull" not shiny. When I contact my cardiologist I was told this was a side effect.
AskAPatient.com / May 16, 2011 / Zocor complaint
Loss of strength in hands, headache's, blurred vision, some fatigue and more hair loss
AskAPatient.com / March 9, 2011 / Zocor Complaint
Hair loss, severe abdominal pain/cramps/tenderness, gas uncomfortable & irregular bowl problems, acne, headaches, vision blurriness, sinus irritation, insomnia, decreased energy, muscle tightness, general crabbiness, mental fogginess
AskAPatient.com / March 4, 2011 / Zocor Complaint
Within the last year have noticed a 10 lb weight gain, tired all the time, hair loss, skin problems, mood swings
AskAPatient.com/ Feb. 19, 2011 / Zocor Complaint
Hair loss, severely chapped lips, dry skin, dry eyes, loss of libido, memory loss, elevated blood sugar.
AskAPatient.com/ Feb. 18, 2011 / Zocor Complaint
Rashes, loss of appetite, muscle spasms, heart palpitations and heart skipping beats.

In 2010, researchers from the U.K. examined data on more than two million statin-users aged 35 to 74. More than 70 percent were taking Zocor. For every 37 women treated with a statin for five years, only one woman would be free of cardiovascular disease (CVD). On the other hand, for every 33 women treated with a statin for five years, one would end up with cataracts – demonstrating that ***the risk of incurring cataracts with statin use was greater than the decreased risk of CVD.***

Similarly, over a five-year period, 33 men would have to be treated with a statin for one man to be free of CVD. Out of 52 men treated with a statin for five years, one man would have cataracts.

Those statistics are not very impressive to say the very least.

Individualising the risks of statins in men and women in England and Wales: population-based cohort study

Julia Hippisley-Cox, Carol Coupland

Accepted 30 March 2010

Table 7 Numbers needed to harm (NNH) or numbers needed to treat (NNT) and numbers of extra or prevented cases, for each outcome over 5 years in patients aged 35–74 free of cardiovascular disease at baseline with QRISK2 score of 20%+ (table reproduced from the BMJ)

	NNH or NNT (95% CI)
Potential benefits in women	
Cardiovascular disease	−37 (−64 to −27)
Cataract	33 (28 to 38)
Potential benefits in men	
Cardiovascular disease	−33 (−57 to −24)
Cataract	52 (44 to 63)

What *is* known is that cholesterol and lipid-bound proteins are vital components of the lens of the eye and are typically reduced in cataracts.

Tobert has a knack for accentuating the positive and dismissing the negative. In a 1987 report, he admitted that cataracts had been observed by physicians in an early clinical trial, but discredited the findings as likely due to bias by the examiners after receiving news that cataracts had been found in Merck's experimental dogs. He further dismissed any cataracts in the same study as due to subjective error by the examiners.

Having made reference to the MER/29 cataracts in the same paper and discrediting those too, Tobert's so-called science is inexcusably unconscionable, especially when cast in the wake of the MER/29 disaster.

> **New developments in lipid-lowering therapy: the role of inhibitors of hydroxymethylglutaryl-coenzyme A reductase**
>
> JA Tobert
>
> treatment with lovastatin. In one early study in 101 patients,[14] an increase in the prevalence of lens opacities was reported; however, this experience is atypical and is probably the result of bias induced by the finding of cataracts in dogs, which were discovered after almost all patients in this study had had their baseline examinations, but before the majority had had their posttreatment examination. (It is well known that the detection of small lens opacities is subjective and depends, for example, on the time the examiner spends and the degree of pupillary dilatation achieved.) Thus it is likely that many, if not all, of the so-called new opacities reported in this study were merely small preexisting opacities missed at baseline.

The MER/29 grand jury discovered that Merrell Company had withheld information from the FDA regarding cataracts in rats. According to Tobert, Merck never saw cataracts in any of their rats or mice:

> **New developments in lipid-lowering therapy: the role of inhibitors of hydroxymethylglutaryl-coenzyme A reductase**
>
> JA Tobert
>
> In dogs, lovastatin produces posterior and anterior subcapsular cataracts in about 10% of treated animals, albeit at doses at least 50 times the maximum therapeutic dose. This phenomenon was not noted in rats or mice.*
>
> *MacDonald JS: Personal communication.

There is an explanation for how Tobert was able to make the above claim. Apparently, it can be very difficult to reproduce cataracts in rats with cholesterol-blocking drugs like MER/29 because the rats die from the drug before cataracts are formed.

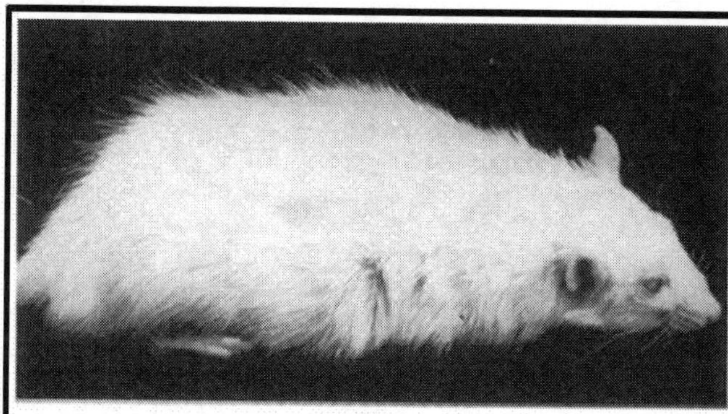

FIGURE 6

The only surviving Sprague-Dawley rat of the pilot studies, 5 weeks after cataracts developed and drug was stopped. Fur is returning to normal and rat is gaining weight but cataracts remain dense.

Apparently, the production of triparanol cataracts in white rats can be difficult and frustrating. With the Sprague-Dawley strain, cataracts could be produced in weanling rats with a dose of 0.05 per cent of body weight given daily for 8 to 9 weeks, but only 5 of 40 rats survived this program long enough to show cataracts. It was decided to use a different strain of rats and to vary the dosage weekly in order to keep as many animals alive as possible until a greater number could produce cataracts.

A dead rat (or no rat) leaves no cataract tracks. And so it is, without batting an eye, the following boldfaced announcement was made to the FDA regarding statins and cataracts in rats or mice:

> **"This phenomenon did not occur in rats or mice" (Jonathan Tobert to the FDA Advisory Committee on Lovastatin, February 19, 1987, transcript page 157).**

Since we can assume that if rat and mice studies had been performed with favorable results, Tobert and Merck would have eagerly shared those details with the FDA. That makes Tobert's side step even more reprehensible.

With Merck's lovastatin, the FDA approval committee was so full of pro-statin NIH and Merck scientists that only one short question was asked about MER/29. The meeting may as well have been held at Merck headquarters in New Jersey rather than the NIH in Bethesda, Maryland.

The deck was clearly stacked from the start.

PART FOUR: 20/20 HINDSIGHT

Chapter 30: Cholesterol – Friend or Foe?

The people who have vilified cholesterol have the most to gain financially by convincing you and me that we would live longer if only our livers made less "bad" cholesterol. So-called evidence-based medicine points to cholesterol as the cause of heart and vascular disease, because, after all, diseased blood vessels become clogged up with oxidized LDL cholesterol. If there's less LDL cholesterol, then there should be less CVD.

Well, at least that's the theory – the lipid theory. The scientific community rightfully threw the lipid theory in the trash around 1960. It was resuscitated by Steinberg, Merck and Sankyo, regardless its being faulty, to sell statins.

Cholesterol is essential to life. Yet because it shows up in clogged arteries, blaming cholesterol for heart attacks is like blaming the fire department for water damage for extinguishing a fire that the homeowner started in the first place. That's because, in large part thanks to the exhaustive work of Linus Pauling and Matthias Rath, cardiovascular disease is more sensibly explained as an antioxidant deficiency – more specifically, a vitamin C deficiency.

Vitamin C is one of the most powerful antioxidants and it serves to keep other antioxidants such as glutathione recharged and recycled. Vitamin C is also required for cells to make collagen. Collagen the glue that connects cells, tissues and joints together. Collagen, which also lines arteries and keeps them smooth and supple, is damaged in CVD.

Collagen literally makes glue, and specialty glues are still made today by boiling collagen from animal skin, blood vessels, bones and tendons. Collagen keeps blood vessels pliable and strong. Signs of collagen deficiency (vitamin C deficiency) surface as if the sufferer is becoming "unglued": weakening of blood vessels (vascular disease), bleeding gums, easy bruising, nose bleeds,

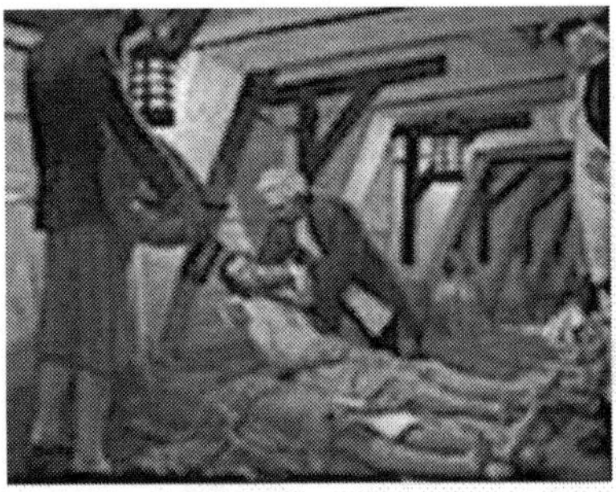

skin sores and, eventually, death by cardiovascular collapse. Another name for collagen deficiency is “scurvy”, which was once the scourge of sailors who ate vitamin C-deficient foods of mostly preserved meats and grains.

Long-term human studies have repeatedly demonstrated that vitamin C and healthy cholesterol levels also go hand-in-hand (references 65-67). Linus Pauling predicted that the constant mechanical pumping of the heart stresses the collagen in blood vessels of the heart; if cells are deficient in vitamin C to replace the worn-out collagen, cholesterol is instead mobilized to fill in the weak spots. He demonstrated that ample vitamin C to make collagen lowers cholesterol and can even reverse cardiovascular disease. In this light, cholesterol-blocking drugs based on the lipid theory make little sense, if indeed elevated “bad” cholesterol is simply an indicator that the body is trying to do the next-best job of holding cells together.

Chlorinated tap water kills fish and other aquatic organisms. Vitamin C, due to its potent antioxidant properties, neutralizes chlorine in water and makes it safe for use in aquariums.

People in developed countries drink the same water that kills fish. CVD rates are rising in developing countries.

Merck told the lovastatin advisory committee that their toxicity data was compromised because lovastatin was given to animals with normal cholesterol levels. There is a reason why Merck didn't simply give animals a “bad” high-cholesterol diet and reproduce CVD in their lab animals. Simply put: they couldn't. Most animals make vitamin C and do not suffer from CVD. Humans, on the other hand, lack the gene to make vitamin C. Scurvy, and all of its complications, is due to a genetic defect in the entire human race. An exception in the animal kingdom are guinea pigs who, like humans, lack the gene to make vitamin C. Guinea pigs share something else in common with humans; they make cholesterol in every cell in their bodies.

Why didn't Merck, then, use guinea pigs? They did; they used human guinea pigs – under the direction of Merck's Jonathan Tobert.

There is no money to be made in promoting Pauling's and Rath's research – but there are billions to be made in convincing gullible physicians that cholesterol rather than oxidation and/or deficiency in antioxidants like vitamin C is at the root of CVD. To this end, the for-profit drug behemoth has not only failed humanity; it has failed humanity miserably.

Four fruits and vegetables have been found to decrease the risk of CVD by more than 25 percent: apples, tomatoes, onions and broccoli. All are highly rich in vitamin C.

You do have a heart-healthy choice: tomatoes or onions.

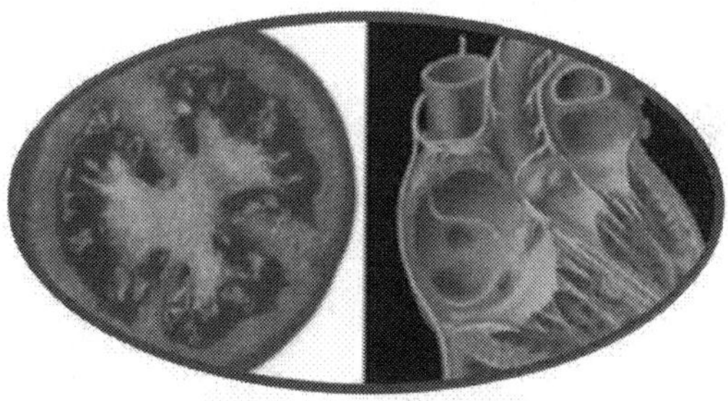

Chapter 31: How Did Statins Make It?

The science was irrefutable. Blocking the mevalonate pathway was a bad idea. The lipid theory had been discarded. MER/29 demonstrated that statins were untenable.

The same bad results as MER/29 had already been observed in lab animals with lovastatin.

After bringing statins to market the same side effects in humans began to surface. Were greed and lust for power really enough to overcome the consciences of what had once been good men and solid scientists? Could the entire medical establishment be so easily duped and corrupted? It became almost incomprehensible, yet the body of evidence is staggering.

Doctors had been fooled before with MER/29.

What became clear is that there was and is a plan. It has been a systematically executed endeavor to take over national health care by hiring and corrupting scientists and infiltrating every pubic health care agency in the country for profit. It is beyond malevolent.

In 2008, a group of Harvard medical students were appalled to find that they were being taught to prescribe medicines by professors who had vested financial interests in the companies who made them (reference 68).

The question, "How did statins make it to the shelves," begs to be answered. The only answer that makes sense is that medicine has lost its way.

The father of one of the authors died in 1960. His death certificate reads that he died from malignant hypertension. By the time he died he had bleeding gums and blood in his urine. He was going blind from leaking blood vessels in his eyes and had bruises all over his body from broken or leaking blood vessels.

He died of scurvy.

Not a single doctor saw it. No one had offered him a single dose of vitamin C. Even if the diagnosis of scurvy had been wrong it would have been a very benign treatment without risk to his life and health. Today, the results would be the same.

Why then would it be a surprise that one of the oldest diseases on earth is commonly missed and bad drugs are instead prescribed to treat symptoms? Simple answer: we trust our doctors who, in turn, trust their drug reps and the FDA.

By the 1950's, the diagnosis of malnutrition had been completely lost to medicine. It was solidly believed that malnutrition had been eradicated in America – *that* only happened in third world countries. Worse, the proponents of nutritional therapies had been relegated to the fringes of medicine. They were called quacks. Brilliant men were scoffed at and discredited. Research monies were declined. Those men and those medicines are the true competition to the drug cartels. It is no surprise that Codex Alimentarious was covertly signed into law in June 2010, by Executive Order making nutritional supplements subject to prescription-only dispensing.

We are made of cells and organelles within cells that comprise organs and yet physicians largely specialize by organs. Where are the cellular specialists who can account for multiple organ failures due to common injury of cells that may surface as multiple complaints in tissues and organs?

There aren't any – except perhaps Dr. Matthias Rath, MD and his colleagues. His specialty is cellular medicine, and like his colleague Linus Pauling, he has been held at arm's length for decades. He has held fast, nevertheless, likely knowing that new revelations are predictably treated with disdain before they become self-evident. It seems to hurt too much to change our minds once we have accepted convention.

In light of statins, the tendency of humans to accept mainstream thinking established by scientists with an agenda for financial gain can be deadly.

There are at least two biochemical pathways, common to all cells of all organs that should never be disrupted in any way by a drug:

1.) The mevalonate pathway
2.) Aerobic metabolism

Notably, the two are interconnected. Statins interrupt both.

The mevalonate pathway makes the products cells need to replicate DNA and divide; it is essential to the life cycle of all cells. Aerobic metabolism, highly dependent upon an ample supply of CoQ10 from mevalonate, is how cells make energy to perform their many functions.

Anything that blocks metabolism, such as carbon monoxide and cyanide, is potentially deadly to cells, organs and the organism. If cells cannot make energy, the heart can stop beating, the diaphragm can stop moving and cardiopulmonary arrest can follow. While blocking CoQ10 production does not *directly* block metabolism like carbon monoxide and cyanide leading to rapid death, it hinders it by depleting CoQ10, leading to slow death – with some exceptions of rapid death by kidney failure.

Mitochondrial alterations in muscle biopsies of patients on statin therapy.

by S Gambelli, M T Dotti, A Malandrini, M Mondelli, M L Stromillo, C Gaudiano, A Federico

Journal of Submicroscopic Cytology and Pathology (2004)

Abstract

Clinical and biopsy study of nine patients on statin therapy suffering from various myopathic syndromes is reported. Biopsy findings showed non specific myopathic signs and mitochondrial changes, such as subsarcolemmal accumulation, morphological alterations, lipid increase and Cox-negative fibers. These findings confirm that statins may cause muscle damage and impair oxidative metabolism.

Studies by researchers at the University of Warwick and USCD have demonstrated that statins lower blood pressure. A heart that pumps less efficiently due to CoQ10 deficiency should propel blood at a lower pressure. Statin trials by the drug companies have touted that statins lower blood LDL levels as well as the incidence of stroke and cardiovascular events. Stroke and LDL levels are not connected, but lower blood pressure *does* decrease the risk of stroke – and heart attacks.

A weakening of the heart muscle with statins due to CoQ10 blockade accounts for the decrease in blood pressure as well as the decreased risk of stroke and cardiovascular events triggered by high blood pressure. What a shame that THAT horrific connection has been overlooked.

Effect of *Atorvastatin* on Left Ventricular Diastolic Function and Ability of Coenzyme Q_{10} to Reverse That Dysfunction

Marc A. Silver, MD, Peter H. Langsjoen, MD, Szabolcs Szabo, MD, Harish Patil, MD, and Allan Zelinger, MD

This study evaluated left ventricular diastolic function with Doppler echocardiography before and after statin therapy. Statin therapy worsened diastolic parameters in most patients; coenzyme Q_{10} supplementation in patients with worsening diastolic function with statin therapy improved parameters of diastolic function. ©2004 by Excerpta Medica, Inc.

(Am J Cardiol 2004;94:1306–1310)

As disturbing as that possibility remains (that the cardiovascular and anti-stroke "benefits" of statins are due to a weakening of the heart muscle by CoQ10 depletion), scientific literature certainly supports the connection. After all, CoQ10 supplementation strengthens the contractility of the heart. It makes sense, then, that CoQ10 depletion weakens the contractility of the heart – and in so doing, lowers blood pressure.

Statins have not lowered the incidence of heart attacks and stroke because they lower LDL cholesterol but because they lower blood pressure by weakening heart muscle (cardiomyopathy). Dr. Abramson, author of “Overdosed America”, puts statins in perspective: heart attacks are traded for other serious illnesses.

If you doubt John Abramson, there’s always David Bilheimer’s voice of reason:

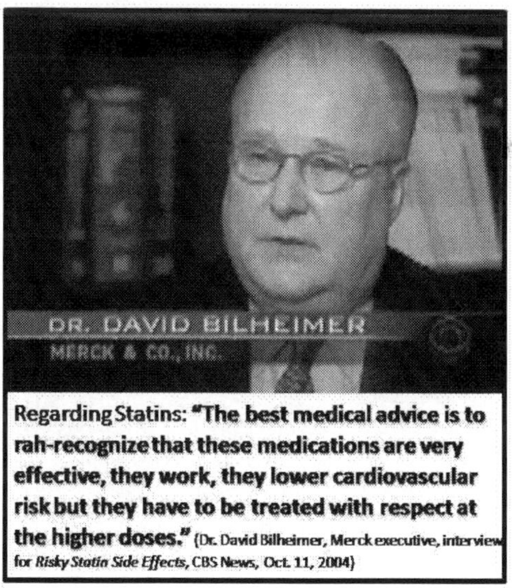

Dr. Siperstein, the cancer researcher, is the real father of the knowledge about the mevalonate pathway. Sadly, it was his work that sent a whole bunch of scientists down the malevolent pathway of statins. But based on his work alone they have no excuses for interfering with mevalonate. They knew better.

If you take the queen bee from a hive, the worker bees furiously go to work to raise a new queen to preserve the hive. If you continue to remove queens as they develop, the whole hive gradually dies. No beekeeper in his right mind would ever keep his queen bee or worker bees from doing their duty or block the development of new queens.

The wise beekeeper will occasionally replace a queen to preserve his hive. He will also move queen cells along with a few workers to start a new hive. But it is always about preservation and propagation. He will never do anything that risks the original hive or the new hive.

The queen bee passes a whole library of information on to her offspring. As they are born they have a plethora of duties that change as they mature. They fan the new nectar to distill it into honey. They become guard bees to protect the hive from robbers. They build new comb and forage for pollen and nectar. They feed the young and have an almost incomprehensible ability to communicate with one another.

Break any part of that chain and the hive dies.

Bees also make a glue-like substance called propolis. Propolis is used to patch holes in the hive and fill voids. Propolis makes it difficult to harvest the honey and inspect the hive. Cleaning up the propolis makes bee keeping real work. Understanding the function of propolis makes it unthinkable to interfere with its production.

LDL cholesterol is not "bad" any more than propolis is "bad". It is essential for life.

Mounting negative studies reveal that the early statin studies were hoaxes, making a moratorium long overdue:

Disappointing Recent Cholesterol-Lowering Drug Trials: Is It Not Time for a Full Reappraisal of the Cholesterol Theory?

Michel de Lorgeril

HeartDisease, WorldRev Nutr Diet. Basel, Karger 2009, vol 100, pp 80-89

Conclusion

For cholesterol experts and the cholesterol industry, recent cholesterol-lowering drug trials have definitely been very disappointing. The most recent trials were either negative (ENHANCE, SEAS, GISSI-HF, CORONA) or not clinically consistent and probably biased (JUPITER) because of premature termination. Taken together, in the light of other negative trials (ASPEN, 4D, PREVEND IT, IDEAL, ILLUMINATE) published after the Vioxx affair in 2005 and the following new clinical research regulations, these trials are puzzling. They suggest that the positive trials published before 2005 and the Vioxx affair should be urgently re-examined. At a minimum, experts independent of industry and free of conflict of interest should be asked to carefully check all the raw data recorded in the datasets and redo the statistical analyses.

The next question would then be: is it not time for a full reappraisal of the cholesterol theory?

While de Lorgeril's thoughts are thought provoking, here is a more definitive question:

Disappointing Recent Cholesterol-Lowering Drug Trials: Haven't Enough Victims Been Killed or Disabled by Statins?

A case involving injury or wrongful death for violation of Consumer Protection Law (i.e., failure to warn, breach of the implied warranty of merchantability, negligent misrepresentation and fraudulent concealment and obfuscation) is strengthened when a lawyer can demonstrate that an alternative design of the product could have prevented or ameliorated the injury or death.

The clearest evidence that Merck knew how dangerous statins were are patents 4,929,437 (May 29, 1990) and 4,933,165 (June 12, 1990) to add CoQ10 to the formula to prevent and reverse muscle and liver damage and multiple experiments on rescuing dying experimental animals with mevalonate. Without CoQ10, or at least mevalonate, cells die.

The concurrent blockade of mevalonate by statins is the mechanism that has caused statin-induced toxicity.

And Merck knew it.

By 1990, Merck had the foresight to predict this complication as documented in their patent request No. 4,929,437 for adding CoQ10 to Merck statins, which states:

> **"Coenzyme Q.sub.10 (2,3-dimethoxy-5-methyl-6-decaprenyl-1, 4-benzoquinone) is a redox component in the respiratory chain and is found in all cells having mitochondria. It is thus an essential co-factor in the generation of metabolic energy and may be important in liver function."**

Adding CoQ10 could have solved for Merck the foreseen design flaw in their statin drugs (disruption of aerobic metabolism by CoQ10 depletion causing liver and muscle damage) as stated in Merck's two patent requests:

> **"In its application to the counteraction of liver damage and, in particular, elevated transaminase levels, the present invention (CoQ10 addition) is accordingly to be understood as providing for the avoidance of liver damage", and, "In its application to the counteraction of myopathy the present invention (CoQ10 addition) is accordingly to be understood as providing for the avoidance of myopathy".**

Bayer voluntarily discontinued Baycol after people died. What remains are less-potent statins that by Merck's own admission cause harm by blocking CoQ10-dependent metabolism as revealed in the following excerpt from Patent No. 4,933,165:

"HMG-CoA reductase inhibitors represent a new class of cholesterol-lowering drugs. Relatively low doses of these drugs effectively reduce plasma cholesterol levels. These drugs are believed to function by inhibiting the chemical transformation HMG-CoA to mevalonate, which is an early and rate-limiting step in the biosynthesis of cholesterol. A branch of the mevalonate cholesterol biosynthetic pathway in mammalian cells leads to the formation of CoQ.sub.10. [reviewed by Brown and Goldstein J. Lipid Res., 21, 505 (1980)]."

This patent excerpt is proof that Merck had indisputable foreknowledge that their statins would cause harm. Masking this as "risks" or "adverse reactions" is fraudulent, deceptive, and deserves full reevaluation in the light of full disclosure.

Mevalonate blockade is the predictable cause of innumerable deaths and injuries, rather than due to random and unexplained secondary or peripheral "adverse reactions" as claimed in Merck's patient and prescriber information sheets. It is the mevalonate blockade that is the source of the design defect and marketing defect of statins.

Merck had knowledge to foresee but did not employ or disclose both the antidote and remedy that would have avoided or ameliorated untold injuries and deaths by their statins.

Merck had a design defect. They knew it. They didn't correct it.

Chapter 32: Bottom Line

Liars use statistics but statistics do not lie.

There are two types of statistics: relative and absolute. For example, if two out of 100 people die from X disease, then the death rate is 2%. That is an absolute statistic on a small sampling. If you give drug Z to 100 people and now only one person dies from X disease, that too is an absolute statistic – a death rate of 1%. If you are a drug company with a profit motive you can say you have proof that by taking drug Z you have a 50% less relative risk of dying from disease X (a 1% death rate rather than 2%). That is misuse of statistics to baffle 'em with BS.

What follows here are absolute statistics on a very large sampling of two million statin users. From 2009 to 2010, two scientists gathered data (published in the BMJ British Medical Journal) on over two million statin users in England and Wales. They extrapolated the statistics for a five-year period and uncovered the following:

One out of 37 women and one out of 33 men taking statins for five years would be free of cardiovascular disease (CVD). Put another way, ***36 of 37 women and 32 of 33 men receive no CVD benefit from statin use after five years***.

On the risk side, 1.2 of those same 37 women will suffer from one or more of the following during that same five-year period:

1. Acute renal failure (potentially fatal)
2. Cataracts (greater chance of cataracts than CVD improvement)
3. Liver dysfunction
4. Myopathy (potentially-permanent loss of muscle function)

And this is tracking only four of the proven negative side effects.

Bottom line:

Using only this data, you have a 2.7% chance of not contracting CVD and a 4.35% increased chance of experiencing one or more of four chronic and potentially fatal diseases after only five years of statin use.

Individualising the risks of statins in men and women in England and Wales: population-based cohort study

Julia Hippisley-Cox, Carol Coupland

Accepted 30 March 2010

Table 7 Numbers needed to harm (NNH) or numbers needed to treat (NNT) and numbers of extra or prevented cases, for each outcome over 5 years in patients aged 35–74 free of cardiovascular disease at baseline with QRISK2 score of 20%+ (table reproduced from the BMJ[5a])

	NNH or NNT (95% CI)	Estimated number of extra cases (or cases prevented) per 10000 patients treated
Potential benefits in women		
Cardiovascular disease	−37 (−64 to −27)	−271 (−374 to −157)
Potential harms in women		
Acute renal failure	434 (284 to 783)	23 (13 to 35)
Cataract	33 (28 to 38)	307 (260 to 355)
Liver dysfunction	136 (109 to 175)	74 (57 to 91)
Myopathy	259 (186 to 375)	39 (27 to 54)
Potential benefits in men		
Cardiovascular disease	−33 (−57 to −24)	−301 (−417 to −174)
Potential harms in men		
Acute renal failure	346 (245 to 539)	29 (19 to 41)
Cataract	52 (44 to 63)	191 (158 to 225)
Liver dysfunction	142 (115 to 180)	71 (56 to 87)

If all the statin-associated diseases were added to the list and all the non-reported statin injuries the numbers would have more likely totaled: “100% chance of statin injury.” That would make more sense. No one has undertaken a study of all statin users nor informed all statin users of the potential for harm. Most statin users and their physicians attribute their ills to normal aging.

Merck knows.

Meanwhile untold billions to trillions of dollars are spent on diagnosing and treating these diseases without our doctors ever suspecting the cause. The loss in human productivity is in the trillions of dollars – with only a supposed 2.4% decrease in CVD.

From the same study, the two scientists took four statin-associated diseases and personalized the risk data as follows:

Example 1

A 64-year-old Caribbean man with type 2 diabetes, hypothyroidism and chronic kidney disease, who is a heavy smoker, with a body mass index of 36.7 kg/m^2, systolic blood pressure of 200 mm Hg, cholesterol/high-density lipoprotein ratio 4.3 would have the following 5 year risks on and off statins:

- Cardiovascular risk 30% risk off statins, 23% risk on statins;
- Acute renal failure 1.8% risk off statins, 2.9% risk on statins;
- Cataract 12.7% risk off statins, 16.4% risk on statins;
- Liver dysfunction 1.8% risk off statins, 2.8% risk on statins;
- Moderate/serious myopathy 0.7% risk off statins, 4.4% risk on statins.

Example 2

A 60-year-old white women, with rheumatoid arthritis, currently prescribed corticosteroids, heavy smoker, with a systolic blood pressure of 190 mm Hg, cholesterol/high-density lipoprotein ratio of 7; body mass index 33.1 kg/m^2 would have the following 5-year risks on and off statins:

- Cardiovascular risk 21% risk off statins, 16% risk on statins;
- Acute renal failure 0.4% risk off statins, 0.7% risk on statins;
- Cataract 7.1% risk off statins, 9.1% risk on statins;
- Liver dysfunction 5.4% risk off statins, 8.2% risk on statins;
- Moderate/serious myopathy 0.2% risk off statins, 0.7% risk on statins.

The man in the above example has over six times the relative risk for myopathy and the woman 3.5 times the relative risk. These are appalling relative statistics.

In light of the irrefutable, universally accepted and peer-reviewed science establishing mevalonate's prime role in DNA replication and cell life, it is likely that scanning-electron microscopic evaluation of tissue samples from statin users would show ***100 percent*** cellular injury to their DNA, endoplasmic reticulum and mitochondria within days to weeks of use.

Furthermore, the largest meta-analysis performed to date on over two million statin users revealed that of ***seventy*** people taking statins, only ***two*** receive a CVD benefit (which might even be secondary to lowered blood pressure from cardiomyopathy). If aspirin had similar results at $10 per pill, no one would take it.

Merck and the FDA have perpetrated the largest pharmaceutical snake-oil scam in medical history.

When Ford started being sued for defective exploding gas tanks in their Pinto an interoffice memo went out to settle those suits out of court because it was cheaper than a recall.

Merck continues to settle out of court and successfully avoids public scrutiny.

Daniel Steinberg is perhaps the best writer of science fiction since Robert Heinline. He describes in glowing well-written persuasive prose his journey to prove the lipid theory (his agenda). First, he got approval to commence a $150,000,000 study called the CPPT. Then he got appointed to set up the parameters of the study. They gathered up 3,800 healthy men with cholesterol higher than 265. The facts as presented by Steinberg, that he touts convinced the NIH consensus panel to recommend the NCEP, was that lowering cholesterol decreased CVD risk by 19%. If that were an absolute statistic it is abysmal but it is not. It is a relative statistic. The absolute statistic was less than a 2% decreased risk in CVD. Steinberg spent $150,000,000 taxpayer dollars to end up with a less than 2% absolute statistic that he then perverted as "proof" to advance his agenda.

After having spent an embarrassing 150 million dollars from the public trust, one can easily understand the motives for the fiction.

Bad motives (agendas) can only result in bad science.

It was based on this study that the lipid theory came back to prominence. It was based on this study that another $150,000,000 was spent to "educate" doctors and the general public. This study made approval of statins possible.

Cholestyramine, the drug used to lower cholesterol in the CPPT study, causes liver toxicity and cancer. There is a good chance there was an elevated liver illness and death rate in the treatment group. No report was made on those small details.

To review the dismal numbers for yourself, see Steinberg's five-part report on the statin controversy (reference 25).

At least Steinberg's manipulated numbers can be scrutinized in the light.

Chapter 33: Efficacious *and* Safe

The FDA charter requires that a prescription drug be efficacious and safe, not efficacious or safe. The whole process breaks down when focusing on one component and not the other.

"To do no harm" is the covenant promise of every physician. Toxins (poisons) have long been used in the practice of medicine. Mercury and arsenic were once used to treat syphilis. Today we use chemotherapy and radiation against cancer. Some antibiotics are toxins. So as to do no harm, toxins are used as a curative last resort. Statins are toxins that are prescribed to prevent CVD. At a 2.4% success rate and a much higher harm rate they are neither efficacious nor safe and violate the most basic principle of medicine. Chemotherapy would never be used to prevent cancer.

By the time the FDA approved statins, a huge body of relative statistics existed that lower LDL cholesterol levels indicated a lower incidence of CVD and stroke. It was natural to assume (make an ass of you and me) that if a drug lowered LDL cholesterol it would benefit the patient.

No requirement was made of Merck to prove the efficacy of lovastatin in reducing the incidence of CVD and stroke. The only caveat imposed by the FDA was, since proof was not available, that Merck could not make the claim of reducing CVD and stroke. The efficacy issue was stepped over on a single assumption that lowering cholesterol would lower CVD risk – even without the proof. It is on that assumption that insurance companies require statin prescriptions as medical protocol and doctors wholesale prescribe statins.

There are benign proven ways to safely lower cholesterol. Vitamin C therapies, niacin, selenium, good nutrition, linoleic acid (safflower oil), natural estrogens, drinking chlorine-free water and exercise are a few. There is very little profit in any of them.

Why would our FDA not require proof of efficacy? Statins were assumed to lower CVD risk and no proof was required. That they stepped over the safety issue is not as surprising as missing the efficacy issue. Once omitting the requirement of efficacy, the safety issue was so corrupted by Merck that statins could not be rejected.

On January 28, 2008 at 2:00 pm, the FDA held a press conference to address the exposed Vytorin scandal. Vytorin, a combination of Merck's Zocor with Zetia, had proven poorly on a study that Merck would not release to the public – and now with the cat out of the bag the FDA had some questions to answer.

Here is a quote on the matter to the press from Dr. Jim Jenkins, Director of the Office of Medical Policy (this interview is posted at the FDA web site):

> **"Our approval of lipid lowering drugs has always been based on a demonstration of lowering LDL cholesterol. And we have not required for initial approval the demonstration of reduction in risk of cardiovascular events such as heart attack or stroke."**
>
> **"Zetia and Vytorin were both approved based on their ability to lower LDL cholesterol. However, they have not been demonstrated to reduce the risk of cardiovascular disease, such as heart attack and stroke. And that information is clearly documented in the labeling, as it has been for all other lipid-lowering agents until they completed a cardiovascular outcome study".**

That is their excuse.

Considering that statins negatively affect every single cell in the body, this is like saying that it is efficacious and safe to remove an entire leg to excise a small basal cell carcinoma (benign skin cancer) on a big toe.

There was no excuse for approving statins without proof that they reduced and/or ameliorated the risk of CVD and stroke – and safely.

High LDL cholesterol is not the enemy. It is not even a proven symptom. Only rarely is it genetic. CVD and stroke kill. That is how we are so easily conned by the drug companies. Everyone wants the magic potion that fixes everything without requiring us to go sane. Insanity in day-to-day life is continuing to do the same old thing and expecting different results. And so we get duped into taking dangerous drugs. That, however, does not excuse the con artists or the FDA.

Dr. Jenkin's statement shows that the FDA suffers the same insanity. Always having done something the same way regardless ongoing revelation that the process is badly broken is inexcusable, especially when hundreds of millions of lives are at stake.

FDA jobs are not at risk for bad science but rather bad publicity. The FDA charter mandates prevention of drug catastrophes. Instead, untold billions are spent reacting to them.

It is common knowledge amongst veterinarians that a few licks of antifreeze can be lethal to pets. Animals ingest it because it tastes sweet. Bottles are clearly labeled POISON. PEG and PPG are antifreeze approved by our FDA for use in foodstuff as preservatives. They are in every package of our beloved Twinkies and ice cream. "FDA-approved" means there was something wrong in the first place. Tomatoes and eggs are not FDA approved. They are safe.

A recently aired TV program followed several families living on the streets due to economic hard times. In the follow-up program Americans had responded to the need and every head of the households had been offered jobs. Every family had been given homes. Over a million dollars had been donated. The children had been provided college scholarships. That is the heart and soul of Americans. We are a good and generous people whether we are Democrats, Republicans, Christian, Muslim or other.

What is our sin in all of this? We are gullible. Every single time a drug or anything else is approved or disapproved by our government we need to be asking the right questions: Who stands to gain by it? Who is behind it? What happens if it turns out to be a bad product or bad idea?

Follow the money.

Capitalism is a good idea and self-corrects but it needs the tight rein of public scrutiny, fairness and justice to properly function. Otherwise it runs amuck and moneyed interests take over everything. Then capitalism mutates into imperialism. That is what happened with statins, Merck and the FDA.

Deregulation is a bad idea. As silly and corrupt as the FDA has become it is a necessary regulatory agency in a capitalistic society. It needs to be revamped to insure the keeping of its original charter.

The FDA once operated with an excess of caution. A public outcry for drugs to slow the HIV epidemic and cure incurable diseases came on like a tidal wave. Some drugs had already been approved in other countries. That has caused an avalanche of dangerous drugs to be approved under suspect conditions. Now we have a lack of caution. This pendulum needs to swing back to center. Statins and many other drugs need careful reexamination.

Failure to disclose known risks must be prosecuted. Studies on efficacy and safety must be done by independent entities without ties to the result. With the evidence of a corrupt process so clear, no one must ever sit on an FDA approval committee who has a vested interest in the outcome. All approval-related meetings, papers and even memos must be done in the sunshine. The internet, where results can be instantly posted, makes it possible.

Our medical system is now like two snakes wrapped around a pole sitting on top of a pile of dung and hissing at us, daring us to require it to change. We need to snatch its twin tails, break its backs and return it to the dung heap.

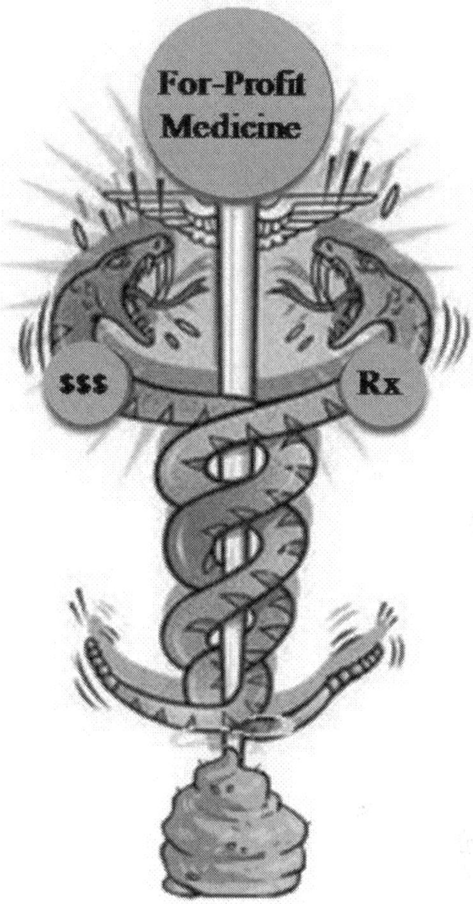

In the meantime, all drug approvals must be suspended until the process can be cleaned up or hauled to the dump.

Chapter 34: Do NOT Touch the Mevalonate Pathway.

Human life is a sexually transmitted terminal disease. None of us gets out of this alive. Neither does any single cell in our body.

Dead cells slough off our skin, hair and eyes and out our bowel tract, urethra and sweat. Every single cell in our body dies. In normal cycles, cells reproduce by splitting and cloning themselves. As they die and slough we do not miss them. Statins eventually result in the consequence of our cells being unable to replace themselves. Take a statin and cells stop reproducing. Death accelerates one cell at a time.

Brown said in his Nobel speech that statins trigger a complex regulatory mechanism that sets a new steady state in cells. He is correct. Statins neutralize reductase then increase reductase and LDL receptors. This shifts LDL cholesterol from the blood to LDL receptors on cells. This satisfies cells' demand for cholesterol but not isoprenoids and sets a new homeostasis for reductase – less elevated than at first but nevertheless still elevated above normal.

Caveat: Cells work overtime and the reproductive cycle of cells remains blocked as long as the mevalonate pathway remains obstructed.

To sum:

1. Statins block cells from making mevalonate.

2. More reductase is made.

3. The elevated reductase stimulates production of LDL receptors that collect circulating blood cholesterol.

4. If isoprenoid synthesis remains blocked, cells die.

That is how statins ***really*** work and kill you one cell at a time. It is truth that Merck's scientists and advisors have muddied.

The great cholesterol myth: unfortunate consequences of Brown and Goldstein's mistake
QJM (2012) 105(2): 214

The mevalonate pathway should have been considered sacrosanct the moment its role was discovered in Dallas by Marvin Siperstein. Based upon its function, the premiere law of "doing no harm" should mandate that a sign be hung in every pharmaceutical company bathroom that advises: "Employees must wash hands before returning to work…and do NOT touch the Mevalonate Pathway!"

Collusion was rampant among employees at Merck, the FDA, the NIH, Siperstein's old lab at Dallas and the AHA. The hard science had been overlooked or in some cases nearly obliterated. Was it for money, power and fame? While those certainly contributed to the nightmare, it was well-educated credentialed people who approved statins just as the well-educated credentialed Southern Politicos had segregated southern blacks and kept them in the bondage of fear and poverty for a century after the Emancipation Proclamation.

The truth cannot be found when you have already decided what it is. The man who thinks he already knows can learn nothing. These men are the Dixiecrats of science.

Men like Steinberg, Endo and Tobert brought prejudice and bias to the process. Cholesterol, the precious essence of life, was the enemy and not heart disease and stroke. They hammered it into the minds and hearts of the public and pushed back the resistance with multi-million-dollar propaganda campaigns paid for from the public treasury. They had the money and resources to do it and they pursued their agenda with a vengeance.

And why wouldn't they block the mevalonate pathway even if they knew what holocaust might follow? Mankind has been blocking the life cycle of the whole planet since before the industrial revolution. The oceans, air, rainforests and even fellow humans are not sacrosanct. Other species are fair game for annihilation. Pride and prejudice seem inherent in our nature and consistently lead to war and other forms of destruction.

Doctors Marvin Siperstein and Van Rensselaer Potter are worth our tribute. Siperstein's meticulous work that unraveled the mevalonate pathway should go down in history as the greatest biochemical discovery of the twentieth century. Potter left us a brilliant treatise on Global Bio-ethics.

Bio means life. Bio-ethics includes a right perspective of life within the universe.

Imagine this one little biosphere from deep space – a speck in one arm of a seven-armed spiral galaxy with billions of stars in a universe with galaxies like grains of sand. The earth is a living organism and mankind is killing it. Mankind is anti-life as statins are anti-life. We are headed for extinction at our own hands. The worst of it is we will probably eradicate all life on the planet in our madness. That is what happens to a species that cannot live in harmony with one another and the precious living things in the biosphere.

It is a natural course for us to allow ourselves to be poisoned or go to war and call it “good”. We are a hair's breadth from extinction. One bad vaccine or one bad medicine can now be approved in jig time and administered in weeks all over the planet. One accidental release of one of the horrible diseases we have weaponized in a lab could end our insanity. Perhaps the living biosphere with all its redundant pro-bios systems will rise up against humankind and stamp us out like a deadly virus.

Is there hope? If there is, it requires a revolution in the minds and hearts of us all, a highly unlikely proposition. We must do the most difficult of all tasks: we must change our minds.

We must see our personal destiny as less important than the destiny of the planet, less important than the destiny of everyone and every living thing. We must see ourselves in the light of the truth that we are less important than the health of the biosphere. Either way, we are born to die. How then shall we live? We are inextricably intertwined with all life and the environment that supports it. It is how we respect all life while we live this moment of time in infinity that decides whether or not we survive as a species.

Being blind to it does not change the outcome. Only opening our minds and hearts gives us a chance.

MEVALONATE PATHWAY

Do NOT touch the mevalonate pathway.

Epilogue by James

Hannah and I started this book with closely aligned motives. Her interest as a medical doctor was that she had become suspicious of statins while still practicing medicine. Mine was as a victim. We discussed the possibility of writing an exposé and eventually made our first attempt.

There are many statin critics but the evidence they presented was a mixture of fact and theory and no one seemed to have the whole story. Also, the statin proponents had published fairly convincing articles to contradict the detractors. People like Steinberg, Brown, Goldstein and Tobert had solid credentials and more credibility than the naysayers.

We believed the cynics anyway – I, because statins had done me so much harm, and Hannah because she had seen the bad results in her patients.

We had not yet discovered a solid body of indisputable evidence. We ourselves did not yet understand the difference in double blind, peer-reviewed drug company science and proven hard science. We could not see through the obfuscations of men like Steinberg. We too had been programmed to believe that lowering LDL blood cholesterol was a good thing. We started with the perspective that prescribers were probably just using a bad drug.

We did not believe in great conspiracies but could imagine a good old boy network. Worst of all, we believed in the FDA. Our writing stalled again and again. I followed my BS detector and Hannah pursued the science.

We traced Brown and Goldstein's cholesterol-related research back to Siperstein and eventually to Van Rensselaer Potter whom Siperstein quoted. The hard science was irrefutable. Statins were not just bad medicine; they were deadly.

Finally, we had it. We could complete the book. We were wrong. More and more questions unveiled themselves.

How could our trusted FDA approve such a piece of dung – and who would even bring it to them? We started with a concern that the FDA must have been lied to. We still did not have a mental equivalent for the corruption. We were wrong again.

We stopped and ordered the FDA transcripts of the lovastatin advisory committee meeting under the Freedom of Information Act.

By then we knew without question that statins were poison. After reading the transcript we had to stop writing. Both of our BS detectors were ringing so loud we could not write for weeks. We paced the floor and cried some for the victims and some for ourselves and the disillusionment. It was all a transparent sham.

We discussed the book endlessly. We had already written and rewritten it from scratch no less than seven times. The evidence continued to contradict our preconceptions of what must be true. We made a conscious decision to let go of our paradigms and let the evidence lead us.

It took us three more attempts.

What we wrote is what we call "obnosis": observing the obvious. It became this book.

James B. Yoseph

References

1. Brown M, Goldstein J. Progress in understanding the LDL Receptor and HMG-CoA Reductase, Two Membrane Proteins that Regulate the Plasma Cholesterol. *Journal of Lipid Research.* 1984: 25:1450-61.

2. White Junod, S. Statins: A Success Story Involving FDA, Academia and Industry. *FDA Web Site:* http://www.fda.gov/AboutFDA/WhatWeDo/History/ProductRegulation/SelectionsFromFDLIUpdateSeriesonFDAHistory/ucm082054.htm

3. Steinberg, D. An Interpretive History of the Cholesterol Controversy (part V). *Journal of Lipid Research.* 2006: 47:1343-5.

4. Ibid., 1343.

5. Ibid., 1344.

6. Sijbrands E, Westendorp R, Defesch J, de Meier P, Smelt A, Kastelein J. Mortality Over Two Centuries in Large Pedigree with Familial Hypercholesterolemia: Family Tree Mortality Study. *BMJ*, 322:1019-23.

7. Williams R, Hasstedt S,, Wilson D, Ash K, Yanowitz F, Reiber G, Kuida H. Evidence That Men with Familial Hypercholesterolemia Can Avoid Early Coronary Death. *JAMA,* 1986: 255(2): 219-24.

8. FDA CDER Interoffice Memo dated August 1, 1997 http://www.jlr.org/content/25/13/1450.full.pdf

9. Heber D. Nutritional Oncology, Chapter 38: Isoprenoids and Novel Inhibitors of Mevalonate Pathway Activities. *Academic Press (Elsevier),* 2006: p. 636. Online (preview): http://books.google.com/books?id=RjVIrQ7aBFQC&printsec=frontcover#v=onepage&q&f=false

10. Kiessliong Karl-Heinz. Biochemical Mechanism of Action of Mycotoxins. *Appl. Chem.*, 1986: 58(2):327-338.

11. ABC News: Statins May Cause Muscle Damage in Some Patients (2009 video).

12. Elsevier web site: elsevier.com/wps/find/authored_newsitem.cws_home/companynews05_01203).

13. http://i.bnet.com/blogs/cert-fda-letter-to-the-president-4-2-09-and-trans-team-1-7-09.pdf.

14. Steinberg, D. An Interpretive History of the Cholesterol Controversy (part IV). *Journal of Lipid Research.* 2006: 47:12.

15. Yudkin, J. *British Medical Journal.* 1977: 2:1477.

16. Revis, N, Osborne, T, Holdsworth, G. "Effect of Chlorinated Drinking Water on Myocardial Structure and Functions in Pigeons and Rabbits," 5th Conf. on Water Chlorination. Eds. R. J. Jolly et al. 1985: 365-373.

17. Enos W et al. Coronary Disease Among United States Soldiers Killed in Action in Korea. *JAMA,* 1953: 152:1090-93.

18. McNamara, J et al. Coronary Artery Disease in Combat Casualties in Vietnam. *JAMA,* 197: 216:1185-87.

19. Ministry of Health, Labour and Welfare: Water Supply in Japan. http://www.mhlw.go.jp/english/policy/health/water_supply/1.html

20. Foley R, Collins A, Herzog C, Ishani A, Kalra P. Serum Phosphorous Levels Associate with Coronary Atherosclerosis in Young Adults. *JASN*, 2009: 20(2): 397-404.

21. Anyanwu E, Ehiri J, Kanu I. High Cholesterol Levels and Chronic Exposure to Toxigenic Molds in Damp Buildings: A High Risk for Cardiovascular Diseases and Stroke. *The Internet Journal of Toxicology,* ISSN: 1559-3916

22. Costantini A. The Fungal/Mycotoxin Connections: Autoimmune Diseases, Malignancies, Atherosclerosis, Hyperlipidemias, and Gout. Etiology of Atherosclerosis and Hyperlipidemia. *The Arthritis Trust of America 28th Annual Meeting Lecture*. October 11, 1993.

23. Steinberg, D. Progress, Prospects and Provender. Chairman's address before the Council on Arteriosclerosis, American Heart Association, Dallas, Texas, November 12, 1969. *Circulation*, 1970: 41: 723–728.

24. 2004 NCEP Guidelines Financial Disclosure.

25. Steinberg, D. An Interpretive History of the Cholesterol Controversy (part V): The Discovery of the Statins and the End of the Controversy. *Journal of Lipid Research*. 2006: 47: 1344.

26. Powell E, Kroon P. Low Density Lipoprotein Receptor and 3-Hydroxy-3 Methylglutaryl Coenzyme A Reductase Gene Expression in Human Mononuclear Leukocytes is Regulated Coordinately and Parallels Gene Expression in Human Liver. *J. Clin. Invest.*, 1994: 93: 2168-2174.

27. Stulnig T, Klocker H, Harwood H, Jürgen G,Schönitzer D, Jarosch E, Huber L, Amberger A,Wick G. In Vivo LDL Receptor and HMG-CoA Reductase Regulation in Human Lymphocytes and Its Alterations During Aging. *Arteriosclerosis, Thrombosis, and Vascular Biology*, 1995: 15: 872-878.

28. Brown M, Goldstein J, Bilheimer D, Ma P, Gil G, Sudhof T. Mevinolin, an inhibitor of cholesterol synthesis, induces mRNA for low density lipoprotein receptor in liver of hamsters and rabbits. Proc. Natl. Acad. Sci., 1986: 83: 8370-8374.

29. Molowa D, Cimis G (Merck). Co-ordinate regulation of low-density lipoprotein receptor and 3-hydroxy-3-methylglutaryl-CoA reductase and synthase gene expression in HepG2 cells. *Biochem. J.,* 1989: 260: 731-736.

30. Rudling M, Angelin B, Ståhle L, Reihnér E, Sahlin S, Olivecrona H, Björkhem I, Einarsson C. Regulation of Hepatic Low-Density Lipoprotein Receptor, 3-Hydroxy-3-Methylglutaryl Coenzyme A Reductase, and Cholesterol 7{alpha}-Hydroxylase mRNAs in Human Liver. *J. Clin. Endocrinol. Metab.*, 2002: 87: 4307-4313.

31. http://i.bnet.com/blogs/cert-fda-letter-to-the-president-4-2-09-and-trans-team-1-7-09.pdf

32. http://hcrenewal.blogspot.com/2007/03/more-on-financial-entangles-of.html

33. Landers, P. Stalking Cholesterol: How One Scientist Intrigued by Molds Found First Statin. *The Wall Street Journal*, January 9, 2006; page A1.

34. Steinberg, D. An Interpretive History of the Cholesterol Controversy (part V). *Journal of Lipid Research.* 2006: 47: 1344-46.

35. Office of Technology Assessment. Pharmaceutical R&D: Costs, Risks and Rewards. *OTA-H522*. February 1993; page 74.

36. White Junod, S. Statins: A Success Story Involving FDA, Academia and Industry. *FDA Web Site: http://www.fda.gov/AboutFDA/WhatWeDo/History/ProductRegulation/SelectionsFromFDLIUpdateSeriesonFDAHistory/ucm082054.htm*

37. Alberts A, Kornbrust D, MacDonald J, Peter C, Duchai D, Stubbs J, Germershausen J. Toxicity of the HMG-CoEnzyme A Reductase Inhibitor, Lovastatin, to Rabbits. *The Journal of Pharmacology* and *Experimental Therapeutics*, 1989: 248 (2): 498.

38. MacDonald J and Halleck M. The Toxicology of HMG-CoA Reductase Inhibitors: Prediction of Human Risk. *Toxicologic Pathology*, 2004, 32.

39. Faust J, Brown M, Goldstein J. Synthesis of Δ^2-Isopentenyl tRNA from Mevalonate in Cultured Human Fibroblasts. *The Journal of Biological Chemistry*, 1980: 256 (14): 6546.

40. Ryan J, Hardeman E, Endo A, Simoni R. Isolation and Characterization of Cells Resistant to ML236B (Compactin) with Increased Levels of 3-Hydroxy-3-methylglutaryl Coenzyme A Reductase. *The Journal of Biological Chemistry*, 1981: 256 (13): 6763.

41. MacDonald J and Halleck M. The Toxicology of HMG-CoA Reductase Inhibitors: Prediction of Human Risk. *Toxicologic Pathology*, 2004: 26, 33.

42. Alberts A, Kornbrust D, MacDonald J, Peter C, Duchai D, Stubbs J, Germershausen J. Toxicity of the HMG-CoEnzyme A Reductase Inhibitor, Lovastatin, to Rabbits. *The Journal of Pharmacology* and *Experimental Therapeutics*, 1989: 248 (2): 498, 504.

43. Siperstein M, Hughes Wiley M, Righetti M, Murrill P. The in Vitro Metabolism of Mevalonate by Sterol and Non-sterol Pathways. *The Journal of Biological Chemistry*, 1976: 251(9): 2716-2721.

44. Siperstein M, Hughes Wiley M, Howton M. The Quantitative Role of the Kidneys in the in Vivo Metabolism of Mevalonate. *The Journal of Biological Chemistry*, 1977: 252(2): 548-554.

45. Endo A. The Discovery and Development of HMG-CoA Reductase Inhibitors. *Journal of Lipid Research*, 1992: (33): 1573.

46. Endo A. A Gift From Nature: The Birth of the Statins. *Nature Medicine.* 2008: 14 (10): xxv. Endo A.

47. Endo A. The Discovery and Development of HMG-CoA Reductase Inhibitors. *Journal of Lipid Research*, 1992: (33): 1574.

48. Ibid.

49. MacDonald J and Halleck M. The Toxicology of HMG-CoA Reductase Inhibitors: Prediction of Human Risk. *Toxicologic Pathology*, 2004, 36.

50. Alberts A, Kornbrust D, MacDonald J, Peter C, Duchai D, Stubbs J, Germershausen J. Toxicity of the HMG-CoEnzyme A Reductase Inhibitor, Lovastatin, to Rabbits. *The Journal of Pharmacology* and *Experimental Therapeutics*, 1989: 248 (2): 498.

51. MacDonald J and Halleck M. The Toxicology of HMG-CoA Reductase Inhibitors: Prediction of Human Risk. *Toxicologic Pathology*, 2004, 32.

52. MacDonald J. Endocrinologic and Metabolic Drugs Advisory Committee, 9:00 a.m., Thursday, February 19, 1987. *Baker, Humes & Burkes Reporting, Inc.,* FOIA Request, 130.

53. Merck Co., Inc. *Zocor (simvastatin) Highlights of Prescribing Information*, 5.

54. Draeger A, Mohaupt M, MD, Karas R, Babiychuk E, Sanchez-Freire V, Monastyrskaya K, Iyer L, Hoppeler H, Breil F. Association Between Statin-associated Myopathy and Skeletal Muscle Damage. *Canadian Medical Association Journal,* July 7, 2009: 181.

55. Merck Co., Inc. *Zocor (simvastatin) Highlights of Prescribing Information*, 5.

56. Sigler R, Dominick M and McGuire E. Subacute Toxicity of a Halogenated Pyrrole Hydroxymethylgluaryl-Coenzyme A Reductase Inhibitor in Wistar Rats. *Toxicologic Pathology* ,1992: 20 (4).

57. MacDonald J and Halleck M. The Toxicology of HMG-CoA Reductase Inhibitors: Prediction of Human Risk. *Toxicologic Pathology*, 2004: 34.

58. Folkers K, Langsjoen P, Willis R, Richardson P, Xia L, Ye C, Tamagawa H. Lovastatin Decreases CoEnzyme Q Levels in Humans. *Proc. Natl. Acad. Sci.,* Nov. 1990: (87): 8931.

59. Dietschy J, Turley S. Thematic Review Series - Brain Lipids: Cholesterol Metabolism in the Central Nervous System During Early Development and in the Mature Animal. *J. Lipid Res.,* Aug. 2004: 45 (8): 1375.

60. MacDonald J, Alberts A, et al. Brain and Optic System Pathology in Hypocholesterolemic Dogs Treated With a Competitive Inhibitor of 3-Hydroxy-3-Methylglutaryl Coenzyme A Reductase. 32: (3).

61. Expert Panel on Detection, Evaluation, and Treatment of High Blood Cholesterol in Adults. Executive Summary of The Third Report of the National Cholesterol Education Program (NCEP) Expert Panel on Detection, Evaluation, and Treatment of High Blood Cholesterol in Adults (Adult Treatment Panel III). JAMA 2001: 285: 2486–2497.

62. Mosca L, Appel JA, Benjamin EJ et al. AHA Guidelines: Evidence-Based Guidelines for Cardiovascular Disease Prevention in Women. *Circulation* 2004: 109: 672–693.

63. Herbert WNP, Braly PS, Barss VA, et al. *ACOG: Guidelines for Women's Health Care.* 2nd ed. Washington, DC: ACOG; 2002: 209–211.

64. US Preventive Services Task Force. Screening for Lipid Disorder in Adults: Recommendations and Rationale. *J. Intern. Med.* 2002: 3(2) www.ispub.com/ostia/index.phpxmlFilePath=journals/ijim/vol3n2/lipid.xml.

65. Ginter E, Cerna O, Budlovsky J, Balaz V, Hruba F, Roch V, Sasko E. Effect of Ascorbic Acid on Plasma Cholesterol in Humans in a Long-Term Experiment. *Int. J. Vitam..Nutr. Res.*, 1977: 47 (2): 123-34.

66. Jacques P, Sulsky S, Perrone G, Schaefer E. Ascorbic Acid and Plasma Lipids. *Epidemiology Resources, Inc.* 1994: 5 (1).

67. Ginter E, Bobek P, Jurcovicova M: Role of Ascorbic Acid in Lipid Metabolism. *Ascorbic Acid, Chemistry, Metabolism and Uses*. Edited by Seith PA, Toblert, BM. American Chemical Society, Washington, DC; 1982: 381-393.

68. Wu C. Harvard Medical Students Push to Codify Conflict of Interest Policies: Classroom conflict of interest sparks movement among first-years to press for disclosure policies. Nov. 14, 2008.

Appendix: Statin Injury Reports

(How blocking mevalonate kills you one cell at a time)

BIRTH DEFECTS

1. Central Nervous System and Limb Anomalies in Case Reports of First-Trimester Statin Exposure (2004)
2. Congenital Abnormalities (VATER) in Baby Born to Mother Using Lovastatin (1992)
3. Developmental Toxicity of the HMG-CoA Reductase Inhibitor, Atorvastatin, in Rats and Rabbits (1994).
4. Gestational Exposure to Lovastatin Followed by Cardiac Malformation Misclassified as Holoprosencephaly (2005)
5. Mechanistic and Epidemiologic Considerations in the Evaluation of Adverse Birth Outcomes Following Gestational Exposure to Statins (2004)
6. Mevalonate Supplementation in Pregnant Rats Suppresses the Teratogenicity of Mevinolinic Acid, an Inhibitor of 3-Hydroxy-3-Methylglutaryl-Coenzyme A Reductase (1983)
7. Pregnancy Outcomes After Maternal Exposure to Simvastatin and Lovastatin (2005)
8. Role of Cholesterogenesis and Isoprenoid Synthesis in DNA Replication and Cell Growth (1994)
9. Simvastatin has Deleterious Effects on Human First Trimester Placental Explants (2005)
10. Statin Drugs and Congenital Anomalies (2005)
11. Statins: Beware During Pregnancy (2006)

EYE INJURY

1. Cataract and Simvastatin: Case Report (1998)
2. Cataract and the Use of Statins: A Case-Control Study (2003)
3. Drug Against High Cholesterol Can Affect Vision (1991)
4. Ocular Hemorrhage Possibly the Result of HMG-CoA Reductase Inhibitors (2004)
5. Ocular Side Effects of the Lipid-Lowering Drug Simvastatin? A One Year Follow-Up (1989)
6. Risk of Cataract in Patients Treated With Statins (2001)

7. Statin Use and Incident Nuclear Cataracts (2006)
8. The Human Lens After 48 Weeks of Treatment with Lovastatin (1990)

INTESTINAL INJURY

1. Atorvastatin-induced severe gastric ulceration: a case report (2005)
2. Pravastatin-induced colitis (2008)
3. Statins and Gastric Cancer Risk (2011)
4. Ulcerative colitis after statin treatment (2002)

KIDNEY FAILURE

1. Cerivastatin and Acute Kidney Failure Caused by Rhabdomyolysis
2. Cerivastatin and Reports of Fatal Rhabdomyolysis (2002)
3. Cerivastatin Monotherapy-Induced Muscle Weakness, Rhabdomyolysis and Acute Renal Failure
4. Combined Organ Failure with Combination Antihyperlipidemic Treatment: A Case of Hepatic Injury and Acute Renal Failure (2007)
5. Fatal Rhabdomyolysis Associated with Simvastatin in a Renal Transplant Patient (2000)
6. Fatal Rhabdomyolysis Caused by Cerivastatin (2001)
7. Fatal Rhabdomyolysis Caused by Lipid-Lowering Therapy (2001)
8. Lovastatin-Induced Acute Rhabdomyolysis (1990)
9. Multiorgan Failure Induced by Atorvastatin (2002)
10. Rhabdomyolysis, Acute Renal Failure and Hepatopathy Induced by Lovastatin Monotherapy (1997)
11. Rhabdomyolysis and Acute Renal Failure Associated with Lovastatin (1994)
12. Rhabdomyolysis and Renal Injury with Lovastatin Use. Report of Two Cases in Cardiac Transplant Recipients (1988)
13. Rosuvastatin-Induced Arrest in Progression of Renal Disease (2004)

LIVER INJURY

1. Acute Cholestatic Hepatitis Associated with Pravastatin (1999)
2. Acute Cholestatic Hepatitis During Simvastatin Administration (1991)
3. Acute Cholestatic Hepatitis Induced by Cerivastatin (2002)

4. Acute Hepatitis Induced by HMG-CoA Reductase Inhibitor, Lovastatin (1994)
5. Atorvastatin as a Trigger of Autoimmune Hepatitis (2004)
6. Autoimmune Hepatitis After Treatment with Fluvastatin (2007)
7. Autoimmune Hepatitis Revealed by Atorvastatin (2003)
8. Autoimmune Hepatitis Triggered by Statins (2006)
9. Cholestatic Hepatitis After Reinitiating Treatment with Atorvastatin (2002)
10. Cholestatic Jaundice During Lovastatin Medication (1991)
11. Clinically Manifest Liver Lesions During use of Simvastatin (1996)
12. Effect of the Magnitude of Lipid Lowering on Risk of Elevated Liver Enzymes, Rhabdomyolysis, and Cancer: Insights from Large Randomized Statin Trials (2007)
13. Hepatitis due to Lovastatin (1996)
14. Hepatotoxicity of Hydroxy-Methyl-Glutaryl-Coenzyme A Reductase Inhibitors (1992)
15. Lipid Lowering Medication and Hepatotoxicity (2001)
16. Liver Fibrosis Attributed to Lipid Lowering Medications: Two Cases (2001)
17. Lovastatin and Cholestasis (1993)
18. Lovastatin-Induced Acute Cholestatic Hepatitis (1995)
19. Lovastatin-Induced Hepatitis (1992)
20. Simvastatin-Induced Hepatitis (1992)
21. Statins and Hepatotoxicity (2007)
22. Statins: Hepatic Disease and Hepatotoxicity Risk (2008)
23. Statin Toxicity: A Situation that Mimics Viral Hepatitis (2005)
24. Rosuvastatin-Associated Hepatitis with Autoimmune Features (2005)
25. Toxic Liver Damage Caused by HMG-CoA Reductase Inhibitor (2000)

LUNG INJURY

1. A Case of Drug-Induced Pneumonia Possibly Associated with Simvastatin (2005)
2. A Case of Interstitial Lung Disease with Atorvastatin (Tahor) and a Review of the Literature About These Effects Observed Under Statins (2006)
3. Basal Respiratory Exchange Ratio Is Altered With Statin Use in Normals (2004)
4. Bilateral Pleural Effusions Associated with Pravastatin Sodium Treatment (2007)
5. Dermatomyositis with Lung Involvement in a Patient Treated with Simvastatin (1995)

6. Hypersensitivity Pneumonitis in a Patient Taking Pravastatin (2001)
7. Interstitial Lung Disease with Pleural Effusion Caused by Simvastatin (1996)
8. Polymyalgia, Hypersensitivity Pneumonitis and Other Reactions in Patients Receiving HMG-CoA Reductase Inhibitors (1999)
9. Potential Link Between HMG-CoA Reductase Inhibitor (Statin) Use and Interstitial Lung Disease (2007)
10. Pulmonary Fibrosis Reported with Statins (2006)
11. Simvastatin-Induced Chylothorax (2003)
12. Statin-Induced Fibrotic Nonspecific Interstitial Pneumonia (2002)
13. Statins and Interstitial Lung Disease: A Systematic Review of the Literature and of Food and Drug Administration Adverse Events Reports (2011)

MEMORY AND COGNITION LOSS

1. Australian National Prescribing Service Factsheet on Statins and Memory Loss
2. Changes in Memory Function and Neuronal Activation Associated with Atorvastatin Therapy (June 2010)
3. Cognitive Impairment Associated with Atorvastatin (2001)
4. Cognitive Impairment Associated with Atorvastatin and Simvastatin (2003)
5. Do Low Dose Statins Affect Cognition? (2006)
6. Effects of Lovastatin on Cognitive Function and Psychological Well-Being (2000)
7. Randomized Ttrial of the Effects of Simvastatin on Cognitive Functioning in Hypercholesterolemic Adults (2004)
8. Short-Term Memory Loss associated with Rosuvastatin (2006)
9. Simvastatin-Associated Memory Loss (2001)
10. Simvastatin-Induced Decline in Cognition (2006)
11. Statins and the risk of dementia (2000)
12. Statin-Associated Memory Loss: Analysis of 60 Case Reports and Review of the Literature (2003)
13. Transient Global Amnesia Associated with Statin Intake (2006)

MENTAL ILLNESS

1. Depressive Symptoms in Hypercholesterolaemic Patients Treated with Pravastatin (1992)
2. Lipid-Lowering Medication Use and Aggression Scores in Women: A Report from the NHLBI-Sponsored WISE Study (2008)
3. Low Cholesterol and Violence (1998)
4. Low Cholesterol and Violent Crime (2000)
5. Psychiatric Disorders with Use of Simvastatin (1993)
6. Serum Cholesterol in Aggressive Conduct Disorder: A Preliminary Study (1984)
7. Serum Cholesterol Levels and Frequency of Aggression (1994)
8. Serum Cholesterol Levels and Severity of Aggression (1993)
9. Severe Irritability Associated with Statin Cholesterol-Lowering Drugs (2004)
10. Statins--The Pattern of Adverse Effects with Emphasis on Mental Reactions. Data from a National and an International Database (1997)

MUSCLE INJURY

1. A Comprehensive Description of Muscle Symptoms Associated with Lipid-Lowering Drugs (2003)
2. Cardiopulmonary Function Is Abnormal After Statin-Induced Rhabdomyolysis and Myositis (2004)
3. Adverse Effects of Statins (2005)
4. An Assessment of Statin Safety by Muscle Experts (2006)
5. Association Between Statin-Associated Myopathy and Skeletal Muscle Damage (2009)
6. Clinical Characteristics of 1053 Patients with Statin-Associated Muscle Complaints (2004)
7. Clinical Perspectives of Statin-Induced Rhabdomyolysis (2006)
8. Coenzyme Q10: A Therapy for Hypertension and Statin-Induced Myalgia? (2010)
9. Decreased Skeletal Muscle Mitochondrial DNA in Patients Treated with High-Dose Simvastatin (2007)
10. Effect of Atorvastatin on Left Ventricular Diastolic Function and Ability of Coenzyme Q10 to Reverse That Dysfunction (2004)
11. Effect of Coenzyme Q10 on Myopathic Symptoms in Patients Treated with Statins (2007)
12. Fatal and Widespread Skeletal Myopathy Confirmed Morphologically Years After Initiation of Simvastatin Therapy (2007)
13. FDA Adverse Event Reports on Statin-Associated Rhabdomyolysis (2002)

14. HMG CoA Reductase-Inhibitor-Related Myopathy and the Influence of Drug Interactions (2002)
15. How Common is Rhabdomyolysis in Patients Receiving Lipid-Lowering Therapy? (2005)
16. Incidence of Hospitalized Rhabdomyolysis in Patients Treated with Lipid-Lowering Drugs (2004)
17. Increased Exposure to Statins in Patients Developing Chronic Muscle Disease: A 2-Year Retrospective Study (2007)
18. Increases in Creatine Kinase After Exercise in Patients Treated with HMG Co-A Reductase Inhibitors (1990)
19. In Vivo and in Vitro Characterization of Skeletal Muscle Metabolism in Patients with Statin-Induced Adverse Effects (2006)
20. Lovastatin Increases Exercise-Induced Skeletal Muscle Injury (1997)
21. Managing Statin-Induced Muscle Toxicity in a Lipid Clinic (2011)
22. McArdle's Disease Diagnosed Following Statin-Induced Myositis (2004)
23. Methods and Compositions for the Treatment and Diagnosis for Statin-Induced Myopathy (2009)
24. Mild to Moderate Muscular Symptoms with High-Dosage Statin Therapy in Hyperlipidemic Patients – The PRIMO Study (2005)
25. Mitochondrial Alterations in Muscle Biopsies of Patients on Statin Therapy (2004)
26. Muscle Abnormalities in Four Patients Taking Statins to Treat Unfavorable Cholesterol Levels (2002)
27. Muscle CoEnzyme Q10 Level in Statin-Related Myopathy (2005)
28. Muscle Symptoms Associated with Statins: A Series of Twenty Patients (2006)
29. Observations from a Statin Myopathy Clinic (2006)
30. Occurrences of Rhabdomyolysis or Myositis Among Statin Users in a Veteran Affairs Population (2004)
31. Outcomes in 45 Patients with Statin-Associated Myopathy (2005)
32. Polymyositis Induced or Associated with Lipid-Lowering Drugs: Five Cases (2004)
33. Polymyositis Associated with Simvastatin (1997)
34. Potential Adverse Effects of Statins on Muscle (2005)
35. Pravastatin-Associated Inflammatory Myopathy (1992)
36. Pravastatin-Associated Polymyositis, a Case Report (2004)
37. Professional Athletes Suffering From Familial Hypercholesterolaemia Rarely Tolerate Statin Treatment Because of Muscular Problems (2004)
38. Risk Factors for Rhabdomyolysis with Simvastatin and Atorvastatin (2006)
39. Risk for Myopathy with Statin Therapy in High-Risk Patients (2003)
40. Severe Polymyositis with Simvastatin Use (2003)

41. Rhabdomyolysis Induced by a Single Dose of a Statin (2004)
42. Rhabdomyolysis Secondary to Lovastatin Therapy (1990)
43. Risk for Fatal Statin-Induced Rhabdomyolysis as a Consequence of Misinterpretation of 'Evidence-Based Medicine' (2005)
44. Severe Muscle Disorders Associated with Statins: Analysis of Cases Notified in France up to the end of February 2002 and Data Concerning the Risk Profile of Cerivastatin (2005)
45. Simvastatin-Induced Rhabdomyolysis in a Patient with Chronic Renal Failure (2000)
46. Simvastatin-Induced Rhabdomyolysis Followed by a MELAS syndrome (1993)
47. Simvastatin (Zocor) Drug Interactions Linked to Increased Risk for Myopathy (2005)
48. Spontaneous Compartment Syndrome in Association with Simvastatin-Induced Myositis (2008)
49. Sporadic Rippling Muscle Disease Unmasked by Simvastatin (2006)
50. Statin-Associated Exacerbation of Myasthenia Gravis (2004)
51. Statin-Associated Muscle-Related Adverse Effects: A Case Series of 354 Patients (2010)
52. Statin-Associated Muscle Adverse Effects (2003)
53. Statin-Associated Myopathy (2001)
54. Statin-Associated Myopathy (2006)
55. Statin-Associated Myopathy with Normal Creatine Kinase Levels (2002)
56. Statin-Associated Rhabdomyolysis (2005)
57. Statin Cardiomyopathy? A Potential Role for Co-Enzyme Q10 Therapy for Statin-Induced Changes in Diastolic LV Performance: Description of a Clinical Protocol (2003)
58. Statin-Induced Apoptosis and Skeletal Myopathy (2006)
59. Statin-Induced Myopathy: A Clinical Perspective (2009)
60. Statin-Induced Myopathy in a Competitive Amateur Cyclist (2008)
61. Statin-Induced Myositis Migrans (2002)
62. Statin Myopathy: An Update (2006)
63. Statin Myopathy as a Metabolic Muscle Disease (2008)
64. Statin Myopathy: Incidence, Risk Factors, and Pathophysiology (2007)
65. Statin Myotoxicity is Associated with Changes in the Cardiopulmonary Function (2004)
66. Statins Induce Calcium-Dependent Mitochondrial Permeability Transition (2006)
67. Statins and Myotoxicity: A Therapeutic Limitation (2006)
68. Statins May Cause Muscle Damage in Some Patients

69. Statins Unmasking a Mitochondrial Myopathy: A Case Report and Proposed Mechanism of Disease (2003)
70. Statin Therapy: Risks vs. Benefit: An Expert Interview with Eliot A Brinton, MD (2004)
71. The Role of Coenzyme Q10 in Statin-Associated Myopathy: A Systematic Review. (2007)
72. Two Different Types of Exercise-Induced Muscle Pain without Myopathy and CK-Elevation During HMG-Co-Enzyme-A-Reductase Inhibitor Treatment (1999)
73. Underappreciated Statin-Induced Myopathic Weakness Causes Disability (2005)

NERVE INJURY

1. Amyotrophic Lateral Sclerosis-Like Conditions Arising in Association with Cholesterol-Lowering Drugs: Hypothesized Role for Oxidative Stress and Mitochondrial Injury (2009)
2. Are Users of Lipid-Lowering Drugs at Increased Risk of Peripheral Neuropathy? (2001)
3. Assessing the Risk of Drug-Induced Neurological Disorders: Statins and Neuropathy (2002)
4. Association of HMG-CoA reductase inhibitors with neuropathy (2003)
5. Atorvastatin-Induced Polyneuropathy (2003)
6. Australian Adverse Drug Reactions Bulletin: Statins and Peripheral Neuropathy
7. Disorder Resembling Guillan-Barré Syndrome on Initiation of Statin Therapy (2004)
8. Lipid Lowering Drugs Prescription and the Risk of Peripheral Neuropathy: An Exploratory Case-Control Study Using Automated Databases (2004)
9. Inhibition of Cholesterol but not of Nonsterol Isoprenoid Products Induces Neuronal Cell Death (1999)
10. Multiple Mononeuropathy Associated to Treatment with Pravastatin (2006)
11. Peripheral Neuropathy and Lipid-Lowering Therapy (1998)
12. Peripheral Neuropathy Associated with Simvastatin (1995)
13. Presymptomatic Neuromuscular Disorders Disclosed Following Statin Treatment (2006)
14. Statins and Peripheral Neuropathy (1999)
15. Statins and Peripheral Neuropathy: Causation or Coincidence? (2011)
16. Statins and Risk of Polyneuropathy: A Case-Controlled Study (2002)

17. Statin-Associated Peripheral Neuropathy: A Review of the Literature (2004)
18. Statin Neuropathy Masquerading as Diabetic Autoimmune Polyneuropathy (2005)
19. Statins, Neuromuscular Degenerative Disease and an Amyotrophic Lateral Sclerosis-Like Syndrome: An Analysis of Individual Case Safety Reports from Vigibase (2007)
20. Statins Provoking MELAS Syndrome. A Case Report. (2007)
21. Statin Therapy and Small Fibre Neuropathy: A Serial Electrophysiological Study (2003)
22. Statin Therapy Inhibits Remyelination in the Central Nervous System (2009)

PANCREATIC INJURY/DIABETES

1. A Case of Simvastatin-Associated Pancreatitis and Review of Statin-Associated Pancreatitis (2006)
2. Acute Onset and Worsening of Diabetes Concurrent with Administration of Statins (2005)
3. Acute Pancreatitis due to Pravastatin Therapy (2003)
4. Acute Pancreatitis Associated With Atorvastatin Therapy (2000)
5. Acute Pancreatitis due to Lipid-Lowering Drugs (2005)
6. Acute Pancreatitis due to SimvastatinTherapy: Increased Severity After Rechallenge (2004)
7. Acute Pancreatitis Induced by Fluvastatin Therapy (2002)
8. A New Case of Simvastatin-Induced Acute Pancreatitis (1991)
9. Drug Induced Pancreatitis Might be a Class Effect of Statin Drugs (2005)
10. High-dose atorvastatin Associated with Worse Glycemic Control: A PROVE-IT Substudy (2004)
11. Pravastatin: A Potential Cause for Acute Pancreatitis (2006)
12. Recurrent Acute Pancreatitis During Pravastatin-Therapy (2006)
13. Recurrent Acute Pancreatitis Possibly Induced by Atorvastatin and Rosuvastatin. Is Statin Induced Pancreatitis a Class Effect? (2004)
14. Simvastatin: A New Drug Responsible for Acute Pancreatitis? (1991)
15. Simvastatin-Induced Acute Pancreatitis: Two Cases (1991)
16. Statins and Pancreatitis: A Systematic Review of Observational Studies and Spontaneous Case Reports (2006)
17. Statins and the Risk of Acute Pancreatitis: A Population-Based Case-Control Study (2006)
18. Statins: Beneficial or Adverse for Glucose Metabolism (2006)

SEXUAL DYSFUNCTION

1. Adverse Drug Reactions Advisory Committee Simvastatin and Adverse Endocrine Effects in Men (1995)
2. Atorvastatin and Male Infertility: Is There a Link? (2005)
3. Do Lipid-Lowering Drugs Cause Erectile Dysfunction? A Systematic Review (2002)
4. Effects of High-Dose Simvastatin on Adrenal and Gonadal Steroidogenesis in Men with Hypercholesterolemia (2000)
5. Effects of Statin Treatment on Serum Sex Steroid Levels and Autonomic and Erectile Function (2008)
6. Erectile Dysfunction and Statin Treatment in High Cardiovascular Risk Patients (2006)
7. HMG-CoA Reductase Inhibitor-Induced Impotence (1996)
8. HMG-CoA Reductase Inhibitors and Sexual Dysfunction (2001)
9. Is Decreased Libido Associated with the use of HMG-CoA-Reductase Inhibitors? (2004)
10. Lipid-Lowering Drugs and Erectile Dysfunction (2002)
11. Lovastatin and Hypospermia (1990)
12. Men Treated with Hypolipidaemic Drugs Complain More Frequently of Erectile Dysfunction (1996)
13. Probable Statin-Induced Testicular Pain (2007)
14. Reductase Inhibitors and Impotence: Two Case Series from the Spanish and French Drug Monitoring Systems (2006)
15. Simvastatin and Impotence (1997)
16. Testicular Function in Hypercholesterolemic Male Patients During Prolonged Simvastatin Treatment (1996)
17. The Effect of Statin Therapy on Testosterone Levels in Subjects Consulting for Erectile Dysfunction (2010)

SKIN INJURY

1. Acquired Ichthyosis with Pravastatin (2007)
2. Acute Generalized Exanthematous Pustulosis Induced by Simvastatin (2003)
3. Alopecia Associated with Atorvastatin (2002)
4. Antilipemic Drug-Induced Skin Manifestations (1995)
5. Atorvastatin-Induced Drug Reaction with Eosinophilia and Systemic Symptoms (DRESS) (2009)
6. Chronic Actinic Dermatitis due to Simvastatin (1998)
7. Chronic Actinic Dermatitis Secondary to Simvastatin (2002)
8. Dermatomyositis-like Syndrome and HMG-CoA Reductase Inhibitor (Statin) Intake (2004)
9. Effects of Systemic Treatment with Statins on Skin Barrier Function and Stratum Corneum Water-Holding Capacity (1996)
10. Eosinophilic Fasciitis Secondary to Treatment with Atorvastatin (2005)
11. Fluvastatin-Induced Dermatomyositis (2005)
12. Generalized Eczematous Skin Rash Possibly due to HMG-CoA Reductase Inhibitors (1993)
13. Ichthyosis Induced by Cholesterol-Lowering Drugs. Implications for Epidermal Cholesterol Homeostasis (1987)
14. Interferon-gamma (INF-gamma) Release Test Can Detect Cutaneous Adverse Effects to Statins (2009)
15. Lichenoid Drug Eruption with HMG-CoA Reductase Inhibitors (2004)
16. Linear IgA Bullous Dermatosis Induced by Atorvastatin (2001)
17. Pravastatin-Induced Lichenoid Drug Eruption (2006)
18. Simvastatin and Thrombotic Thrombocytopenic Purpura (1998)
19. Simvastatin-Induced Lichenoid Drug Eruption (2004)
20. Skin Lesions Due to Treatment with Simvastatin (2003)
21. Statins and the Skin (June 2011)
22. Thrombocytopenic Purpura During Therapy with Simvastatin (1992)
23. Thrombotic Thrombocytopenic Purpura and Simvastatin (1998)
24. Thrombotic Thrombocytopenic Purpura Associated with Statin Treatment (2004)
25. Toxic Epidermal Necrolysis from Atorvastatin (1998)

TENDON INJURY

1. Four Cases of Tendinopathy in Patients on Statin Therapy (2001)
2. Reproducible Tendinitis-Like Symptoms Related to Statin Therapy (2006)
3. Shoulder Stiffness: A Common Adverse Effect of HMG-CoA Reductase Inhibitors in Women? (2001)
4. Tendinous Disorders Attributed to Statins: A Study on Ninety-Six Spontaneous Reports in the Period 1990-2005 (2008)

THYROID INJURY

1. Asymptomatic Hypothyroidism and Statin-Induced Myopathy (2007)
2. HMG-CoA Reductase Inhibitors (Statins) Might Cause High Elevations of Creatine Phosphokinase (CK) in Patients with Unnoticed Hypothyroidism (2006)
3. Hypothyroidism and Lovastatin-Induced Myositis (2005)
4. Interaction Between Simvastatin and L-Thyroxine (2005)
5. Radioiodine Studies, Low Serum TSH, and the Influence of Statin Drugs (2009)
6. Simvastatin-Induced Bilateral Leg Compartment Syndrome and Myonecrosis Associated with Hypothyroidism (2007)
7. Simvastatin Induced Rhabdomyolysis and an Important Clinical Link with Hypothyroidism (2007)

OTHER

1. Adverse Side Effects of Statins in the Oral Cavity (2008)
2. Cholesterol-Lowering Therapy and Cell Membranes: Stable Plaque at the Expense of Unstable Membranes? (2009)
3. Does Pravastatin Promote Cancer in Elderly Patients? A Meta-Analysis (2007)
4. Drug Interactions with Lipid-Lowering Drugs: Mechanisms and Clinical Relevance (2006)
5. Evidence for Caution: Women and Statin Use (June 2007)
6. Golf-Inhibiting Gynecomastia Associated with Atorvastatin Therapy. (2006)
7. Gynecomastia due to Pravastatin (1999)
8. Gynecomastia Possibly Induced by Rosuvastatin (2008)
9. Insights from Large Randomized Statin Trials (2007)

10. Lupus Erythematosus and Other Autoimmune Diseases Related to Statin Therapy: A Systematic Review (Jan. 2007)
11. Lupus-Like Syndrome Associated with Simvastatin (1998)
12. Lupus-Like Syndrome Associated with Statin Therapy (2004)
13. Maternal Exposure to Statins and Risk for Birth Defects: A Case Series Approach (Oct. 15, 2008)
14. Meta-Analysis of Drug-Induced Adverse Events Associated with Intensive-Dose Statin Therapy (2007)
15. Reversal of Statin Toxicity to Human Lymphocytes in Tissue Culture (2003)
16. Safety and Statin Therapy: Reconsidering the Risks and Benefits (2003)
17. Should There Be A Moratorium on the Use of Cholesterol Lowering Drugs? (1992)
18. Simvastatin-Induced Lupus-Like Syndrome (2000)
19. Statins and Breast Cancer in Postmenopausal Women Without Hormone Therapy (Dec. 2009)
20. Statin-Related Adverse Events: A Meta-Analysis (2006)
21. Statin Safety: An Assessment Using an Administrative Claims Database (2006)
22. Systematic Review and Meta-Analysis of Clinically Relevant Adverse Events from HMG CoA Reductase Inhibitor Trials Worldwide from 1982 to Present (2007)
23. Treatment of Statin Adverse Effects with Supplemental Coenzyme Q10 and Statin Drug Discontinuation (2005)

MEDIA RELEASES

1. ABC30.com story: Sorting Out Statins (Nov. 13, 2006)
2. ABC News: Statins May Cause Muscle Damage in Some Patients (2009)
3. Business Week Online: Statins Could Cause Legal Headaches (August 2, 2006)
4. CBS News: Risky Statin Side Effects (Oct. 11, 2004)
5. CBS Evening News: Statins' Mind-Boggling Effects (May 24, 2004)
6. Daily Mail (UK): Statins: Side Effects of Anti-Cholesterol Drugs Questioned (June 27, 2006)
7. Daily Mail (UK): Statins: The Truth (January 29, 2007
8. Idaho Observer: The Horrors of Statin Drugs: The Misguided War on Cholesterol (Oct. 2007)
9. John Hopkins Health Alert: Statins and Cataract Risk (2007)
10. KTVU.com: Experts Warn of Side Effects from Cholesterol Meds (Sept. 14, 2006)
11. Los Angeles Times: The Downside of Statin Drugs (June 23, 2003)
12. Medical Science Today: Dallas Scientists Discover Statins May Falsely Indicate Thyroid Problems (Feb. 20, 2009)
13. Milwaukee Journal Sentinel: Doubts Raised Over Drugs for Cholesterol (March 28, 2004)
14. News 8 (Austin): Statins Have Risk (Feb. 5, 2005)
15. New York Daily News: Lipitor Ripped. Pfizer Downplay Side Effects of Drug. Suit Charges (June 9, 2006)
16. New York Times: Researcher Links Reduction in Cholesterol with Violent Death (March 17, 1998)
17. New York Times: Seeking a Fuller Picture of Statins (July 20, 2004)
18. People's Pharmacy: Are Statins Linked to Lou Gehrig's Disease? (Aug. 25, 2009)
19. People's Pharmacy: Statin Memory Loss Misdiagnosed as Alzheimer's (Feb. 10, 2006)
20. San Diego Union Tribune: Two San Diego Scientists Raise Questions About Cholesterol-Cutting Drugs (May 28, 2001)
21. San Diego Union Tribune: Remedy & Risk (July 14, 2004)
22. San Diego Union Tribune: Trouble with Statins? Tell USCD (Oct. 31, 2006)
23. San Francisco Chronicle: Doubts Raised on Wider Sales of Statins: Over-the-counter Marketing Push for Cholesterol Drug (Jan. 2005)
24. Science Daily: Statin Drugs May Risk for Peripheral Neuropathy (May 14, 2002)
25. Science Daily: Muscle Damage May Be Present in Some Patients Taking Statins (July 6, 2009)

26. Scientific American: It's Not Dementia, It's Your Heart Medication: Cholesterol Drugs and Memory (Oct. 19, 2010)
27. Scientific American: Cholesterol Conundrum: Changing HDL and LDL Levels Does Not Always Alter Heart Disease or Stroke Risk (Oct. 25, 2011)
28. Smart Money: The Lipitor Dilemma (Nov. 2003)
29. The Patient Tort Report: Study: Statins and Lung Disease (2011)
30. The Seattle Times: Concerns over Statins and ALS (Aug. 30, 2009)
31. The Telegraph: Statins Raise Chances of Kidney Failure and Cataracts (May 21, 2010)
32. The Washington Post: Study Links Statins to Nerve Damage (Sept. 10, 2002)
33. Wall Street Journal: Researchers Ask Patients to Help Fill Gap in Data on Side Effects of Statins (Oct. 3, 2006)
34. WebMD: Statins May Lower Testosterone, Libido: Men with Erectile Dysfunction on Statin Therapy are Twice as Likely to have Low Testosterone, Study Finds (April 16, 2010)
35. WFTV.com: Controversy Over Use of Cholesterol Drugs (Nov. 29, 2006)

WEBSITES & LINKS

1. Ask A Patient: Medical Ratings and Health Care Opinions
2. Dr. Graveline's Website: SpaceDoc.com
3. FDA MedWatch
4. Message Board - High Cholesterol Messages (HealthBoards.com)
5. Message Board - All Aspects of Cardiovascular Diseases (Google groups)
6. Message Board – Lipitor (Atorvastatin and Related) RxBoard
7. Public Citizen - Health Research Group
8. StatinAlert.org
9. Statin Effects Study Group: StatinEffects.com
10. The International Network of Cholesterol Skeptics: THINCS.org

EXPERTS

1. John Abramson, MD
2. Richard J. Cenedella, PhD
3. Annette Draeger, MD
4. Beatrice Golumb, MD, PhD
5. David Graham, MD
6. Julie Hippisley-Cox, MD
7. Joel M. Kauffman, Professor Emeritus
8. Malcolm Kendrick, MD
9. Peter H. Langsjoen, MD
10. Gwen Olsen
11. Joseph M. Price, MD
12. Matthias Rath, MD
13. Julian Whitaker, MD
14. Dave Woynorowski, MD

Papers on the Marvelous Mevalonate Pathway by Marvelous Marvin Siperstein:

1953: Biliary End-Products of Cholesterol Metabolism
1958: Studies on the Relationship Between Glucose Oxidation and Intermediary Metabolism. 1. The Influence of Glycolysis on the Synthesis of Cholesterol and Fatty Acid in Normal Liver
1958: Studies on the Relationship Between Glucose Oxidation and Intermediary Metabolism. II. The Role of Glucose Oxidation in Lipogenesis in Diabetic Rat Liver
1959: Studies on the Site of Feedback Control of Cholesterol Synthesis
1963: Feedback Control of Cholesterol Synthesis in Man
1964: Deletion of the Cholesterol-Negative Feedback System in Liver Tumors
1966: A Gas-Liquid Chromatographic Procedure for the Measurement of Mevalonic Acid Synthesis
1966: Feedback Control of Mevalonate Synthesis by Dietary Cholesterol
1966: Further Studies on the Deletion of the Cholesterol Feedback System in Hepatomas
1970: Cholesterol and Cancer
1971: The of Cholesterol Biosynthesis to Cancer
1971: Loss of Feedback Control of Hydroxymethylglutaryl Coenzyme A Reductase in Hepatomas
1973: 3-Hydroxy-3-Methylglutaryl Coenzyme A Reductase
1973: Studies of the In Vivo Metabolism of Mevalonic Acid in the Normal Rat
1974: Properties of 3-Hydroxy-3-Methylglutaryl Coenzyme A Reductase Solubilized from Rat Liver and Hepatoma
1976: The In Vitro Metabolism of Mevalonate by Sterol and Non-sterol Pathways
1977: The Quantitative Role of the Kidneys in the in Vivo Metabolism of Mevalonate
1979: Sex Differences in the Sterol and Nonsterol Metabolism of Mevalonate
1980: Influence of Thyroid Hormone Status on Mevalonate Metabolism in Rats
1981: Isopentenyladenine as a Mediator of Mevalonate-Regulated DNA Replication
1983: Dual Role of Mevalonate in the Cell Cycle
1984: Role of Cholesterogenesis and Isoprenoid Synthesis in DNA Replication and Cell Growth

UPDATE: 2018 Neuropathy Treatment Protocol

The following free eBook is available for download at:

HannahYoseph.com

Neuropathy Treatment:
3 Natural Remedies for Neuropathy
And How They Work

Hannah Yoseph, MD

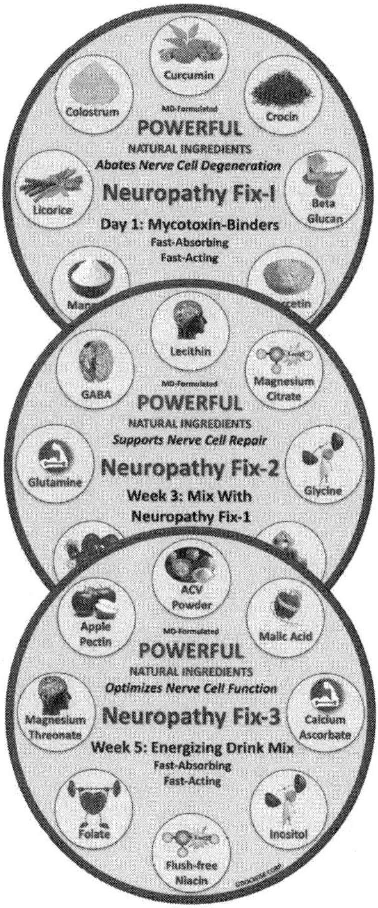

Preface

In most of my self-help medical books, James would word-smith both the Introduction and Epilogue. His pen offered the easiest reading and practical wisdom to my dry science.

Two years ago, James was wheeled away for a routine pacemaker implant. We had not been advised of any bad outcome, so when a weeping surgeon announced that James' heart had stopped after insertion of the lead wire, I was totally unprepared. I resisted. "Oh noooooo; James can't die – you don't understand. Go back and throw everything you have at him. *Death is not an option!*"

The cardiologist, who had come to love James as did everyone who peered into his naked, open heart, wheeled around and with a quick assurance retorted, "Okay, but this will take some time."

James died. Mercifully released from two decades of suffering from statin-drug (mycotoxin) poisoning and multifocal motor neuropathy, he took with him the truth on how to prevent and reverse his illness which his doctors should have known.

This book is a gross simplification of what we discovered and detailed in two coauthored books: ***Conquering Lou Gehrig's Disease: The ALS Diet*** and ***How Statin Drugs Really Lower Cholesterol (And Kill You One Cell at a Time)***. Refer to these books for exhaustive evidence that supports what is simply stated here where the greater focus is on REMEDY rather than cause.

The cause for ALS and various neuropathies has been known for many years. It is well documented in this book. That statin drugs induce ALS and peripheral neuropathy serves to further cement the connection between mycotoxins and neuropathy. The logical and simple mode of remedy follows proven cause.

Hannah Yoseph, MD
August 11, 2018

Introduction: Poisoned (NOT Genetics)!

Many types of mycotoxins induce ALS and other non-traumatic neuropathies. Layers of evidence make this is inarguable.
-H. Yoseph

Ubiquitous toxins that cannot be sensed are slowly and imperceptibly debilitating us. These poisons are in our food, in the air and in our medicine cabinets. They are *everywhere* with one exception: our medical textbooks – the type that medical doctors read.

Unlike medical doctors, veterinarians are well-informed of these universal toxins that seep into animal feed, causing wobbly legs ("staggers") and sometimes a slow, nerve-destroying, paralyzing death. Pharmaceutical stakeholders, who structure medical curricula by funding university-based drug studies, have more to gain by keeping human doctors in the dark.

These universal toxins – so tenacious that they can survive a round trip to the moon and then wipe out an entire species – are spawned by fungi. They are called *mycotoxins* ("myco" means "fungus"). *Mycotoxicosis* is poisoning caused by mycotoxins.

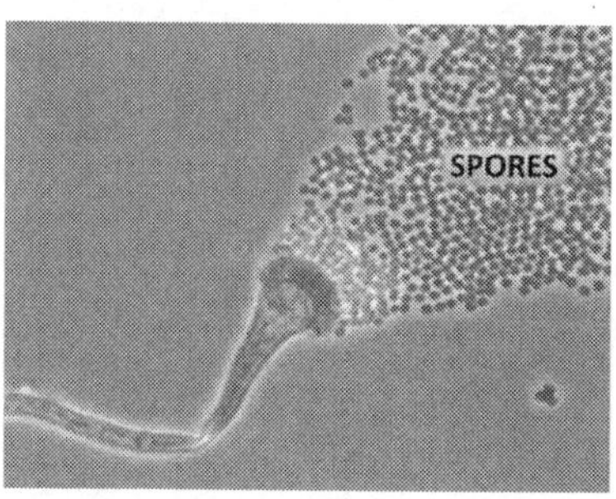

Of the three types of fungi (molds, yeasts and mushrooms), the vast majority are molds that proliferate in wet acidic environments. Molds are spread all over the earth by invisible germinated spores that suspend in turbulent air for an indefinite time until a moist acidic environment invites them to spawn. The air we breathe is a virtual jungle of them. Even so, a healthy alkaline body normally resists them – but an acidic body does *not* (dark colas are ten thousand times more acidic than normal alkaline blood).

In mummification, the body is made alkaline and dry. The wet internal organs are removed and the body is dehydrated and salted. This removes the moist acidic environment that supports mold and subsequent decay. Western dietary habits, which include regular ingestion of soda drinks, promote an acidic environment that supports decay by mycotoxins.

Upon landing on moist and acidic organic matter, spores release mycotoxins that digest cells into microscopic subcellular parts that seep into the fungus as food. Mold "eats" this decayed soup and is nourished; what remains is returned to the earth. Without fungi, the earth's biomass such as leaves and dead bodies would stockpile. Simply put, fungi cause cells to rot and die because ***that is what fungi do***. Fungal spores, and the mycotoxins they release to cause cells to decay, are essential to the life cycle of the planet.

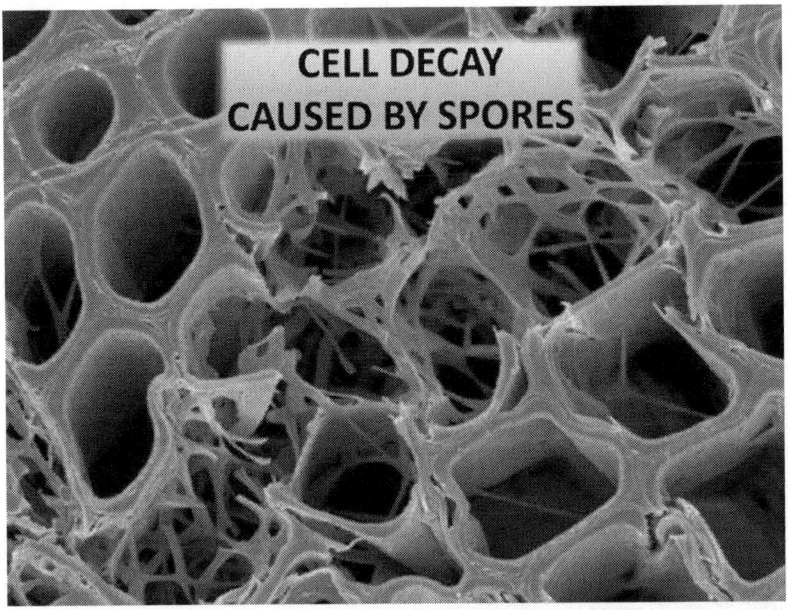

If given the opportunity, mycotoxins could turn all of the earth's biomass into rot for reuse. This doesn't happen because spores require damp acidic environments to grow and proliferate. They may live forever, however, waiting for that opportunity to present itself. And so it is that airborne mold spores inevitably find their way into any stored damp food - grains, fruit, coffee beans, nuts – *anything* organic.

Mycotoxins can degenerate most everything organic (alive, dead or dying) that they touch. Physicians are taught that most chronic degenerative diseases are due to "genetics". This unsupported explanation is a crutch to lean upon when left without a sound diagnosis to explain any debilitating condition (such as that caused by mycotoxins inside an acidic moist host).

Mycotoxin-induced degenerative disease is not due to genetics. However, genetics is at the root of degenerative disease caused by mycotoxins. Some mycotoxins destroy the genetics housed inside cells by disrupting the DNA. This causes cells and the genetic material housed in the DNA to rupture. This is, after all, what mycotoxins do – cause cellular decay.

The nucleus that contains DNA is "command central" of any type of cell including nerve cells. If this is disrupted and the cell is ruptured, a live victim starts to degenerate, one poisoned cell at a time. If the cells are nerve glial cells, the victim experiences increasing neuropathy (loss of normal nerve function). Because DNA is unique to each individual, people respond to mycotoxin poisoning differently. For some, the insult is increasingly debilitating (such as motor neuron disease) while others have minor discomfort (such as muscle pain). Because different mycotoxins induce different types of decay, a host of degenerative diseases, including chronic neuropathies, affect different people differently.

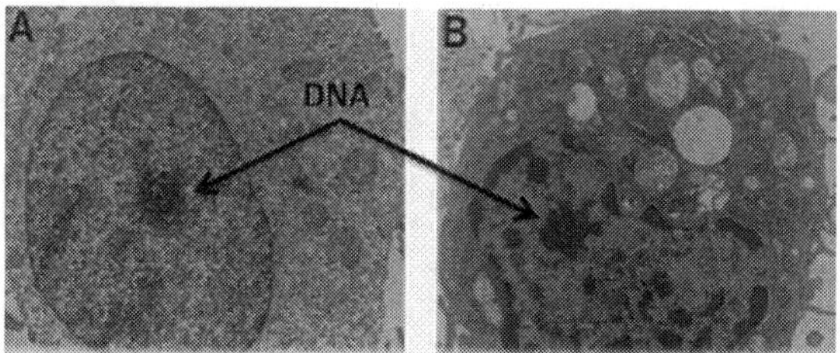

A: Normal Nucleus with condensed DNA

B: Nucleus falling apart 24 hours after exposure to mycotoxin

Degenerative disease by mycotoxicosis is not due to genetics. Rather, genetic disruption and cell degeneration are at the root of mycotoxicosis.

When cells are destroyed by mycotoxins, antibodies are made to "flag" specific dead and dying cell parts for destruction by white blood cells (called macrophages).

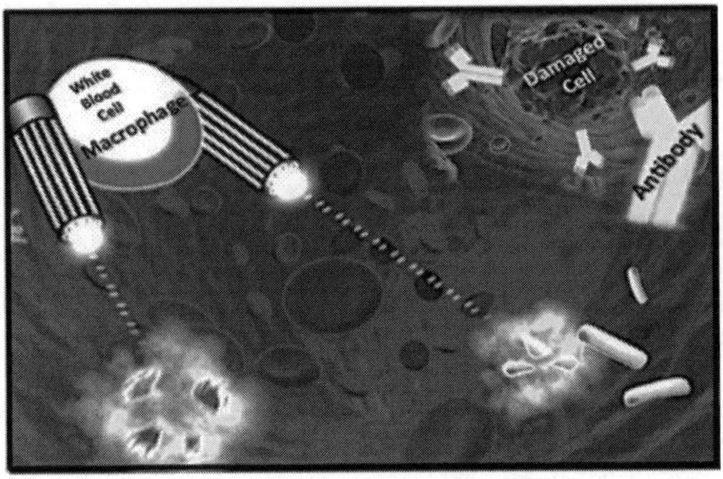

If DNA is destroyed, *anti-DNA antibodies* are made. If the nucleus (which houses DNA) is ruptured, *anti-nuclear antibodies* mark the debris for removal. If cell membrane phospholipids are destroyed, *anti-phospholipid antibodies* are made. Macrophages "see" the antibodies and dispose of the damaged cell parts.

When these antibodies are discovered by lab tests, the patient is diagnosed with an "autoimmune disease". It appears that the body is attacking itself by making antibodies against normal cells. In fact, the body is doing what it is designed to do – remove dead and dying cell parts that have been destroyed by the undetected mycotoxins that are EVERYWHERE in our air, food and buildings! Toxic drugs are then prescribed to block an immune system that is *simply doing its job*. To date, there remains no known cause for cancer or autoimmune disease, and there never will be. There is essentially no training in mycotoxicosis. When the connection is made, it is suppressed.

Some mycotoxins block DNA replication rather than degrade the DNA. When DNA replication is blocked in living cells, cells reflexively respond in a life-or-death attempt to override the blockade. This can lead to an out-of-control replication of cells called *cancer*. This is why some molds are implicated in cancer, as well as why some drugs that are disease-causing mycotoxins (such as statin drugs for lowering cholesterol) can induce cancer.

If a cell cannot override the DNA blockade, it dies. The degenerative disease that follows is as varied as there are different types of cells. But the root cause is the same.

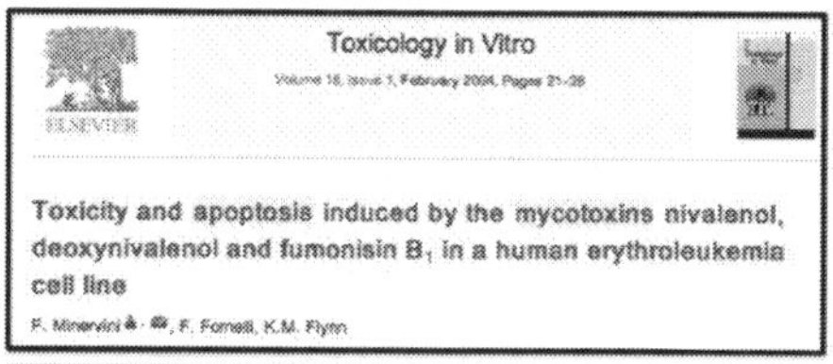
Toxicology in Vitro

Volume 18, Issue 1, February 2004, Pages 21-28

Toxicity and apoptosis induced by the mycotoxins nivalenol, deoxynivalenol and fumonisin B_1 in a human erythroleukemia cell line

F. Minervini, F. Fornelli, K.M. Flynn

Apoptotic activity induced by the mycotoxins ochratoxin A and zearalenone in bovine lymphocytes

M.B. Lioi[1], A. Santoro[1], R. Barbieri[1], S. Salzano[2], M.V. Ursini[3]

Ital.J.Anim.Sci. vol. 2 (Suppl. 1), 94-96, 2003

Mycotoxins can rupture cells by a process called *apoptosis*. Human cells that die by apoptosis leave behind pits, ulcers and scars. If this happens to stomach cells, we see ulcers. If this happens to glial cells that make myelin in nerves, "multiple scars" are seen on MRI scans. If this happens to red blood cells, it causes anemia or, if enough blood cells are ruptured, death by asphyxiation.

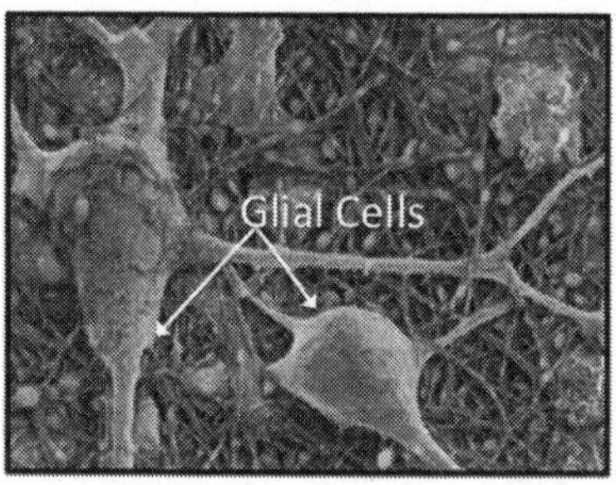

All nerves are protected by living interconnecting cells called "glial cells". These fat-rich cells wrap around and insulate nerves just like plastic protects electrical wire. If glial cells are destroyed by glial toxins, then normal electrical conduction to muscles and organs is interrupted. This results in shaking and weakness. The tremors and muscle weakness are like faulty conductions in electrical wires with missing portions of protective plastic wrap. For this reason, ALS and other neuropathies have been linked to glial toxins from mycotoxins and various other nerve toxins.

Because mold can be seen, mold-contaminated foods are readily treated. But mycotoxins that ooze from mold spores onto food are invisible, and more often than not, are left intact after treatment methods destroy the mold *but not the unseen toxins.* For this reason, a milk cow that has eaten moldy feed can have mycotoxin-contaminated milk that is not purified by pasteurization. The same applies to grains sprayed for mold after mycotoxins have already penetrated the hull. (This begs the question: Is grain intolerance due to gluten or is it unseen and untested-for mycotoxins?)

> Bonn 2010
>
> **Analysis of the genetic potential of the sponge-derived fungus *Penicillium chrysogenum* E01-10/3 for polyketide production**
>
> **Fungal mycotoxins**
>
> Mycotoxins are known as low-molecular-weight natural products (i.e. small molecules) produced as secondary metabolites in filamentous fungi. These metabolites represent a chemically heterogeneous group, but they all exhibit high toxicity. By definition mycotoxins are synthesised in filamentous fungi and are toxic to vertebrates and other animal groups in extremely low (i.e. microgram) concentrations [15]. When present in food, these fungal metabolites can have toxic effects with acute (e.g. liver or kidney deterioration) and chronic (e.g. liver cancer) symptoms. Due to their mutagenic and teratogenic profile, exposure to fungal metabolites may result in skin irritation, immunosuppression, birth defects, neurotoxicity and death [16]
>
> The members of the statin family of secondary metabolites are potent inhibitors of 3-hydroxy-3-methylglutaryl-coenzyme A (HMG-CoA) reductase, the key enzyme in cholesterol biosynthesis in humans [87].

The above excerpt from the book ***How Statin Drugs Really Lower Cholesterol (And Kill You One Cell at a Time)*** is one of many layers of evidence that the number one-selling drug for lowering cholesterol is actually a deadly mycotoxin that was originally used in cancer research to demonstrate how cancer-inducing mycotoxins predictably lower cholesterol before causing cancer (low cholesterol precedes various forms of mycotoxin-induced cancers; this is due to accelerated cell replication that reduces blood cholesterol). Physicians are ill-equipped to recognize mycotoxin poisoning or the dietary habits that promote it. They have no training in mycotoxicosis (mycotoxin poisoning), only a few hours of training on nutrition and wrong training on pH (acid vs alkaline blood) which serves to resist, support or exacerbate mycotoxicosis.

To diagnose and reverse mycotoxicosis requires KNOWLEDGE of:

1. **Mycotoxins (MDs have NONE)**
2. **Nutrition (MDs have MINIMAL)**
3. **pH (MDs have it WRONG)**

One day in medical school, a group of colleagues and I were handed a message to appear at the Dean of Surgery's office. We speculated why the normal schedule had been interrupted for this odd meeting, only to find that the entire class had been divided into eight groups for a focused two-day lesson on blood pH balance. Because multiple students had complained that the recent lessons on pH balance did not make sense, the class was divided into smaller sections for a do-over. But after two days and four hours of exhaustive instruction by the Dean, my colleagues and I insisted that the blood pH formulas *still* did not make a lick of sense.

I can now look back on that meeting and know that the reason we did not understand the formulas for blood pH balance is that western medicine has it wrong. I discovered this after working in New Zealand where physicians measure blood pH with a *direct* measurement of the four alkaline minerals: sodium, potassium, calcium and magnesium. In the USA, pH is *indirectly* calculated by measuring blood gases (such as carbon dioxide and oxygen) that are altered by these four alkaline minerals. This is not intuitive, and is the reason my then fellow-students complained that the formulas for calculating blood pH defied common sense.

Nothing is more important to plant health than the pH of the soil. How much more, then, for the *human* soil – the blood – to have a proper pH balance that resists, rather than promotes, mycotoxin poisoning and for physicians to understand it correctly!

In violation of consumer safety laws, MANY prescription drugs are made from known disease-causing mycotoxins…and both prescribers and consumers are woefully uninformed. This is indisputably proven in my book, ***How Statin Drugs Really Lower Cholesterol (And Kill You One Cell at a Time).***

The pharmaceutical machine can support patent chemicals (Rx drugs) only because trustworthy medicine – vitamins and whole foods – cannot be patented. Trillions have been invested over the past century in medical schools, clinics and hospitals, to provide a polished illusion of credibility that merits unconditional trust.

This illusion of pharmaceutical medicine's reliability is a clear danger to the masses. Prescribers are grievously uninformed about how mycotoxins, nutrition and pH interact to promote cellular health or disease. Whether this ignorance is by design does not matter, because the inevitable result is the same: repeat failures to diagnose mycotoxicosis and/or nutritional deficiencies that induce chronic degenerative disease (therefore blaming genetics) and continuing to chase symptoms and posturing oneself as an authority to support the mystique of credibility.

For example, arteries and joints are lined with collagen, which provides strength and pliability. Collagen is made of three proteins wound together by vitamin C like a rope. Vitamin C deficiency predictably results in weakening of collagen, and therefore weakening of the blood vessels and joints. This can manifest as bleeding and receding gums, frequent infections, sore joints, hemorrhoids, varicose veins and high blood pressure. This nutritional deficiency is called "scurvy" and is no longer recognized by physicians or dentists (no money to be made in advising patients to eat more fruit). The remedy used to be oranges or onions, fed to smoking ancient mariners to prevent death by cardiovascular disease on the high seas. But modern prescribers have been so dumbed down in regard to nutritional deficiencies and disease that if you complain of bleeding gums, your dentist will tell you to use a softer tooth brush. If you present with elevated blood pressure, your physician will give you an unknown chemical that will block the body's normal response to weakening blood vessels. But at what cost? Mycotoxins and snake venom, after all, also lower blood pressure by weakening the heart muscle.

Even penicillin, the so-called medical wonder-drug, remains the singular number-one cause of drug-induced death. Physicians are taught that this is due to an allergic reaction causing the patient to stop breathing. Penicillin is a mycotoxin that, in some people (due to their genetics) causes red blood cells to rupture (lack of blood cells to carry oxygen = lack of breath). If the patient survives, normal gut bacteria may learn to survive the poisoning by shedding their protein coat and morphing into forms that have been implicated in autoimmune diseases of all kinds. This medical mayhem continues for one simple reason: physicians are taught only what patent drugs *do* – not what they *are*.

Most autoimmune diseases, cancer and some cases of Type 2 diabetes (which all express various types of neuropathies) are caused by nutritional deficiencies and mycotoxin poisoning. It is the same for ALS. I have collected hundreds of pages of evidence on this matter, available in the following two books:

1. ***How Statin Drugs Really Lower Cholesterol (And Kill You One Cell at a Time)***
2. ***Proof for the Cancer-Fungus Connection***

In this book, I am presenting the underlying cause of ALS (mycotoxicosis) and various neuropathies, backed by decades of research and connecting the dots in order to restore James to health after two decades of mycotoxin poisoning by prescription statin drugs. I refer you to these two books for more detailed science than will be covered in this book, where the focus is more on remedy than cause. Here are a few published studies proving the connection between mycotoxin poisoning and nerve disease of various kinds ("tremorgenic" means "to cause tremors or shaking"):

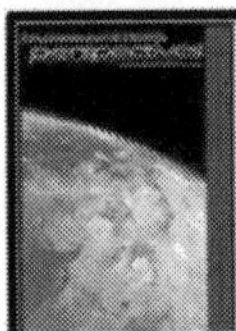

Aflatrem: A Tremorgenic Mycotoxin With Acute Neurotoxic Effecits

Valdes J, Cameron J and Cole R.

"A group of fungal metabolites collectively known as tremorgenic mycotoxins have been identified as the causative agents of a neurological disease of cattle known as "staggers syndrome". This disease is characterized by muscle tremors and hyperexcitability, and similar responses have been observed in laboratory animals treated with the mycotoxins. The fungi which product these compounds have been isolated from corn, silage and various forages, and so pose a health threat for both livestock and humans who consume these commodities."

Environmental Health Perspectives, 1985 (62): 459-63.

Territrems, Tremorgenic Mycotoxins of Aspergillus terreus

Ling K H, Yang C K and Peng F T.

Applied and Environmental Microbiology, 1979: 37 (3): 355.

Territrem B, a Tremogenic Mycotoxin That Inhibits Acetylcholinesterase with a Noncovalent yet Irreversible Binding Mechanism

The Journal of Biological Chemistry., 1999: 274 (49): 34916-923

Since mycotoxicosis is the missing diagnosis in ALS and various non-traumatic neuropathies (including sciatica and diabetic neuropathy), the first natural remedy is a blend of mycotoxin binders to remove the toxins from INSIDE the poisoned nerve cells.

The connection between mycotoxins and neuropathy is not up for debate. There are also many other mycotoxin-like toxins that damage the nerves. Nevertheless, the first step remains the same: identify the toxin source and remove the toxin load.

STEP ONE: BIND THE TOXINS.
The FIRST STEP is Neuropathy Fix-1.

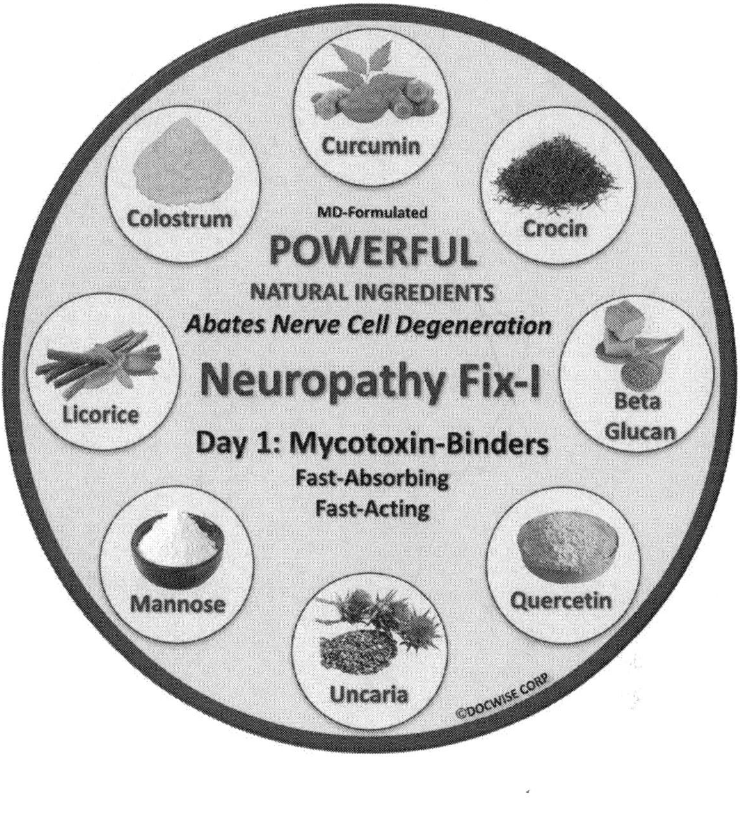

1. Neuropathy Fix-1: Mycotoxin Binders

"The doctor of the future will give no medicine, but will interest his patients in the cause and prevention of disease."
-Thomas Edison

Before taking any kind of remedy for a chronically debilitating neurological condition not caused by trauma, toxin *sources* must first be eliminated. Prevention MUST precede remedy.

There are five main mycotoxin sources implicated in nerve cell degeneration:

1. Mycotoxin-contaminated food and/or buildings
2. Rx drugs that are mycotoxins
3. Occupational toxins
4. Acid blood pH (primarily from drinking colas)
5. Excess alcohol ingestion

Eliminate these potential sources one at a time:

1. Mycotoxin-contaminated food and/or buildings

Any moldy food can cause mycotoxin poisoning. The most common source is grains (rice and cereals) stored in silos.

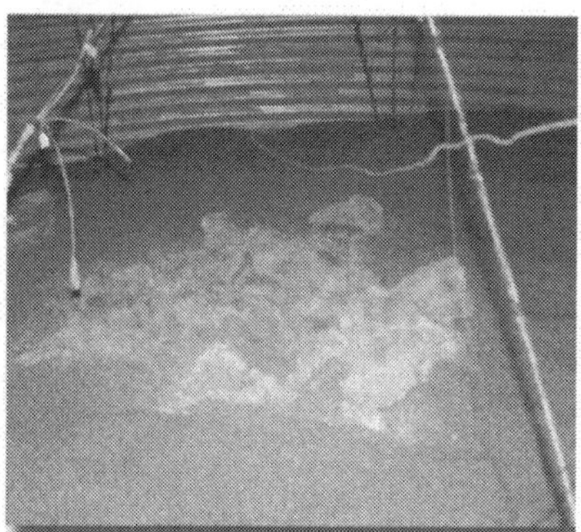

Mold in wheat storage bin. Photo: Winnipeg Cereal Research Centre, Agriculture and Agri-Food Canada

Many mycotoxins are neurotoxic. Fumonisins, penetrems and territrems, for example, are universally present in peanuts, corn and wheat products. These can cause tremors, convulsions, limb weakness, and ataxis (unsteady gait) – similar to symptoms of ALS and various neuropathies such as Multiple Sclerosis (MS).

Most physicians would diagnose mycotoxicity and its resultant tissue damage by apoptosis (causing spasms and shakes) as one or more of the following:

1. Amyotrophic Lateral Sclerosis (ALS – a nerve destroying muscle wasting condition).
2. Parkinson's disease (shaky muscular condition).
3. MS (another nerve scarring muscular condition).

Because of varied symptoms caused by different toxins, there are as many different diagnoses to account for the symptoms. Most MDs would agree, nevertheless, that the neuromuscular trouble is attributed to some "genetic proclivity" rather than possible mycotoxicity from common food molds. Mycotoxicosis is the missing diagnosis.

Do your own research here to look for a potential source of contamination in your diet. Keep in mind that foods that are stored long-term, such as in silos, are at high-risk for mold contamination. Consider other sources of environmental mold exposure such as cancer-causing black mold found in public buildings and homes. (Noteworthy, the Jewish-Christian scriptures include a mandate in Leviticus 14:34-48 to destroy clothing and buildings irreversibly contaminated by mold.)

2. Rx drugs that are mycotoxins

The most commonly-prescribed Rx drugs that are mycotoxins are statin drugs (Lovastatin, Lipitor, etc.) for lowering cholesterol. If your doctor knew that these drugs are mycotoxins, he or she would *never* prescribe them for long-term use.

Chem. Rev. 2009, 109, 3909-3990

Chemistry and Biology of Mycotoxins and Related Fungal Metabolites

Table 2. Mycotoxins Produced by *Aspergillus* sp.

fungus	mycotoxin produced
Aspergillus terreus	Territrem A,[25] Citreoviridin, Citrinin (2), Gliotoxin (527), Patulin (3), Terrein, Terreic acid, Terretonin, Itaconic acid, Aspulvinone, Asterric acid, Asterriquinone, butyrolactone I, Emodin (573), Geodin, Itaconate, Lovastatin,[26] Questin, Sulochrin, Terrecyclic acid.

Again, doctors know only what drugs *do*; they do not know what most of them *are*. Other drugs that are high on the mycotoxin suspect list are those that induce autoimmune disease and cancer. These drugs cause cells to decay, which triggers an antibody response. This includes over 70 drugs such as:

- Statins (Lipitor)
- Sulfadiazine
- Hydralazine
- Procainamide
- Isoniazid
- Methyldopa
- Quinidine
- Minocycline
- Cyclosporin
- Chlorpromazine

All of the above are antibiotics (as is penicillin, which is a mycotoxin-based antibiotic and the most common cause of drug-induced death by apoptosis/rupture of red blood cells). Other mycotoxins such as statin drugs (Lovastatin) rupture nerve cells (glial cells):

Lovastatin-Induced Proliferation Inhibition and Apoptosis in C6 Glial Cells[1]

JAE W. CHOI and SUNG E. JUNG
Department of Pharmacology, Yonsei University College of Medicine, Seoul, Korea

In this study we demonstrated that the cytotoxic effects of lovastatin fall into two categories: suppression of cell growth and induction of apoptosis of C6 glial cells...In conclusion, our data demonstrate that lovastatin can inhibit cell proliferation and induce apoptosis in C6 glial cells, which highlights the importance of the mevalonate pathway on the regulation of cell proliferation and prevention of apoptosis.

Statins, Neuromuscular Degenerative Disease and an Amyotrophic Lateral Sclerosis-Like Syndrome

An Analysis of Individual Case Safety Reports from Vigibase

I. Ralph Edwards, Kristina Star and *Anne Kiuru*

The WHO Foundation Collaborating Centre for International Drug Monitoring, the Uppsala Monitoring Centre (UMC), Uppsala, Sweden

Results: 'Upper motor neurone lesion' is a rare adverse event reported in relationship to drugs in Vigibase (a database containing nearly 4 million ICSRs). Of the total of 172 ICSRs on this reported term, 43 were related to statins, of which 40 were considered further: all but one case was reported as ALS. In 34/40 reports a statin was the sole reported suspected drug. The diagnostic criteria were variable, and seven of the statin cases also had features of peripheral neuropathy.

Drug Safety 2007; 30 (6): 515-525
0114-5916/07/0006-0515/$44.95/0

If you have neurodegenerative disease and are taking any of these drugs, do some investigating and make an educated decision as to whether a prescription drug may be the source of the damage to your nerves. If the prescription drug you are taking has been linked to "drug-induced Lupus" or "drug-induced autoimmune disease" then it is highly suspect as the source toxin for any neuropathy. Most autoimmune illnesses involve some type of neuropathy and increased risk of cancer. Again, some mycotoxins are *indisputably linked to autoimmune disease and cancer*.

3. Occupational Toxins

Mycotoxins are now marketed as "Fungal Biological Control Agents" or FBCA. They are used as herbicides and pesticides for farm crops. We spray mycotoxins everywhere and have been doing so for decades.

FBCA are sold as "all-natural" insecticides. They are dusted on crops for bug control, coated on fruit to extend shelf life and sprayed on ball fields to kill weeds without any regard for the athletes who then roll in it.

Predictably, many studies demonstrate a relationship between exposure to FBCA agricultural chemicals and ALS:

Severely Increased Risk of Amyotrophic Lateral Sclerosis Among Italian Professional Football Players.

Brain, 2005: 128 (3): 472-76.

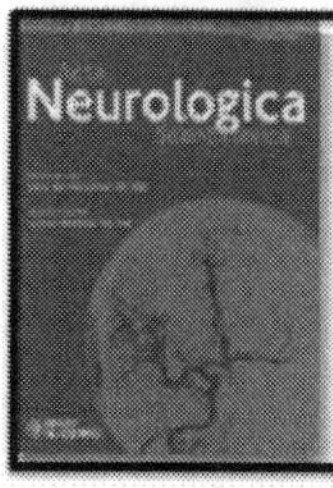

Amyotrophic Lateral Sclerosis in Sweden in Relation to Occupation

Gunnarsson L, Lindberg G, Soderfeldt B, Axelson O.

Acta Neurologica Scandinavica, 1991: 83 (6): 394-98.

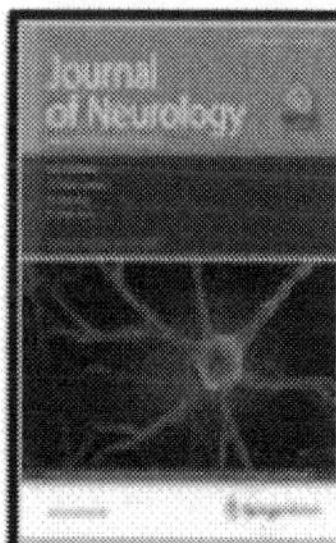

Amyotrophic Lateral Sclerosis, Rural Environment and Agricultural Work in the Local Health District of Ferrera, Italy, in the years 1964-1998.

Govani V, Granieri E, Fallica E, Casett I.

Journal of Neurology, 2005: 252 (11): 1322-27.

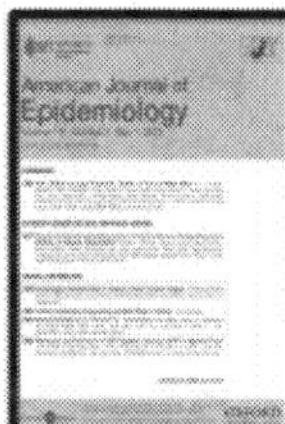

Occupational Exposures and Amyotrophic Lateral Sclerosis. A Population-based Case-Control Study

"These findings suggest an association between ALS and agricultural chemicals in men".

McGuire *et al.* Am J. Epidemiololgy, 1997: 145 (12): 1076-88.

4. Acid blood pH (primarily from drinking colas)

We are born with alkaline blood (normal pH is 7.4) and we die acidic (pH less than 7). Upon death, the body immediately begins to become acidic. This causes unseen microbes in the blood to transform into fungi that release mycotoxins that turn the body to dust. This is why a vacuum-sealed dead body will still decay. The body rots from the inside-out, not the outside-in.

Dark sodas (including "diet" versions) are made with phosphoric acid that is 10,000 times more acidic than normal blood. The heart is like an alkaline battery that functions optimally only when bathed in alkaline blood. Acid sodas, when drunk without food, are quickly absorbed through the empty stomach wall into the bloodstream. Some people discount this hazard, reasoning that stomach acid is more acidic than a cola drink. But stomach acid is *not* released when soda is ingested without food. When stomach acid is *not* released, the pancreas is *not* stimulated to release neutralizing enzymes which would neutralize the acid drink. What a mess!

Phosphoric acid-containing sodas should NEVER have been approved for human consumption.

The body is intricately designed to neutralize acidic drinks that are absorbed into the blood (so that the heart does not stop) by mobilizing alkaline minerals (calcium and magnesium) from bone and muscle for release into the blood. In time, the ill effects of daily calcium and magnesium loss from bone and muscle surface as a collapsed spine and fragile bones (osteoporosis) and stiff or sore muscles (fibromyalgia or MS). Prove the connection for yourself by asking anyone with any type of muscle, nerve or bone disease (and eventually cancer, including childhood leukemia) how many phosphoric acid-containing colas they drink every day (or serve to their children).

Depending on the bone mass and soda-drinking habits of the individual, mineral reserves become depleted so that the body can no longer compensate for acid fluids entering the blood without risking complete collapse of the skeleton or complete destruction of the muscles and nerves. The blood begins to become acidic at this point, greatly increasing the risk of heart attack and stroke (acid blood forms clots more easily than normal alkaline blood) and all types of degenerative disease including neuropathy.

Acid blood mimics the condition of death. Remember, we are born with alkaline blood and die with acid blood. Upon death and no longer breathing oxygen, the body fluids increasingly turn acidic, toxins (similar to mycotoxins) are released into the blood and the body decays. In this light, autoimmune disease and cancer are conditions that mimic death – because cells are decaying and antibodies are being released to clean up the debris. All autoimmune diseases have a higher incidence of cancer which is a continuum of the degenerative death process.

Processed solid foods that cannot completely metabolize into energy form dietary acids that, in time, will change the blood to a disease-promoting acid pH. To learn more about how solid foods can also transform a healthy body into a degenerating wasteland (which in turn can cause mycotoxins to be made from within) see my book: ***Fat is a Four Letter Word: ACID***.

5. Excess alcohol ingestion

Excess alcohol intake depletes B-vitamins that are required to metabolize alcohol from the body but which are also essential to nerve health. Grain-derived alcohols, such as beer, are also at risk of environmentally-derived mycotoxin contamination from every stage of processing: growth, harvest and storage (silage).

FIRST STEP: Neuropathy Fix-1

After identifying all toxin sources, the FIRST STEP to arresting non-traumatic neuropathy is to BIND THE TOXINS. All of the ingredients in **Neuropathy Fix-1** are potent mycotoxin/toxin binders. These organic and natural ingredients include:

- Colostrum
- Beta Glucan
- Glutamine
- Glycine
- Silibinin
- Curcumin
- Crocin
- Quercetin
- Licorice
- Mannose
- Uncaria
- Honey Granules

All of these natural ingredients are powerful toxin binders. Most are plant compounds uniquely employed by plants to prevent cell-wall destruction by mold-derived toxins. All of the plant flavonoids additionally suppress the JNK gene which is activated in many types of neuropathies.

New research reveals that ALS and various neuropathies involve *activation* of the JNK gene that is linked with the nucleus of human cells. Certain mycotoxins infect human cells and stimulate those cells to turn on the DNA replication machinery via the JNK pathway. Any kind of stress activates the JNK gene. When the JNK gene is turned on, the DNA replication mechanism is also activated (the JNK gene is part of the replication machinery). *This is why stress (emotional, hormonal or environmental) can exacerbate many types of neuropathies.*

Neuropathy Fix-1 is specifically formulated to suppress this activated JNK pathway with a combination of plant flavonoids (pigments) that protect each plant from mycotoxin poisoning by mold. The result is a blend that is much more effective than each individual plant compound alone.

Published clinical studies have demonstrated the activation of the JNK (c-Jun) gene with neuropathy and ALS as follows:

Mol Cell Biochem. 2013 Jan;372(1-2):241-8. doi: 10.1007/s11010-012-1465-x. Epub 2012 Sep 24.

The JNK/c-Jun signaling axis contributes to the TDP-43-induced cell death.

Suzuki H[1], Matsuoka M.

J Neuropathol Exp Neurol. 1997 Dec;56(12):1314-22.

c-Jun, JNK/SAPK kinases and transcription factor NF-kappa B are selectively activated in astrocytes, but not motor neurons, in amyotrophic lateral sclerosis.

Migheli A[1], Piva R, Atzori C, Troost D, Schiffer D.

Molecular Neurodegeneration

HOME ABOUT ARTICLES SUBMISSION GUIDELINES

RESEARCH ARTICLE | OPEN ACCESS

C-Jun N-terminal kinase controls TDP-43 accumulation in stress granules induced by oxidative stress

Jodi Meyerowitz[†], Sarah J Parker[†], Laura J Vella, Dominic CH Ng, Katherine A Price, Jeffrey R Liddell, Aphrodite Caragounis, Qiao-Xin Li, Colin L Masters, Takashi Nonaka, Masato Hasegawa, Marie A Bogoyevitch, Katja M Kanninen, Peter J Crouch and Anthony R White

c-Jun N-terminal Kinase 3 Deficiency Protects Neurons from Axotomy-induced Death *in Vivo* through Mechanisms Independent of c-Jun Phosphorylation*

Elizabeth Keramaris[‡], Jacqueline L. Vanderluit[‡], Mohammad Bahadori[‡], Kambiz Mousavi[§], Roger J. Davis[¶], Richard Flavell[|], Ruth S. Slack[‡] and David S. Park[‡**]

Simply put, blocking JNK activity also blocks mycotoxins from interfering with normal function of the cell nucleus that houses the DNA. But, that is not all! Blocking an over-active JNK gene not only blocks mycotoxin destruction of nerve cells but also improves brain function, provides pain relief, decreases cancer risk, enhances repair of damaged blood vessels and improves nerve function.

Here are three such reports:

1. ***JNK: A Putative Link Between Insulin Signaling and Alzheimer's Disease* (Rodriguez-Perdigon).**

2. ***SP600125, a selective JNK inhibitor, protects ischemic renal injury via suppressing the extrinsic pathways of apoptosis* (Wang).**

3. ***Neuroprotection against focal ischemic brain injury by inhibition of JNK and attenuation of the mitochondrial apoptosis-signaling pathway* (Gao).**

All of the ingredients in **Neuropathy Fix-1** have been demonstrated in published clinical studies to suppress the JNK gene. This proprietary formula includes silibinin, curcumin, crocin, quercitin, licorice and uncaria. Because these flavonoids suppress the JNK gene that mycotoxins activate to destroy glial cells, **Neuropathy Fix-1** improves nerve problems associated with sciatica, tinnitus (ringing in the ears), peripheral neuropathy (and effects such as shaking, burning and sensitivity to touch) motor neuron disease (muscle weakness) and autonomic neuropathy (bowel, bladder or digestive problems and changes in blood pressure that may cause dizziness or lightheadedness).

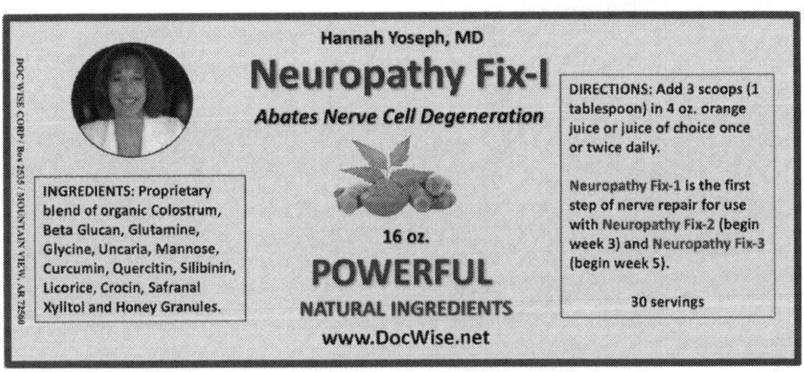

The most effective way to realize the benefits of any natural medicine is to enhance the absorption of the product through the stomach and small intestine. This way, more of the medicine reaches the blood stream and less is lost as waste. For this reason, **Neuropathy Fix-1** is *not* encapsulated but instead packaged in its native powdered form without any anti-caking agents or other fillers. To prevent the powder from caking, refrigerate after opening (although this is not required). To enhance absorption of **Neuropathy Fix-1** through the gut, mix it with orange juice or juice of your choice once or twice daily. You can also mix it with cottage cheese, yogurt, apple sauce or a smoothie.

Neuropathy Fix-1 is POWERFUL medicine based upon cutting edge research that has repeatedly shown how a wide variety of plant compounds neutralize and thus inactivate many different types of mycotoxins via a wide variety of strategies.

Neuropathy Fix-1 should be taken daily as directed for a minimum of 8 weeks (each jar has 30 servings which will last one month if taken once daily) and taken for as long as needed. After 8 weeks, if neuropathy symptoms (tremors, weakness, difficulty breathing or swallowing, pain, etc.) return after discontinuing use, then restart the treatment and try reducing the dose.

Toxins affect nerve cells (glial cells) based upon genetics. Therefore, toxins are reversible in some people and not reversible in other people. So while your neuropathy is likely NOT due to genetics, genetics plays a role in recovery time which can not be predicted. This is the basis for the recommendation to discontinue or decrease **Neuropathy Fix-1** after 8 weeks and see if any neuropathy-related symptoms return. Some nerve toxins bind irreversibly to nerve cells. If this proves to be the case for you, **Neuropathy Fix-1** is safe to take indefinitely if needed.

Neuropathy Fix-1 is a toxin binder for NON-TRAUMATIC (not accident-related) types of central (brain and spinal cord) and peripheral (everything else) neuropathy, including nerve problems related to diabetes, ALS-related neuropathy, MS-related neuropathy, transverse myelitis, autoimmune neuropathy, sciatica, tinnitus (ringing in the ears), etc. It is also safe for children.

Remember, it is *imperative* to identify the source of the toxin(s) causing neuropathy in the first place (this includes dietary sources). If you are unsure of the root toxin(s) inducing your nerve problems, consider a face-to-face Skype consult with me at **www.DocWise.net**.

Neuropathy Fix-2 should be started after two weeks of taking **Neuropathy Fix-1** and can be mixed with **Neuropathy Fix-1**. **Neuropathy Fix-2** is a special blend of nutrients designed to repair damaged nerve cells. Nerve myelin is made of LIVING CELLS which, when provided the needed nutrients to make myelin, can repair damaged nerve cells.

Neuropathy Fix-2 is KEY to repairing damaged nerves only AFTER the toxin source has been identified and removed from the diet or environment, and the toxin load bound and eliminated or reduced with **Neuropathy Fix-1. Neuropathy Fix-1** is thus formulated to **stop** the nerve damage. Step two, then, is to **repair** the toxin-induced damage to nerve cells with **Neuropathy Fix-2**.

STEP TWO: REPAIR THE DAMAGED NERVES.
The SECOND STEP is Neuropathy Fix-2.

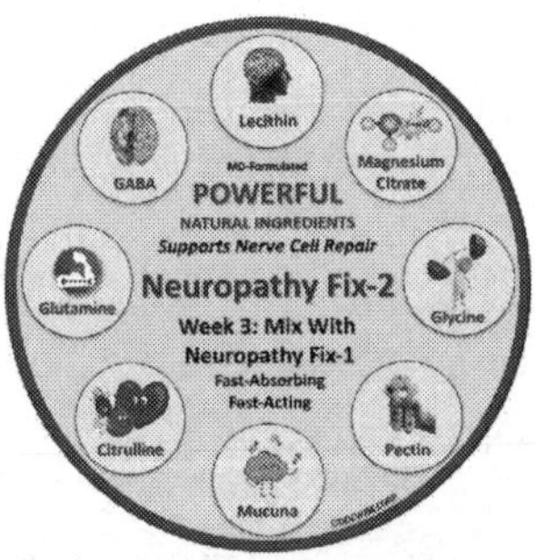

2. Neuropathy Fix-2: Nerve Cell Repair

"No army can withstand the strength of an idea whose time has come."
-Victor Hugo

Destruction of myelin in any neurodegenerative disease interrupts normal nerve impulses to nerves and muscle, gradually paralyzing the body. The resultant dreaded symptoms include tremors, muscle weakness, incoordination, burning pain, slurred speech, difficulty with swallowing and increasing shortness of breath (in ALS, mechanical breathing machines may be required to extend life). Prescription drugs can help alleviate symptoms, but do not reduce the progression of the disease.

While most nerve cells are slow to regenerate, glial nerve cells are not. Glial cells make up to 90 percent of the brain and support the entire nervous system. ***Glial nerve cells rapidly replicate when there is injury.*** This is good news for anyone with ALS, MS or any neurodegenerative disease, because glial cells make myelin – and lots More accurately, glial cells ARE myelin. "Glia" means "glue". Glial cell outgrowths are what make

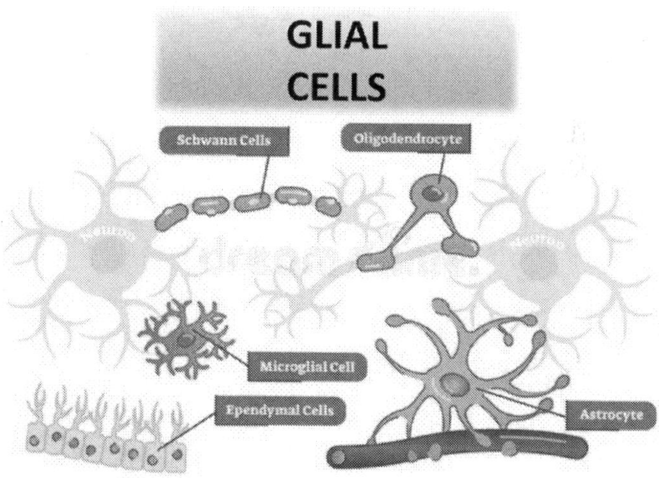

myelin. When glial cells are damaged or destroyed, nerves become “unglued.” This leaves scars. If multiple glial cells are destroyed, the result is nerve and muscle damage (neuropathy and myopathy). Because nerves innervate muscles, neuropathy and myopathy go hand-in-hand.

When toxin-poisoned glial cells die by apoptosis and are blocked from replicating (and therefore replacing) myelin, what remains are degenerated nerves. If the nerves are central (involving the brain and spinal cord), the resulting symptoms are more like MS (Multiple Sclerosis) or transverse myelitis. If the nerves are motor nerves that innervate muscle, the symptoms are more like ALS (Amyotrophic Lateral Sclerosis).

In some demyelinating neuropathies, the myelin sheath has become “scarred” – hence the “S” in ALS and MS which stands for “sclerosis” or “scars” (Multiple Sclerosis = Multiple Scars). Again, mycotoxins and other nerve toxins cause the glial cells that comprise the myelin to rupture by “apoptosis” which appears as “scars”. The source of glial cell poisoning must be found and stopped for glial cell health to be maximally restored.

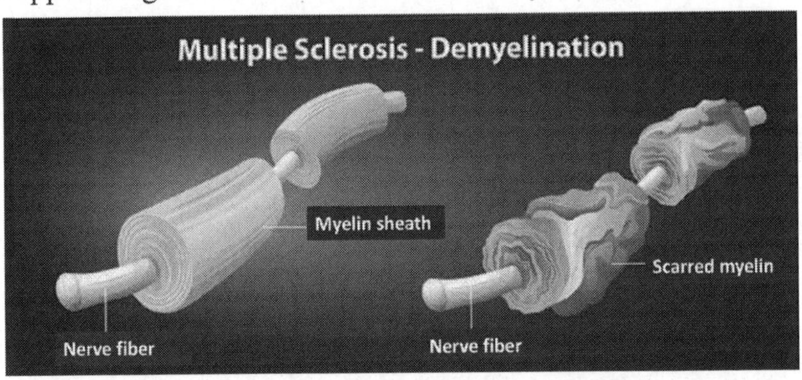

Myelin, which is mostly fat, *insulates* nerve impulses from neighboring nerve fibers, and it increases the speed of impulses sent through nerve axons. Part of supporting glial cells that make myelin is knowing what to do and what not to do. Do not drink any phosphoric acid-containing colas. Do not ingest anything that blocks glial cells from making myelin or causes glial cells to become unglued. You would do well to follow these suggestions while taking **Neuropathy Fix-2**:

- Avoid all oxidizers such as smoke, chlorine, fluoride and phosphoric acid (in dark colas) that destroy nerve cell membranes.

- Avoid all acidic drinks. This means NO soft drinks (diet or regular), no black coffee and no black tea. If you have problems with caffeine-withdrawal headaches, add plenty of milk or cream to your coffee or tea (do not use non-dairy creamer which does not have neutralizing calcium).

- Avoid all bottled drinks, juices and sports drinks. Avoid vitamin B-depleting alcohol during recovery from neuropathy. Glial cells need vitamin B.

- Drink clean well water or bottled spring water. Do not drink bottled water that has been purified by "reverse osmosis" or "distillation". These so-called "purification" techniques remove alkaline mineral such as calcium and magnesium from water.

- Try to always drink home-made fruit juice (any kind).

For glial cells to maintain or repair myelin, they need to quickly replicate. You CANNOT take a statin drug that lowers cholesterol and expect success with myelin repair. Statin drugs block nerve cells from making isopentenyl adenine which is essential for DNA to replicate. Furthermore, myelin is 70% fat and much of that is cholesterol – another simple reason you do not want to take any prescription drug for lowering cholesterol and why cholesterol-lowering statin drugs can cause neuropathy. There are many natural antioxidants such as CoQ10 that will normalize high blood LDL cholesterol and support rather than hinder myelin repair.

After two weeks of taking **Neuropathy Fix-1**, it is time to fuel nerve cells with building blocks to make and maintain new myelin. At the start of week 3, add **Neuropathy Fix-2** to your morning dose of **Neuropathy Fix-1**. Follow the directions provided on the label and the package instructional sheet.

Neuropathy Fix-2 is formulated to provide glial cells the basic nutrients needed to make myelin and includes other amino acids that support cell growth and repair. Other nutrients, such as lecithin, are added to stimulate growth of new myelin sheath which protects nerves and serves to prevent shaking. It is a powerful mix of ingredients, designed to boost the body's natural ability to make growth hormone, which helps to strengthen muscles and nerves. The ingredients include:

- lecithin
- glycine
- glutamine
- colostrum
- citrulline malate
- magnesium citrate
- calcium ascorbate
- mucuna
- GABA
- ribose

Here are a few case backgrounds and testimonies:

Case 1 Background: Female, mid-40's with rapid-onset peripheral neuropathy and motor weakness in the lower extremities.

Suspect toxin: Hyaluronic acid injections (Botox-like "fillers").

Case 1 Testimony: "I had a Skype consultation with Dr. Yoseph to address my peripheral neuropathy. She reviewed all my medical records (over 100 pages). Prior to meeting with her, I had spent a year and a half with no answers and thousands of dollars racked up in testing. After 6 weeks of **Neuropathy Fix-1**, I was dramatically improved (about 80%). The numbness in my feet decreased and my balance improved. Shaking in my hands is diminishing and I have more energy. The haze I felt I was in is lifting and I feel clearer minded. She is extremely knowledgeable about myelin sheath and cells as well as the nervous system." After starting **Neuropathy Fix-2** she reported:

"It's helping…this is so cool!!! It's only been ten days I'm taking it (**Neuropathy Fix-2**) but feeling is returning to my toes and the comforter used to feel so heavy almost painful when it was on my feet at night and now I am FINE. I truly think it's curing the neuropathy. I am excited to see additional developments over time. If so, I have to meet Dr. Yoseph to thank her in person!"

Case 2 Background: Female, mid-80's, with bilateral bicep fasciculations (involuntary twitches), hand tremors, increasing breathlessness (unknown etiology with normal pulmonary and cardiac tests), increasing weakness and imbalance.

Suspect Toxin: ACE Inhibitors

Case 2 Testimony: "One year ago I felt like I was quickly dying. As a retired nurse, I have access to extensive medical care, but no one could account for my breathing problems and failing health even after three hospital admissions and multiple tests which all showed normal lung and heart function. After starting **Neuropathy Fix-1** one month ago, I could tell after a couple of weeks that my breathing had improved and my blood pressure normalized enough to stop taking prescription drugs. Although the number one side effect with the ACE inhibitor I was taking is breathlessness, no one except Dr. Yoseph considered that this was the cause of all of my problems. I have been taking **Neuropathy Fix-2** for three weeks now. The twitches in my arms have decreased and my strength is improved. Shaking has also decreased. My voice is stronger and sounds more normal. I will be celebrating a family reunion next month at the beach so I am looking forward to the opportunity to test how far I am able to walk at the shore which was impossible one year ago.

Case 3: Male, mid-50's with tinnitus, intermittent high blood pressure and increased swelling and pressure in neck.

Suspect Toxin: Prescription thyroid hormone.

Second-Person Testimony: After three weeks of **Neuropathy Fix-1** the tinnitus is almost resolved (still faint ringing in ears but improved), BP is normalized and pressure in neck is gone.

Here is a list of the types of symptoms that are improved with **Neuropathy Fix 1/2/3:**

- Burning, freezing, sharp and/or throbbing pain
- Extreme sensitivity to touch or pain
- Reduced sensitivity to touch
- Prickling in feet or hands, spreading upwards
- Shaking/tremors and slow reflexes
- Lack of balance, lack of coordination and falling
- Muscle loss
- Muscle weakness and cramping
- Bowel, bladder or digestive problems
- Changes in blood pressure causing lightheadedness
- Ringing in the ears
- Pain in Gluteus maximus ("sciatica")

Because nerve cells require very large amounts of energy to make neurotransmitters, step three in restoring nerve function is formulated to maximize nerve cell energy production.

**STEP THREE: MAXIMIZE NERVE CELL ENERGY.
The THIRD STEP is Neuropathy Fix-3.**

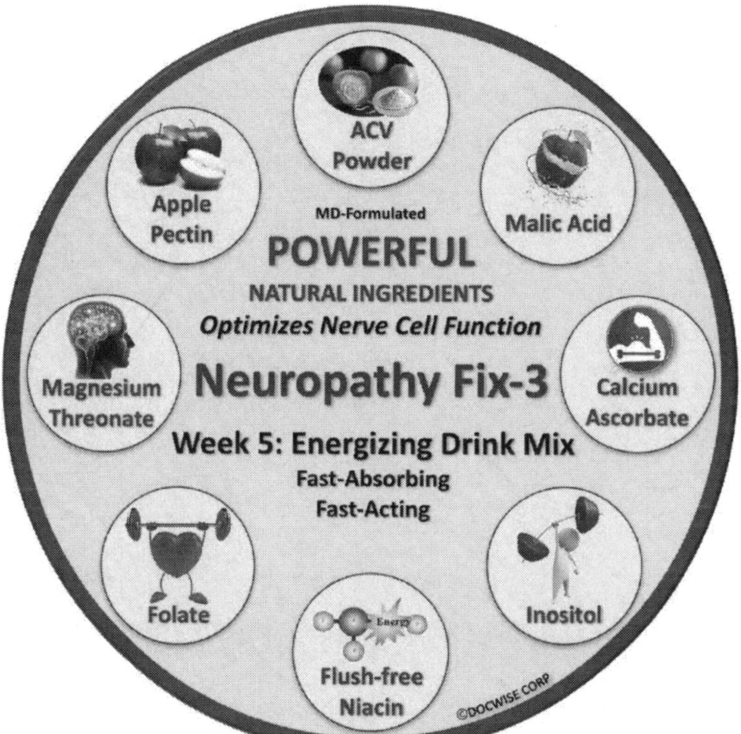

3. Neuropathy Fix-3: Nerve Cell Energy Mix

"Health is real wealth and not gold and silver."
-Mahatma Gandhi

Cellular metabolism (the making of energy) must be optimized for nerves to function normally and to make sufficient neurotransmitters, which are the chemicals of the nervous system to control the entire body.

Certain types of cells require much more energy than others – and nerve cells are at the top of the list. One key sign that nerve cells are not making sufficient energy to function normally is difficulty sleeping. This is because nerve cells are not likely making sufficient neurotransmitters required for restorative sleep.

Neuropathy Fix-3 is begun on week 5. Follow the directions provided on the label and the package instructional sheet.

Because this tasty energizing drink mix increases cellular metabolism (and the making of neurotransmitters), you should notice one or more of the following:

- Improved sleep
- Improved sense of well-being
- Increased energy and focus
- Improved bowel function
- Relief from acid reflux
- Improved strength
- Improved balance
- Less breathlessness

It's been said not to mix apples with oranges, but that is exactly what nerve cells do to make energy in the form of a molecule called ATP. Every nerve cell is energized by ATP and most kinds of neuropathy can be caused or exacerbated by a lack of ATP. The brain and nervous system have a huge demand for ATP to function optimally.

ATP is made from carbohydrate foods. The "carbo" portion is exhaled as carbon dioxide and the "hydrate" part (hydrogen) is converted into ATP.

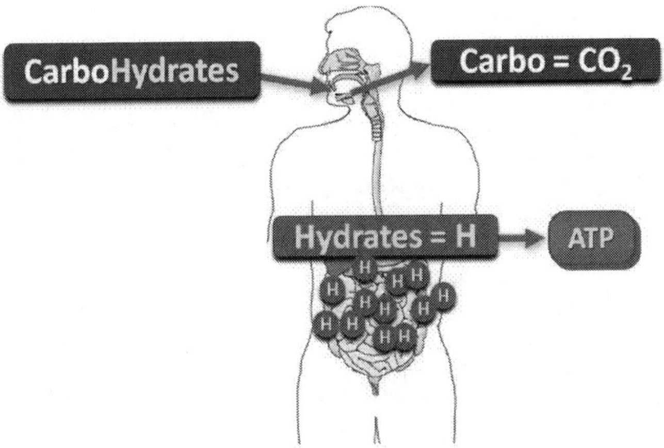

Hydrogen, from carbo*hydrates* (raw nuts, fruits and vegetables) is what lights up your life by energizing every nerve cell in your body. Not all carbs, however, are equal hydrogen doners and thus equal ATP makers!

Carbohydrates that make the most hydrogen make the most energy for nerve cells. The most energy-producing carbohydrates are NOT processed and have little to no shelf life. Due to all the active nutrients, these carbohydrates (mostly fruits and vegetables) rot in less than two weeks and are preferably eaten raw. Simply put, if you want to know if a carbohydrate is "good" for making ATP, if it can sit on your shelf for more than a month, then it probably does not qualify. There are two exceptions to this rule: Canned or jarred tomato products and apple cider vinegar.

In the final analysis, it is apple cider vinegar that makes more hydrogen (ATP) than any other food or drink. Here's why: Carbohydrate foods are broken down or metabolized by nerve cells into vinegar (called acetyl CoA). Vinegar then reacts with an apple acid (malic acid) stored in cells to make citric acid which is the acid found in citric fruit. Citric acid is metabolized to make carbon dioxide which you exhale. Citric acid is also metabolized into hydrogen which is converted into ATP. Again, ATP is what all nerve cells use to operate a very complex nervous system.

The release of carbon dioxide and hydrogen converts citric acid back into malic acid, which then reacts with the vinegar from the good carbohydrates that you eat – making citric acid again. This is how the nerve cell energy cycle (called the "citric acid cycle) is repeated.

While eating apples (malic acid) and oranges (citric acid) is a great way to supply your nerve cells with the ingredients they need to make ATP, nothing is as effective as apple cider vinegar, which has malic acid and vinegar – the two ingredients that nerve cells need to make citric acid. Drinking apple cider vinegar, then, is like throwing hot coals into the energy furnaces of your nerve cells!

No wonder, then, that there are so many positive reports about the amazing health benefits of apple cider vinegar. But vinegar, even if mixed with honey, can be hard on the taste buds, cause stomach upset and damage the dentine layer of teeth.

Powdered apple cider vinegar, on the other hand, has none of the negative effects of liquid apple cider vinegar and retains all of the health-promoting benefits. **Neuropathy Fix-3** is formulated with powdered apple cider vinegar, malic acid, citric acid and eight other ingredients that nerve cells need to make optimal ATP.

One of the key ingredients is inositol nicotinate, an active form of vitamin B3 that nerve cells need to convert hydrogen into ATP. While a different form of vitamin B3 called niacinamide is added to cereals and vitamin supplements, studies have shown that this is not the form of B3 that nerve cells prefer to make ATP.

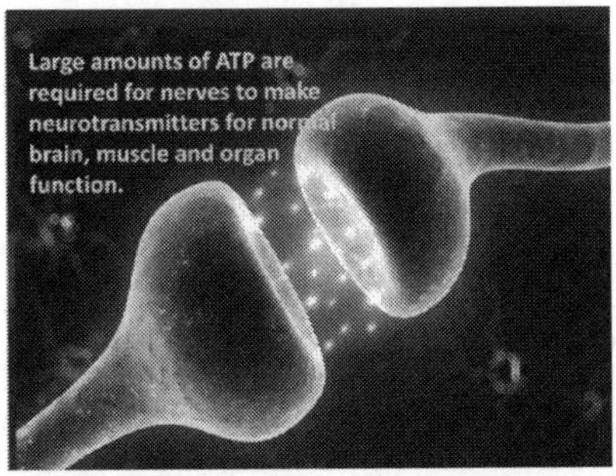

ATP works like a rechargeable battery that makes energy for every cell. ATP is the fuel you need to move, eat, think and sleep. Without sufficient ATP, you simply cannot be healthy. And, more likely than not, you will also be overweight, sore, tired and frequently sick.
Because nerve cells require large amounts of ATP to function normally, **Neuropathy Fix-3** is a MUST to optimize nerve cell ATP production.

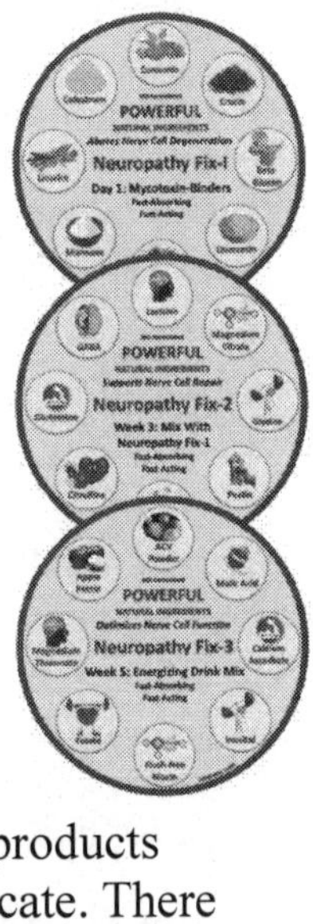

Optimum ATP production is the key to overall health – period! When nerve cells have more energy, YOU have more energy and you have better health.

Neuropathy Fix-1, **Neuropathy Fix-2** and **Neuropathy Fix-3** work synergistically to:

1. **Bind toxins**
2. **Support nerve cell repair**
3. **Optimize nerve cell ATP production**

Maximizing the effectiveness of these three natural products requires a basic review of how nerve glial cells replicate. There are certain foods you can include in your diet to increase the efficiency of the nerve cell replication pathway called the "mevalonate path".

The mevalonate path makes glial cell fats such as cholesterol that make up the myelin sheath. Let's take a quick look at the mevalonate path and how it helps make myelin and stimulate glial cells to replicate – a **KEY** biochemical path to support if your goal is to restore damaged and scarred nerves back to health. More on these fats of life…

4. Fats of Life

"Let food be your medicine."
-Hippocrates

There are two biochemical paths that support nerve cell life:

1. **Metabolism path** (makes energy)
2. **Mevalonate path** (makes fats and replicates cells)

The **metabolism path** is supported by **Neuropathy Fix-3** and a diet rich in raw carbohydrates (fruits, vegetables and raw nuts).

The **mevalonate path** is also supported by **Neuropathy Fix-3**. To further enhance REPLICATION and GROWTH of fat-rich glial nerve cells that make fat-rich myelin, the mevalonate path can be further optimized by making food your medicine.

Made of 60% fat, the brain is the fattest organ in the body. Glial cells use mevalonate to make fats such as cholesterol, which is the most abundant fat in brain tissue. Cholesterol is also the most abundant fat in myelin, which is 70% fat and 30% protein.

Mevalonate is the precursor to fatty CoQ10 which helps convert hydrogen into ATP via the metabolic path.

Mevalonate is not something you can buy at the store. Rather, nerve cells readily make it when:

1. The mevalonate path is open – not blocked by mycotoxins or drugs such as statins for lowering cholesterol.
2. The correct ingredients are provided in the diet.

The ingredients in **Neuropathy Fix-3** provide the building blocks that glial cells need to make mevalonate. Even so, is important that you make careful food choices to further optimize the mevalonate path.

Glial cells make fatty molecules that are necessary for a healthy nervous system via the mevalonate path. Other key mevalonate products that glial cells *cannot* make must instead be obtained from dietary plants; these include vitamins A, E and K, as well as antioxidants and pigmented fats that needed for nerve health.

Plants make fatty molecules from mevalonate, such as the oily vitamins A, E and K that are essential for nerve health. All vitamins are "vital" because they cannot be made inside human cells and must therefore be obtained from food. Vitamin E is a powerful antioxidant with anti-cancer and heart-protective properties. Vitamin E deficiency can cause painful neuropathy.

Orange and red plant pigments are rich in vitamin A. Green pigments are rich in vitamin K. Nuts and seeds are rich in vitamin E. Vitamins are best absorbed into the nervous system when the source is a natural food rather than a manufactured supplement. (Note: An exception is a multi-B vitamin supplement that should be taken daily with food during recovery from any neuropathy. Studies show that vitamin B6 can promote nerve health in diabetics. Vitamins B12, B9 and B1 are also important to the structural integrity of the fats found in the myelin.)

The following plant foods are excellent sources for nerve-healthy "fatty" vitamins A, E and K:

- Sweet potato – Vitamin A
- Winter squash (butternut and acorn) – Vitamin A
- Carrot – Vitamin A
- Tomato – Vitamins A and K
- Greens (kale, collards and turnip) – Vitamins A and K
- Green vegetables – Vitamin K
- Sunflower seeds and raw nuts – Vitamin E
- Sunflower and Safflower cooking oils – Vitamin E

Many plant-derived fats and fatty acids from mevalonate are natural antioxidants that support nerve health and prevent cancer. Include these in your diet:

- Allixin (garlic)
- Danielone (papaya – consider dried papaya slices)
- Pterostilbene (blueberries)
- Ellagic acid (pomegranates)
- Resveratrol (grapes)

Mevalonate-derived fats are important to nerve health because electrons flow through fats. The flow of electrons through fatty cell membranes is how nerve cells (how all cells) work and communicate. Fats made from mevalonate are the "fats of life" because normal, healthy nerve cell function cannot happen without them. The most LIFE PROMOTING or DEADLY food choices we make are the fats and oils we consume. Fats and oils are incorporated into nerve and other cell membranes. The brain, spinal cord and entire nervous system is wired via fat-rich cell membranes through which electrons flow.

Half of the fats in nerve cell membranes are saturated with hydrogen (solid oils) and the other half are unsaturated (liquid oils). Two-thirds of unsaturated oils are omega-6 type fats and one-third is omega-3 type fats. Your diet, then, should reflect the same ratio.

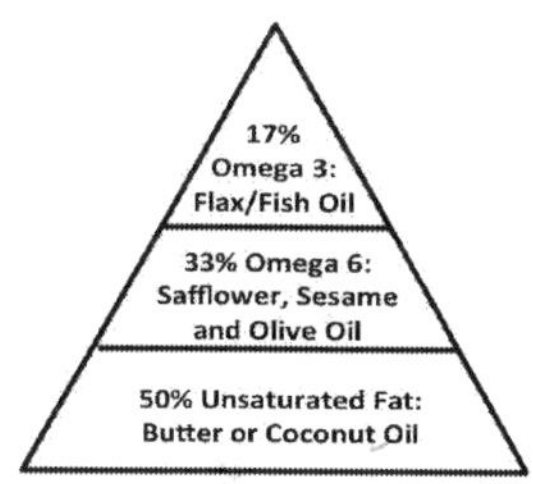

Eating energizing fats in proper balance will be as easy as 1-2-3 if every day you use 1 part flax oil, 2 parts safflower oil and 3 parts coconut oil and/or butter as follows:

1 Tablespoon of flax oil mixed in cottage cheese or applesauce.
2 Tablespoons of safflower oil for salads or to sauté.
3 Tablespoons of coconut oil to fry; butter to flavor or bake.

Flax oil is one of the most important oils you can add to your daily diet during the phase of nerve repair. Flax oil is super-unsaturated which means ELECTRONS FLOW EASILY through this life-giving oil. I have used flax oil mixed in apple sauce or cottage cheese to restore dangerous heart rhythms back to normal within minutes. Oils are more-easily absorbed through the small intestine if they are mixed with cottage cheese (add fruit as you like) and/or applesauce. I recommend Barlean's flax oil with lignan taken daily this way rather than cooking with it because heat will destroy (oxidize) this temperature-sensitive oil that lights up the nervous system (you will feel energy flow within minutes!).

I also recommend adding one tablespoon of phosphatidyl choline oil (by Body Bio at Amazon) to your daily mix of flax oil and cottage cheese or applesauce. Phosphatidyl choline is a key ingredient of myelin and your nerves will thank you. Do this daily for at least the first eight weeks of recovery from neuropathy. **Neuropathy Fix-1** is also taken for a minimum of eight weeks. As an alternative to mixing **Neuropathy Fix-1** in juice, you can add it to your flax oil and phosphatidyl choline oil and applesauce (or cottage cheese) mixture.

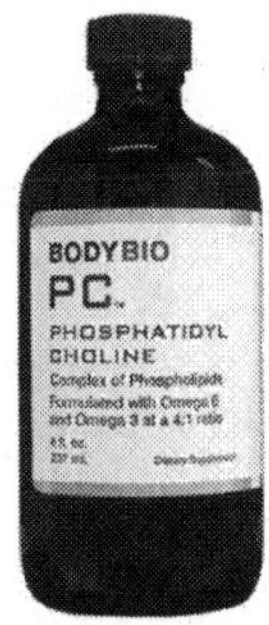

AVOID MAN-MADE saturated fats that make membranes rigid and less fluid; these include margarine, shortening (Crisco) and oils that are made with industrial solvents (vegetable oils and canola oil).

Mevalonate not only makes fatty substances that are key to healthy myelin; it is also the essence of cell renewal. In all cells, mevalonate travels down the mevalonate pathway to make cholesterol and myelin-essential fats. This stimulates a glial cell to grow, replicate the DNA and divide into two cells. This is the "cell cycle". This is life at the cellular level and what keeps glial cells young and healthy.

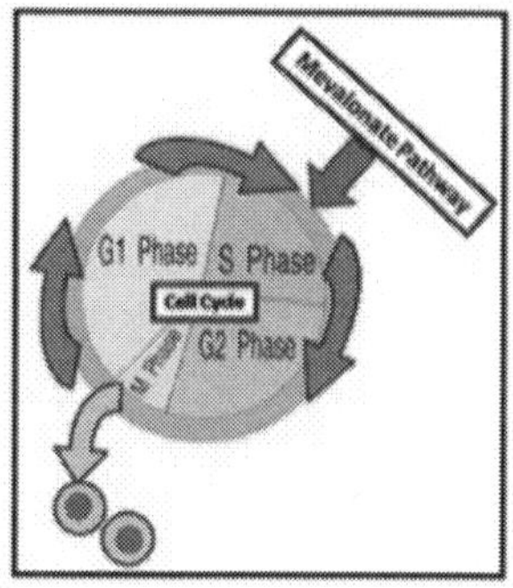

For a glial cell to cycle, it must grow (G1), replicate its DNA (S phase) grow some more (G2) and divide into two new glial cells (M phase). Cell renewal, or turnover, varies for different types of cells. Cells lining the gut are replaced every five days, skin cells are recycled every two weeks, red blood cells last four months, bone cells last a decade and cells from the brain's vision center are as old as the individual. While glial cell turnover is poorly understood, ***about 28% of all glial cells are replaced every year***.

Glial cells replicate, and glial cells are the living matrix that makes up myelin (in other words, glial cells do not just make myelin, they ARE the myelin). Therefore, if you have a demyelinating neuropathy then you should have plenty of hope that the myelin, in time, can be restored. If 28% of glial cells are replaced every year, then in four years you should have all new glial cells IF the toxin that has been destroying these cells has been properly identified and eliminated.

To sum: Cell cycles work in concert with cholesterol and fats made from the mevalonate pathway. Without mevalonate's fats, none of this happens. No glial cell cycle means no glial cell life which means no myelin renewal.

The mevalonate path supports glial cell growth and replication.

Do NOT take drugs that block glial cells from making cholesterol! Eat plenty of cholesterol-rich and choline-rich foods such as eggs (do NOT throw away the yolk). This way your glial cells won't have to make so much cholesterol and choline from scratch.

Cholesterol in food does NOT raise cholesterol. It is oxidation, caused by consuming smoke products, dark colas containing phosphoric acid and drinking chlorinated city water, that destroys LDL cholesterol. This does not happen with HDL ("good") cholesterol because it is a larger and heavier fatty molecule, making it less sensitive to destruction by oxidation. Because the liver must replace oxidized LDL cholesterol, it produces *higher than normal* levels in order to offset the ongoing damage. The connection between elevated cholesterol and cardiovascular disease and stroke is OXIDATION. Oxidation both destroys LDL cholesterol and hardens the fat-rich membranes that line the inside walls of arteries. Lighter-weight LDL cholesterol is simply more sensitive to damage by oxidation than heavier-weight HDL. LDL is not bad. All cholesterol is GOOD! It is *oxidation* that is bad.

Cholesterol, both LDL and HDL, are good, good, GOOD for a healthy, well-myelinated nervous system. If you read my book, ***How Statin Drugs Really Lower Cholesterol (And Kill You One Cell at a Time)*** you will find layers of indisputable evidence to support this. The health of your nervous system hangs in the balance of this uncontestable truth. Get informed!

The mevalonate pathway, then, is the pathway of glial cell life. It is what keeps glial cells replicating and renewed to make new myelin. The mevalonate pathway is, in fact, the "fountain of youth" for every cell in your body. The more efficiently this pathway operates, the younger your cells – which means a younger and healthier *you.*

The three steps of the Neuropathy Fix product line are:

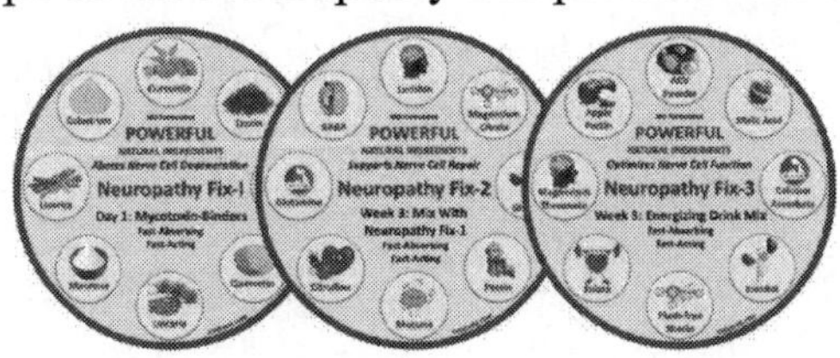

1. **Neuropathy Fix-1**: Binds the myelin-destroying toxins
2. **Neuropathy Fix-2**: Supports nerve cell and myelin repair
3. **Neuropathy Fix-3:** Optimizes nerve cell ATP production

Other neurodegenerative diseases that are well-served with **Neuropathy Fix** include Parkinson's Disease, Huntington's Chorea and Alzheimer's which are all associated with abnormally folded nerve proteins.

All three products promote a lean and energized body. They are also safe for children, with half the recommended dose for children age 6 to 12 and one-fourth the dose for children under 6. They can be consumed for conditions such as ADD, ADHD and autism (with or without seizures), which involve a wide spectrum of neurological deficits. The dietary recommendations are also safe for children, including the flax oil and phosphatidyl choline oil mixtures at the same lower doses.

Again, eat foods and oils that support the mevalonate path used by glial cells to make myelin's fatty nerve insulation, especially eggs that are rich in cholesterol and choline. Stop drinking alcoholic drinks during recovery from neuropathy because alcohol depletes the myelin-dependent B-vitamins (and take a daily multi-B supplement with food). Finally, avoid oxidizers such as smoke, phosphoric acid in colas and chorine in city water, all of which destroy nerve cell fats.

This protocol is simple, but not easy! Every step is backed by conventional science. Having made a thorough investigation, it is time to take the first step and start your journey back to health.

5. What to Expect

"The best doctor uses the least medicines."
-Benjamin Franklin

Conquering any type of non-traumatic neuropathy requires adopting protocols that are based on proven science. Myelin is made of living cells that replicate and make the fatty matrix that insulates nerves. Stop losing your nerve with myelin-destroying toxins and support your glial cells so that they can perform their normal functions optimally. That is the message of this book and the basis for the protocols herein.

One of the keys to recovery is patience. Chemistry students quickly learn that more is not always better when conducting chemical reactions in a controlled setting. Chronic illnesses don't develop overnight and neither does the recovery process.

As you fuel your body with real medicine and real food, there are outward signs that signal nerve cell health is being restored:

1. Nails will grow faster and become less brittle.
2. A white-coated tongue will become healthy and pink.
3. Dry, dull and thinning hair will become thick and shiny.
4. Thick scaly skin on the knees and elbows will clear up.
5. A butterfly rash will dissipate.
6. Recurrent bladder infections will lessen and stop.
7. Nail fungus will disappear as new nails advance.
8. Bowel function will regulate.
9. Breathlessness will decrease.
10. Muscle strength will increase and tremors will subside.
11. Psychiatric and emotional problems will balance out.
12. Libido will increase.
13. Clarity of thought (focus) and memory will improve.
14. Muscle and joint pain will subside.
15. Grip strength will improve.
16. Teeth sensitivity and bleeding gums will resolve.

17. Hemorrhoids will heal faster, recur less and/or stop.
18. Swollen ankles will improve.
19. Blood pressure will normalize.
20. Ringing in the ears and/or imbalance will decrease.

If you have drug-induced ALS neuropathy from taking a statin drug, know that the difficulty with recovering from statin use is that some damage is slow to heal and other damage may not repair at all. No one knows for sure. Consider bringing a copy of ***How Statin Drugs Really Lower Cholesterol (And Kill You One Cell at a Time)*** to your doctor for a second opinion. He or she, after all, might also be a victim of trust in the medical system and have a second thought about prescribing you or anyone else another statin.

Take charge of your own wellness. Good health is more than physical; it is mental, emotional and spiritual. It is very difficult to be patient and hopeful when feeling sick and tired of being sick and tired, especially when one's needs are so demanding. Try it anyway.

Please feel free to share with me your journey on the road to conquering neuropathy. Take this road map with you and be well.

Much care,

Hannah Yoseph, MD
Doc@docwise.net

6. Other Books by Hannah Yoseph, MD

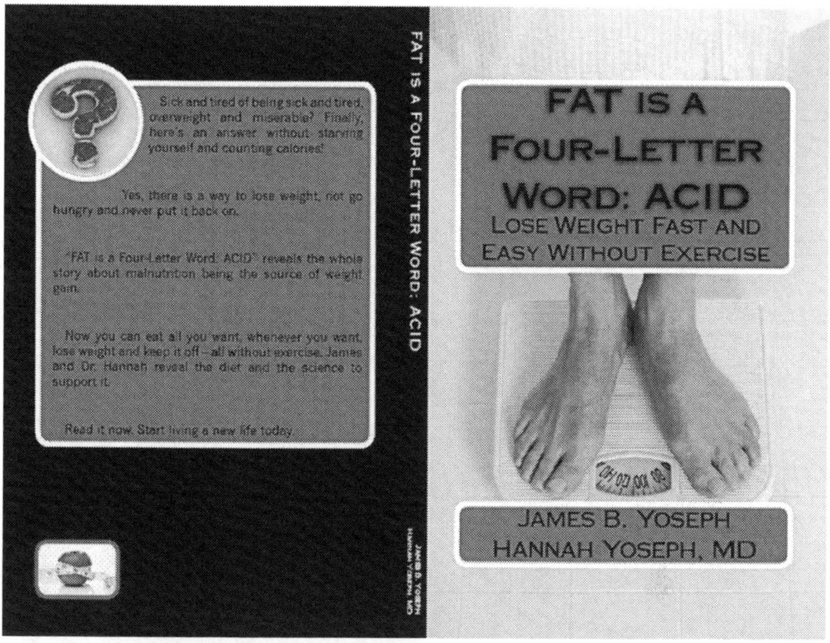

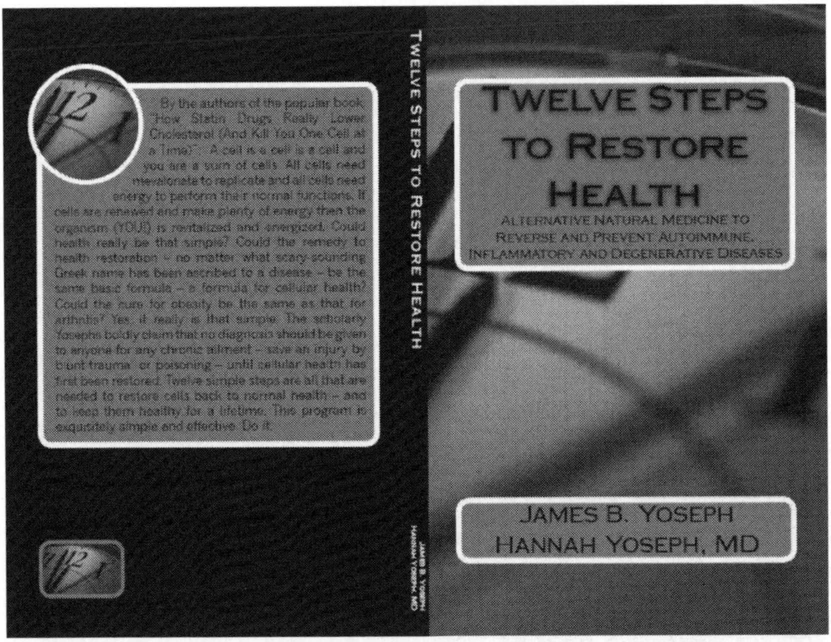
TWELVE STEPS TO RESTORE HEALTH
TWELVE STEPS
TO RESTORE
HEALTH
ALTERNATIVE NATURAL MEDICINE TO
REVERSE AND PREVENT AUTOIMMUNE,
INFLAMMATORY AND DEGENERATIVE DISEASES
JAMES B. YOSEPH
HANNAH YOSEPH, MD

CONQUERING LOU GEHRIG'S DISEASE
CONQUERING
LOU GEHRIG'S
DISEASE
THE ALS DIET
HANNAH YOSEPH, MD
INTRODUCTION BY JAMES B. YOSEPH

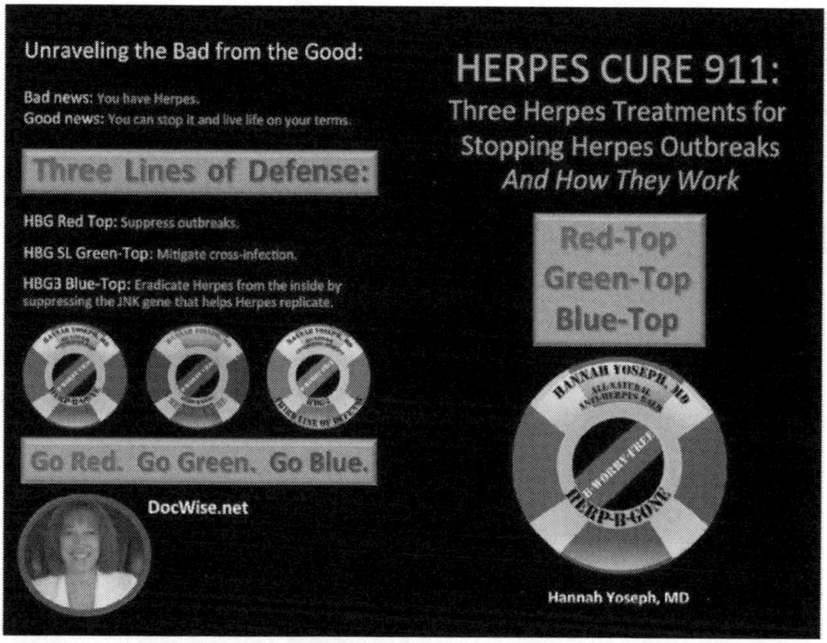
Unraveling the Bad from the Good:
Bad news: You have Herpes.
Good news: You can stop it and live life on your terms.
Three Lines of Defense:
HBG Red Top: Suppress outbreaks.
HBG SL Green-Top: Mitigate cross-infection.
HBG3 Blue-Top: Eradicate Herpes from the inside by suppressing the JNK gene that helps Herpes replicate.
Go Red. Go Green. Go Blue.
DocWise.net
HERPES CURE 911:
Three Herpes Treatments for Stopping Herpes Outbreaks
And How They Work
Red-Top
Green-Top
Blue-Top
HANNAH YOSEPH, MD
HERP-B-GONE
Hannah Yoseph, MD

You've been told by your doctor you have Sjögren's Syndrome and that there is no cure. Dr. Yoseph dares to challenge the naysayers. She explains how Sjögren's is not a diagnosis but a description, and without a proper diagnosis there can be no remedy. Toxic drugs to suppress painful symptoms are the best that modern medicine can offer in its current system of belief. Here, layers of evidence are provided to unlock the so-called mystery of Sjögren's. Remedy is made straightforward when the axe is taken to the root of the tree. Dare to be well, stump your physician and stomp out Sjögren's – for life.
SJÖGREN'S SYNDROME HANNAH YOSEPH, MD
SJÖGREN'S SYNDROME
CAUSE AND RECOVERY IN TEN SIMPLE STEPS
HANNAH YOSEPH, MD

Neuropathy Fix is available at:

www.DocWise.net

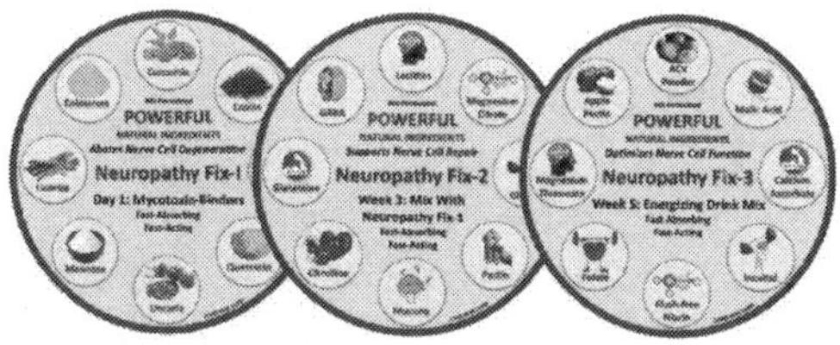

Neuropathy Fix can be used to improve:

ADD, ADHD and Autism
Alcoholic Neuropathy
Alzheimer's and other Dementias
Autoimmune-related Neuropathy
Autonomic Neuropathy
Central Neuropathy
Chemotherapy-induced Neuropathy
Cranial Neuropathy
Demyelinating Neuropathy (ALS, MS, etc.)
Diabetic Neuropathy
Focal Neuropathy
Idiopathic Neuropathy
Inflammatory Neuropathy
Mood Disorders
Motor Neuron Disease
Neurodegenerative Neuropathy
Parkinson's, Huntington's and other Tremors
Peripheral Neuropathy
Post-Infection Neuropathy
Sciatica
Seizure Disorders
Tinnitus
Transverse myelitis

32829452R00230

Made in the USA
Lexington, KY
06 March 2019